1997 Honda CR-V

Mercury Tracer
Mitsubishi Diamante
Oldsmobile Cutlass Ciera
Saab 9-5
Saturn LW
Saturn SW
Subaru Impreza/Outback Sport
Subaru Legacy
Subaru Outback
Suzuki Aerio
Suzuki Esteem
Toyota Camry
Toyota Corolla
Volkswagen Jetta
Volkswagen Passat
Volvo 850
Volvo 960/V90
Volvo V40
Volvo V70
Volvo Cross Country

MINIVANS

Chevrolet Astro
Chevrolet Lumina
Chevrolet Venture
Chrysler Town & Country
Chrysler Voyager
Dodge Caravan
Dodge Grand Caravan
Ford Aerostar
Ford Windstar
GMC Safari
Honda Odyssey
Isuzu Oasis
Kia Sedona
Mazda MPV
Mercury Villager
Nissan Quest
Oldsmobile Silhouette
Plymouth Grand Voyager
Plymouth Voyager
Pontiac Trans Sport/Montana

Toyota Previa
Toyota Sienna
Volkswagen EuroVan

PICKUP TRUCKS

Cadillac Escalade EXT
Chevrolet Avalanche
Chevrolet C/K 1500
Chevrolet Silverado
Chevrolet S-10
Dodge Dakota
Dodge Ram
Ford Explorer Sport Trac
Ford F-150
Ford Ranger
GMC Sierra C/K 1500
GMC Sonoma
Isuzu Hombre
Mazda B-Series
Nissan Truck/Frontier
Toyota T100
Toyota Tacoma
Toyota Tundra

SPORTS/SPORTY CARS

Acura Integra Coupe
Acura RSX
Audi TT
BMW 318ti
BMW M3
BMW Z3
Chevrolet Camaro
Chevrolet Corvette
Dodge Stealth
Dodge Viper
Eagle Talon
Ford Mustang
Ford Probe
Ford Thunderbird
Honda Civic del Sol

Honda Prelude
Honda S2000
Hyundai Tiburon
Mazda MX-5 Miata
Mazda MX-6
Mercedes-Benz SLK
Mercury Cougar
Mitsubishi 3000GT
Mitsubishi Eclipse
Nissan 200SX
Nissan 240SX
Nissan 300ZX
Plymouth Prowler
Pontiac Firebird
Porsche 911
Porsche Boxster
Saturn SC
Subaru SVX
Toyota Celica
Toyota MR2
Toyota Paseo
Toyota Supra

COUPES

Acura CL
BMW 8-Series
Buick Riviera
Cadillac Eldorado
Chevrolet Monte Carlo
Chrysler Sebring
Dodge Avenger
Ford Thunderbird
Lexus SC300/SC400, SC430
Lincoln Mark VIII
Mercedes-Benz CLK
Mercury Cougar
Toyota Camry Solara
Volvo C70

SPORT-UTILITY VEHICLES

Acura MDX
Acura SLX
BMW X5
Buick Rendezvous
Cadillac Escalade
Chevrolet Blazer
Chevrolet Suburban
Chevrolet Tahoe
Chevrolet/Geo Tracker
Chevrolet TrailBlazer
Dodge Durango
Ford Bronco
Ford Escape
Ford Excursion
Ford Expedition
Ford Explorer

GMC Envoy
GMC Jimmy
GMC Suburban
GMC Yukon
GMC Yukon XL
Honda CR-V
Honda Passport
Hyundai Santa Fe
Infiniti QX4
Isuzu Amigo, Rodeo Sport
Isuzu Axiom
Isuzu Rodeo
Isuzu Trooper
Jeep Cherokee
Jeep Grand Cherokee
Jeep Liberty
Jeep Wrangler
Kia Sportage
Land Rover Discovery
Land Rover Freelander
Land Rover Range Rover
Lexus LX450/LX470
Lexus RX300
Lincoln Navigator
Mazda Tribute
Mercedes-Benz M-Class
Mercury Mountaineer
Mitsubishi Montero
Mitsubishi Montero Sport
Nissan Pathfinder
Nissan Xterra
Oldsmobile Bravada
Pontiac Aztek
Saturn VUE
Subaru Forester
Suzuki Sidekick
Suzuki Vitara/Grand Vitara/XL-7
Toyota 4Runner
Toyota Highlander
Toyota Land Cruiser
Toyota RAV4
Toyota Sequoia

1998 Toyota Tacoma

Consumer Reports

USED CAR
BUYING GUIDE
2003

THE EDITORS OF CONSUMER REPORTS

Published by Consumer Reports ◆ A Division of Consumers Union ◆ Yonkers, New York

First printing, January 2003
Copyright © 2003 by Consumers Union of United States, Inc., Yonkers, New York 10703.
Published by Consumers Union of United States, Inc., Yonkers, New York 10703.
All rights reserved, including the right of reproduction in whole or in part in any form.
ISSN: 1042-9476
ISBN: 0-89043-974-5

Manufactured in the United States of America

1999 Mazda MX-5 Miata

TABLE OF CONTENTS

1999 Honda Odyssey

2000 Toyota Tundra

2000 Subaru Legacy

Chapter 5 Car Care & Tires

Profiles of 256 used cars, trucks, minivans, and SUVs

Recalls & Technical Service Bulletins

1996 Nissan Pathfinder

Your One-Stop Used-Car Guide

Buying a used vehicle is a greater risk than buying a new one. This guide can help minimize that risk by steering you toward the better-performing, more reliable models and away from those with a troubled past or substandard performance. Chapter 1, "How to Buy a Used Car," starting on page 11, takes you step by step through the buying process from selection to shopping strategies, vehicle inspection, negotiation techniques, and closing the deal. We give details about the checks you can perform—and tell you how to find a good mechanic if you can't or don't want to perform these various checks yourself. Other chapters cover topics such as reliability, insurance, safety, and more—everything you need to help get you behind the wheel of a reliable used car.

The major part of this book is devoted to the "Profiles" of 256 cars and trucks, representing all the major 1995 through 2002 models. Each of the profiles contains a photo from a representative year and a writeup of the vehicle. The profile pages also include reliability histories, crash-test data, and the model years when key safety gear was added and when a major redesign took place. The profiles start on page 81.

ABOUT CONSUMER REPORTS

For more than 65 years the nonprofit Consumers Union has had a single mission: to test products, inform the public, and protect consumers. In that time, CU has grown into the world's largest and most comprehensive test center for evaluating consumer products and services.

Our magazine CONSUMER REPORTS, the ConsumerReports.org web site, and our other magazines and books accept no advertising. We anonymously buy all the products we test, just as consumers do. Our income is derived solely from the sale of our publications and services, and from nonrestrictive, noncommercial contributions, grants, and fees. We do not allow anyone to use our reports or Ratings for commercial purposes.

The automobile information developed by CONSUMER REPORTS comes from three sources: formal hands-on tests conducted by experienced automotive engineers and technicians; extensive reliability surveys to measure how cars hold up as they age; and expert analysis and buying guidance. Together, those resources provide you with the tools you need to make a wise and informed choice about your next car.

HOW CONSUMER REPORTS TESTS CARS

The performance judgments in the profiles and throughout this book are based on tests CONSUMER REPORTS engineers run throughout the year. Tests are conducted at the specially equipped CONSUMER REPORTS auto-test center, a 327-acre facility in rural Connecticut, as well as on surrounding public roads.

Unlike other publications, which mainly test cars borrowed from the manufacturer, CONSUMER REPORTS staffers anonymously buy the test vehicles from dealers, so they're the same quality as those *any* buyer would purchase. Posing as ordinary shoppers, the auto-test staff buys the selected vehicles—usually 40 to 50 per year—and bargains over price, much as you might. They don't tell the dealer it is intended for CONSUMER REPORTS until they take delivery.

As soon as a new car arrives, CR technicians make a thorough inspection using a 50-item checklist. They check fluid levels, wheel alignment, headlight aim, and other such things and make minor adjustments as needed to bring it within the manufacturer's specifications. But if there's a major defect, the car is taken back to the dealer for repair.

The staff breaks in each car with several thousand miles of everyday driving, gathering experience with the vehicle. Then it's inspected again. If everything checks out, CR engineers begin the process of formal testing. They conduct more than 40 tests on each vehicle. These include a range of performance tests, such as acceleration, braking, and handling, including our collision-avoidance maneuvers. They also evaluate comfort, convenience, interior noise levels, and fuel economy. Those tests reveal things you just can't learn even from the most thorough test drive at a car dealership. The time our testers spend with a car—typically six months or more—is also important, because it gives sufficient time for first impressions to fade and for the vehicle's true character to emerge.

Safety is a central theme. One aspect of safety is how well a car can avoid a crash,

Handling is evaluated in several types of tests, including on a high-speed handling course, above. At right: An avoidance-maneuver test simulates how a vehicle would handle in emergency situations.

something our drivers judge in a series of emergency-handling tests. Those judgments, combined with published crash-test results, come together in the CONSUMER REPORTS Safety Assessment, described in Chapter 3.

Safety considerations are a major reason CR takes note of a vehicle's ergonomics—how well the cockpit fits the human form. A poor driving position, for instance, is not only uncomfortable, but also can cause fatigue, reducing your concentration and preventing you from reacting effectively in an emergency. The driver's seat should support your body so that you don't need to flex any muscles to drive the car, even for extended periods. You should also be able to reach and use any controls, such as the wiper, headlights, and audio controls, without fumbling for them or taking your eyes off the road.

A hydroplaning test, performed as part of tire testing, measures how well tires stick to the road surface when driving through standing water.

Besides testing new cars, CR's engineers also test tires, usually once or twice per year. The key tire tests gauge each model's cornering, emergency-handling, and braking performance in wet and dry conditions as well as its ride comfort, noisiness, and resistance to hydroplaning. We also test tires in snow and ice, both at our own facility and at a skating rink and a ski slope in Vermont. We conduct braking tests for tires much as we do for cars, on both wet and dry pavement on our test facility's long straightaway.

GAUGING RELIABILITY

A new car comes with a comprehensive warranty, so if things go wrong you have some recourse. Some used cars are also sold with a limited warranty (See "The Certified Option," page 16), but in most cases you're on your own. For that reason, reliability should be a key concern with any used car. No matter how much money you save, a car that spends its life in the shop or leaves you stranded is no bargain. That's where CONSUMER REPORTS' annual surveys of car owners can help. Each year, readers tell us how trouble-free or trouble-prone their cars have been. Those survey responses cover hundreds of thousands of vehicles.

◆ For most models profiled in this book, data from those surveys has been distilled into a Reliability History. This shows how the model fared in 14 problem areas over eight model years.

◆ The Reliability Verdict symbols at the bottom of each Reliability History chart give a quick overview year by year.

Our survey results, of course, apply to a model in general terms and not to an individual vehicle. The typical Honda Accord or Toyota Camry, for example, has had top-notch reliability, but the one you're looking at on a dealer's lot or in somebody's driveway could have been poorly maintained or even turn out to be an outright lemon. Conversely, a model that has been shown to be troublesome in our survey, such as the Chevrolet Blazer, might turn out to be trouble-free, but the risk you take with such vehicles is greater. For more on reliability, see Chapter 2. Before you buy, also check recalls. We list about a decade's worth of government recalls, starting on page 209.

OTHER BOOKS FROM CONSUMER REPORTS

The Used Car Buying Guide is one of a series of annual publications devoted to automobiles and other products. Here are other current publications.

AUTOMOTIVE PUBLICATIONS:

- ◆ New Car Buying Guide
- ◆ New Car Preview
- ◆ Sport Utility Special
- ◆ Used Car Yearbook
- ◆ Road Tests

OTHER PRINT PUBLICATIONS:

- ◆ Best Buys for Your Home
- ◆ Consumer Drug Reference
- ◆ Consumer Reports Buying Guide
- ◆ Guide to Baby Products
- ◆ Digital Buying Guide
- ◆ How to Clean (and Care for) Practically Anything
- ◆ Travel Well for Less

1

How to Buy a Used Car

From initial research to driving it away, here are the tools you need to find your next car.

WHY SMART SHOPPERS BUY USED CARS

Buying a used car, particularly a late-model used car, often makes more sense than buying a new car. It's not just that the initial price is lower. Buying used also means that items pegged to the car's value, such as collision-insurance and taxes, will be lower. If the car is less than three years old it's probably still covered by the factory warranty. What's more, buying used is also a way to get a better-equipped vehicle than you'd be able to afford new.

Recession, over-supply, low interest rates, and easy credit have made this a particularly good time to look for a used car. Used-car prices have been declining slowly but steadily since the beginning of 2001. At the used-car departments of new-car dealers, where the choicest used cars are usually to be found, the average car sold for about $12,500 at the beginning of 2001 and for about $11,000 at the end of 2002. At independent used-car dealers the average price declined from about $9,000 to about $7,000—a hefty 22-percent drop.

SEVEN STEPS TO GETTING THE BEST DEAL

Buying a used car is in some ways more challenging than buying a new one. While new cars are somewhat like commodities, with thousands of similar units to choose from, every used car has its own unique history. Be wary but open-minded. Finding the right car at the right price needn't be terribly difficult. All it takes is a little knowledge and a methodical approach. The process can be divided into seven steps that anyone can follow. The seven steps are these:

NARROW YOUR CHOICES. You must first decide what sort of vehicle you're looking for—sedan, wagon, sporty car, minivan, SUV, or pickup. This book can tell you something about vehicles in each of those categories, which ones were highly rated when tested new, and which have proved reliable.

FIND THE BEST PRICE. The value of a used car differs, depending on its condition and where it is sold. We'll tell you how to find the best price in your area.

KNOW WHERE TO SHOP. We summarize here the different shopping venues: new-car dealers, independent used-car dealers, private parties, and the Internet.

INTERVIEW THE SELLER. Call the seller and ask some pointed questions about the car and its history. What you can learn from asking the right questions may save you a fruitless trip.

INSPECT AND TEST DRIVE. Since every used car has the potential to be troublesome, it's vitally important to give it a thorough going-over. We'll tell you what you should look for—inside and out—and on the road.

NEGOTIATE EFFECTIVELY. Some people enjoy dickering, some do not. We'll give some pointers on how to get the best price no matter what your style.

TIE UP LOOSE ENDS. At the end of any transaction there are always some details to nail down, such as paperwork, insurance, and registration. We'll take you through the processes.

Step 1: Narrow your choices

The inside front cover of this book, Vehicles by Category, lists most of the models made in the last eight years, by type. Those lists are a handy starting place to remind yourself of what's out there. Looking for a luxury car? A sports car? An SUV? A small sedan? Start with these lists. The vehicles CONSUMER REPORTS regards as "Good Bets" are printed in **boldface** type. Those are the models that have both performed well in CONSUMER REPORTS tests and consistently recorded better-than-average reliability.

Once you've chosen a few candidates, you can find a description of each vehicle in the Profiles section beginning on page 81. There you will also find its reliability history—a key consideration when choosing any used car. We explain how the reliability judgments work in Chapter 2. That chapter also lists the most and least reliable used cars in CR's latest (2002) survey.

Safety is another key consideration. Chapter 3 discusses safety equipment and how to interpret crash-test scores. For newer cars you'll find the Consumer Reports Safety Assessment. The CRSA gives overall safety scores, based on judgments of a car's accident-avoidance capabilities from CR tests as well as its crash-test performance.

After you've selected some likely candidate cars, you can check out their history of safety recalls in the Recalls & Technical Service Bulletins section starting on page 209.

Step 2: Find the right price

Used-car price information is available from many sources, both electronic and in print. Many web sites give either rough prices or detailed estimates tailored to specific venues

BEST FOR THE BUCK

From overlooked gems to good cars aging gracefully, some models make exceptionally good values. Here are some that performed well when new, have at least average reliability, and sell for reasonable sums. Prices are average asking prices at auto dealers.

SMALL AND ECONOMICAL

The 1996 Honda Civic EX sedan ($8,750) did almost everything well in CR's tests. The 1999 Mazda Protegé ES ($9,350) was another well-rounded design that's holding up well.

SPORTY SEDANS

The now-discontinued Acura Legend was always a good performer. Figure $13,750 for a 1995 model. The nimble Infiniti G20 was well put together and inexpensive. Look for a 1996 with a manual transmission (about $9,200). The 1998 Mazda Millenia S ($15,150) has a small cockpit but boasts a plush interior and excellent reliability.

FAMILY HAULERS

For a midsized family sedan, it's hard to beat a 1996 Toyota Camry XLE V6 ($11,000), which came loaded and was virtually a Lexus in all but name. The 1998 Honda Accord LX V6 ($13,150) is another good choice, with sound handling, a quality interior, and a good view out. For more passenger and cargo space, consider the 1995 to 1998 Honda Odyssey minivan, smaller and less powerful than the current Odyssey but roomy enough. A 1997 EX model goes for about $14,700. The quiet, comfortable 1998 Toyota Sienna LE is another good choice; expect to pay around $16,000 for a 3-door, $17,500 for a 4-door XLE.

PLUSH CRUISERS

Lincolns have depreciated so rapidly that some are bargains used. For about $14,400, you can buy a spacious and feature-laden 1998 Town Car Executive. The Acura RL offers more refinement. A 1996 runs about $15,300. Essentially a stretched Camry, the Toyota Avalon offers the

Mazda Miata

refinement and quiet competence of its smaller sibling in a roomy and polished package. Look for a 1998 XLS, for about $16,000. For the ultimate in relaxed cruising, consider the opulent Lexus LS400. A good 1995 example can be found for about $19,000. One size smaller is the excellent Mercedes-Benz E320. Figure about $18,500 for a 1995 model. Another top choice is the zesty but civilized BMW 530i ($18,250 for a 1995 model).

FUN TO DRIVE

Among affordable sporty cars, the Mazda Miata has few peers. While woefully short on comfort, convenience, and trunk space, this tiny two-seat convertible is thrilling to drive. A 1995 model goes for about $7,800; a redesigned 1999 for

Honda Odyssey

Nissan Pathfinder

about $14,000. The Toyota Celica is another sporty contender, with enjoyable handling and excellent quality. A choice Celica is the 1995 GT coupe, at about $9,350.

SUVs

For a traditional-design SUV with proven reliability, the 1998 Nissan Pathfinder SE ($16,000) and the 1998 Toyota 4Runner SR5 ($18,200) are both good choices. The Pathfinder's cabin is a bit small, however. For those who value everyday driving comfort over off-road brawn, the car-based Subaru Forester L is a good choice ($13,600 for a 1998 model). The Toyota RAV4 ($12,350 for a 1998 four-door AWD) offers fine foul-weather credentials in an agile, maneuverable package.

STATION WAGONS

For best value in a station wagon, the reliable all-wheel-drive Subaru are tops. Even plain-vanilla models are well designed. The small Impreza L wagon goes for about $9,250 for a 1997, while the larger Legacy runs about $13,000 for a 1998 L.

THE BEST VEHICLES UNDER $15,000

These days $15,000 will buy only the cheapest of new cars, usually a small sedan or hatchback without many features or frills. That same money will go a lot further when you buy a used car. It can net you a late-model family car, SUV, or mini-van, or even a luxury model of a slightly older vintage.

CONSUMER REPORTS' list of top choices under $15,000 includes 1995 or newer vehicles that have demonstrated above-average reliability and also did well in CR tests when they were new. Price ranges are approximations.

$12,000-$15,000
Acura Integra '98-99,
   TL '96-'97
Honda Accord '98-99,
   Civic '00, CR-V '97-98,
   Odyssey '96-97
Infiniti I30 '97
Isuzu Oasis '97-98
Lexus ES300 '95
Mazda Millenia '98
Nissan Maxima '98-99,
   Pathfinder '96-97
Subaru Impreza '00-01,
   Forester '98,
   Legacy '97-98
Toyota 4Runner '96,
   Avalon '97-98,
   Camry '98-99, Celica '97,
   RAV4 '98-99

$10,000-$12,000
Acura Integra '97
Chevrolet Prizm '01
Honda Accord '97, Civic '99,
   Odyssey '95

Infiniti I30 '96
Isuzu Oasis '96
Mazda Protege '01
Nissan Maxima '97
   Pathfinder '95
Toyota 4Runner '95, Avalon
   '96, Camry '97, Celica
   '96, Corolla '00-01,
   RAV4 '97

Less than $10,000
Acura Integra '95-96
Chevrolet Prizm/Geo Prizm
   '95-00
Honda Accord '95-96,
   Civic '95-98
Infiniti G20 '95-96
Mazda Millenia '96
Nissan Maxima '95
Subaru Impreza '95-98,
   Legacy '97
Toyota Avalon '95-96,
   Camry '95-96, Celica '95,
   Corolla '95-99, RAV4 '96

such as dealers and private sales. See the "Online Resources" guide on page 18. Printed guides include the Kelley Blue Book, the Edmund's guide, and the NADA Official Used Car Guide, among others. You can often find them at newsstands, bookstores, libraries, and from the loan officer at your bank. You'll also find online versions of these guides.

When you calculate a used-car price, you will want to specify important factors such as mileage, condition, and the level of optional equipment. The CONSUMER REPORTS Used Car Price Service gives such customized used-car price information. It notes those things as well as giving different price ranges for trade-ins or purchases from a dealer. CR's Used Car Price Reports can be ordered either on the phone or from ConsumerReports.org (see the ad on page 239).

Different cars command varying prices depending on the region, the season, the city, and maybe even the neighborhood within that city. The important information for you is what price a car sells for in the place you're shopping.

Whatever your source of price information, keep in mind that to some extent all used-car prices are local, and in the end you'll probably wind up bargaining over the price.

You can gauge local prices by scanning newspaper ads and classified-ad publications. You can also refer to Internet used-car sites to scope out prices within regions or across the whole country (see "Online Resources," page 18.)

FINANCE AND INSURANCE. How much it will cost to finance and insure your next car may affect your choice. We discuss financing and insurance options in Chapter 4.

THE DEPRECIATION FACTOR. One of the major reasons that used cars are as widely sold as they are (the used-car market is about twice the size of the new-car market) is because new cars depreciate so rapidly. Cars lose value most quickly in their first several years on the road. After that, the depreciation curve levels out some. The average model, CONSUMER REPORTS research shows, loses more than 43 percent of its value in its first three years.

Depreciation hits different car segments differently. On average, sedans lose nearly 45 percent of their value in the first three years. Large domestic luxury cars tend to lose money even faster—more than half their value in the first 36 months. While that's bad news for new-car buyers, it's great news when you're buying those vehicles used. Likewise, vehicles that hold their value well—including many small or sporty cars, sport-utility vehicles, and pickup trucks—cost their original buyers less in depreciation, but are hardly bargains secondhand. You can see how age affects price in the profiles of 256 models, which start on page 81, where we give the approximate price range for each model and year covered.

Step 3: Where to shop for a used car

The spread of retail leasing, the advent of the used-car superstore, and the burgeoning Internet have changed the retail landscape for both consumers and dealers. A fiercely competitive new-car market has made used cars potentially more profitable for dealers than new ones. That means that a dealer's used-car operation is more important than ever before, and a buyer may find more selection and more flexible financing options.

Here are the major used-car venues to check out:

NEW-CAR DEALERS. Nearly all franchised dealers have a used-car department that sells vehicles they have taken as trade-ins or that have come back at the end of a lease. Such departments tend to feature late-model vehicles, two or three years old, many of which have just come off lease and are sold with a limited warranty (see "The Certified Option," page 16). Many new-car dealers don't bother with very old cars or ones that are difficult to sell, so their used vehicles tend to be expensive.

SUPERSTORES. The used-car superstore chain was a novel selling system that has had a bumpy ride. The concept involves selling huge lots of good used cars at no-haggle prices. Of the two national chains that tried this, CarMax, a Circuit City subsidiary, is the only one still going. AutoNation, the other big chain, is now the biggest owner of new-car dealerships, but its used-car superstores have been phased out. The company continues to sell used cars through its many new-car dealerships.

There are also individual independent dealers who call themselves superstores. Whether they specialize in low-pressure, one-price selling, or want you to bargain the old-fashioned way, their key advantage is size and the variety of the stock.

INDEPENDENT USED-CAR DEALERS. Independent used-car dealers are apt to handle any and all vehicle brands. Their merchandise can run the gamut from the almost-new to the should-be-scrapped. A used-car dealer offers the benefits and drawbacks of any other local merchant. If the dealer has been around for a long time and has a good reputation, that's a good sign. A local used-car dealer may take the trouble to locate a specific vehicle for you. Traditionally, used-car dealers are accustomed to arranging financing for people who don't have much to spend.

Still, caution is the watchword. Both price and quality tend to be lower than at a new-car dealership. Repair facilities tend to be less sophisticated, so expect to take the car elsewhere for major servicing.

SERVICE STATIONS. Many service stations have a sideline business selling used cars. They may not have all that many cars to sell, but prices are often better than those you'll find at a dealership. If the station has serviced the car throughout its life, you may have access to the repair history—a real plus.

PRIVATE OWNERS. You can usually get the best price if you buy a car directly from its previous owner. A private party doesn't have to cover the overhead of a business and frequently just wants to get rid of the vehicle.

Buying from a private owner, however, also carries the biggest risk. Even the most honest

THE CERTIFIED OPTION

Are you buying someone else's problems?

That's always been a big concern for used-car shoppers. Manufacturers and some dealers have now developed "certification" programs to give buyers a greater sense of confidence in their wares. Certified used cars are billed as the cream-of-the-crop, inspected and reconditioned according to a strict checklist. Nearly all the major brands now have manufacturer-certification programs. Of course, dealers charge extra for "certified" cars.

As it happens, there are a lot of candidate vehicles for these programs. The huge increase in car leasing in the late '90s has saddled the carmakers' financing subsidiaries with millions of late-model, well-maintained off-lease cars that they must dispose of. Certification, with its higher prices, helps maintain the resale value of the leased vehicles, which in turn helps the finances of the leasing business look rosier.

The term certification doesn't actually mean much. Any used-car dealer can call any car "certified." The term has no legal definition, and no watchdog agency polices its use.

As a result, you'll sometimes see a car labeled "certified" that has not undergone any reconditioning process. It may carry only a service contract, the cost of which is rolled into the vehicle's asking price.

You might also see aftermarket warranty programs that look like manufacturer certification. These "dealer certification" programs are underwritten by one of a number of warranty companies, essentially insurers, that sell a program to dealers who then resell it to consumers. Because the quality and terms of such contracts vary widely, it's especially important to read the fine print skeptically.

Many are culled, fewer are chosen

All manufacturer programs require that candidate cars be under a specified age and mileage, typically no more than five years old with less than 60,000 or 70,000 miles. Manufacturer programs routinely exclude cars that have a suspicious title history or other serious flaws.

With a typical manufacturer-certification program, the dealership screens, inspects, and reconditions cars according to stringent manufacturer guidelines. The automaker then certifies that the car is sound and gives it a manufacturer-backed warranty. Terms differ significantly. Some extend or reinstate all or part of the car's original warranty, with coverage lasting from three months to several years. Others begin when you buy the certified vehicle.

Certification programs also typically throw in enhancements such as roadside assistance and trip-interruption insurance. Since these items are generally available elsewhere, the extras probably shouldn't be a deciding factor.

Peace of mind or piece of paper?

You needn't assume that a certified car is worth the big premium a dealer may ask. If you're buying a late-model, low-mileage car, you should expect it to be in good condition. Negotiate the price as you would any other used car.

The major value of certification is its warranty. Look for the longest and fullest warranty you can find.

The best warranties are those called "comprehensive," which cover the most items. Luxury nameplates tend to offer the fullest and longest warranties, which makes sense since one of the luxuries you buy with such a car is a good warranty.

Recommendations

Before buying a certified used car, compare the price with that of noncertified cars of the same age and mileage. When considering any such car, ask the dealer some specific questions:

◆ Is the vehicle covered by a manufacturer-certified program or by a third-party plan sold by the dealer? Nonmanufacturer plans are wild cards because they can vary greatly in quality.

◆ What does the warranty cover, and for how long? Ask to see a copy of the warranty contract, not just a glossy brochure.

◆ Is there a deductible? If there is a charge for service, find out how much it is, and whether you must pay it for each item serviced or for each service call.

◆ Who provides the service? Ask if you have to bring the car back to the original dealer for warranty work, or will any same-brand dealership do the work for you. Ask what you're required to do in an emergency.

If you are buying a well-maintained car with a good record of reliability, then you aren't taking much of a risk if you skip the certification route. But you should always try to have the vehicle thoroughly inspected by an independent mechanic.

citizen may be unaware of trouble signs or may suffer a sudden bout of amnesia when asked about problems with a car he is selling. If you're buying a car privately, shop wisely. Check local newspapers, weekly classified-ad publications, and specialized car-sales-oriented publications.

Limit your choices to cars with a good history of reliability, and be sure to make a thorough inspection in broad daylight. The checklist on page 22 can help. It's a good idea to have any used car, particularly one bought privately, inspected by a mechanic as well. The problems the mechanic uncovers can be used as bargaining chips should you decide you still want the car.

Shopping online

Buying—or at least researching—used cars online opens up a world of possibilities. Locating a specific vehicle online is like using a sophisticated version of classified advertising. Its major advantage is your ability to search, sort, and check the marketplace without leaving home. While that's a real convenience, you may find the offerings slim and located far from home. Used cars also aren't any cheaper online, but the web does provide a way to find out what various models are selling for in your area.

Web resources go far beyond vehicle shopping. You can also shop for insurance and financing, or look up safety information. You'll also find innumerable sites for hobbyists, do-it-yourselfers, collectors, and private sellers.

A car-purchase web site typically asks you to fill in some search parameters: the make and model you're interested in, the price range you're shopping in, and the geographic area (based on your ZIP code) where you'd like to shop. You then get a list of vehicles that fit your buying criteria, along with the sellers' e-mail addresses or phone numbers. Because many of the current sellers are car dealers, most of these specialized sites offer direct links to the dealers' web sites. Most services also let you place a classified ad for selling your old car, either free or for a small fee.

One of the keys to shopping online to avoid searching a broader area than you're willing to drive to inspect a vehicle. Problems we've noticed with online offerings include the freshness of the information and the clutter of annoying ads.

Sellers must constantly update their web offerings as inventories change. If they don't, the sites grow stale and inaccurate. That can make locating even common models a challenge. Always call before visiting any dealer, to make sure the vehicle you're looking for is still in stock.

Advertising provides much of a selling site's revenue. Sometimes the ads show up as windows posing as links to information resources when in fact they're just links to an advertiser, such as an insurance or finance company.

Being able to search the country and compare prices from region to region does have its uses, but more for research than for actual buying. Except in unusual circumstances, such as collecting a classic, it usually isn't helpful to know about a car for sale hundreds or thousands of miles away from home.

The biggest limitation to shopping for a used car online is that you can't test drive it. In our experience, a close personal inspection is absolutely vital, even if you think you've covered all the bases by phone or e-mail.

ONLINE GUIDE. You'll find a list of web sites helpful to car shoppers below. CONSUMER REPORTS does not endorse or recommend any of the sites appearing on this list except its own site, ConsumerReports.org.

Step 4: Interview the seller

Once you've located some candidates for purchase, it's time to interview the owner, either a private party or a car dealer. The answers you get to basic questions about a used car—even over the telephone—can help you avoid a lot of trouble later. That's especially true when you're buying from a private party. Any strange, far-fetched, or odd-sounding answers to routine questions should put you on guard.

'WHAT COLOR IS THE CAR?' Color may or may not be important to you, but this question

ONLINE RESOURCES

The Internet is handy for researching most aspects of buying a vehicle. This list of major providers of auto information and services covers the waterfront but is by no means exhaustive. CONSUMER REPORTS has not rated and does not endorse the businesses listed here. All web addresses begin with "www."

CONSUMERREPORTS.ORG
CONSUMER REPORTS offers online assistance at **ConsumerReports.org.** Site subscribers get unlimited access to our extensive archives, including full road tests, and an interactive vehicle selector for new and used cars. The free area of the Autos section provides an array of articles, ranging from the latest trends and technology to in-depth expert advice on buying, leasing, safety, and more. **CR New Car and Used Car Price Reports,** with model-specific information, are designed to help you get the best deal on your vehicle purchase, and can be ordered online.

PRICING: NEW & USED CARS
Look here for new-car retail prices and used-car values. Some sites also provide dealer invoice, incentives, and other pricing variables for new cars.

AutoSite . . . . .autosite.com
Edmunds . . . . .edmunds.com
Intellichoice . . . . .intellichoice.com
Kelley Blue Book . . . . . . .kbb.com
National Automobile Dealer
 Association . . . . .nada.com
VMR (used cars only) . .vmrintl.com

**VEHICLE REVIEWS
& COMPARISONS**
Different sources have varying points of view. Read a range.

Automobile . . .automobilemag.com
Car and Driver . . .caranddriver.com

Carpoint . . . . .carpoint.com
Epinions . . . . .epinions.com
Motor Trend . . . . . .motortrend.com
Road & Track . . . .roadandtrack.com

NEW-CAR BUYING
These sites can provide prices for specific models and put you in touch with participating dealerships.

Autobytel . . . . .autobytel.com
Auto Trader . . . . . . .autotrader.com
AutoVantage . . . .autovantage.com
Autoweb . . . . .autoweb.com
CarBargains . . . . .checkbook.org
Carpoint . . . . .carpoint.com
Cars.com . . . . .cars.com
CarsDirect . . . . . . .carsdirect.com
InvoiceDealers.com
 . . . . .invoicedealers.com
StoneAge . . . . .stoneage.com

USED-CAR BUYING
These sites are like online classified ads that allow you to search over as broad an area as you like.

Autobytel . . . . .autobytel.com
Auto Trader . . . . . . .autotrader.com
Autoweb . . . . .autoweb.com
Dealernet . . . . .dealernet.com
Cars.com . . . . .cars.com
Ebay . . . . .ebaymotors.com
Imotors . . . . .imotors.com
StoneAge . . . . .stoneage.com
Used Cars Online . . . .ausedcar.com

**LEASING DEALS
& INFORMATION**
Automotive Lease Guide . . .alg.com

LeaseSource . . . . .leasesource.com
Intellichoice . . . . .intellichoice.com

AUTO LOAN RATES & LENDERS
Bank Rate Monitor . . . .bankrate.com
E-Loan . . . . .eloan.com
LendingTree . . . . . .lendingtree.com
Household Auto householdauto.com
Peoplefirst . . . . . . .peoplefirst.com
VirtualBank . . . . . .virtualbank.com

CREDIT REPORTS
Experian . . . . .experian.com
Trans Union . . . . . .transunion.com
My Credit . . . . . . .mycreditfile.com

**MAINTENANCE/
OWNERSHIP COSTS**
Intellichoice . . . . .intellichoice.com

VEHICLE HISTORY REPORTS
Carfax . . . . .carfax.com
Experian . . . . .autocheck.com

SAFETY/CRASH-TEST RESULTS
National Highway Traffic Safety
Administration . . . . . .nhtsa.dot.gov
Insurance Institute for
Highway Safety . . . . . .hwysafety.org

**EPA FUEL ECONOMY/
EMISSIONS**
Green-vehicle ratings
 . . . . .epa.gov/greenvehicles
Fuel-economy
 estimates . . . . . .fueleconomy.gov

AUTOMAKER WEB SITES
Acura . . . . .acura.com

Audi . . . . .audiusa.com
BMW . . . . .bmwusa.com
Buick . . . . .buick.com
Cadillac . . . . .cadillac.com
Chevrolet . . . . .chevrolet.com
Chrysler . . . . .chrysler.com
Daewoo . . . . .daewoous.com
Dodge . . . . .dodge.com
Ford . . . . .fordvehicles.com
GMC . . . . .gmc.com
Honda . . . . .honda.com
Hyundai . . . . . . .hyundaiusa.com
Infiniti . . . . .infiniti.com
Isuzu . . . . .isuzu.com
Jaguar . . . . .us.jaguar.com
Jeep . . . . .jeep.com
Kia . . . . .kia.com
Land Rover . . . . . .landrover.com
Lexus . . . . .lexus.com
Lincoln . . . . . .lincolnvehicles.com
Mazda . . . . .mazdausa.com
Mercedes-Benz . . . . . . .mbusa.com
Mercury . . . . .mercuryvehicles.com
Mini . . . . .miniusa.com
Mitsubishi . . . . .mitsubishicars.com
Nissan . . . . .nissanusa.com
Oldsmobile . . . . . . .oldsmobile.com
Pontiac . . . . .pontiac.com
Porsche . . . . .porsche.com
Saab . . . . .saabusa.com
Saturn . . . . .saturn.com
Subaru . . . . .subaru.com
Suzuki . . . . .suzukiauto.com
Toyota . . . . .toyota.com
Volkswagen . . . . .vw.com
Volvo . . . . .volvocars.com

can break the ice. Whatever the answer, follow up with, "Are the body and upholstery in good shape?" You want to get a general idea of the car's condition.

'HOW IS IT EQUIPPED?' Whether they're listed in the ad or not, ask about key features: number of doors; transmission type; air conditioning; antilock brakes; air bags; sound system; power windows, locks, seats, or mirrors; cruise control; sunroof; upholstery material; and so forth. Double-checking on these could produce some telling comments.

'HAVE YOU OWNED IT SINCE IT WAS NEW?' You want to be able to piece together as much of the car's service history as you can. Be concerned about a car that's changed hands quite a bit—three or four times in two years, say.

'ARE YOU THE PERSON WHO DROVE IT THE MOST?' Ideally, you want to meet the car's principal driver or drivers to see if they strike you as responsible people. Be wary of a car that has spent time in the hands of a teenager.

'HOW MANY MILES DOES IT HAVE?' If the mileage is higher than, say, 20,000 per year or lower than 5,000, ask why. If a car has high mileage because its owner had a long highway commute to work, that's better than if a car was used for a lot of short trips, stop-and-go driving, or a delivery route. Low mileage is a good thing, but a low odometer reading is no guarantee of gentle care.

'HAS IT EVER BEEN IN AN ACCIDENT?' If so, ask about the extent of the damage, cost of repairs, and the sort of shop that did the work. Don't worry too much about minor scrapes, but think twice about buying a car that has been in a serious accident.

'DO YOU HAVE SERVICE RECORDS?' You want a car that has been well cared-for. That means that it should have had recommended maintenance performed at the manufacturer's specified service intervals. If the owner says he did the maintenance himself but can't produce any receipts for parts, be skeptical. You also want to see the receipts for any new muffler, brakes, tires, or other "wear" parts that have been replaced. Repair-shop receipts normally note the car's odometer reading, helping you verify the car's history. Also ask if any safety-recall work was performed or, more importantly, *needs* to be performed. Dealers keep records of that, and also note the mileage when such work was performed. (See "Recalls & Technical Service Bulletins," page 209.)

'WHY ARE YOU SELLING THE CAR?' Look for a plausible explanation rather than an interesting story. If the answer sounds evasive, be wary.

If you're buying from a dealer, you probably won't be able to glean all that much information about the car's history because the dealer simply may not know it. Take with a grain of salt any tale about how the previous owner pampered the car. But you should still ask to see service records and other evidence that the car was maintained properly.

Step 5: How to inspect and test drive

Whether you buy from a dealer or a private party, always inspect the vehicle thoroughly and try to take it to a mechanic for a final inspection. To check for known defects, see the recalls section starting on page 209.

You don't have to be an expert to give a car a good, revealing going-over. You can learn a great deal just by using your eyes, ears, and nose. Dress in old clothes and take along a friend to help you out. Do your inspection in broad daylight on a dry day or in a well-lit garage. The car must be parked on a level surface and shouldn't have been driven for at

WHERE THERE'S SMOKE...

A little smoke from the tailpipe in the first seconds after startup is nothing to worry about. Smoke that persists is cause for concern.

After driving awhile at highway speeds, take your foot off the accelerator for a few seconds and check the rear-view mirror for exhaust smoke. Step firmly on the accelerator and then look back again.

◆ Black smoke comes from partially burned fuel. This indicates that the fuel system needs to be serviced.

◆ Blue smoke indicates burning oil–a bad sign. Clouds of blue smoke on startup may indicate worn valve guides, seals, or pistons rings, which can mean a cylinder-head or engine rebuild is needed.

◆ Billowy white smoke may indicate that coolant is getting into the engine–another bad sign. However, it's normal when starting an engine in cold weather for condensation in the exhaust pipe to blow out as a whitish vapor.

least an hour before you take a look. Bring along a copy of the "Used-Car Checklist" you'll find on page 22.

CHECK OUT THE EXTERIOR. First, walk around the car and see if it's standing level. Bounce each corner up and down. If the shock absorbers are in good shape, the car should rebound just once or twice. Then grab the top of each front tire and tug it back and forth. If you feel play in it or hear a clunking or ticking sound, the wheel bearings or suspension joints may be shot.

Body condition. Check each body panel and the roof, looking for scratches, dents, and rust. Examine the lines of the fenders and doors. Misaligned panels or large gaps can indicate either sloppy assembly at the factory or shoddy repair. Paint color and finish should be the same on every body panel.

If you think a dent may have been patched up, use a magnet to see if it sticks to the suspect area. If a dent in a steel panel was filled with plastic body filler, the magnet won't stick. If parts of the car have been repainted, there may be signs of "overspray," or paint adhering to the rubber seals around the hood and trunk lid.

Minor cosmetic flaws are no cause for concern, but rust is. Look particularly for blistered paint or rust spots around the wheel wells and rocker panels (the sheet metal beneath the doors) and the bottoms of the doors themselves. Use a flashlight to look inside the wheel wells for rust and corrosion caused by salt.

Open and close each door, the hood, and the trunk. Gently lift and let go of each door, particularly the driver's door. If the door is loose on its hinges, the car has seen hard or long use. Also inspect the rubber seals around all openings.

Lights and lenses. Have a friend stand outside the car and confirm that all lights are working. Make sure all light lenses are intact and not cracked, fogged with moisture, or missing.

Tires. You can tell a lot from the tires. If the car has less than, say, 20,000 miles on the odometer, it should probably still have its original rubber. If a car with low miles on the odometer has new tires, be suspicious. The odometer may have been rolled back.

Tread wear should be even across the width of the tread. It should also be the same on the left and right sides of the car. Ask if the tires have been rotated front-to-rear regularly. If not, the wear is usually more severe on the drive wheels.

An aggressive driver tends to put heavy wear on the outside shoulder of the front tires, at the edge of the sidewall. If it's badly worn, assume that the car has been driven hard.

Check the tread depth, either with a tread-depth tool (available at auto-parts stores) or with a penny. To be legal, tires must have at least $\frac{1}{16}$ inch of tread. If you don't have a tread gauge, insert a penny into the tread groove, with Lincoln's head down. If you can see the top of Abe's head, the tire should be replaced.

Examine the sidewalls for scuffing, cracks, or bulges, and look on the edge of each rim for dents or cracks. And be sure to check the spare.

Glass. Look carefully at the windshield and other windows to make sure there are no cracks. A small stone chip may not be cause for alarm, though you should bring it up, as a bargaining point in negotiations. But cracks in the windshield often grow worse over time and can lead to a costly repair.

CHECK OUT THE INTERIOR. It's the inside of a car that may matter most in the long run, since that's where you'll be spending the most time with the car.

Odor. When you first open the car door, sniff the interior. A musty, moldy, or mildewy smell could indicate water leaks. Remove the floor mats, and feel and sniff for wet spots on the carpet beneath. Odors can be hard to get rid of. If there's doubt, find another car.

Pedal rubber. The rubber on the brake, clutch, and gas pedals gives an indication of use. A car with low miles shouldn't show much wear. If the pedal rubber is worn through in spots—or brand new—it indicates high miles.

Instruments and controls. Start the car and let it idle. Note if it's hard to start when cold. Note too whether the engine idles smoothly. Then methodically try out every switch, button, and lever.

With the engine running, turn on the heater full blast and see how hot it gets, how quickly. Switch on the air conditioning and make sure it quickly blows cold.

Try the sound system. Check radio reception on AM and FM, and try loading, playing, and ejecting a tape or compact disc if there is a tape or CD player.

Seats. Try out all the seats even though you may not plan on sitting in the rear. Upholstery shouldn't be ripped or badly worn, particularly in a car that's supposed to have low miles on it. Try all the driver's seat adjustments to make sure you can find a good driving position.

LOOK IN THE TRUNK. The trunk is another place to use your nose as well as your eyes. Again, sniff and look for signs of water entry. See if the carpeting feels wet or smells musty. Take up the trunk floor and check the spare-tire well for water or rust.

WATCH OUT FOR REBUILT WRECKS

A growing problem in the used-car market is that of "rebuilt wrecks." Most are vehicles that have been heavily damaged in an accident and subsequently declared a "total loss" (that is, more expensive to repair than to replace) by the owner's insurance company. After paying off the policy-holder's claim, the insurance company usually obtains a "salvage" title for the vehicle, then auctions it off to a dismantler (for parts), a scrap processor, or, increasingly, a rebuilder. The rebuilder puts the car back together—often as cheaply as possible—and attempts to resell the car at a profit.

While it is possible to return a totaled car to safe operating condition, especially if the damage was more superficial than structural, there's no guarantee that the rebuilder will do so. And, unfortunately, most states require only a cursory inspection before deeming a rebuilt vehicle roadworthy.

In addition to their suspect durability and questionable crashworthiness, rebuilt wrecks represent a singularly poor investment: When a vehicle is issued a salvage title, its value typically drops by 50 percent or more.

You can usually tell whether a car has been wrecked and rebuilt by checking the title, but some states make it easier than others. Among the best is Washington state, which requires "WA REBUILT" in large type running diagonally across the title. Among the worst: Colorado, where salvage titles are distinguished only by a small "R" in front of the vehicle's make.

Call your local Department of Motor Vehicles office to find out how to spot a salvage title in your state.

USED-CAR CHECKLIST

VEHICLE DESCRIPTION

Year_____   Make_____   Model_____   Trim line_____

Body   ❏ Sedan   ❏ Coupe   ❏ Convertible   ❏ Wagon   ❏ Van   ❏ Truck   ❏ SUV

Engine: Cylinders_____   Displacement_____(liters)   Odometer reading_____

Color: Exterior_____   Interior_____

No. of doors_____   No. of seats_____   Upholstery material   ❏ Cloth   ❏ Leather   ❏ Vinyl

Vehicle Identification Number (VIN)_____

Owner's name_____   Town_____   Phone number_____

INSPECTION

◆ EXTERIOR

❏ Shocks and struts rebound just once or twice after bouncing   ❏ No play in wheel bearings

Finish: ❏ Paint smooth, not peeling or blistered   ❏ No dents   ❏ No scratches   ❏ No rust   ❏ Body panels fit well   ❏ Color and finish match

❏ No damage evident on underside of hood or trunk

Doors, hood, trunk lid: ❏ Open and close smoothly   ❏ Hinges tight   ❏ Rubber seals intact

Body condition notes:_____

Lights working: ❏Front   ❏ Rear   ❏ Brake   ❏ Backup   ❏ Fog lights   ❏ License plate light(s)   ❏ Lenses intact

Tires: ❏ Same brand all around   ❏ Wear even   ❏ Rims not dented or rusted   ❏ Tread depth OK (use penny test)   Tire size_____

Glass: ❏ No chips or cracks

◆ INTERIOR AND INSTRUMENT PANEL

❏ No musty smell   ❏ Carpets OK   ❏ Floor mats present   ❏ Carpet/underlayment under mats dry   ❏ Wear on pedal rubber agrees with odometer

❏ Upholstery in good shape   ❏ Seats in good shape   ❏ Driving position comfortable

Controls working: ❏ Headlights   ❏ Turn signals   ❏ Horn   ❏ Windshield wiper/washer   ❏ Climate system   ❏ Air conditioner

❏ Seat heater   ❏ Dome/map/panel lights   ❏ Window cranks or switches   ❏ Seat adjustments   ❏ Power seat(s)   ❏ Sunroof

❏ Power locks   ❏ Power mirrors   ❏ Key-fob remote   ❏ Sound system: ❏ AM   ❏ FM   ❏ Tape   ❏ CD

Interior notes:_____

_____

◆ TRUNK

❏ Spare tire OK   ❏ Full-sized spare   ❏ Limited-service spare   ❏ Jack and all tools present   ❏ No moisture or rust in spare-tire well

General condition:_____

◆ ENGINE COMPARTMENT

❏ Wiring-harness plastic armor flexible   ❏ Wiring connectors neat   ❏ No aftermarket wiring   ❏ Rubber hoses supple

Fluids: ❏ Oil OK   ❏ Transmission fluid OK   ❏ Power steering fluid OK   ❏ Brake fluid OK   ❏ Radiator coolant greenish

❏ Battery liquid/color of "eye" OK   ❏ Automatic transmission fluid OK (check with engine running)   ❏ Windshield washer fluid OK

◆ UNDERNEATH

❏ No drips beneath car   ❏ Constant-velocity boots intact   ❏ Tailpipe residue gray, not black or oily   ❏ Pipes, muffler, and catalytic converter OK

NOTES

_____

_____

_____

_____

Permission is granted to photocopy this page.

Check the condition of the spare tire. (If the car has alloy wheels, the spare-tire rim is often plain steel.) Also be sure the jack and all the jack tools are present.

UNDER THE HOOD. If the engine has been off for a few minutes, you can do most under-the-hood checks. Look first at the general condition of the engine bay. Dirt and dust are normal, but watch out if you see lots of oil spattered about, a battery covered with corrosion, or wires and hoses hanging loose.

Hoses and belts. Try to squeeze the various rubber hoses running to the radiator, air conditioner, and other parts. The rubber should be firm and supple, not rock-hard, cracked, or mushy. Feel the fan belt and other drive belts to determine if they are frayed.

Fluids. Check all the fluid levels. The owner's manual will point out where to look. The engine oil should be dark brown or black, but not too dirty or gritty. If the oil is honey-colored, it was just changed. White spots in the oil cap indicate water is present. Transmission fluid should be pinkish, not brown, and smell like oil, with no "burnt" odor. It shouldn't leave visible metal particles on your rag—a sign of serious problems. With most cars, you're supposed to check the automatic-transmission fluid with the engine warmed up and running. On some, the transmission-fluid dipstick has two sets of marks for checking when the engine is either cold or warm. Also check the power-steering and brake-fluid levels. They should be within the safe zone.

Radiator. Check the coolant by looking into the plastic reservoir near the radiator. The coolant should be greenish, not a deep rust or milky color. Greenish stains on the radiator are a sign of pinhole leaks.

Battery. Some "maintenance-free" batteries have a built-in charge indicator. A green indicator eye usually means the battery is in good shape while yellow or black usually means the battery is dying or dead. But because these indicators reveal the condition of just one cell, it may not give an accurate reading on how healthy the whole battery is.

If the battery has filler caps, wipe off the top of the battery with a rag, then carefully pry off or unscrew the caps to look at the liquid electrolyte level. If the level is low, it may not mean much, or it may mean that the battery has been working too hard. Have a mechanic check out the charging system and do a "load test" on the battery.

UNDER THE CAR. Spread an old blanket on the ground, so you can look under the engine at the pavement. Use a flashlight. If you see oil drips, other oily leaks, or green or red fluid, it's not a good sign. If you can find the spot where a car was habitually parked, see if that part of the garage floor or driveway is marred with puddles of gasoline, oil, coolant, or transmission fluid.

Don't be alarmed if some clear water drips from under the car on a hot day. It's probably just water condensed from the air conditioner.

Examine the constant-velocity-joint boots behind the front wheels. They are round, black rubber bellows at the ends of the axle shafts. If the rubber boots are split and leaking grease, assume that the car has or shortly will have bad CV joints—another item that's costly to repair.

Feel for any tailpipe residue. If it's black and greasy, it means the car is burning oil. The tail-pipe smudge should be dry and dark gray. Look at the pipes. Some rust is normal. Heavy rust is sometimes normal but could mean that a new exhaust system might be needed soon.

Take a test drive

If you're still interested in the car, ask to take it for a test drive. Plan to spend at least 20 minutes behind the wheel, to allow enough time to check the engine's cooling system and the car's heater and air conditioner.

COMFORT. Make sure the car fits you. Set the seat in a comfortable driving position and attach the safety belt. With an air-bag-equipped car, make sure that you can sit at least 10 inches back from the steering wheel and can still fully depress all the pedals. Make sure that you can reach all the controls without straining, that the controls are easy to use, and that the displays are easy to see. Adjust the mirrors and make sure you can see well to the rear. Look over your right shoulder, too, to see if that view is obstructed.

STEERING. With the engine idling before you start your test drive, turn the steering wheel right and left. You should feel almost no play in the wheel before the tires start to turn on the pavement.

Once under way, the car should respond to the helm quickly and neatly, without lots of steering-wheel motion. At normal speeds, the car should maintain course without constant steering corrections. If the wheel shakes at highway speed, suspect a problem with tire wear, wheel balance, or front-end alignment, which are all easily remedied, or with the driveline or suspension, which may not be.

ENGINE AND TRANSMISSION. When you accelerate, there should be no appreciable hesitation between the engine's acceleration and the car's. If there is, it's an almost sure sign of transmission or clutch wear—and a costly fix down the road.

With a manual transmission, the clutch should fully engage well before you take your foot all the way off the pedal. If there isn't at least an inch of play at the top of the pedal's travel, the car may soon need a new clutch.

BRAKES. Test the brakes on an empty stretch of road. From a speed of 45 mph, apply the brakes hard. The car should stop straight and quickly, without pulling to one side and without any unusual vibration. The pedal feel should be smooth and not grabby, and stopping the car shouldn't take a huge effort. If the car has antilock brakes, you should feel them activate with a rapid pulsing underfoot when you push hard on the brake. (It's easier to make the antilock braking system activate on a stretch of wet road.)

Try two or three stops; the car should stop straight and easily each time. Then pull into a safe area, stop, and step firmly on the brake pedal for 30 seconds. If the pedal feels spongy or sinks to the floor, there may be a leak in the brake system.

LOOK, LISTEN, FEEL. At a steady speed on a smooth road, note any vibrations. You shouldn't feel shuddering through the steering wheel, nor should the dashboard shake or the image in your mirrors quiver noticeably.

Drive at 30 mph or so on a bumpy road. You want a compliant, well-controlled, quiet ride. If the car bounces and hops a lot on routine bumps and ruts, it may mean the car has suspension problems or the car's chassis wasn't designed well in the first place. Listen, too, for rattles and squeaks—they're annoying to live with and often difficult to track down and fix.

Take it to a mechanic

Try to have the car checked out by a good mechanic. A dealer should have no problem lending you the car for that purpose as long as you leave some identification; a private owner, though, may be reluctant. If the inspection can be done while you wait, you may leave your old car as assurance you're coming back. Or you may caravan to the mechanic with the seller. A thorough diagnosis should cost around $100. Ask for a written report detailing the car's condition, noting any problems found and what it would cost to repair them. You can then use the report in the negotiation with the seller, should you decide to buy the vehicle.

LOOKING FOR MR. GOODWRENCH. It can be a challenge to locate a qualified mechanic. The best recommendation is a referral from someone who has had dealings with the garage. You might also try asking for mechanics' names at a good local auto-parts store.

The Yellow Pages should list shops that advertise auto-diagnostic work. An organization called the Car Care Council also certifies shops that do diagnostic work. If you're an American Automobile Association (AAA) member, use its recommended facility.

The garage should look clean and well maintained. There should be up-to-date electronic diagnostic equipment next to the service bays. Look for framed certificates or window decals from AAA or the National Institute of Automotive Service Excellence (ASE). AAA-certified garages must meet certain quality standards. ASE grants certificates to mechanics who pass exams in any of eight areas of expertise. Look also for signs of membership in the local Better Business Bureau.

Step 6: Negotiate effectively

In general, negotiating to buy a used car is less harrowing than buying a new car. If you're buying from a car dealer, there are fewer opportunities for the dealership to load up the deal with extra-cost items and nonobvious charges. If you're buying from a private party, that person is unlikely to have the experience and resources to play all the games a dealer might try.

If you've followed the recommendations in Step 2, above, then you already have a good idea of what a car like the one you're looking at sells for in your area.

Always assume that any advertised price is negotiable. The best way to negotiate is to say as little as possible for as long as possible. Begin by making an offer that is realistic but still, say, 25 percent lower than what you are willing to pay.

You might start by itemizing all the legitimate things you have found wrong with the car. If you have a mechanic's report, use it to show how much it will cost to bring the car up to what you consider an acceptable level. Be polite about it. Then name your offer and say no more until the person you're negotiating with responds.

Whatever counteroffer you receive, respond that your original figure is fair and is what you're prepared to pay today. Say nothing more and see what happens. Don't smile, don't fidget. Just be courteous and businesslike.

If you must move your offer up, do it in small increments. If the gap between the two sides is, say, $1,000 or less, move your bid $100 at a time. When you get close to your target price, make it clear that the game is almost over. State clearly when you have reached the highest price you have budgeted. Once you've made your last offer, stick to it. Don't be afraid to say that your offer is firm and final, and good for the next 24 hours only. If the other person does the same, walk away. With luck, nobody walks away and the actual negotiation will be over within a few minutes.

Step 7: Tying up the loose ends

A car purchase always ends with a good deal of paperwork. Satisfy yourself that all is in order before you commit your money.

First, check that the car's vehicle identification number, VIN, is the same as the VIN number printed on the car's title. It's stamped on a metal tag attached to the dashboard, on the driver's side, near the base of the windshield.

Make sure you have a clear title before you hand over a check, and talk this over with the seller. If the seller still owes money on the car, make sure the loan is paid off and that the seller has the actual title in his or her possession. If the seller needs your money to pay off the loan first, then talk to the lender, with the seller's permission of course, and explain that you need a release-of-lien at the time you pay for the car.

You may need to stop at your bank and get a certified check for the purchase price—something you cannot do outside of banking hours.

Before you actually pick up the car, talk to your auto-insurer and find out what insurance documentation you need. It may take only a phone call to get you covered, but you might need an insurance ID card as well. Depending on the state, you may need to talk to your local Department of Motor Vehicles about getting a license plate for the car, and whether you need to get a permanent or temporary plate in order to drive the car home.

The seller should also create a bill of sale, giving the description of the car as it appears on the car's identity papers, the name and address of the seller, the name and address of the buyer, the price paid, and the date.

BUYING CARS FOR TEENS

Things to consider when choosing a set of wheels for a first-time driver.

When buying any vehicle, it's important to consider safety, reliability, and value. Because a young, first-time driver usually has neither a lot of money nor driving experience, these considerations become even more important when buying a car for a teen.

Despite sobering statistics about teenage drivers—they have a much higher collision rate than any other age group, and close to 40 percent of deaths among 16- to 19-year-olds are from traffic accidents—driving is one of the rites of passage into adulthood.

The key is to reduce the risk as much as possible. Seatbelts should be worn at all times. Parents should limit who is allowed to ride in the car and establish a curfew on nighttime driving.

You'll want a model that comes with key safety equipment, but it's often not possible or practical for a teen to buy a brand-new car with the latest safety equipment. A used vehicle is usually the only practical choice. Here are some suggestions from CONSUMER REPORTS auto experts.

Cars that offer both good reliability and a moderate price include most models from Honda, Nissan, Subaru, or Toyota. A six- or seven-year-old midsized car is a good choice. So is a small, car-based SUV such as the Subaru Forester or Toyota RAV4.

With any car, make sure that the driver can see out well, and that frequently used controls such as the audio and climate-control systems are close at hand.

Condition is everything. Examine any used car thoroughly. Even the best vehicle can become a lemon if it's poorly maintained.

Many parents pass along their old car to the kids when they buy a new one. That makes sense if the car has been reliable and well maintained.

Looking for safety

No car can be considered safest. You can look for safety equipment, however. The profile pages in this publication note the years when manufacturers introduced such equipment as side air bags. (Safety issues are discussed in detail in Chapter 3.)

Crash protection, accident-avoidance capabilities, and rollover propensity all affect safety. People in a bigger, heavier car have less risk of injury in a collision with a smaller, lighter one.

Among sedans, some big old-fashioned cruisers like the Buick LeSabre have proved reliable and done well in crash tests. Large vehicles, however, can be unwieldy and guzzle gas.

Big pickups and SUVs are heavy, too, but their extra height relative to their width makes them more prone to rollover than vehicles with a lower center of gravity. They're not a good choice for an inexperienced driver.

Many young drivers are responsible and attentive, but driving experience takes time to acquire. Parents might consider enrolling their teenager in an advanced-driving course. The accident-avoidance skills acquired there can yield benefits for life.

The sports-car trap

Sports cars and muscle cars are a poor choice for young drivers. They beg to be driven too fast and they're astronomically expensive to insure. If driving fun is important, consider an agile, fun-to-drive small car, such as mid-1990s versions of the Acura Integra, Honda Civic, Nissan Sentra SE-R, or Subaru Impreza.

HOW TO SELL YOUR OLD CAR

In general, you can sell a car in the same ways that you can buy a car: through a dealer, through a service station, or in a private transaction. There are two reasons why someone would buy your car: Either they want it for themselves, or they believe they can resell it at a profit. If the buyer plans to resell your car, don't count on getting top dollar.

You're apt to get the best price if you sell it privately, but experience the least hassle if you sell it to a dealer. People who buy used cars every day, as dealers do, know what they are willing to pay, and they'll have the necessary paperwork—and the money—ready at hand. Selling a car privately involves placing an ad or displaying the car someplace with a "For Sale" sign on it, and being prepared to field phone calls. It also means you'll have to show the car to strangers and perhaps let them into your home.

MAKE IT PRESENTABLE. Regardless of how you try to sell your car, make it as clean as you can, inside and out. Wipe or vacuum all surfaces you can reach, including the trunk and engine compartment. If you're due for an oil change, have that done.

Clean the upholstery with a carpet cleaner or pet-spot remover. If the car is worth several thousand dollars, it may be worthwhile to invest $200 or so to have a body shop buff and touch up the exterior.

Pull together your service records and repair receipts and any other proof you have that the car was maintained properly. If the car has any faults that make it illegal or dangerous, such as bald tires, a leaking exhaust system, or missing lights, have those things repaired or disclose them fully to the buyer.

FIND THE PRICE. To determine what your old car is worth, use the CONSUMER REPORTS Used Car Price Service mentioned on page 18 or one of the price services available on the web. Check local classified ads to get an idea of the retail asking prices for cars like yours.

You might also want to find the wholesale price. That will help in your negotiations if you decide to sell or trade in your car to a dealer. Take your spiffed-up car to the used-car department of local car dealers, particularly those that sell your brand. Ask the used-car manager what the dealership would give you in a straight-out sale. This, too, is a negotiation, so counter the first offer with a higher figure. Try for a price around 80 percent of the retail price. The dealer may not budge much, but it doesn't hurt to ask. Once you've visited several dealers, you'll have a good idea of your car's true wholesale value in your area. You may even decide that a quick, sure sale is worth forgoing the best price you could obtain.

TRADE-IN STRATEGY. If you're trading in an old car on the purchase of a new one, try to get the best price on both cars. The temptation is to make your best deal on the new car, and then talk trade. The trouble with that approach is that once you're committed to the new car, the dealer has every incentive to try to "lowball" you—offer a ridiculously low price—on the trade. And after the intense emotion of the new-car negotiation, you might not have the stomach to fight back. It may make more sense to negotiate the trade-in price first. Tell the salesperson that you're ready to buy a new vehicle, but the deal hinges on getting a good trade-in price.

If the dealer refuses to give you a figure for the trade-in or if the figure is just too low, consider selling your car elsewhere. If you get an offer you can live with, go to work on negotiating for the new car. Start from scratch, as if the trade-in didn't exist. Bargain up from the dealer's cost, and make it clear you want the lowest markup the dealership will allow.

Remember, no matter how tired you are of your old car, the dealership is not doing you a favor. If it buys your old car, it's because it plans to make a profit when selling it.

SELLING TO A PRIVATE PARTY. This requires the most work on your part, but it's the best way to get the most money. Check classified-ad publications and local newspapers. That should give you an idea of where and how to advertise, and what sort of prices people in your area ask for cars like yours. If you don't want strangers to come to your home, offer to meet the buyer at a neutral location. Answer all questions honestly but briefly. Be prepared to provide service receipts, and to accompany a prospective buyer on a lengthy test drive.

BILL OF SALE

Date: _____

Received from:

Seller's name _____

Street address _____

City _____ State _____ ZIP _____

Phone _____

Co-owner's name (if any) _____

in consideration of $ _____, receipt of which is hereby acknowledged,

Do hereby transfer to:

Purchaser's name _____

Street address _____

City _____ State _____ ZIP _____

Phone _____

Co-purchaser's name (if any) _____

The following described motor vehicle:

Year _____ Make _____ Model _____

Body style (e.g., 4-dr. sedan) _____ No. of cylinders _____

Color _____ Odometer reading _____

Vehicle ID No. (VIN) _____

Certificate of Title No. _____

_____   _____
Signature of seller   Signature of buyer

Permission is granted to photocopy this page.

2

Finding a Reliable Used Car

CONSUMER REPORTS reliability information helps you separate the cream puffs from the lemons.

Buying a used car always entails an element of risk: You can never be quite sure what you're getting, and most used cars are not covered by any significant warranty. Accordingly, the promise of reliability is arguably the single most important criterion for choosing a car.

To help guide buyers to a smart choice, CONSUMER REPORTS offers the most detailed and revealing used-car reliability information available anywhere. The reliability information you'll find on these pages is presented in two ways:

♦Lists of the most- and least-reliable vehicles (see pages 32-34).

♦Individual reliability histories on most makes and models sold in the last eight years, starting on page 81.

The reliability data indicates not only which have been the best makes and models overall, but also points you to specific problem areas to watch out for in the car you may consider.

CONSUMER REPORTS gathers its data from an extensive and detailed annual survey of the magazine's four million subscribers, from which it typically gets about a half million responses. CR has been conducting this annual survey for more than 40 years.

The major and most heartening trend in the last couple of decades has been the continuously improving quality and reliability of automobiles, Whether you look back five, ten, or twenty years, it's clear that all brands and car types are getting better. Detroit-based autos have improved the most, although they had the most improving to do. American automakers have substantially reduced, but not eliminated, the reliability gap between themselves and most Japanese and European competitors. Today you can buy many American cars with reasonable confidence.

Back in 1980, the average trouble rate for new vehicles was 88 problems reported for every 100 cars. By 2000, that trouble rate had dropped to just 20 problems—an astounding 70 percent improvement. The improvement in sport-utility vehicles and pickup trucks was also pronounced, dropping from 99 problems in 1980 to 20 in 2000.

For most makes, the improvement rate flattened out between 1990 and 1995. The average trouble rate for new vehicles stayed at about 30 problems in that period. But since then the pace of progress picked up again. We suspect problems that came from some of the computer-controlled systems introduced in the late 1980s and early 1990s offset reliability improvements in other areas. But now, many of the kinks have been worked out of in-car computer systems.

The overall improvement is attributable to a series of major and minor breakthroughs in design, technology, materials, and manufacturing.

Solid-state electronics, for instance, which now control everything from a car's engine and transmission to its emissions and safety systems, are less vulnerable to wear and vibration than the mechanical systems they replaced. Steel body panels are galvanized on both sides and coated with baked-on finishes for rust resistance. Specialized high-strength metals, ceramics, plastics, and long-life lubricants cut down on the need for frequent maintenance while extending the life of components.

Overall, we've seen sharp reductions in problems such as rust and peeling paint. Likewise, ignition systems, transmissions, and air conditioners are much more reliable than they used to be. Many models of recent vintage, if well cared for, can be expected to go 200,000 miles and more.

This is not to say that things won't go wrong. Squeaks and rattles remain a common problem, and sooner or later you'll have to replace "wear parts" such as tires, mufflers, and brakes.

You may also have to cope with bigger headaches. Frequently these days the repair itself is no big deal but the diagnostic time required to find the fault is. If it takes a dealer's service department several hours to track down a corroded ground wire, for instance, then making that simple repair can wind up costing hundreds of dollars. As a result, it's more important than ever to find a car that doesn't need to go to the shop very often.

HOW CONSUMER REPORTS ASSESSES RELIABILITY

Every year, Consumer Reports mails its Annual Questionnaire to subscribers, asking them to check off problems they've had with their own vehicles in the preceding 12 months. The latest (2002) survey of owners generated information on almost 480,000 cars, minivans, sport-utility vehicles, and pickup trucks. Those reports enable us to predict the reliability of new vehicles and zero in on trouble spots found in older ones.

From analyzing the survey results, we are able to provide reliability information for you in several different ways:

CR GOOD BETS. Listed on page 32, these are the cream of the crop—all performed well in Consumer Reports road tests when they were new, and have consistently had few problems,

USED CARS TO LOOK FOR

THESE ARE CR'S LISTS OF RELIABLE CARS AS OF THE 2002 SURVEY. BELOW ARE CARS THAT HAVE PROVED RELIABLE YEAR IN AND YEAR OUT. AT RIGHT ARE THE CARS WITH ABOVE-AVERAGE RELIABILITY FOR SPECIFIC MODEL YEARS.

CR Good Bets

These are the best of both worlds: models that have performed well in CONSUMER REPORTS tests over the years and have proved to have better-than-average overall reliability. They are listed alphabetically.

Acura Integra	Mercury Tracer
Acura RL	Nissan Altima
Acura TL	Nissan Maxima
Ford Escort	Nissan Pathfinder
Geo/Chevrolet Prizm	Saab 9-5
Honda Accord	Subaru Forester
Honda Civic	Subaru Impreza
Honda CR-V	Subaru Legacy/Outback
Honda Odyssey	Toyota 4Runner
Infiniti G20	Toyota Avalon
Infiniti I30	Toyota Camry
Isuzu Oasis	Toyota Camry Solara
Lexus ES300	Toyota Celica
Lexus GS300/GS400, GS430	Toyota Corolla
Lexus LS400, LS430	Toyota Echo
Lexus RX300	Toyota RAV4
Mazda Millenia	Toyota Sienna
Mazda MX-5 Miata	Toyota Tacoma
Mazda Protegé	Toyota Tundra

The lists on these pages are compiled from overall reliability data covering 1995 through 2002 models with better-than-average reliability. CR Good Bets include only the models for which we have sufficient data for at least three model years. Models that were brand new in 2001 or 2002 do not appear. Problems with the engine, engine cooling, transmission, and drive system were weighted more heavily than other problems.

Reliable used cars

Listed by price group, and alphabetically within groups. Price ranges are what you'd pay for a typically equipped car with average mileage.

LESS THAN $6,000

Ford **Escort** '97-98
Geo **Metro** '95 • **Prizm** '95-96 • **Tracker** '95
Mazda **Protegé** '96
Mercury **Tracer** '97-98
Subaru **Impreza** '95
Suzuki **Sidekick** '95 • **Swift** '95
Toyota **Tercel** '95

$6,000-$8,000

Chevrolet **Prizm** '98
Ford **Escort** '99-00 • **Ranger (2WD)** '95-97
Geo **Prizm** '97
Honda **Civic** '95-96
Mazda **B-Series (2WD)** '95 • **MX-5 Miata** '95 • **Protegé** '97-98
Mercury **Tracer** '99
Nissan **Altima** '96 • **Sentra** '97
Saturn **SL/SW** '98-99
Subaru **Impreza** '96 • **Legacy** '95
Toyota **Corolla** '95-97 • **Tercel** '96-97

$8,000-$10,000

Acura **Integra** '95
Buick **Century** '98
Chevrolet **Prizm** '99-00
Ford **Crown Victoria** '97 • **Escort** '01 • **Explorer (2WD)** '95-96 • **F-150 (2WD)** '95 • **Ranger (2WD)** '98
Honda **Accord** '95 • **Civic** '97
Infiniti **G20** '95-96
Lincoln **Town Car** '95
Mazda **B-Series (2WD)** '96-98 • **MX-5 Miata** '96-97 • **Protegé** '99-00
Nissan **Altima** '97-98 • **Maxima** '95-96 • **Pickup** '95-96 • **Sentra** '99
Saturn **SL/SW** '01
Subaru **Impreza** '97-98
Toyota **Avalon** '95 • **Camry** '95-96 • **Celica** '95 • **Corolla** '98-99 • **Echo** '00-01 • **RAV4** '96

$10,000-$12,000

Acura **Integra** '96-97
Chevrolet **Prizm** '01
Ford **Crown Victoria** '98

Honda Accord '96 · Civic '98-99
· Odyssey '95
Infiniti I30 '96
Isuzu Oasis '96
Lincoln Continental '96
Mazda 626 '98-99 · Protegé '01
Mercury Grand Marquis '97-98
Nissan Altima '99 · Maxima '97 ·
Pathfinder '95 · Pickup '97
Saturn SL/SW '02
Toyota 4Runner '95 · Avalon '96
· Camry '97 · Celica '96 · Corolla '00-
01 · Echo '02 · Previa '95 · RAV4 '97
· T100 '95 · Tacoma '95-96

$12,000-$14,000
Acura CL '97 · Integra '98 · TL '96
Chevrolet Prizm '02
Ford Crown Victoria '99 · F-150 (2WD)
'97-98
Honda Accord '97-98 · Civic '00
· CR-V '97-98 · Odyssey '96
Hyundai Sonata '01
Infiniti I30 '97
Isuzu Oasis '97
Lexus ES300 '95
Lincoln Town Car '96
Mazda 626 '00 · Protegé '02
Mercury Grand Marquis '99
Nissan Altima '00-01 · Frontier '98-99
· Maxima '98 · Pathfinder '96-97
Subaru Forester '98 · Impreza '00
· Legacy/Outback '97
Toyota Avalon '97 · Camry '98 · Celica
'97 · Corolla '02 · RAV4 '98 · T100
'96-97 · Tacoma '97-98

$14,000-$16,000
Acura 3.5RL '96 · CL '98 · Integra '99
· Legend '95 · TL '97
BMW 3-Series '95
Buick Century '01
Ford F-150 (2WD) '99 · F-150 (4WD) '97
Honda Accord '99 · Civic '02 · CR-V
'99 · Odyssey '97
Hyundai Sonata '02
Infiniti G20 '99
Isuzu Oasis '98
Lexus ES300 '96
Lincoln Town Car '97
Mazda Millenia '98 · MX-5 Miata '99
Nissan Frontier '00 · Maxima '99

Subaru Forester '99 · Impreza '01
· Legacy/Outback '98
Toyota 4Runner '96 · Avalon '98
· Camry '99 · Camry Solara '99
· Celica '99-00 · RAV4 '99-00
· Sienna '98 · Tacoma '99

$16,000-$18,000
Acura Integra '00
Buick Century '02 · Regal '00
Chevrolet Impala '02
Chrysler PT Cruiser '01
Ford Expedition (2WD) '97 · F-150
(2WD) '00 · F-150 (4WD) '98
Honda Accord '00 · CR-V '00
· Odyssey '98
Infiniti I30 '98 · QX4 '97
Lincoln Continental '99 · Town Car '98
Mazda MPV '00 · MX-5 Miata '00-01
Nissan Frontier '01 · Maxima '00
· Pathfinder '98
Subaru Legacy/Outback '99
Toyota 4Runner '97 · Avalon '99
· Camry '00-01 · Camry Solara '00
· Celica '01 · Tacoma '00

$18,000-$20,000
Acura 3.5RL '97 · CL '99 · Integra '01
· TL '98
BMW Z3 '97
Buick Regal '01
Ford Expedition (2WD) '98 · F-150
(4WD) '00
Honda Accord '01 · CR-V '01
Infiniti G20 '00-01 · I30 '99 · QX4 '98
Lexus ES300 '97 · LS400 '95 ·
SC300/SC400 '95
Mazda Millenia '99 · MPV '01
Mercedes-Benz C-Class '97
Nissan Maxima '01 · Pathfinder '99
Subaru Forester '01-02
· Legacy/Outback '00
Toyota 4Runner '98 · Camry Solara '01
· Celica '02 · Prius '01-02 · RAV4
'02 · Sienna '99 · Tacoma '01-02

$20,000-$22,000
Acura 3.5RL '98 · TL '99
BMW Z3 '98
Buick Regal '02
Chrysler PT Cruiser '02
Ford F-150 (2WD) '02

Honda Accord '02 · CR-V '02
Hyundai Santa Fe '02
Infiniti G20 '02 · QX4 '99
Lexus ES300 '98
Lincoln Continental '00 · Town Car '99
Mazda Millenia '00 · MPV '02
Nissan Maxima '02
Subaru Legacy/Outback '01
Toyota 4Runner '99 · Avalon '00
· Camry Solara '02 · Sienna '00
· Tundra '00

$22,000-$26,000
Acura 3.5RL '99 · CL '01 · TL '00-01
Ford F-150 (4WD) '02
Infiniti I30 '00-01 · QX4 '00
Lexus ES300 '99 · GS300/GS400 '98
· LS400 '96
Lincoln Town Car '00
Mazda Millenia '01
Nissan Pathfinder '00-01
Saab 9-3 '00-01
Subaru Legacy/Outback '02
Toyota 4Runner '00-01 · Avalon '01-02
· Highlander '01 · Sienna '01-02
· Tundra '01-02

$26,000-$30,000
Acura 3.5RL '00 · TL '02
Ford Expedition '02
Honda Odyssey '01-02 · S2000 '00
Infiniti QX4 '01
Lexus ES300 '00-01 · GS300/GS400
'99 · IS300 '01 · LS400 '97
· RX300 '99
Mercedes-Benz C-Class '00
Nissan Pathfinder '02
Saab 9-5 '00
Toyota 4Runner '02 · Highlander '02

$30,000 and up
Acura 3.5RL '02 · MDX '01-02
BMW 5-Series '99 · 7-Series '01 · Z3 '01
Honda S2000 '01
Lexus ES300 '02 · GS300/GS400 '00
· GS300/GS430 '01 · LS400 '98-
99 · LS430 '01-02 · RX300 '00-02
Porsche Boxster '00
Saab 9-5 '01-02
Toyota Land Cruiser '00
· Sequoia '01-02

USED CARS TO AVOID

Unreliable models year by year

Derived from the 2002 survey, these are CR's lists of unreliable cars. They are listed alphabetically, by make, model, and year.

Audi A4 '97, '00, '02 • **A6 (V6)** '97-99 • **A6 (V6, Turbo)** '00 • **TT** '00-01
BMW 3-Series '00-01 • **X5** '01-02
Buick Park Avenue '97-98, '01-02 • **Rendezvous** '02 • **Riviera** '95 • **Roadmaster** '95-96
Cadillac Catera '97-01 • **DeVille** '95-98, '00-01 • **Escalade** '02 • **Seville** '95-02
Chevrolet Astro '95-02 • **Blazer** '95-02 • **C1500** '96-97 • **Camaro** '96-00 • **Caprice** '96 • **Cavalier** '96-97, '02 • **Corsica, Beretta** '95 • **Corvette** '00-01 • **Express 1500** '96-01 • **K1500** '96-99 • **Lumina Van** '95 • **Malibu** '97-00 • **Monte Carlo** '95 • **S-10 (4-cyl.)** '95 • **S-10 (V6)** '96-02 • **Silverado 1500 (4WD)** '99-02 • **Suburban** '96-00 • **Tahoe** '96-98, '00 • **Tracker** '00 • **TrailBlazer** '02 • **Venture (ext.)** '97-00, '02• **Venture (reg.)** '99-00
Chrysler 300M '99, '02 • **Cirrus (V6)** '99 • **Concorde** '95-99 • **New Yorker, LHS** '95-96 • **LHS** '97, 99 • **Sebring Conv.** '98, '00, '02 • **Sebring (V6)** '01 • **Town & Country (reg.)** '96-97, '99 • **Town & Country (2WD)** '95-97, '00-01 • **Town & Country (AWD)** '97, '99-01 • **Voyager** '01-02
Dodge Caravan (4-cyl.) '95-98, '01-02 • **Caravan (V6)** '95-97, '99, '01-02 • **Dakota (2WD)** '98-99, '02 • **Dakota (4WD)** '96-01 • **Durango** '98-02 • **Grand Caravan (V6, 2WD)** '95-97, '00-01 • **Grand Caravan (V6, AWD)** '97, '99-01 • **Intrepid** '95-99 • **Neon** '95-00 • **Ram 1500 (2WD)** '97-98, '01-02 • **Ram 1500 (4WD)** '96-00, '02 • **Stratus (4-cyl.)** '96-98 • **Stratus (V6)** '99, '01
Ford Contour '95-96 • **Contour (V6)** '97-98 • **Crown Victoria** '02 • **Econoline Wagon, Van 150** '96-97 • **Escape (V6)** '01-02 • **Expedition (4WD)** '99 • **Explorer** '98-02 • **Explorer Sport Trac** '01-02 • **Focus** '00-01 • **Mustang** '01-02 • **Probe** '95-96 • **Ranger (4WD)** '97-01 **Ranger** '02 • **Taurus** '95 • **Windstar** '95-02

GMC Envoy '02 • **Jimmy** '95-'01 • **S-15 Sonoma (4-cyl.)** '95 • **S-15 Sonoma (V6)** '96-02 • **Safari** '95-02 • **Savana Van 1500** '96-01 • **Sierra 1500 (2WD)** '96-'97 • **Sierra 1500 (4WD)** '96-02 • **Suburban** '96-99 • **Yukon** '96-98, '00 • **Yukon XL** '00
Honda Passport '96-97, '99-01
Isuzu Rodeo '96-'97, '99-01
Jaguar S-Type '00-01 • **X-Type** '02
Jeep Cherokee '00-01 • **Grand Cherokee** '95-02 • **Wrangler** '97-02
Lincoln LS '00-02 • **Town Car** '01
Mazda B-Series (4WD) '97-01 • **B-Series** '02• **Tribute (V6)** '01-02
Mercedes-Benz C-Class '95, '01 • **CLK** '00-02 • **E-Class** '98, '00 • **M-Class** '98-02 • **S-Class** '00-01 • **SLK** '01
Mercury Cougar '99 • **Grand Marquis** '02 • **Mountaineer** '98-02 • **Mystique** '95-96 • **Mystique (V6)** '97-98 • **Sable** '95
Mitsubishi Eclipse '01 • **Galant** '01
Nissan Sentra '00
Oldsmobile 88 '97 • **Alero** '99-01 • **Aurora** '95-98, '01-02 • **Bravada** '97-99, '02 • **Cutlass** '97-99 • **Intrigue** '02 • **Silhouette (ext.)** '97-00, '02 • **Silhouette (reg.)** '95, '99-00
Plymouth Breeze '96-98 • **Grand Voyager (V6)** '95-97, '00 • **Neon** '95-00 • **Voyager (4-cyl.)** '95-98 • **Voyager (V6)** '95-97, '99
Pontiac Bonneville '95, '97, '00-02 • **Firebird** '96-00 • **Grand Am** '95-02 • **Grand Prix** '97 • **Montana (ext.)** '99-00, '02 • **Montana (reg.)** '99-00 • **Sunfire** '96-97, '02 • **TransSport** '95 • **TransSport, Montana (ext.)** '97-98
Saturn L-Series '00-01
Suzuki Vitara '00
Volkswagen Golf '99-01 • **Jetta** '95-02 • **New Beetle** '98-01 • **Passat (4-cyl.)** '98 • **Passat (V6, AWD)** '00, '02
Volvo 960 '96-97 • **S40/V40** '00 • **S80** '99-01 • **S90/V90** '98 • **V70 (except XC)** '01 • **V70 Cross Country** '98-99

Reliability risks

These cars showed multiple years of much-worse-than-average overall reliability. The list covers 1995 to 2002 models. Many are siblings —essentially similar models sold under different nameplates. Models are listed alphabetically.

Cadillac Catera
Cadillac Seville
Chevrolet Astro
Chevrolet Blazer
Chrysler New Yorker, LHS
Chrysler Town & Country (AWD)
Dodge Caravan (4-cyl)
Dodge Dakota 4WD
Dodge Durango
Dodge Grand Caravan (AWD)
Dodge Neon
Ford Focus
Ford Windstar
GMC Jimmy
GMC Safari
Jeep Grand Cherokee
Lincoln LS
Mercedes-Benz M-Class
Oldsmobile Alero
Oldsmobile Bravada
Oldsmobile Cutlass
Plymouth Grand Voyager
Plymouth Neon
Plymouth/Chrysler Voyager (4-cyl)
Pontiac Grand Am
Volkswagen Jetta
Volkswagen New Beetle
Volvo S80

The lists on this page are drawn from reliability data on 1995 through 2002 models with below average reliability. Reliability risks include only models on which we have sufficient data for at least three model years. Models that were brand new in 2001 or 2002 do not appear. Problems with the engine, engine cooling, transmission, and drive system were weighted more heavily than other problems.

according to the reliability surveys. Consider them first.

RELIABLE USED CARS. This list (pages 32-33) can help you find the more reliable cars in various price ranges, from less than $6,000 to $30,000 or more.

UNRELIABLE MODELS YEAR BY YEAR. These are the ones you want to steer clear of if you can. Listed by make, model, and year, these are the less reliable cars (page 34).

RELIABILITY RISKS. Any model can have one bad year. Some cars are unreliable year in and year out. This list identifies vehicles that have had multiple years of much-worse-than-average reliability (page 34).

RELIABILITY HISTORY CHARTS. Included in the vehicle profiles for most models, these charts highlight problem rates for 1995 through 2002 models in 14 trouble spots. The vehicle profiles begin on page 81.

The most common complaints across all model years involve the electrical system (such as wiring), power equipment (power accessories), body hardware (including window and door mechanisms), and body integrity (squeaks and rattles).

For more on what the trouble spots include—and on how well the average car ages—see pages 79-80.

CHECK-MARK RELIABILITY VERDICT. Part of the Reliability History charts found on each model's profile page, these verdicts sum up our findings for each model, year by year. Those with above-average reliability for their age earn a red check (✔); average models earn a black check (✔); and below-average models get no check mark.

WHAT'S BEEN GOOD LATELY?

The 2002 survey brought a few surprises. Most notable among them was a great improvement in the most recent two to three model years for Hyundai vehicles and for some General Motors pickups and SUVs. At the same time, some of the top Japanese brands' recently redesigned cars dropped from better-than-average to average in overall reliability. Older (pre-2002) Japanese-nameplate cars still had a stellar record, though.

Hyundai, South Korea's largest automaker, had been dogged for years by a reputation for shoddy workmanship. Ten years ago the Hyundai Sonata finished at the very bottom of CR's reliability survey. But Hyundai has gradually reversed that record. CONSUMER REPORTS engineers had already noted the much-improved build quality of recent Hyundais. Now the reliability survey has borne that out. For the first time in CR's survey, reliability had improved to average or better. The improvement was seen across the board, from the small Accent to the midsized Elantra and larger Sonata sedans and the Santa Fe SUV.

The other good-news story involved the General Motors truck platform that supplies the underpinnings for seven separate models: the Chevrolet Silverado pickup and Tahoe and Suburban SUVs, along with their GMC equivalents the Sierra, Yukon, and Yukon XL, and the Chevrolet Avalanche. In their first couple of years on the road, reliability was fairly abysmal. Now they've improved to average overall—at least for 2001 and later models.

Another turnaround involved Volvo. Its midsized wagons, the V70 and Cross Country, also improved to average. Volvo is one of the few European nameplates that improved noticeably in this survey.

THE MERELY AVERAGE JAPANESE. Japanese makers Honda, Nissan, Subaru, and Toyota have finished near the top of CR's reliability standings for decades, and they finish near the top this year as well. However, the survey turned up an odd pattern: The Nissan Altima, Subaru Impreza, and Toyota Camry, which were all redesigned for 2002, scored as merely average in their first year on the road. The major complaints for all three: squeaks, rattles, and loose trim. Based on these brands' track record, CR experts think it's likely that those problems will be fixed by the time the next annual survey is conducted.

For the Japanese makes, the "average" showing was disappointing. But to put that finding into context, note that an average reliability score in one model year still leaves these "disappointing" Japanese cars as good as some of the best from the Big Three and from Europe.

EUROPE A MIXED BAG. The Saab 9-5, with above-average overall reliability, was one of the few bright spots for the European brands, although it was outranked in its class by the Japanese makes.

BMW and Mercedes-Benz models had mixed results. Older models were mostly average or better, but some of the newer models were below average.

Jaguar also failed to pull ahead. The newest Jags in the survey, the S-Type and X-Type, were designed under the aegis of Jaguar's owner, Ford. Both turned out to be far below average.

Finally, consider Volkswagen. Volkswagens have hovered between average and below-average reliability for many years. They turned in a mediocre showing for 2002. Only the Passat continued to maintain an average reliability assessment across the model years. Volkswagen's luxury-brand Audi A4 and A6 also had a spotty showing.

THE FINE PRINT

While CONSUMER REPORTS collects data for most models in the eight-year range covered by the survey, not every car makes the final cut. To make a judgment, CR's statisticians require a minimum sample size of around 100 vehicles of each make, model, and year. Big-selling vehicles such as the Honda Civic and Ford Explorer may generate thousands of responses, while more-exotic cars like the Jaguar XJ8 may generate only a handful. On the Reliability History charts that accompany the car profiles we give those with a below-minimum sample size the notation "insufficient data."

Once the survey data is gathered, CR statisticians perform a vigorous screening and analysis operation. For instance, the data is "standardized" for mileage. Since cars can be expected to have more problems as they are driven more miles, our statisticians adjust the problem rates of a car according to a standard mileage distribution for a given model year. This levels the playing field for a fair comparison.

3

Making Sense of Safety Info

It's not always easy to shop for safety or to interpret the crash-test results.

GETTING THERE SAFELY

Year in and year out for the last quarter century, roughly 30,000 people riding in motor vehicles have died on U.S. roads. A further 10,000 or so traffic deaths per year have involved pedestrians, cyclists, and others not considered "vehicle occupants." When safety engineers talk about life-saving designs and equipment, it is usually some of those 30,000 vehicle occupants they are aiming to save.

Though the fatality figures are certainly grim, they conceal a very positive development. The number of cars and drivers has risen dramatically, and the number of miles traveled roughly doubled between 1975 and 2000. Consequently, the death rate per mile has been cut in half. In other words, a person is only half as likely to die in a motor vehicle today as 25 years ago.

Several factors have contributed to the declining death rate: better roads, more and better safety equipment, safer vehicle designs, better medical aid, stiffer penalties for drunk driving, and a higher percentage of older, more experienced drivers. In addition, more people are using seat belts, which safety experts identify as the single most important step you can take to preserve your life.

The federal government estimates that belt use for front-seat passengers has now reached 75 percent nationwide—and more in states that enforce belt-use vigorously. The government calculates that the 2 percent rise in belt use seen in the past two years accounts for 500 lives saved per year.

KEY SAFETY FEATURES

Every year, new safety features and technology show up to help drivers avoid an accident or help protect occupants during a collision. Systems that were available only on luxury cars just a few years ago are now common on less expensive cars as well. Here's a rundown of some of the more important safety features:

ANTILOCK BRAKING SYSTEM (ABS). Antilock brakes prevent the wheels from locking up during a hard stop, something that can take away steering control and cause a vehicle to slide sideways. In typical usage, ABS almost always provides shorter stops. More than that, ABS helps keep the vehicle straight on slick surfaces. It also allows the driver to retain steering control while braking, so that a driver can maneuver more safely, say, around an obstacle. CONSUMER REPORTS highly recommends ABS.

BRAKE ASSIST. This adjunct to ABS senses the speed or force with which the brake pedal is depressed, tries to determine if the driver wants to make an emergency stop, and if so, activates the ABS fully, even if the driver is too tentative using the brake pedal. It may be found on some Audi, Lexus, Mercedes-Benz, Nissan, and Toyota vehicles, among others.

TRACTION CONTROL. Now commonly available on two-wheel-drive cars, this system limits wheel-spin during acceleration so that the drive wheels have maximum traction. It's particularly useful when starting from a standstill in wet and icy conditions but will not improve ultimate traction the way that all- or four-wheel drive does.

STABILITY CONTROL. Electronic stability control, common on luxury cars, is finding its way to sport-utility vehicles and less costly cars. Stability control uses the ABS system and additional sensors to help keep the vehicle under control when it is on the verge of a slide or skid during cornering. It selectively applies brakes to one or more wheels to keep the car on a controllable path. It is highly recommended, especially for SUVs where it can help prevent a rollover.

FRONT AIR BAGS. By law, front air bags have been standard on all new vehicles for several years. They started appearing in upscale cars at the end of the 1980s and were pervasive by the mid-'90s. The latest development in front air bags is dual-stage and three-stage deployment. Generally, in a low-level collision, the bags may not inflate or may inflate less aggressively. In a higher-speed collision, the bags are fully inflated more quickly to protect the occupant. With a three-stage system, both the low- and high-speed inflators deploy simultaneously in the severest collision.

SIDE AIR BAGS. Front side air bags, which started showing up in luxury cars a few years ago, are becoming more common, and some automakers are now offering side air bags for the rear seats as well. The basic side-impact air bag is a cushion that protects the torso. There is some concern that a child leaning against the door may be hurt by a deploying bag—yet another reason why children should be properly restrained and, where possible, located in the center rear seat.

The more-sophisticated systems use additional side air bags that protect the head as well. The most common design uses curtain-type side air bags, which spread across both front and rear side windows. The side-curtain bags keep occupants from hitting their heads and can also help prevent an occupant from being ejected in a rollover accident.

OCCUPANT SENSORS. Electronic occupant sensors are showing up on some new cars. These sensors can detect if the front passenger seat is occupied by someone below a specified weight, and also whether that person is leaning into an air bag's deployment path. The sensors then disable the front or side air bag to prevent injury from the bag itself.

SAFETY-BELT PRETENSIONERS. Some features are helping safety belts do their job more effectively. Pretensioners, for instance, take up the slack in the belt. In a frontal crash, pretensioners are activated by crash sensors, and retract the safety belts slightly, removing any slack and helping to hold a person more securely during the initial impact of the crash.

SAFETY-BELT FORCE-LIMITERS. A companion feature on many vehicles with pretensioners, force limiters relax the safety-belt tension slightly following the initial impact, so they can help absorb some of a person's forward thrust, and help prevent chest and internal injuries caused by a more rigidly held belt.

CHILD-SEAT ATTACHMENTS. If you'll be using a child-safety seat, we recommend the use of a top tether, part of a new standardized child-safety-seat system called LATCH, designed to simplify installation and enhance child safety. Top tethers limit how much a child seat can lurch forward in a crash. Kits make it possible to retrofit many older vehicles with top-tether anchors. In newer (1999 and later) cars there may also be sturdy attachment brackets in the crease between the seatback and the cushion. LATCH-equipped child seats and cars are designed to be easier to secure. For more, see "Child-safety car seats," page 48.

WHAT MAKES A CAR SAFE

One of the questions many car buyers ask is "Which is the safest car?" But there's no single or simple answer. For example, different vehicles fare differently in a crash depending on the circumstances. Comparing cars' overall safety potential involves pulling together and making sense of many disparate pieces of information—handling characteristics, crash-test results, vehicle weight, and so on.

The Consumer Reports Safety Assessment (see page 42, and the table on pages 43-45) assigns an overall safety score to many cars. Other safety issues include a vehicle's propensity for rollover, and how much load a vehicle is designed to safely carry. The analyses on the following pages can help you put all those factors into perspective.

Accident avoidance

A vehicle's ability to help keep you out of an accident can be just as important as its ability to protect you in a crash. Several factors contribute to a vehicle's accident-avoidance capability; braking and emergency handling are most important.

BRAKING. A vehicle's braking system has to stop the vehicle in as short a distance as possible and keep the vehicle under control and on a controllable path. Our tests measure braking performance on both dry and wet pavement, and evaluate the effectiveness of a vehicle's antilock braking system (ABS).

EMERGENCY HANDLING. The more controllable and secure a vehicle is when pressed to its handling limits, the better able you'll be to avoid an accident—say, by steering around an obstacle without losing control. We rate emergency handling on the basis of three tests. In one, we perform a series of double-lane-change maneuvers that simulate a driver trying to steer around an obstacle on the road. In the other tests, vehicles are pushed to their cornering limits around our skidpad and our handling course.

OTHER ACCIDENT-AVOIDANCE FACTORS. Acceleration, driving position, visibility, and even seat comfort also can affect accident avoidance. A vehicle that accelerates quickly can make it easier to merge safely into highway traffic and to escape from a potential crash. The driving position can affect both visibility and comfort. The better that drivers can see out, the more aware of other vehicles and conditions they can be. Seat comfort plays a role (although smaller) because a driver who is fatigued or uncomfortable may concentrate less on the road.

Crash protection

If a crash does happen, a vehicle's ability to protect its occupants becomes key. No one can say for sure what will happen in an actual crash, but the best indications come from crash tests. The two organizations that perform those tests are the federal government's National Highway Traffic Safety Administration (NHTSA), and the Insurance Institute for Highway Safety (IIHS), a private research group supported by auto insurers.

How well a vehicle protects its occupants from injury depends primarily on its design and safety equipment, including safety belts and air bags. Every vehicle has "crumple zones," which are designed to collapse in a way that helps absorb the crash energy and minimize any deformation of the cabin. The better the vehicle manages this energy, the less chance the driver and passengers will suffer serious injury.

THE SIZE AND WEIGHT FACTOR. On the highway, many if not most collisions involve vehicles of different weight, size, and shape, often with predictable results. As the IIHS states, "All else being equal, larger and heavier vehicles are safer than smaller, lighter ones" in a crash. This is because larger, heavier vehicles absorb less of the total crash energy than do other vehicles, at the smaller vehicles' expense. This, in turn, helps to better protect the bigger vehicles' occupants.

Vehicle weight isn't the only difference. In a crash, the higher bumper on many larger vehicles, such as sport-utility vehicles and trucks, hits a typical passenger car above the car's bumper line and crumple zone, exerting its force into weaker portions of the smaller vehicle and inflicting greater damage.

What government tests show

The government's most widely known crash-test program, and the one whose results are most frequently seen, is called the New Car Assessment Program, or NCAP ("Encap"). Every year the NCAP team conducts crash tests of almost 100 passenger vehicles, in two different series.

One is a full-frontal crash into a rigid barrier at 35 mph. It simulates two crash scenarios simultaneously: a serious collision with a fixed object like a concrete wall and a head-on collision between two vehicles of the same weight traveling at the same speed. Instrumented crash-test dummies in the driver's and front passenger's seat record crash forces on different parts of their bodies, and those numbers are ultimately translated into a ratings score. The driver and front passenger are assigned one to five stars, representing the likelihood of injury or death; one star denotes the greatest likelihood of harm, five stars, the least.

Another NCAP test series is side-impact crash testing. This is a test that simulates a vehicle traveling at 17 mph being hit on the side by a 3,000-pound car traveling at 34 mph.

Scores for this test are assigned to the driver and the left-rear passenger.

Safety experts believe that NHTSA's full-frontal crash into a rigid, unyielding barrier may not be representative of many real-world crashes but is still a very good gauge of how well a vehicle's restraints protect front occupants. The rigid barrier gives a car less time to slow down than an impact into a softer "deformable" barrier would.

What the insurance tests tell you

The Insurance Institute for Highway Safety conducts a different sort of front-impact test, called an "offset test." A vehicle is crashed at 40 mph into a deformable barrier, a test that mimics a car colliding with another car. Instead of engaging the whole front end of the car, though, only the part in front of the driver hits the barrier. The IIHS maintains that such offset crashes are more common in the real world than full-frontal crashes. The major European crash-test programs also rely on offset crashes.

In any case, there is wide agreement in safety circles that an offset test is better able than a full-frontal test to show how well the vehicle's structure can protect the driver. The IIHS believes that its 40-mph test speed allows the test to cover serious collisions in which a collapsing vehicle structure contributes to injury.

Both the NHTSA and IIHS frontal-crash results are only comparable within a vehicle's weight class. If the vehicle crashed into a car that was much heavier or much lighter than itself, the results could be very different.

WHAT THE CRASH TESTS DON'T SAY

While the crash tests the government and the IIHS have conducted provide valuable information, it's important to understand their limitations as well. Crash-test results cannot guarantee anyone's survival. At best, they give the relative probability of sustaining injury in a serious collision. Some other caveats apply as well:

♦ Published NHTSA and IIHS test results apply best to average-sized adult males, since that's the size approximated by the crash-test dummies used up to now. The test results may not apply as well to smaller or larger men or to women or children.

♦ Crash-test scores can only be compared within vehicles of the same weight category.

♦ Current tests don't address a vehicle's ability to resist a rollover that happens while the vehicle is being driven. (See page 46.)

♦ No tests address crash protection from rear impacts. While such crashes account for only 6 percent of fatal accidents, they cause more than 20 percent of all injuries.

♦ The crash-test database is incomplete. Currently NHTSA and IIHS crash-test information exists for about 75 percent of the vehicles sold; the rest go untested. That's because, in order to get the most bang for their limited testing dollars, the testing agencies focus on models that represent the most sales.

Behind the scenes

The star ratings from government-conducted crash tests and insurance-industry ratings are the published results that car-buyers see. But vehicles must also pass government "certifica-

OFFSET CRASH
The IIHS offset-frontal crash impacts just part of a vehicle's front end.

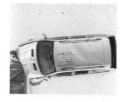

tion" tests. These are crash tests the automakers themselves must conduct before a model can be sold. Those test results are not published. They are pass/fail tests, and use unbelted crash dummies. That determines how well a vehicle protects unbelted occupants—a crucial concern since a significant percentage of the driving population still doesn't buckle up.

Part of Federal Motor Vehicle Safety Standard 208, the federally mandated tests set a minimum performance level. Carmakers have to certify that the unbelted dummies didn't sustain the human equivalent of serious or fatal injuries. Until a few years ago, carmakers conducted these tests in a way that closely resembled the NCAP frontal tests: Entire vehicles were rammed into a fixed barrier, though at 30 mph instead of 35 mph. The speed difference is significant: A 35-mph collision is about one-third more severe than a 30-mph crash.

In 1997, the test criteria were changed in order to address the issue of deaths and serious injuries attributed to over-aggressive air bags. The industry successfully argued that the test standard should be lowered, since that was the quickest way to allow for less-powerful air bags. NHTSA permitted the industry to substitute a simulated crash test that used just part of a vehicle, mounted on a sled, rather than crashing real cars. The less-severe sled test was one that vehicles could pass with "depowered" air bags, which began appearing in all cars in 1998-model vehicles.

NHTSA has since promulgated new rules, but they won't apply before the 2004 model year. The new rules will revert back to full-vehicle crash testing, though at 25 mph. But the range of tests will be greatly expanded:

♦ Tests will involve five crash dummies, simulating different-sized people including a medium-sized adult male, a 108-pound adult female, and children ages 1, 3, and 6 years.

♦ Dummies will be tested both belted and unbelted, in both full-frontal and offset crashes. That puts added emphasis on protecting belted occupants while still evaluating what happens to unbelted people of different sizes.

♦ Frontal air bags will be tested with dummies positioned close to them. Vehicles will pass only if both belted and unbelted dummies are protected from severe "injury."

♦ Crash-test data will include expanded neck- and chest-injury results.

Having to pass this expanded repertoire of tests would appear to make vehicle design tougher for automakers. Bob Lange, a high-ranking safety engineer for General Motors, explained to CONSUMER REPORTS some of the trade-offs involved:

"A structure stiff enough to prevent cabin deformation at high speed means that it's a stiff front at lower speed, too. So at lower speeds there is less crush in the front [and] more of the crash energy is transferred to the occupants." The result of making a vehicle too stiff, he explained, can be injury to children and small or frail adults.

THE CR SAFETY ASSESSMENT

To compare overall safety among different vehicles in the same category, CONSUMER REPORTS created the CR Safety Assessment, which in this book presents information on the latest models (see pages 43 to 45). The tables note the model years for which the CRSA judgments are applicable. The Safety Assessment itself consists of three parts:

ACCIDENT-AVOIDANCE RATING. This rating is determined by combining CONSUMER

REPORTS test results for braking, emergency handling, acceleration, driving position, visibility and seat comfort.

CRASH-PROTECTION RATING. This is determined by combining IIHS crash-test scores with all available NHTSA results.

OVERALL SAFETY SCORE. The accident-avoidance and crash-protection ratings are combined on an equal basis to produce an overall safety score.

Models with a lower score are not inherently unsafe. But a higher-scoring vehicle can improve your chances of avoiding or surviving a crash compared with a lower-scoring model. Given the range of choices, there's no reason to accept a vehicle that doesn't perform well in all safety areas.

MAKE AND MODEL	MODEL YEARS	TRIM	OVERALL CRSA SCORE	ACCIDENT AVOIDANCE	CRASH PROTECTION	COMMENTS
SMALL CARS						
Volkswagen Golf	2000-2002	TDI		◒	◉	Excellent frontal- and offset-crash results. Secure handling, very good brakes and driving position.
Honda Civic	2001-2002	EX		◉	◉	Good offset-crash result. Nimble handling, excellent brakes.
Volkswagen Jetta	2000-2002	GLS 2.0		◒	◉	Excellent results in all crash tests. Very good brakes and driving position.
Volkswagen New Beetle	1998-2002	2.0		◒	◉	Excellent offset- and driver-side crash results. Very good handling, brakes, and driving position.
Ford Focus	2000-2002	ZTS		◉	◒	Agile and safe handling. Good offset-crash result.
Mazda Protegé	1999-2001	ES		◒	◒	Unimpressive driver side-crash result.
Toyota Corolla	1998-2002	LE		◒	◒	Unimpressive side-crash result (even with side air bags). Somewhat sloppy emergency handling.
Nissan Sentra	2000-2002	GXE		○	◒	Mediocre braking, so-so tire grip.
Dodge Neon	2000-2002			◉	○	Marginal offset-crash result. Excellent brakes.
Saturn SL2	2000-2001			○	◒	Mediocre side-crash result. Seat and driving position too low.
Hyundai Elantra	2001-2002	GLS		◒	○	Poor offset-crash result. ABS hard to find.
Kia Sephia	1999-2001	LS		○	○	Poor offset-crash result. ABS hard to find.
Chevrolet Cavalier	2001-2002	LS		◒	◖	Poor offset- and driver-side crash results.
Pontiac Sunfire*	2001			◒	◖	Poor offset- and driver-side crash test results.
FAMILY CARS						
Volkswagen Passat	1998-2002	GLS V6		◉	◉	Very good overall performer.
Chrysler Sebring	2001-2002	LX V6		◒	◉	Very good frontal- and offset-crash results and braking.
Dodge Stratus*	2001-2002	SE V6		◒	◉	Very good frontal- and offset-crash results and braking.
Chevrolet Impala	2000-2002	LS		◒	◉	Impressive frontal- and offset-crash results. Secure emergency handling.
Toyota Camry	1998-2001	LE V6		◒	◒	Unimpressive side-crash results (even with side air bags). Good driving position. Very good overall.
Honda Accord	1998-2002	EX V6		◒	◒	Very good crash results and driving position.
Mazda 626	2000-2002	LX V6		◒	◒	Good offset-, but unimpressive side-crash results.
Honda Accord	1998-2002	EX 4		◒	◒	Very good crash results and driving position.
Ford Taurus	2000-2002	SE		○	◒	Excellent frontal- and offset-crash results. Unimpressive side-crash results. Braking stops were long.
Mercury Sable*	2000-2002	LS		○	◒	Excellent frontal- and offset-crash results. Unimpressive side-crash results. Braking stops were long.

CR Safety Assessments — Within categories, in performance order

Excellent ● Very good ◒ Good ○ Fair ◖ Poor ●

0 — 100 : P F G VG E

CR Safety Assessments

Within categories, in performance order

Excellent Very good Good Fair Poor

MAKE AND MODEL	MODEL YEARS	TRIM	OVERALL CRSA SCORE	ACCIDENT AVOIDANCE	CRASH PROTECTION	COMMENTS
FAMILY CARS *continued*						
Subaru Legacy	2000-2002	L		○	◐	Emergency handling can be tricky.
Nissan Maxima	2000-2002	GXE		◐	◐	Very good overall performer.
Mitsubishi Galant	1999-2002	ES V6		◐	◐	Excellent braking. Secure emergency handling.
Hyundai Sonata	2001-2002	GLS V6		◐	◐	Excellent braking. Very good crash results.
Mitsubishi Galant	1999-2002	ES 4		◐	◐	Very good overall performer.
Mazda 626	1998-1999	LX 4		○	◐	Acceptable offset- and unimpressive side-crash results.
Nissan Altima	2000-2001	GXE		◐	◐	Unimpressive side-crash result. Sound performer.
Chevrolet Malibu	2000-2002	LS		◐	○	Mediocre crash results. Predictable handling.
Dodge Intrepid	1998-2002	Base		○	◐	Unimpressive passenger-side crash result.
Pontiac Grand Prix	1997-2002	SE		◐	○	Mediocre side-crash result. So-so brake performance.
Oldsmobile Intrigue	2000-2002	GL		◐	○	Disappointing results for passengers in frontal and side crashes.
Saturn LS1	2000-2001			○	○	Disappointing driver-side crash result, unimpressive braking and emergency handling.
Oldsmobile Alero	1999-2002	GL2 V6		●	○	Poor offset-crash result, but secure handling and excellent braking.
Buick Regal	1998-2002	LS		○	○	Disappointing side-crash result. Sloppy emergency handling.
Oldsmobile Alero	1999-2002	GL 4		○	○	Poor offset-crash result. Mediocre handling.
Pontiac Grand Am	1999-2002	SE 4		○	○	Poor offset-crash result. Mediocre handling.
Daewoo Leganza	1999-2002	CDX		○	◒	Poor offset- and mediocre frontal-crash results.
UPSCALE AND LARGE CARS						
Volvo S80	1999-2002	2.9		◐	●	Excellent crash results. Secure handling, strong brakes.
Lincoln LS	2000-2002	V6		◐	●	Excellent crash results. Very good handling and brakes.
Volvo S60	2001-2002	2.4T		◐	●	Good offset-crash result. Very good frontal result. Secure handling.
Acura 3.2TL	1999-2002			◐	◐	Good offset-crash test. Very good frontal- and side-crash results. Able handling.
Oldsmobile Aurora	2001-2002	4.0		◐	◐	Good offset-crash result, but mediocre driver-side crash result.
Toyota Avalon	2000-2001	XLS		◐	◐	Disappointing driver-side frontal-crash result. Excellent offset- and side-crash results.
Pontiac Bonneville	2000-2002	SE		○	◐	Very good crash results. Not very agile.
Buick Park Avenue	1998-2002	Ultra		○	◐	Very good crash results. So-so emergency handling.
Infiniti I30	2000-2001			◐	◐	Very good crash results. Solid performer.
Buick LeSabre	2000-2002	Limited		○	◐	Very good crash results. Sloppy handling.
Chrysler 300M	1999-2000			◐	○	Poor offset-crash result for 1999-2000; acceptable from 2001. Secure handling.
Chrysler Concorde	1998-2002	LXi		○	◐	Reasonable frontal-crash result. Braking is disappointing.
COMPACT CREW-CAB PICKUPS						
Toyota Tacoma	2001-2002	TRD		○	○	Good brakes and acceptable offset-crash result.
Nissan Frontier	2001-2002	SC		○	○	Poor offset-crash result, but excellent side-crash result.
Dodge Dakota	2001-2002	SLT		◒	○	Subpar brakes and poor offset-crash result.
Chevrolet S-10	2001-2002	LS		◒	○	Subpar crash-test results. Sloppy handling.
GMC Sonoma*	2001-2002			◒	○	Subpar crash-test results. Sloppy handling.
FULL-SIZED PICKUPS						
Toyota Tundra	1999-2002	SR5 4.7		○	◐	Good offset-crash result.
Chevrolet Silverado 1500	1999-2002	LS 5.3		○	○	No side-crash test. Marginal offset-crash result.

CR Safety Assessments

Within categories, in performance order

Legend: Excellent ◉ Very good ◑ Good ○ Fair ◒ Poor ●

MAKE AND MODEL	MODEL YEARS	TRIM	OVERALL CRSA SCORE	ACCIDENT AVOIDANCE	CRASH PROTECTION	COMMENTS

FULL-SIZED PICKUPS continued

MAKE AND MODEL	MODEL YEARS	TRIM	ACCIDENT AVOIDANCE	CRASH PROTECTION	COMMENTS
GMC Sierra 1500*	1999-2002		Good	Good	No side-crash test. Marginal offset-crash result.
Ford F-150	1999-2002	XLT 5.4	Fair	Good	Poor offset-crash result. Excellent side- and very good frontal-crash results.

MINIVANS

Honda Odyssey	1999-2002	EX	Fair	Excellent	Excellent crash-test results. Well-rounded performer.
Toyota Sienna	1998-2002	LE	Fair	Excellent	Excellent crash-test results. Very good overall performer.
Ford Windstar	1999-2002	SE Sport	Good	Excellent	Excellent crash-test results. Ungainly handling.
Mazda MPV	2000-2001	LX	Fair	Fair	Excellent side-crash results.
Chrysler Town & Country*	2001		Fair	Good	Poor offset-crash result for 2001 model, acceptable for 2002.
Dodge Grand Caravan	2001	Sport	Fair	Good	Poor offset-crash result for 2001 model, acceptable for 2002.
Chevrolet Venture	2001-2002	LS	Good	Good	Poor offset-crash result. Good frontal- and side-crash results.
Oldsmobile Silhouette*	2001-2002		Good	Good	Poor offset-crash result. Good frontal- and side-crash results.
Pontiac Montana*	2001-2002		Good	Good	Poor offset-crash result. Good frontal- and side-crash results.
Mercury Villager	1999-2000	Base	Good	Good	Poor offset-crash result. Sloppy handling, mediocre brakes.
Nissan Quest*	1999-2000	GXE	Good	Good	Poor offset-crash result. Sloppy handling, mediocre brakes.

SMALL SPORT-UTILITY VEHICLES

Toyota RAV4	2001-2002		Excellent	Fair	Agile handling. Excellent side-crash result.
Subaru Forester	2001-2002	S	Fair	Excellent	Impressive crash-test result. Very good brakes.
Ford Escape	2001-2002	XLT	Excellent	Fair	Marginal offset-crash result. Excellent braking and secure handling.
Mazda Tribute	2001-2002	LX V6	Excellent	Fair	Marginal offset-crash result. Excellent braking and secure handling.
Suzuki Grand Vitara	1999-2002	JLX+	Good	Fair	No side-crash result. Reasonable frontal-crash protection. Very good braking.
Honda CR-V	1997-2001	EX	Good	Fair	Marginal offset-crash result. Sloppy handling.
Chevrolet Tracker	1999-2002	2.0	Good	Fair	Reasonably good crash protection. Mediocre brakes, slow handling.

MIDSIZED SPORT-UTILITY VEHICLES

Mercedes-Benz ML430	2000		Fair	Excellent	No side-crash results. Impressive frontal and offset performance. Very good overall performer.
Lexus RX300	2001-2002		Fair	Excellent	Excellent crash-test results. Secure handling with stability control.
Acura MDX	2001-2002		Good	Excellent	Excellent crash results. Needs stability control, which is not available.
Toyota 4Runner	2001-2002	SR5	Fair	Fair	Very good crash-test results. Secure handling with stability control.
Nissan Pathfinder	2001-2002	LE	Fair	Fair	Very good performer.
Jeep Grand Cherokee	1999-2002	Limited V8	Fair	Good	Marginal offset-crash result. Predictable handling.
Dodge Durango	2001-2002	SLT Plus	Good	Fair	Good crash-test results, but sloppy handling.
Nissan Xterra	2000-2002	SE V6	Fair	Fair	Good crash-test results. Sloppy handling.
Jeep Grand Cherokee	1999-2002	Laredo 6	Good	Good	Mediocre performer with 6-cylinder engine.
Honda Passport*	1998-2001	LX	Fair	Good	Poor offset-crash test result. Sloppy emergency handling.
Isuzu Rodeo	1998-2001	S V6	Fair	Good	Poor offset-crash test result. Sloppy emergency handling.
Chevrolet Blazer	1998-2002	LT	Fair	Good	Poor offset-crash test result. Sloppy emergency handling.
GMC Jimmy*	1998-2001	SLT	Fair	Good	Poor offset-crash test result. Sloppy emergency handling.

*Model is a twin—or essentially similar model— of a tested model.

ROLLOVERS AND LIGHT TRUCKS

Taller vehicles such as SUVs and pickup trucks have a higher center of gravity than ordinary cars do, and that makes them more top-heavy than one that sits lower. In a situation where a vehicle is subjected to strong sideways forces it's easier for a taller vehicle to roll over. Rollovers are deadly: People are frequently ejected or partly ejected through a window, and killed as a result. Rollovers are involved in some 10,000 traffic fatalities per year, NHTSA estimates.

According to NHTSA, SUVs have a rollover rate that is two to three times that of passenger cars. The rollover propensity of SUVs is of particular concern because they are often used as the family car.

To put this in perspective, note that SUVs as a group fare about the same as cars in overall death rates, according to NHTSA. The largest SUVs, those weighing more than 5,000 pounds, such as the Chevrolet Suburban and Lincoln Navigator, have lower fatality rates overall than other passenger vehicles. The death rate for small SUVs (under 3,000 pounds) is higher than for all but the smallest cars. Midsized SUVs, such as the Jeep Grand Cherokee, in the 3,000-to-5,000 pound range, have a mixed safety record.

Keep in mind, too, that a given vehicle's death rate is greatly influenced by the type of driver likely to be found behind the wheel. Sports cars and small SUVs, for example, may have a disproportionately high death rate because they tend to appeal to young males rather than to a more cautious crowd, such as middle-aged parents.

Sport-utility-vehicle occupants survive more often in multivehicle crashes than in single-vehicle accidents—the reverse of what's true for car occupants. That's partly because most SUVs weigh more than most cars do. An SUV's heavier weight transfers more crash energy to the lighter car in a collision. In addition, the higher bumper height of a tall SUV means it can transfer the crash energy into a lower car at a point on the car that's not optimized to absorb it. NHTSA studies show that people driving in cars are about five times as likely to die if an SUV hits them head-on or on the driver's-side door than if a car hits them the same way. So SUVs unfairly gain at least part of their apparent safety advantage in crashes at the expense of the occupants of the other vehicle.

ROLLOVER RATINGS. NHTSA has developed a five-star rating of vehicle stability, called the Rollover Resistance Rating. It's based on a vehicle's static stability factor, which is the ratio of half the track width to the center-of-gravity height. While the usefulness of this method is limited, it does give a rough indication of a vehicle's inherent stability. NHTSA's web site (*nhtsa.dot.gov/hot/rollover*) currently covers some 2001 and newer vehicles.

Because it's based on measurements of a stationary vehicle rather than on one being driven, the Rollover Resistance Rating doesn't account for a vehicle's suspension design, choice of tires, or the presence of an electronic stability-control system—any of which can significantly affect a vehicle's behavior in an emergency situation.

At the direction of Congress, NHTSA has proposed a dynamic on-road rollover test that involves subjecting vehicles to a series of sharp turns on a test track. At this writing NHTSA has proposed a series of tests designed to push vehicles to their handling limits. CR applauds the action of Congress and NHTSA for this proposal and is urging its prompt implementation.

LOAD CAPACITY: HOW MUCH CAN YOU SAFELY CARRY?

A vehicle's load-carrying capacity is the maximum combined weight of people and cargo that the vehicle is designed to handle safely. Vehicle owners should be aware of this limit.

CONSUMER REPORTS publishes the load capacity on every vehicle it tests. The vehicles here are listed alphabetically within categories. The figures are for the model CR tested in the version specified. For other versions, use this table as a rough guide only.

Make & model	Model year	Max. load, lbs.
SPORT-UTILITY VEHICLES		
Acura MDX	2001	1,265
BMW X5 4.4	2000	1,290
Buick Rendezvous CXL	2002	1,215
Chevrolet Blazer LT	1998	1,040
Chevrolet Suburban 1500 LT	2000	1,610
Chevrolet Tahoe	2002	1,390
Dodge Durango SLT Plus	2001	1,590
Ford Excursion XLT	2000	1,630
Ford Expedition XLT	1997	1,710
Ford Explorer XLT	1997	1,025
Ford Explorer XLT	2002	1,325
GMC Envoy SLE	2002	1,090
Infiniti QX4	1998	795
Isuzu Rodeo S	1998	915
Jeep Grand Cherokee Laredo (6-cyl)	2001	1,100
Jeep Grand Cherokee Limited (V8)	1999	1,150
Land Rover Discovery	1999	1,330
Lexus RX300	2001	840
Lincoln Navigator	1999	1,350
Mercedes-Benz ML430	2000	1,340
Mercury Mountaineer	1998	1,080
Mitsubishi Montero Limited	2001	1,020
Nissan Pathfinder LE	2001	1,030
Toyota 4Runner SR5	2001	1,115
Toyota Highlander Limited (V6)	2001	925
Toyota Land Cruiser	1999	1,240
Toyota Sequoia Limited	2002	1,320
WAGONS		
Audi A6 Avant	1999	1,210
Audi Allroad	2001	1,280
BMW 528i Sportwagon	1999	1,090
Chrysler PT Cruiser Limited	2001	865
Ford Focus SE	2000	880
Ford Taurus	1997	1,200
Mazda Protegé5	2002	850
Mercedes-Benz E320 4MATIC	1999	1,050
Saab 9-5 (V6)	1999	920
Saturn LW300	2000	925
Subaru Impreza Outback Sport	2002	900
Subaru Outback H6 VDC	2001	900
Subaru Outback Limited	2000	900
Volkswagen Jetta GLS 1.8T	2002	1,000
Volkswagen Passat GLS (4-cyl)	2000	1,000
Volkswagen Passat GLX 4Motion	2001	1,070
Volvo V40	2000	825
Volvo Cross Country	2001	1,075

Make & model	Model year	Max. load, lbs.
SMALL SPORT-UTILITY VEHICLES		
Chevrolet Tracker 2.0	1999	870
Ford Escape XLT (V6)	2001	900
Honda CR-V EX	2002	850
Hyundai Santa Fe GLS (V6)	2001	880
Jeep Cherokee Sport	1997	1,360
Jeep Liberty Sport (V6)	2002	1,150
Jeep Wrangler Sahara	1997	820
Kia Sportage EX	1999	860
Land Rover Freelander SE	2002	905
Mazda Tribute LX (V6)	2001	900
Nissan Xterra SE (V6)	2000	885
Saturn VUE (V6)	2002	825
Subaru Forester S	2001	900
Suzuki Grand Vitara JLX+	1999	895
Suzuki Sidekick Sport	1996	770
Suzuki XL-7 Touring	2002	1,170
Toyota RAV4	2001	760
MINIVANS		
Chevrolet Venture LS	2001	1,365
Dodge Caravan LE	1996	1,150
Dodge Grand Caravan Sport	2001	1,150
Ford Windstar SE Sport	2001	1,360
GMC Safari SLE	1996	1,425
Honda Odyssey EX	2001	1,250
Mazda MPV LX	2000	1,190
Mercury Villager	1999	1,450
Toyota Sienna LE	2001	1,160
COMPACT PICKUP TRUCKS		
Chevrolet S-10 LS (crew cab)	2001	1,000
Chevrolet S-10 LS (extended cab)	1998	1,210
Dodge Dakota SLT (crew cab)	2001	1,100
Dodge Dakota SLT (extended cab)	1997	1,320
Ford Explorer Sport Trac	2001	1,190
Ford Ranger XLT (4.0)	1998	1,210
Nissan Frontier SC (crew cab)	2001	915
Toyota Tacoma TRD (crew cab)	2001	1,225
FULL-SIZED PICKUP TRUCKS		
Chevrolet Avalanche 1500	2002	1,190
Chevrolet Silverado 1500 LS (5.3L)	1999	1,465
Dodge Ram 1500 SLT (4.7L crew cab)	2002	1,350
Dodge Ram 1500 SLT (5.2L extended cab)	1999	1,265
Ford F-150 XLT (5.4L extended cab)	1999	1,290
Ford F-150 XLT (5.4L crew cab)	2002	1,455
Toyota Tundra SR5 (4.7L)	2000	1,340

THE LOAD FACTOR

Many people buy an SUV because it has lots of room for cargo. And it's natural to assume that if a vehicle has a large cargo area then you should be able to fill it without worrying about overloading the vehicle. But that's not always the case. Some vehicles have a large cargo area but a relatively low load-carrying capacity—the maximum combined weight of people and cargo that the vehicle is designed to handle safely.

Overloading a vehicle can compromise safety, degrading its handling, stressing its brakes, and possibly overheating its tires, which increases the risk of tire failure. If a tire is underinflated, that risk increases still further. In addition, any loading of an SUV raises its center of gravity; overloading only makes matters worse. Most automakers provide load-capacity data for cars (usually on a door-jamb sticker) but not for pickups, SUVs, or mini-vans. Some exceptions include Chrysler, Honda, Mercedes-Benz, and Toyota, which provide this information in their owner's manuals or on the vehicle itself on newer models.

In addition, the load capacity can vary depending on the trim level, options, type of transmission, and even the amount of sound-deadening material. That's why a higher trim level can have a lower load-carrying capacity than the base model.

Even when well within safe load limits, avoid putting heavy cargo on the roof of an SUV. Cargo on the roof raises the overall center of gravity, which can make a rollover more likely. For a listing of load capacities for recently tested vehicles, see the table on page 47.

CHILD-SAFETY CAR SEATS

Child-safety seats save lives and should be used until a child is big enough to fit the vehicle's regular safety belt. Car seats protect children in all but the most severe crashes. To be effective, though, the car seat has to be installed and used properly and used on every trip, long or short. And it's important to use the right seat for the child's size. NHTSA has estimated that, largely because of installation issues, as many as 8 in 10 seats may not adequately protect the children riding in them.

Using a vehicle's safety belt to cinch up a child car seat can be difficult: Many seats are simply incompatible with some cars. To cinch a seat tightly you may have to climb into the car, place all your weight on the child seat to position it properly, then fuss with the seatbelt to tighten it. CONSUMER REPORTS found that extra padding, such as a rolled towel or a foam pool noodle, needs to be placed beneath a rear-facing child seat to achieve the right recline angle. Sometimes you'll need to use a locking clip on the belt to secure the seat properly.

TOP-TETHER STRAPS. A top-tether strap provides additional security for front-facing seats by limiting how much the seat can lurch forward in a crash. CONSUMER REPORTS highly recommends them. Federal rules mandated top-tether anchors in cars and a top tether strap on all front-facing child seats manufactured on or after Sept. 1, 1999. The top tether hooks to an anchor in a car's rear deck, floor, roof, or seatback.

Most automakers sell kits that allow you to retrofit older vehicles with top-tether anchors. They are inexpensive—often free or priced at $10 to $20 installed. In fact, all cars made after Sept. 1, 1989, have points where a retrofit tether anchor is supposed to be attached. Often these are essentially holes drilled in the metal bracing somewhere behind the rear seat. You can install them yourself or have a mechanic do it. Anchor hardware is available at car dealers.

LOWER ANCHORS. A federal rule in place as of September 2002 is supposed to provide a simpler, universal system. The system is known as LATCH, for Lower Anchors and Tethers for Children. It consists of a top tether and two lower attachments in the crease between the backrest and seat cushion. Lower anchors were phased in by law starting in 2000 and are now required in all cars and light trucks under 8,500 pounds, and in all child-safety seats made on or after Sept. 1, 2002. Many auto manufacturers supplied their cars with upper and lower anchors much earlier than those deadlines.

LATCH was designed to eliminate the struggle with the vehicle's safety belts. Unfortunately, parents and other caregivers may still wrestle with car-seat installation. As CONSUMER REPORTS tests more of the new style of LATCH-equipped cars and child seats, the testers are discovering that incompatibilities between cars and car seats still exist. For instance, it can be tough to hitch the child seat's lower hooks to the car's lower anchors.

The new LATCH-equipped child car seats will still work with vehicle safety belts found in older vehicles. If you don't use the top tether, be sure to secure it so it doesn't fly around and hit someone in the event of a crash.

Seat types

Whichever child seat you use, make sure it's the right type for your child's age, weight, and height. It should fit securely in your car and be easy to get your child into and out of it. Here are the basic types:

INFANT SEATS. Babies should stay in rear-facing infant seats that support the head, neck, and back until age 1. Most hold babies weighing up to 20 or 22 pounds. Seats with a base can be used with or without a base that stays in the car. The seat itself can snap in and out of the base and double as an infant carrier. Some seats that are part of a "travel system" can also snap into a stroller.

An infant may outgrow the weight limit of an infant seat within six to nine months. He or she should then be placed in a convertible seat with a higher weight limit but should remain in the rear-facing position until his or her first birthday.

CONVERTIBLE SEATS. For infants, especially larger ones who are not yet 1 year old, a convertible seat used in the rear-facing position is the answer. This is also an option as a first car seat for a newborn, though it can't double as a carrier. When the child weighs more than 20 pounds and is at least 1 year old, you place the seat facing forward and can continue to use it until the child weighs about 40 pounds.

TODDLER/BOOSTER SEATS. These are booster seats with an internal harness. Use these seats with the internal harness for children 1 year old and up and weighing 20 to 40 pounds (some car-seat makers say 22 to 40 pounds). When the child weighs more than 40 pounds, remove the harness. Then you can use the seat as a belt-positioning booster seat for properly positioning the child to use one of the car's rear lap-and-shoulder belts. Safety experts advise that, given a choice between a lap belt only and a lap-and-shoulder belt, always choose the lap-and-shoulder belt.

REGULAR BOOSTERS. These work without an internal harness (the child is secured by the vehicle belts) and are usually used for children weighing between 40 and 80 pounds.

LATCH

The LATCH installation system (shown below as typically installed), is now appearing on many models and on newer cars. With LATCH, no safety belts are required to install a seat. The seat attaches directly to lower anchors and a top-tether anchor in the car. The goal is to simplify installation and improve compatibility with different cars.

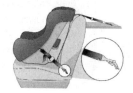

INSTALLING A CHILD CAR SEAT

The federal government says child seats that don't conform to the new LATCH standard (usually those made before Sept. 1, 2001) are still safe so long as they are free of recalls, have not been in a crash, and are properly installed. Read the child seat's instructions and pertinent portions of your car owner's manual to make sure you use all belts, buckles, and clips correctly.

In any car, the center rear is statistically the safest place for children in a car seat, but any rear spot is better than the front passenger seat. For kids too big for a car seat, a lap-and-shoulder belt, even in the front, is better than a center seat with a lap belt only.

When installing a child seat, firmly push it into the vehicle's seat cushions while pulling all slack out of the safety belts. This step is necessary for a secure fit. With some lap-and-shoulder belts, you may need a locking clip to secure a child-safety seat properly. Safety belts anchored forward of the seatback may prevent a car seat from being anchored securely to the vehicle seat.

BUILT-IN (INTEGRAL) CHILD SEATS. Some vehicles, usually minivans or wagons, offer a built-in child restraint as an option. Chrysler, Ford, GM, Mitsubishi, Nissan, Saab, Toyota, and Volvo have offered them on various models, although lately some manufacturers have dropped them. Usually these are toddler/booster seats for children older than 1 year and weighing more than 20 pounds. You get a perfect fit with the car, and no installation is needed. But you must still make sure that the seat is suitable for your child.

CONSUMER REPORTS hasn't tested these seats, but because they're integrated with the car, and the child sits farther back than in a separate car seat, we believe they are likely to perform very well. They also must be in compliance with all applicable safety standards for child car seats. One potential drawback with integrated child seats is that when they are folded away into the seat, they can form a not-so-comfortable seat back for adult passengers.

TRAVEL SYSTEMS. Many infant car seats can be bought as part of a travel system that includes a companion stroller. The child seat snaps into the stroller. One design—the Safeline Sit n' Stroll—transforms from car seat to stroller and back. As a car seat, it can be used rear-facing until a child reaches 22 pounds and then front-facing up to 40 pounds.

Features

Internal harnesses are adjustable and come in several varieties. Infant seats have either a three-point harness (a harness with two shoulder straps that meet and buckle at the crotch) or a five-point system (two shoulder straps, two strap sections over the legs, and a crotch strap that includes a buckle to connect the five sections). Most recently available infant seats come with a five-point system.

Convertible seats and toddler/booster seats typically use a five-point harness with three height positions. Some seats have a label certifying them for use on airplanes, but airlines do not accept all seat types.

Seats generally have removable, machine-washable cloth covers. Some seats used for infants have a leveling indicator to help install the seat at a safe reclining angle.

How to choose

The best choice is a seat appropriate for a child's age, weight, and height that also fits your car easily. Try before you buy.

Until your child is big enough to use the vehicle's safety belt on its own, you'll need to buy at least two sizes of car seats. You can usually start with an infant seat or a convertible seat. If you start with an infant seat, which you can also use as a carrier, you'll have to graduate to a convertible seat when the child reaches 20 or 22 pounds, depending on seat type.

If you start with a convertible seat, choose one with a five-point harness that won't obstruct a small baby's head. There are many fine choices. When the child outgrows the convertible, move to any type of booster seat.

CR TESTS. In the summer of 2001 CONSUMER REPORTS had an outside laboratory perform crash tests slightly more stringent than those the government uses. Dummies of various sizes and weights were strapped into seats mounted on sleds and run through a course simulating a head-on collision at 30 mph. Electronic sensors measured forces to the head and chest. Using high-speed cameras, we could see, for example, if a dummy's head moved so far forward that in real life a child might have been injured. In our labs, we also judged how easy each seat was to use and whether it could be installed securely in vehicles with different seat configurations and safety-belt systems.

PERFORMANCE WARNING. All the seats did fine in the crash tests and most were quite easy to use. The only notable problem we uncovered had to do with the shoulder-belt guides on some toddler/booster seats and on one convertible that could be used as a booster. Sometimes the vehicle's shoulder belt jammed in the seat's belt guide, leaving slack around the child, thereby compromising the child's protection in a crash. When the Cosco Alpha Omega 02-531, a convertible model, was used as a booster seat, it had this jamming problem.

Of the toddler/booster seats, three Century models required care so that the belt guide didn't lock in any slack. They were the Century NextStep SE 44905, Breverra Classic 44865, and Breverra Metro 44850.

With four other toddler/boosters, the design of the belt guide made it easy for a child to create belt slack regardless of how careful a parent might be with the installation. We don't recommend them if the child's size requires the use of the belt guides. They were the Cosco Adventurer II 02-448 and High Back Booster 02-422; the Evenflo Express Comfort Touch 2481183; and the Graco Cherished CarGo 8480. The problem seats were fine when we tested them with their internal harnesses and without using the belt guide for taller kids.

BOOSTER-SEAT PERFORMANCE. Also called "belt-positioning boosters," these seats are analogous to putting a phone book on a dining-room chair. Intended for children weighing between 40 and 80 pounds, they use the car's safety belt to protect a child and do not include their own internal harness. The models CR tested didn't exhibit the belt-guide problems that the toddler/booster seats did.

Financing & Insurance

Interest payments and insurance premiums are two major ongoing costs of car ownership. Here's how to save.

Used-car prices have fallen appreciably lately, thanks in part to the hefty rebates and cut-rate financing deals piled onto new cars in the past year. Because rebates and other incentives effectively lower the price of new cars, that immediately lowers the value of older versions of the same car. Other factors, such as a deluge of off-lease cars entering the market, have further depressed used-car prices. That's good news for the used-car shopper.

Even if it's a buyer's market right now, most shoppers still need to borrow money for a car purchase. Again the news is good for shoppers, because interest rates are low right now, and that directly translates into cheaper loans and lower monthly payments. But you must still watch for the really good finance deals. On the following pages you'll find guidance on how to bring home the best loan rates when you bring home that next car.

FIVE KEYS TO GETTING THE BEST LOAN RATES

Auto loans are relatively easy to get. First, lending institutions know they'll be able to get their money back because the loan is backed by the collateral of the vehicle. If you don't make the payments, the lender will repossess the car. Second, auto dealers will bend over backwards to sell you a car, and getting you financed is not only part of the process, it's also a major source of profit for the dealership.

The trick is to get a loan for the lowest interest rate you can. The auto experts at CONSUMER REPORTS offer these five keys to getting the best loan rate:

1. Shop around before you visit the dealership.

Compare interest rates at various financial institutions, such as banks and credit unions, as well as at the dealership. It's often an advantage to be preapproved for a loan so that you can keep the financial arrangements out of the vehicle-price negotiations at the dealership.

If you're borrowing money to buy a car, the figure to focus on is the annual percentage rate (APR), which can vary from day to day. You can get a quick read on the prevailing rates at such online sites as Bank Rate Monitor (*www.bankrate.com*), E-Loan (*www.eloan.com*), Lending Tree (*www.lendingtree.com*), and Household Auto (*www.householdauto.com*).

2. Keep an eye on the total cost of the loan.

The term (duration) of a loan determines your monthly payment and the total purchase price of the vehicle. A shorter term means higher monthly payments but less money paid overall. Try to keep the length of the loan as short as you can afford. A three-year loan costs you far less overall than a four- or five-year loan at the same interest rate. For instance, if you borrow $20,000 at 7.5 percent APR for 36 months, your monthly payment will be $622 and the total interest you will pay over the life of the loan will be $2,396. If you finance the same amount at the same interest rate for 60 months, your monthly payment would be only $401, but you'd end up paying a total of $4,046 in interest. You need to balance the total cost of the loan against a monthly payment you can afford. The web sites mentioned above have calculators that can help you determine these figures before you sign on the dotted line.

3. Don't let low interest dictate your car choice.

During the last year a number of automakers have provided zero percent and other very low rates on new cars. That has also prompted low rates on used cars. Such deals can save you money, but approach them with some skepticism.

Not surprisingly, the most attractive deals are often attached to the slowest-selling and least-desirable models. Low interest rates are no bargain if they persuade you to buy a car that you won't be happy with or that doesn't hold up well. It may make better financial sense over the long term, for instance, to buy a consistently reliable model at a little higher interest than an unreliable model at zero percent. (You'll find CONSUMER REPORTS' lists of reliable and unreliable cars in Chapter 2.)

4. Be aware that your credit record affects your interest rate.

If in doubt, check your credit score before you start looking for a loan. Having a sterling credit score can get you a better interest rate than having a poor score. The cheapest rates are typically available only to buyers with good credit scores. You can check your credit record online at Experian (*www.experian.com*), Trans Union (*www.transunion.com*), or My Credit (*www.mycreditfile.com*). If there are errors, it's advisable to fix them before you apply for a loan. Many lenders and dealers will work with buyers who are considered credit risks, but such loans have a much higher interest rate. Cleaning up any credit problems before you buy should result in a lower interest rate.

5. Keep financing separate from price negotiations.

If you plan to finance your car through the dealership, nail down the price for the vehicle before you bring up the loan. Many salespeople like to mix the vehicle price and loan together as one negotiation, often by focusing on the monthly payment figure. Don't be drawn into doing this. You want to beat down the cost of the car as low as you can first and talk about financing second. If you let the two negotiations get intermingled, it's a recipe for confusion. Salespeople can exploit that confusion by giving you a favorable figure in one area while inflating a figure in another area.

WHY DEPRECIATION MATTERS

A car is almost never a good investment. Most of the time it's an asset that loses value year after year. Depreciation is a much more ferocious enemy for a new-car buyer than for a used-car buyer. The typical new car loses thousands of dollars in value the first day it's driven off the dealer's lot. It continues to lose value quickly for the next two or three years, then the depreciation curve levels out.

Knowing about depreciation can help a savvy used-car buyer. Some cars depreciate a lot faster than others. If one of those happens to be a good-performing car that just doesn't have much of a resale market for some reason, then that can be a good deal. The Mazda Millenia and Infiniti Q45 fit in that category. Both are pretty good luxury cars that never caught on with the car-buying public.

Numerous large domestic sedans are also notorious for losing value quickly. They include the big Buicks, Cadillacs, Chryslers, and Lincolns. By age three they have usually lost 45 to 55 percent of their initial value.

Some mass-market mainstream sedans choke the used-car market, particularly those that were popular with commercial and rental-car fleets. For instance, you'll see lots of Ford Tauruses, Mercury Sables, and Chevrolet Malibus selling for low prices. Those three, at least, are relatively good cars for their respective niches. Others, like the Buick Century, Chevrolet Cavalier, and Pontiac Grand Am are also steep depreciators, but they were unexceptional cars even when they were new.

Historically, most sport-utility vehicles have held their value well, even if they were rough, crude vehicles such as the ever-popular Jeep Wrangler. The Jeep Wrangler hangs in there, thanks perhaps to its cult-car status. (Even Barbie has one!) However, some widely sold, mostly old-tech and dated SUVs are not doing as well in the depreciation sweepstakes: The Chevrolet Blazer, GMC Jimmy, Kia Sportage, Mitsubishi Montero Sport, and Oldsmobile Bravada prices are sinking fast.

Of the cars that hold their value exceptionally well, the best tend to be sporty vehicles: The Chevrolet Corvette, Honda S2000, Porsche Boxster, and Toyota Celica and MR2 are outstanding examples. Some SUVs continue to hold their own, including the posh BMW X5 and Lexus RX300 and the behemoth Chevrolet Suburban, sometimes referred to as the "national car of Texas."

CR's advice: Look first at the quality and reliability of the car. Quick depreciation may make something look like a bargain, but more often than not these cars are cheap because they aren't very good.

HOW TO SHOP FOR AUTO INSURANCE

Besides buying the car itself, insuring it is usually the steepest car-related expense you'll incur. You should get an idea of what your insurance costs would be for a particular vehicle before you sign on the dotted line for your next car. You don't want to go through the process of shopping and arranging financing, only to find that a high insurance premium puts the car out of reach.

Many people stick with the same insurance carrier for years, never realizing they could get a better deal just by asking. Blind loyalty to one insurer can cost you dearly: You may be paying twice as much as you need to.

How they rate you

Insurers have always been cagey about the standards they apply when deciding whether to sell or renew a policy. Some may disqualify you if you have just one speeding ticket; others decline coverage only if the ticket was for reckless speeding. And many won't insure you if your driving record includes multiple moving violations. Along with your driving history, insurance-company computers look at personal factors that enable them to peg your premium to your risk. These include your age, sex, neighborhood, home ownership, and even your credit rating. Details about anyone else on the same policy—your spouse's and children's ages and driving records, for example—also affect what you pay.

If there's an upside to all that snooping, it's lower premiums for consumers with good driving records and other low-risk attributes. Added data is also benefiting drivers insurers have shied away from. The portion of drivers relegated to assigned-risk pools, which traditionally cover people considered uninsurable, has dropped dramatically in recent years.

How you can rate them

Choosing an insurance carrier is largely a matter of finding a reputable company that offers you good rates. But a low price isn't everything. Prompt service and claims payment count too. If you're happy with your insurer, you may want to stay. That doesn't mean, however, that you shouldn't routinely fish for new quotes and then run them by your current insurer to see if you can get a lower bid.

Comparing premiums should be easy, since many Internet services promise to get you instant quotes. CONSUMER REPORTS found in a recent study, though, that the quality of the information, and the range of premiums quoted varied a lot from site to site.

Out of six sites surveyed, *InsWeb.com* was the best of the lot, followed by *Insurance.com*, *Insure.com*, *Progressive.com*, *Esurance.com*, and *NetQuote.com*.

You should check, too, with your state's insurance department. Most can provide examples of comparative rates for different companies doing business in your state. State insurance departments are usually listed in the state-government pages of telephone directories, and usually have web sites as well.

Another avenue to shop for rate quotes is through local insurance agents, which you can find in the Yellow Pages. Local insurance agents can take a few days to get back to you, but it's worth inquiring. Try to get a price check-up every year.

To get an accurate quote, you'll need to provide details about the car you're considering: the make, model, year, trim line, and the vehicle identification number (VIN). You'll also need to give the age, sex, and recent driving record of all potential drivers.

Who pays more for insurance

The young and the reckless typically pay the most. On the whole, males under 25, particularly teenagers, are charged the highest premiums because they are involved in more than their fair share of accidents and moving violations. Middle-aged women pay the least. Other factors affecting your premium include:

LARGE FAMILIES. Any increase in the number of drivers in your family will boost your auto premium, especially when you add a teenager to your policy. Still, it's usually cheaper to have the kids on your own policy rather than on policies of their own.

Much depends on your individual circumstances, however. For example, a middle-aged person with a conviction for driving while intoxicated can expect to pay heavily for insurance regardless. In some places, such as Chicago and New York, a married couple with two cars will pay more than two single people, while in other places, the reverse is true.

CITY DWELLERS. It's no surprise that urban drivers pay more for auto insurance than suburban and rural residents, due to the greater congestion and higher crime endemic to cities. Still, city residents who choose their insurer carefully can shave their insurance bill by hundreds of dollars.

COMMUTERS. Change jobs, and the chances are good that you will change your daily commute. That could increase what you pay for coverage. More miles usually mean a higher premium.

ACCIDENT-PRONE. Simply put, if you cause an accident, your rates are likely to go up.

Are you overinsured?

Auto insurance is meant to protect you against catastrophic losses, such as a major accident or the theft of your car. Many people overinsure their vehicles with a low deductible—the portion of a claim you're responsible for—or by simply buying coverage they don't need. Still others make the more-serious mistake of buying too little coverage for their needs. Here are some tips on separating the insurance essentials from coverage you can probably live without.

Coverage you must have

BODILY INJURY LIABILITY. Should you cause an accident, this pays the medical, rehabilitation, and funeral bills of your passengers, the other driver, his or her passengers, and any pedestrians hurt. It also covers pain and suffering awards as well as legal costs.

Get at least $100,000 per person and $300,000 per accident. If you have sizable assets, such as a large stock portfolio or an expensive home, consider increasing those limits to

$250,000 per person and $500,000 per accident. This added coverage will raise your premium roughly 10 percent. We also recommend that people with a high net worth have a separate "umbrella" policy to insure against a major lawsuit seeking an amount that exceeds their auto policy's limits.

PROPERTY DAMAGE. This pays to repair or replace another person's vehicle or other property damaged by your car. States typically require only $10,000 to $25,000; buy coverage of $100,000.

UNINSURED MOTORIST. This coverage pays legal bills, rehabilitation, and funeral costs, as well as losses for pain and suffering incurred by you or passengers in your car if an accident is caused by a hit-and-run driver or someone who has little or no insurance. Get at least $100,000 per person and $300,000 per accident—more if you carry higher coverage for bodily injury liability.

Coverage you'll probably need

COLLISION AND COMPREHENSIVE. Collision pays to repair or replace your car no matter who caused the accident. Comprehensive pays if it's stolen or if it's damaged as a result of a storm or other natural disaster. Coverage kicks in for the amount above your deductible.

Choose the highest deductible you can afford—as a general rule no less than $500. Then cancel this coverage once its cost equals 10 percent of your vehicle's book value, since your vehicle's market worth is all you'll collect, no matter how much you've pampered it. Antique vehicles or cars with collector value should be insured through a separate rider.

PERSONAL INJURY PROTECTION. Also known as "PIP," this reimburses you for lost wages and in-home care needed as a result of an accident. Stick to the state-required minimum. Your health and disability policies should cover the balance of your needs.

MEDICAL-PAYMENTS. Known as med-pay, this covers medical bills for you and your passengers, regardless of who's at fault. You may not require any if you have good health insurance. But you may want to carry at least $5,000 to protect your passengers who may not have their own health coverage. The extra cost will be minimal.

Coverage you can probably skip

ROADSIDE ASSISTANCE. This coverage pays to have your vehicle towed. If you already have an auto-club membership or your car's manufacturer provides this service for free, it's probably excess coverage.

RENTAL REIMBURSEMENT. This coverage typically costs $30 per year and pays for a rental car if yours is stolen or is in the shop for repairs after an accident. There's usually a cap on the amount you're reimbursed per day and per occurrence.

Strategies to reduce your premiums

CHECK SPECIFIC MODELS. The difference in premiums between one car or truck and another can be striking, even if the vehicles cost the same to buy. Much of that has to do with the cost of repairing collision damage, which can vary greatly. But individual models' record of damage claims can also have a bearing: Some models get into more accidents than their peers, and insurance companies may charge more to insure them.

ASK FOR THE TOP TIER. Insurers sort customers according to how likely they are to file a claim, then assign them to one of several categories commonly referred to as tiers. Top-tier customers who have the cleanest driving records and live in neighborhoods where auto-theft rates are low, for example, can easily save 15 percent or more. But if you're not sure, ask if you qualify for top-tier status.

GET A VOLUME DISCOUNT. Most insurers will give you a multiple-policy price break if you let them write your auto, home, and personal-liability coverage.

HIT THE BOOKS. Completing a certified defensive-driving course can reduce your premium in some states. And if you have children who drive, you'll save if they get good grades or if they attend a school located more than 100 miles from your home and don't use the car there.

EQUIPMENT DISCOUNTS. You may qualify for extra discounts if your car has current safety equipment such as air bags, antilock brakes, and anti-theft equipment.

GROUP DISCOUNTS. Insurers may award discounts—sometimes sizable—to low-risk consumers who share an affiliation, say members of a company pension fund or an alumni group.

KEEP YOUR REPAIR OPTIONS OPEN. Some insurers insist you use generic replacement parts or suggest you bring your vehicle to certain body shops in an effort to cut claims costs. This arrangement may lower your premium, but may not be the best route. Sometimes the cut-rate repairs are cheap because they use inferior parts. If you want to be sure your damage is repaired with good-as-new parts, insure with a company that lets you decide which parts are used and who does the repairs.

Car Care & Tires

With a little care you can keep your car running (almost) forever.

PROTECTING YOUR INVESTMENT

One of the reassuring qualities of contemporary cars is that they need much less-frequent service to keep them running well. Changing the spark plugs, breaker points, and condenser used to be a seasonal exercise, and body rust was accepted as a normal if unfortunate hazard of aging. Now many spark plugs can go 100,000 miles between changes. Electronic ignition has done away with the points and condenser. Chassis, suspensions, and even some transmissions are lubed for life. And factory rust-through warranties typically run six years or longer. What's more, reliability has improved significantly. The result is that most late-model cars and trucks should be able to go 200,000 miles with regular upkeep. Here are a few simple, periodic checks and procedures you can do that will help you get there.

Three key tasks

CHECK THE ENGINE OIL. Do it regularly—monthly for a vehicle in good condition; more often if you notice an oil leak or find you need to add oil routinely. The car should be parked on level ground so you can get an accurate dipstick reading. Don't overfill. And if you do have a leak, find and fix it soon.

　　CHECK TIRE AIR PRESSURE. Once a month and before any extended road trips, use an accurate tire-pressure gauge to check the inflation pressure in each tire, including the spare. Do this when the tires are cold (before the vehicle has been driven or after no more than a couple of miles of driving). Use the inflation pressure recommended by the vehicle's manufacturer, not the maximum pressure embossed on the tire's sidewall. The recommended pressure is usually found on a placard on a front doorjamb, in the glove compartment, or in the owner's manual. Also be sure to inspect tires for abnormal or uneven wear, cuts, and any sidewall bulges you can see.

CR advises that digital tire-pressure gauges (which cost about $15 to $25) are probably the best bet overall because they will give an accurate reading or none at all. Many pencil-type gauges (typically $10 to $15) are good as well. Note that to check the pressure in a temporary spare tire, which is often 60 psi, you will need a gauge that goes higher than that—say from 0 up to 90 pounds.

GIVE IT A WASH. Try to wash the car every week, if you can. Wash the body and, if necessary, hose out the fender wells and undercarriage to remove dirt and road salt. It's time to wax the finish when water beads become larger than a quarter.

Other checks at each oil change

For normal driving, many automakers recommend changing the engine oil and filter every 7,500 miles or six months, whichever comes first. This is sufficient for the majority of motorists. For "severe" driving—with frequent, very cold starts and short trips, dusty conditions, or trailer towing—the change interval should be shortened to every 3,000 miles or three months. (Check your owner's manual for the specific intervals recommended for your vehicle.) Special engines such as diesels and turbocharged engines may need more-frequent oil changes.

CHECK THE AIR FILTER. Remove the air-filter element and hold it up to a strong light. If you don't see light, replace it. Regardless, follow the recommended service intervals.

CHECK THE CONSTANT-VELOCITY-JOINT BOOTS. On front-wheel-drive and some four-wheel-drive vehicles, examine these bellowslike rubber boots, also known as CV boots, on the drive axles. Immediately replace any that are cut, cracked, or leaking. If dirt contaminates the CV joint it can quickly lead to an expensive fix.

SEVEN WAYS TO LOWER THE COST OF DRIVING

A few simple habits can keep costs in check.

1. Keep a notebook in the car. For a few months, write down everything you spend on driving—fuel, maintenance, tolls, and parking. Knowing where the money goes is the best guide to finding significant places to save.

2. Don't linger long. With most gasoline engines, it's more efficient to turn off the engine than to idle for 30 seconds or longer.

3. Accelerate and brake smoothly. Smooth driving not only saves fuel, but extends the life of the engine, transmission, and brakes.

4. Stay warm. An engine runs most cleanly and effi-ciently when it's warm. Avoid lots of short trips and unnecessary cold starts.

5. Use regular fuel. If your car is supposed to run on regular fuel, don't buy premium in the mistaken belief that your engine will run better. Furthermore, many cars that recommend premium fuel also run well on regular.

6. Stay tuned. A poorly tuned engine can cut gas mileage by 10 to 20 percent. In older cars, a clogged air filter can cause a marked increase in fuel consumption. Follow the maintenance schedule in your owner's manual.

7. Shop for insurance. Some insurers charge twice as much as others for the same coverage. See page 55.

INSPECT THE EXHAUST SYSTEM. If you're willing to make under-car inspections, check for rusted-through exhaust parts that need replacing. Also tighten loose clamps. Do this while the car is up on ramps. If a shop changes your oil, have them make these checks. Listen for changes in the exhaust sound while driving. It's usually advisable to replace the entire exhaust system all at once rather than to repair sections at different times.

LOOK AT THE BRAKES. For most people it makes sense to have a shop check and service the brakes. If you handle your own brake work, remove all wheels and examine the brake system. Replace excessively worn pads or linings, and have badly scored rotors or drums machined or replaced. The brakes should be checked at least twice per year; more often if you drive a lot of miles.

CHECK THE FLUIDS. On many newer cars, the automatic transmission is sealed. On cars where it is not sealed, check the transmission dipstick with the engine warmed up and running (see the owner's manual for details). Also check the power-steering-pump dipstick (it's usually attached to the fluid-reservoir cap) and the level in the brake-fluid reservoir. If the brake-fluid level is low, top it up and have the system checked for leaks.

CLEAN THE RADIATOR. Prevent overheating by removing debris with a soft brush and washing the outside of the radiator with a detergent solution.

CHECK THE BATTERY. Check the battery's terminals and cables to make sure they are securely attached, with no corrosion. If the battery has removable caps, check its fluid level every few months—especially in warmer climates.

Regular maintenance every two to four years

DRAIN AND FLUSH THE COOLING SYSTEM. Considering the hassle of collecting and safely disposing of old antifreeze, you may want to leave this to a shop.

CHANGE THE AUTOMATIC-TRANSMISSION FLUID. Many models require that you replace the fluid and filter every 36,000 miles—sooner if the normally pink fluid takes on a brownish tint. With some cars the fluid and, if applicable, the filter can go 100,000 miles or more. With other late models, the transmission fluid never needs to be changed. Check your owner's manual for this information.

REPLACE THE DRIVE BELTS AND HOSES. Do this every two to three years, even if they don't show any wear. If a belt becomes noisy, have it adjusted.

CHANGE THE TIMING BELT. If your vehicle has a belt instead of a chain, stick to the manufacturer's recommended replacement interval—usually every 60,000 to 80,000 miles. Check the owner's manual or consult a dealer. Failure to change the timing belt can result in a very expensive engine repair if the belt should break.

HOW TO GIVE YOUR OLD CAR NEW LIFE

The old adage, "a clean car runs better," may hide a profound truth. It may be that people who take the trouble to keep their car clean also take the trouble to maintain it. Or it could be that it's easier to spot car problems if you're looking at a clean and orderly area. In either case, making an older car look like new can pay dividends by maintaining the car's value and increasing personal satisfaction.

BASIC FACTS ON TOWING

For the uninitiated, towing a trailer can be intimidating. It's hard enough to get used to towing a trailer straight ahead, since the weight of the trailer tends to hold you back when you're going uphill and shove you forward when you're going downhill. But backing up a trailer without jackknifing takes real skill. Practice before you hit the road.

If you plan to tow a trailer, choose a vehicle with a factory towing package, if you can find one. Manufacturers' towing gear is specifically designed to work with the given vehicle. The package will likely include towing hardware such as the hitch receiver and transmission oil cooler, as well as wiring for the trailer's brakes and brake lights. New-vehicle dealers may be able to supply you with specifics about towing packages and the vehicle's load limits.

Use the right hitch. The types include Class I (up to 2,000 pounds), Class II (2,000 to 3,500 pounds), Class III (3,500 to 5,000 pounds), Class IV (5,000 to 10,000 pounds), and Class V (over 10,000 pounds). Be sure the trailer-ball size is correct for the trailer. Typical sizes are 1⅞-, 2.0-, and 2⁵⁄₁₆-inch. Be sure the vehicle has large side mirrors that allow you to see around the trailer.

Things to consider before towing

The first rule is that you shouldn't try to tow a load that's heavier than your vehicle can manage. Doing so can erode the handling and overstress both your vehicle's drivetrain and brakes. Towing a trailer that's too heavy is like having a big guy pushing you down the stairs. To check the towing capacity of a specific vehicle, look at its window sticker or in its owner's manual.

In addition to the trailer weight, consider the added weight of fuel, water, gear, and people, and make sure the total doesn't exceed the vehicle's gross combined weight rating (GCWR). Don't be misled by a model's maximum towing capability. Often, a vehicle needs to be equipped

---

MATCH THE VEHICLE TO THE LOAD

If you'll be towing regularly, the size load you intend to haul can influence your choice of vehicle.

LIGHT LOAD
(up to 1,000 pounds)
such as a catamaran, two off-road motorcycles, an ATV, a snowmobile, or a personal watercraft.

It needn't cost a lot to transform shabby into chic. As with most other do-it-yourself projects, the more elbow grease you are willing to invest yourself, the less you'll need to pay someone else. Here are some tips to help you go about it.

OUTSIDE APPEARANCES. The first step to getting the body looking good is to give it a thorough cleaning with car-wash soap and water. Once it's completely dry, look over the paint surface and assess any damage you see. Note any scratches, stone chips, dings, and dents in the sheet metal.

You can touch up small scratches and chips yourself with touch-up paint, available for a few dollars at your car dealership and at some auto-parts stores. Make sure you get an exact color match. Touch-up paint usually comes in a small bottle with an applicator brush in the lid. Otherwise, use a small, pointed artist's brush and cover the scratch by going over it in tiny dabs. Let this paint dry for at least a day or two before polishing the car.

To remove or minimize the many fine surface scratches most cars accumulate over time, you can have the car professionally buffed at a body shop or car wash. This buffing, also called "detailing," will take out minor scratches and greatly improve the car's overall appearance. But for a buff and touch-up, you can expect to spend about $200.

If you want to do the job yourself, consider polishing the car by hand if you don't have

with optional equipment or a special towing package before it can handle the maximum load.

Front drive vs. rear. On the whole, rear-wheel-drive vehicles are better suited for towing than front-drivers are. That's because a trailer tends to bear down on the rear of your vehicle, which reduces traction at the front. Front-drive cars and minivans also tend to have unibody (formed sheet metal) construction that's usually not as rugged as the typical truck's full-frame construction.

Hitting the brakes. Light-duty trailers usually have no brakes of their own, and depend instead on the tow-vehicle's braking system. Heavier-duty trailers must by law have their own braking system.

Trailer brakes come in two basic types: electric brakes and hydraulic "surge" brakes. Electric brakes draw power from your tow vehicle's charging system and can be adjusted to the load on the trailer. Surge brakes are hydraulic brakes built into the trailer that are activated by compression of the trailer's tongue. When you slow down, the trailer's towing tongue telescopes a little, activating a hydraulic brake piston. On the whole, electric brakes are superior to surge brakes.

**SMALL LOAD
(up to 2,000 pounds)**
such as a small boat (up to 14 feet), a small camper trailer, or two ATVs, snowmobiles, personal watercraft, or motorcycles.

**MIDSIZED LOAD
(up to 3,500 pounds)**
such as a medium-sized boat (up to 20 feet), large camper trailer, or small travel trailer.

**LARGE LOAD
(up to 5,000 pounds)**
such as a car transport (up to 24 feet long) or medium travel trailer.

**HEAVY-DUTY LOAD
(7,000 pounds or more)**
such as a large Airstream-type travel trailer, larger boat trailer, or two-horse trailer.

---

experience using an electric buffer. Old T-shirts make good polishing cloths. If you still want to use an electric buffer, you can borrow, rent, or even buy one. Good ones start at about $40. If you don't know what you're doing, though, it's easy to mark or even burn through the paint with a buffer.

Most cars made in the past eight to ten years have a "clearcoat" paint finish. That means a thin color layer is coated with a thicker layer of a clear, lacquerlike coating. Whether you are polishing with a buffer or by hand, make sure the polish you use is safe for clearcoat finishes if that's what's on the car. You shouldn't use the old-fashioned, abrasive polishing compounds on them.

DENT REMOVAL. Minor dents and dings in body panels can be very unsightly, but getting them fixed at a body shop can be costly. One viable alternative is so-called paintless dent removal. This type of service, which is sometimes franchised under names such as "Dent Doctor" or "DentPro," uses special tools to massage out small dents from the inside. You can usually find a dent fixer by talking to a local mechanic or body shop, or using the Yellow Pages. Figure on paying about $50 to make a golf-ball-sized dent disappear.

The quality of these repairs is very much dependent on the skill of the operator. Before engaging the dent-removal artist, get a recommendation from a satisfied customer or other experienced person.

FIXING WINDOW GLASS. It's very common for a windshield to pick up "star" or "bull's eye" damage from a flying stone. Sometimes those chips are merely cosmetic annoyances, but other times, if left unaddressed, such damage may grow worse. As with paintless dent repair, there is a cottage industry in auto-glass repair.

A glass-repair person uses a suction-cup device, tiny drills, and special sealers to fill and fix a damaged area. This can shrink the blemish from pea size to pinhead size, and stop the damage from spreading. Again, figure $50 to treat a small glass ding. Of course, if the damage is more than minor to start with, this sort of repair won't work and you'll need a new windshield or side window.

Before springing for a new windshield, consult your auto-insurance policy. If you have glass coverage the replacement is free, and normally there's no deductible.

THE INSIDE DIRT. Even neat people can live in squalor when it comes to the family car. Carpets get loaded with ingrained mud, sand, and debris. Upholstery can gather unrivaled stains from food, children, and the warehouse grit of shopping trips and general travel.

You can buy special car-interior cleaners, but for plastic surfaces you can use any hard-surface cleaner such as Fantastic or Formula 409. Once you've wiped, swiped, and vacuumed the inside of the car, you may still have to deal with upholstery stains.

EARLY WARNING SIGNS OF TIRE FAILURE

Visually inspect your tires on a regular basis. If you note any of the following early warning signs, have a professional inspection performed, check and correct items that may be causing the condition, or replace your tires.

♦ **Cracking or cuts in the sidewalls.**

♦ **Uneven tread wear.** This can be caused by improper inflation, misaligned wheels, damaged tires, or by problems with suspension parts.

♦ **Excessively worn tread.** Tires have tread-wear indicator bars running across the tread, which signal the minimum allowable tread depth of $\frac{1}{16}$-inch. When the tread wears down to these bars, it's time for new tires. Check tread depth by using a tread-wear gauge or a penny. Insert the penny into a tire groove with Lincoln's head toward the tire. If you see the top of Abe's head, the tread is too worn.

♦ **Bulges or blisters in the sidewall.** These signal potential weak spots that could lead to tire failure.

♦ **Excessive vibration.** This may be a sign a wheel is misaligned, unbalanced, or bent. It could also signify internal tire damage. Service the vehicle at once.

ARE YOU DEFLATED?

All tires lose air over time. Usually, though, air leaks out so slowly that many people don't realize it has happened. CONSUMER REPORTS recently tested more than 100 brand-new all-season tires for air loss. They were mounted on rims, properly inflated to 30 psi, and stored under ideal conditions for one year. In that time they lost an average of 6.6 psi and some more than 12 psi.

Seasonal temperature changes may also cause tire pressure to drop. A 10° F drop in outside temperature lowers a tire's pressure by about 1 psi.

Why should you worry about underinflation? Because it can affect a car's handling, making it harder to control. Underinflation also worsens fuel economy and allows damaging heat to build up, which can shorten a tire's life and possibly cause a failure.

♦ **Don't judge the pressure by eyeballing a tire.** Modern radial tires bulge slightly, making them look a little underinflated, even when they're not.

♦ **Once a month, use a pressure gauge to check all four tires and the spare.**

♦ **Measure the pressure with the tires cold.** As the vehicle is driven more than a mile or two, the tires heat up and the pressure rises, which makes it more difficult to set them to the correct cold-tire pressure.

If you tackle this job yourself, try using carpet-cleaning spray or pet-spot remover on the seats (about $6 for an aerosol can).

You may find carpeted floor mats very tough to clean. If the nap on them is still in good shape, take them to a carpet-cleaning service. Figure on paying roughly $15 per pair. If they're badly worn, think about getting new ones.

Ridding a car of odors can be another challenge. Various forms of dirt, from tobacco smoke to mold and spilled food products can sully the atmosphere in the cabin. The first step is to get all the interior fabrics clean with pet-spot cleaner or another odor-fighting cleaning product. Don't forget to wipe down the headliner, the cloth covering inside the roof. (Make sure the fabrics are colorfast first.)

Some commercial deodorizers claim they eliminate rather than merely mask odors from mold, smoke, and other causes. Large auto-parts stores carry such products. Or you can use a familiar product like aerosol Lysol and its relatives. Clean inside the trunk and spare-tire well too.

You can also try cleaning odors from the climate-system ducts by spritzing odor eliminator into the system's air intake. That's usually located beneath the hood cowl, near where the windshield wipers park. Then run the air conditioner full blast for at least ten minutes.

UNDER THE HOOD. Cleaning the outside of the engine and other under-hood components can be a knuckle-scraping, tedious chore. But it's good to have a sparkling clean engine bay if you are about to sell the car, and your mechanic will appreciate it in any case. Consider this a nicety rather than a necessity.

If the battery terminals are growing a fuzz of white encrustation, you should clean the battery with a damp rag soaked with a solution of water and baking soda. Use a stiff toothbrush dipped in the baking-soda solution for the tough parts. (Wear eye protection and gloves when working around the battery.) You can then coat the terminals with a dialectric (non-conducting) protective grease, and spray the outside of the battery with a clear sealer. Both these products are available at auto-parts stores.

You can clean engine parts with plain soap and water or with a commercial degreasing product like Gunk. Be careful, though, not to get electrical connections wet. Be particularly careful to keep water away from the fuse box, cable junctions, and the large electrical connectors near the firewall.

Steam cleaning is another way to get an engine clean. You can find steam-cleaning services at some garages and car washes. But steam cleaning can short out the car's computer or other electrical gadgets if it's not done with great care. The risk of damaging electronic parts has made this cleaning method a less attractive option than it used to be.

HOW TO BUY TIRES

Today, tire manufacturers offer more choices and better performance than ever before. New tires can greatly improve how your car or truck rides, handles, and stops, and how well it keeps its footing on wet roads. No tire does everything perfectly, however. Tire makers usually emphasize one quality or another for each product line. Some tires deliver superior traction on dry or wet roads. Others bite into snow. Still others are noted for crisp steering response, a smooth ride, or long tread life. Which to choose still depends largely on what you drive, where you live, and which characteristics are most important to you. You'll find Ratings of various tire types starting on page 75.

What's available

Major brands include BFGoodrich, Bridgestone, Cooper, Dunlop, Firestone, Goodyear, Kelly, Michelin, Pirelli, and Yokohama. Each of the leading tire manufacturers sells several lines with major performance and price differences. The variants are proliferating, as tire manufacturers create new categories and blur the old distinctions. Knowing the various types and designations will help you buy the right tires for your vehicle and your typical driving conditions.

Where to buy

You have your pick of places to buy tires. When comparing prices, be sure to consider the cost of mounting and balancing.

One promising venue is the mail-order route. Mail-order houses, with their online stores, offer shop-at-home convenience and generally low prices. But you may have to pay extra for shipping, say $6 to $12 per tire. And you'll have to pay a local shop to mount them. It may make sense to ship the tires directly to that shop.

Tire dealers are another good venue. They typically offer low prices along with mounting

---

HOW TO READ A TIRE

On any tire's sidewall, you'll see a multipart size designation, such as P195/70R14 90S. Deciphering the codes is key to buying tires that fit your car or truck and deliver the performance you want. Here's what they mean:

Size. The first letter signifies the tire type—P for passenger-car tire (some light-truck tires have LT instead). The next three digits are the tire's cross-section width in millimeters: 195 mm in the example. Then comes the "aspect ratio"—the ratio of sidewall height to cross-section width. The 70 means the sidewall height is 70 percent of the width. (Performance tires tend to have a relatively low "profile," or sidewall height, providing better steering response, but a firmer ride.) R means radial-ply construction. The next two digits—14—represent the diameter in inches of the wheel on which the tire fits.

Load index and speed rating. A three-figure code such as 90S is typical. The 90 is an index figure that reflects the maximum load a tire can carry (89 equals 1,312 lbs.) The S is the speed rating, specifying the top speed the tire can sustain, in this case, 112 mph. It mostly addresses how well a tire dissipates heat. However, tires with higher speed ratings tend to handle better at normal highway speeds as well.

Treadwear. The treadwear rating compares a tire's expected tread life with that of a reference tire. The 440 here indicates a tread life more than four times that of a tire graded at 100. This is a loose guide. Your driving style, car, and local pavement coarseness affect wear, too.

Traction and temperature. These are scores for government-specified tests that gauge a tire's ability to stop on wet pavement and to resist overheating. AA is the best for traction, A, for temperature. Winter tires aren't required to have traction, temperature, and treadwear ratings.

and alignment service, and often the mounting is free. Car dealers, department stores, and discount warehouse clubs are other options.

Car tires

There are four major types: all-season, winter, touring performance, and performance tires. Paying more doesn't necessarily buy a better tire or a longer warranty.

ALL-SEASON TIRES. These are the most popular tires by far. Standard equipment on most sedans and minivans, they're designed to handle most conditions, including wet and dry pavement and light snow, reasonably well. They also emphasize a comfortable and quiet ride, predictable handling, and long wear. That makes them a sound choice for most drivers, except where winters are severe. Price range: about $30 to $80 per tire for most brands, mostly S- and T-speed rated. (See "Speed Ratings," page 68.)

WINTER TIRES. Winter tires are the new name for snow tires. They feature tread designs and special rubber compounds made to grip well in deep snow and on ice. But the tradeoff is often quick wear and compromised ride and handling on dry roads. Use winter tires during winter months only. Price range: $60 to $100.

TOURING PERFORMANCE TIRES. Touring tires fall somewhere between all-season and performance tires in grip, comfort, tread life, and price. They're marketed as all-season tires with added cornering and braking performance. They're a step up in price from regular all-seasons, with added emphasis on handling. The best we've tested did nearly everything well, though the trade-off can be shorter tread life. Price range: $60 to $80, mostly H-speed rated.

PERFORMANCE TIRES. Performance tires deliver the ultimate in dry- and wet-weather grip and handling. But the penalty is often a stiff ride, poor winter traction, short tread life, and a hefty price tag. Price range: $70 to $120 for most, which are above V-speed rated.

Light-truck tires

Tires for SUVs and pickups tend to be larger than car tires. You'll find four types:

ALL-SEASON TRUCK AND SUV TIRES. These are very popular. Their characteristics are similar to those for all-season car tires. They aren't designed for heavy off-roading, but that's something few SUV drivers do. And because many SUVs come with 4WD or AWD, these tires should be adequate in snow. Price range: about $60 to $100.

ALL-TERRAIN TIRES. All-terrain tires are the second major category of tires for light trucks. They're designed mostly for on-road driving, though their chunky tread is intended to provide off-pavement capability. In our tests, this type did about as well overall as all-season light-truck tires. Price range: $60 to $100.

PREMIUM SUV ALL-SEASON TIRES. This is an expanding category for SUVs and other light trucks. These tires combine aggressive looks with a smooth, quiet ride and long tread life. Despite their looks they don't have special off-road capabilities. Price range: $80 to $120. These are intended for luxury and car-based SUVs.

LT AND OTHERS. Other light-truck categories include off-road and performance models. You'll also find heavy-duty work tires with an LT (light-truck) size designation. They're intended mainly for large SUVs, pickups, and vans that haul heavy loads. Prices vary.

SPEED RATINGS

A speed rating is a tire specification that rates the maximum road speed a tire is designed to sustain. These are the speed ratings for typical tires:

Q ...99 mph

S ...112 mph

T ... 118 mph

H ... 130 mph

V ... 150 mph

ZR ... beyond 150 mph

W ... 169 mph

Y ... 188 mph

How to choose

PERFORMANCE DIFFERENCES. The duration of an all-season tire's warranty doesn't always reflect the tire's braking, handling, and traction performance or its price. CONSUMER REPORTS has found that several all-season tires with 40,000- to 50,000-mile warranties performed nearly as well as high-scoring tires with 60,000- to 100,000-mile warranties. All-terrain tires and all-season truck tires had about the same level of performance.

RECOMMENDATIONS. Be sure your new tires are the same size and have at least the same speed and load ratings as the ones your vehicle originally came with. Check the tire's sidewall, the label on the door jamb, or fuel-filler door. Another location is the owner's manual.

Some automakers recommend keeping the same tire type for SUVs, since switching can adversely affect the handling of these tall vehicles or potentially lower their resistance to rollover. Check your owner's manual for specific recommendations.

Note that all treadwear warranties are prorated; the more the tread is worn, the less of the original price you'll receive back. And warranties usually don't cover damage from potholes and road hazards.

AUTO BATTERIES

The time to think about buying a new auto battery is before the old one fails. Once you're stranded by a dead battery, you probably won't want to spend time shopping around for another. At the first sign that your current battery is growing weaker, have a garage perform a "load test" to see if it's holding a charge properly. If it isn't, find a new battery.

All car batteries aren't created equal. A battery's size, rated capacity, and its age help determine how it will perform.

What's available

Most auto batteries are made by just three manufacturers, Delphi, Exide, and Johnson Controls Industries. Each makes batteries sold under several different brand names.

Delphi makes ACDelco and some EverStart (Wal-Mart) models. Exide makes Champion, Exide, Napa, and some EverStart batteries. Johnson Controls makes Diehard (Sears), Duralast (AutoZone), Interstate, Kirkland (Costco), Motorcraft (Ford) and some EverStarts.

Service centers such as Firestone, Goodyear, Pep Boys, and Sears tend to have a large, fresh inventory and relatively low prices. They also handle installation. Stores such as Kmart, Target, Trak Auto, and Wal-Mart may have the lowest prices, but not all of them can install a battery for you. Service stations and tune-up shops sell batteries too, and they offer convenient and comprehensive service, but their selection tends to be limited. And their stock may not be fresh. For cars and trucks still under warranty, a franchised dealer is your first choice, particularly if the vehicle warranty covers the battery. For older vehicles, though, a dealership is probably the last resort—it's the most expensive service venue. The two most crucial factors in choosing a battery are its "group size" and "cold-cranking amps," or CCA.

GROUP SIZE. A group size defines the batteries' outside dimensions and the placement of the terminals on them. For instance, group size 75 fits mainly General Motors cars. Size 65 applies to most large Ford, Lincoln, and Mercury products. Newer Hondas, Nissans, and Toyotas use size 35. Most Chryslers use 34. You'll also see combinations like 34/78, which has two sets of terminals and will fit either Chryslers or some GM models.

Choose the group size recommended by your car's manufacturer. (Reference guides at places where batteries are sold can tell you which group size your car needs.) The wrong size may not fit securely.

COLD-CRANKING AMPS. CCA is a measure of a battery's ability to start a car in cold weather, when thickened engine oil and slowed chemical reactions make starting hardest. CCAs denote how much current the battery can deliver to the starter at 0° F. Don't confuse CCA with CA, which stands for Cranking Amps. That's a measure taken at 32° instead of 0° and is typically much higher than the CCA rating.

Key considerations

Reserve capacity is another important measure of battery quality. It indicates how many minutes your car might run using the battery alone, should the car's alternator fail. You may have to check product literature rather than the battery's labeling to find the reserve capacity.

Buy a fresh battery—one less than six months old. Batteries are stamped with a date code, either on the battery's case or an attached label. The vital information is usually in the first two characters—a letter and a digit. Most codes start with the letter indicating the month: A for January, B for February, and so forth. The digit denotes the year—say 0 for 2000. For example, B3 stands for February 2003.

WARRANTIES. Like CA ratings, battery warranties can sound better than they are. You'll see two numbers, one for the total warranty period, and one for the free-replacement period (usually three months to three years.) The free-replacement period is key. If the old battery fails after this period expires, you get only a prorated credit toward a new battery.

How to choose

PERFORMANCE DIFFERENCES. Our tests of batteries regularly show wide variations between and within brands. You'll find Ratings of auto batteries on page 73.

RECOMMENDATIONS. Check the battery group size and CCA for your vehicle. Not every brand comes in every CCA level. To get the brand you want you may need to go a bit above your car's CCA requirements.

Steer clear of batteries with a CCA rating below the one specified for your vehicle, as well as those rated 200 amps or more higher than the specified rating. It's a waste of money to go too high. Buy a battery with the longest reserve capacity you can find. If it's not printed on the battery (and it usually isn't), ask store personnel or check product literature. Should your car's charging system fail, a longer capacity can make the difference between driving to safety and getting stuck.

BATTERY BOOSTERS

Think of a portable battery booster as a spare car battery with built-in jumper cables. A booster contains a sealed, leakproof battery, usually the lead-acid kind. You can carry one around in the trunk of your car or keep it handy at your home.

BATTERY CHECK

On maintenance-free batteries, there are no filler caps. Instead, check the color of the "eye" on the top of the battery. It should be green or blue. If the battery is weak, the eye will be black or not visible. A clear or light-yellow eye means the battery should be replaced.

What's available

Boosters usually come in one of two sizes, standard or compact. Standard-sized boosters are about the size of a large pocketbook and weigh 12 to 19 pounds. They can crank a car engine, or, say, a lawn tractor, motorcycle, or boat engine. They can also power various DC appliances, such as an air compressor or electric picnic cooler. With an optional AC inverter they can power a laptop computer, radio, or television set, making a booster handy both in the wild and in a power blackout back home. They're priced at about $70 to $100 at retail.

Compact units are about half the size and weight of the larger ones, and run $50 to $90. They usually lack a DC appliance socket, and they don't have nearly as much power as the larger models.

Key features

The handiest boosters come with a feature called "smart charging." This lets you keep the unit plugged in all the time to keep it charged. With others, you have to unplug them to avoid damaging them. Clamps should be shielded with insulating material to avoid shorting or sparking. A separate on-off switch, sometimes called a switched-power feature, allows you to power up the cables only after they're attached to the battery you want to boost. For reaching tight places, look for a long cord.

How to choose

PERFORMANCE DIFFERENCES. In CONSUMER REPORTS tests, standard-sized boosters generally performed much better than the compacts. They have more power, last longer, and can be used to power DC appliances, such as a portable air compressor—something most compact units aren't designed for.

RECOMMENDATIONS. A compact unit may be fine if you ask little of it. It should be able to help start a car in warm weather—provided that a run-down battery is the only problem. But if some mechanical problem makes the car hard to start, or if the unit is cold—as it would be if left in the trunk during the winter—then the compact units can poop out long before a recalcitrant engine fires up.

Whether you keep a booster in the home or in a vehicle, remember that you'll have to keep it charged up—typically something you need to do every three months or so.

MOTOR OIL

Some years ago, CONSUMER REPORTS tested a variety of motor oils using a fleet of 75 New York City taxicabs. The lessons learned from those tests are still applicable. The most important lesson was that any name-brand motor oil should be fine, as long as you change your oil regularly.

Here's how the test worked: CONSUMER REPORTS put identical rebuilt engines with precisely measured parts into the 75 cabs at the beginning of the test, and changed their oil every 6,000 miles. That's about twice as long as the automakers recommend for the severe service taxicabs see, but that interval was chosen to accelerate the test results and provide worst-case conditions. After 60,000 miles (which translated into 10 to 12 months of use), the engines were disassembled and checked for wear and harmful deposits. The test conditions were grueling. The typical Big Apple cab is driven day and night, in heavy traffic, in stop-and-go driving.

Along with the taxicab tests, CONSUMER REPORTS had the oils' chemical and physical properties analyzed by an independent lab. At each oil change, a sample of the old oil was analyzed to check its viscosity and to look for evidence of worn metals and other contaminants. Every oil CONSUMER REPORTS tested was good at doing what motor oil is supposed to do.

Choosing viscosity

One of a motor oil's key attributes is its viscosity, or ability to flow at a given temperature. The two most commonly recommended viscosity grades are 10W-30 and 5W-30. Automakers specify grades according to the temperature range expected in the climate in which the car is used. The lower the number, the thinner the oil and the more easily it flows.

In 5W-30 oil, for example, the two numbers mean it's a "multiviscosity," or "multigrade," oil that's effective over a range of temperatures. The first number, 5, is an index that refers to how the oil flows at low temperatures. The second number, 30, refers to how it flows at high temperatures. The W designation means the oil can be used in winter.

A popular old-fashioned belief is that 5W-30 oils are too thin to protect vital engine parts when they get hot. One of CONSUMER REPORTS' laboratory tests measured the viscosity of oils under high-temperature, high-stress conditions and found essentially no difference between 5W-30 oils and their 10W-30 brandmates. At low temperatures, the 5W-30 oil flowed more easily. Viscosity grade is important, so be careful. Recommendations vary with the make, engine, and model year of the car, so check your owner's manual and be sure to use the proper grade of oil.

Choosing brands

No brand—not even the expensive, synthetic motor oils—did significantly better or worse in our tests. The wear on key metal parts within the engine averaged only 0.0026 inches, about the thickness of a magazine page. Even the engines with the most wear didn't reach a level at which CONSUMER REPORTS could detect operational problems. Two maladies motor oil is supposed to prevent are sludge (a mucky sediment that can prevent oil from circulating freely and make the engine run hotter) and varnish (a hard deposit that remains on engine

MORE THAN JUST OIL

Motor oil does more than merely lubricate. It helps cool the engine, keep it clean, prevent corrosion, and reduce friction to improve fuel economy. To do all that, refiners blend in various additives, which account for 10 to 25 percent of the product you buy. The oil industry has devised a starburst symbol to certify that a particular motor oil meets the latest industry requirements for protection against deposits, wear, oxidation, and corrosion. The starburst on the label means the oil meets the latest (API) American Petroleum Institute service requirements. Service SJ is the most advanced formulation. Beware of oils without the starburst; they may lack the full complement of additives needed to keep modern engines running reliably.

Here are some of the additives found in modern oils:

- Viscosity-index improvers modify the oil so its viscosity is more consistent over a wide temperature range.
- Antioxidants prevent the oil from thickening when it runs hot for extended periods.
- Dispersants keep contaminants suspended so they don't form deposits in the engine.
- Detergents help prevent buildup of varnish and sludge on engine parts and neutralize acid formed in the engine.
- Rust and corrosion inhibitors protect metal parts from acids and water formed in the engine.
- Foam inhibitors collapse bubbles churned up by the crankshaft (foam reduces lubricating effectiveness).
- Pour-point depressants help the oil flow in a cold engine, especially in cold weather.
- Friction modifiers strengthen the oil film and prevent unlubricated contact between moving parts.
- Antiwear agents provide lubrication when oil is squeezed out from between moving engine parts.

parts if you wipe off the sludge; it can make moving parts stick). All the oils tested proved excellent at preventing sludge, perhaps because sludge is more apt to form during cold start-ups and short trips—conditions the test cabs rarely experienced. Some varnish deposits were heavy enough to lead to problems eventually, but no brand consistently produced more varnish than any other.

Buying advice

Buy the viscosity grade recommended in your owner's manual, and look for the starburst emblem on the container. Expensive synthetic oils (typically $3 or $4 a quart) worked no better than conventional motor oils in our taxi tests, but they're worth considering for extreme driving conditions—high or very low outdoor temperatures and high engine loads.

HOW TO USE THE RATINGS

First, read the report on the product you're interested in. The page numbers for these reports are noted on each Ratings page. The Overall Ratings gives the big picture in performance. Notes on features and performance for individual models are listed under "Recommendations and notes." Use the handy key numbers to locate the details on applicable models to connect them to the descriptive paragraphs.

We verify availability for most products especially for this book. Some tested models may no longer be available.

AUTO BATTERIES

Check the battery group size and CCA for your vehicle, then choose a battery that scored well overall. Sears' Diehard batteries consistently provided long life across sizes and topped the Ratings in four of the five size categories.

Excellent	Very good	Good	Fair	Poor
●	◕	○	◑	●

Overall Ratings   In performance order

BRAND & MODEL	PRICE	OVERALL SCORE	LIFE TEST	COLD-CRANKING AMPS (CCA) MFR.	COLD-CRANKING AMPS (CCA) TEST	RESERVE CAPACITY	WARRANTY (MONTHS) FREE/TOTAL
GROUP SIZE 75 *Fits most four- and six-cylinder GM vehicles.*							
Diehard WeatherHandler (South) 30375 [1]	$60		●	525	○	◑	18/72
Napa The Legend 75 Professional Line 7575 [1]	60		◑	630	◑	●	18/75
Exide Nascar Select 75-84N [1]	80		◑	630	◑	●	24/84
Interstate Mega-Tron MT-75 [2]	80		◑	650	◑	◑	18/60
Motorcraft Test Tough Max BXT-75 [4]	80		○	700	◑	○	36/100
ACDelco Professional 75-7YR [1] [3]	90		◑	650	◑	○	18/72
GROUP SIZE 65 *Fits most large six- and eight-cylinder Ford vehicles.*							
Diehard Gold (South) 33165 [1]	80		●	700	●	◑	36/100
Exide Nascar Select 65-84N [1] [2]	90		○	750	●	◑	24/84
Interstate Mega-Tron MT-65 [2]	80		●	675	○	◑	18/60
Napa The Legend 75 Professional Line 7565 [1] [2]	80		◑	850	○	◑	18/75
ACDelco Professional 65-7YR [1] [3]	90		◑	850	◑	◑	24/84
GROUP SIZE 35 *Fits newer Hondas, Nissans, and Toyotas.*							
Diehard WeatherHandler (South) 30335 [1]	60		○	480	●	○	18/72
Exide Nascar Select 35-84N [1] [2]	80		○	570	○	●	24/84
Napa The Legend 75 Professional Line 7535 [1] [2]	75		◑	570	○	●	18/75
Interstate Mega-Tron MT-35 [2]	75		○	550	○	◑	18/60
EverStart 35-3	40		◑	525	◑	◑	24/72
Motorcraft Test Tough Max BXT-35 [2] [4]	80		○	550	○	○	36/100
Diehard WeatherHandler (North) 30035 [1]	60		◑	500	◑	◑	18/72
Champion CH35 [2]	40		●	570	○	●	36/108
Kirkland Signature 12865 [1] [5]	41		◑	640	◑	◑	36/100
Duralast Gold (North) 35-DG	70		●	640	○	○	36/96
GROUP SIZE 34 *Fits most Chrysler vehicles.*							
Diehard WeatherHandler (North) 30034	60		◑	540	●	○	18/72
Diehard WeatherHandler (South) 30334	60		○	525	◑	◑	18/72

Ratings key: Excellent ◉ Very good ◒ Good ○ Fair ◖ Poor ●

Overall Ratings, cont.

BRAND & MODEL	PRICE	OVERALL SCORE	LIFE TEST	COLD-CRANKING AMPS (CCA) MFR.	COLD-CRANKING AMPS (CCA) TEST	RESERVE CAPACITY	WARRANTY (MONTHS) FREE/TOTAL
GROUP SIZE 34/78 *Can replace size 34 batteries in Chrysler vehicles and 78 batteries in GM vehicles.*							
Motorcraft Test Tough Max BXT-3478 [4]	$80	▭	○	800	◒	◉	36/100
Optima Red Top 34/78-1050 [1]	140	▭	◉	750	◒	◒	24/72
Duralast Gold (North) 34DT-DGN	75	▭	◒	900	○	◉	36/96
Napa 75XDT800 [2]	100	▭	○	850	◒	◒	18/75
Champion 4X4 DT34	60	▭	◒	770	○	◒	36/108
Duralast Gold (South) 34DT-DGS	75	▭	◒	800	◒	○	36/96
Exide Nascar Select 78DT-84N [1]	70	▭	◒	770	◖	◉	24/84
Diehard SUV, Truck & Van (North) 39890 [1][6]	90	▭	○	900	◖	◉	36/100
ACDelco Professional 78DT-7YR [1][3]	90	▭	◖	850	○	◒	24/84
EverStart Maxx-1N	60	▭	◖	900	○	○	36/108
EverStart High Power DT-3	40	▭	◖	630	◖	◖	24/72

[1] *Manufacturer claims no maintenance required; for other models, periodically check the electrolyte-fluid levels.*
[2] *No handle.* [3] *Has charge indicator.* [4] *Formerly the Premier Silver Series.* [5] *Formerly the 207250.* [6] *Formerly the RangeHandler.*

See report, page 68. Based on tests published in Consumer Reports in October 2002.

The tests behind the Ratings

We tested five samples of each battery, including at least two for battery life. Under **brand & model,** we note cold- or hot-weather batteries sold only in the North or South. **Overall score** combines life-test performance, reserve capacity, and performance based on claimed cold-cranking amps (CCAs). Scoring is based on relative performance within each group size. **Life test** reflects a battery's ability to endure repeated charge and discharge cycles at high heat; the more cycles it handled relative to others its size, the higher its score. For **cold-cranking amps,** we list claimed CCA **(mfr.)** and performance **(test)** based on that claim. **Reserve capacity** reflects how long a battery can run an engine without the alternator. **Warranty** shows the **free** replacement and **total** (prorated) in months. **Price** is approximate retail.

TIRES, ALL-SEASON

Check the overall scores in the Ratings. Then look at the key performance judgments under Three-Season Driving and Winter Driving to see which tire is best for the kind of driving you typically do. The Dunlop SP Sport A2, $70, and the Michelin Energy MXV4 Plus, $120, deliver the best combination of year-round performance. The Michelin is pricey and lacks a tread-wear warranty, however. For better handling, consider the Continental ContiTouringContact CH95, $70, which did well overall. A caveat: Wet stops with the antilock braking system (ABS) disengaged were long—a concern if you drive a non-ABS vehicle.

Overall Ratings — In performance order

Key to ratings: Excellent, Very good, Good, Fair, Poor

KEY NO	BRAND & MODEL	PRICE	OVERALL SCORE	Three-Season Driving — Dry Braking	Wet Braking	Handling	Hydroplaning	Winter Driving — Snow Traction	Ice Braking
1	**Dunlop** SP Sport A2	$70		Excellent	Excellent	Very good	Very good	Good	Very good
2	**Michelin** Energy MXV4 Plus	120		Excellent	Very good	Very good	Very good	Good	Very good
3	**Continental** Conti TouringContact CH95	70		Good	Good	Excellent	Excellent	Good	Good
4	**Kelly** Charger HR	70		Very good	Good	Good	Good	Good	Very good
5	**Cooper** Lifeliner Touring SLE	60		Excellent	Fair	Very good	Good	Good	Fair
6	**Toyo** Proxes TPT	85		Excellent	Fair	Very good	Excellent	Good	Poor
7	**Yokohama** Avid H4	70		Excellent	Fair	Good	Very good	Good	Fair
8	**Goodyear** Eagle LS	80		Fair	Very good	Good	Excellent	Good	Good
9	**Uniroyal** Tiger Paw Touring HR	70		Good	Fair	Very good	Good	Good	Very good

See report, page 65. Based on tests published in Consumer Reports in November 2002.

The tests behind the Ratings

Overall score is based on 14 tests, with braking, emergency handling, hydroplaning, and winter performance weighted most heavily. **Snow traction** reflects how far the test vehicle had to travel to accelerate from 5 to 20 mph on flat, moderately packed snow. **Ice braking** is done from 10 mph on an ice rink. **Dry braking** is done from 60 mph, and wet braking, from 40 mph. Most braking scores shown are with the antilock brake system (ABS) engaged (ABS was disengaged for touring-performance ice braking); instances where turning ABS off significantly affected the score are noted above. **Handling** includes how well tires did in an avoidance maneuver that involved a swerve to the left, right, then left again, as well as wet and dry cornering performance and steering feel. **Hydroplaning** reflects the speed tires reached before they began to skim over water on our course. We also judged tire noise and ride comfort on the road, and measured rolling resistance for touring-performance tires with a dynamometer. **Price** is approximate retail for sizes tested. Most winter tires are Q- and H-rated; others are noted above.

Recommendations and notes

1> **DUNLOP** SP Sport A2 **An excellent all-around choice, with the best overall braking.** Good rolling resistance. 50,000-mile tread-wear warranty.

2> **MICHELIN** Energy MXV4 Plus **An excellent all-around choice, though pricey.** Excellent cornering and rolling resistance. No tread-wear warranty.

3> **CONTINENTAL** Conti TouringContact CH95 **An impressive-handling tire.** Very good cornering grip and rolling resistance. 60,000-mile tread-wear warranty.

4> **KELLY** Charger HR **Competent overall, though cornering grip was weakest of this group.** Fair rolling resistance. 40,000-mile tread-wear warranty.

5> **COOPER** Lifeliner Touring SLE **A very good dry-weather choice.** Poor rolling resistance. 50,000-mile tread-wear warranty.

6> **TOYO** Proxes TPT **A very good choice where winters are mild.** Very good rolling resistance. Stiff and relatively noisy ride. 65,000-mile tread-wear warranty.

7> **YOKOHAMA** Avid H4 **Competent overall, though unexceptional in most areas.** Fair rolling resistance. 45,000-mile tread-wear warranty.

8> **GOODYEAR** Eagle LS **Competent overall, though dry stops were longest of this group.** Excellent rolling resistance. No tread-wear warranty.

9> **UNIROYAL** Tiger Paw Touring HR **Competent overall, though wet stops were longest of this group.** Excellent rolling resistance. 55,000-mile tread-wear warranty.

TIRES, WINTER

Use the overall scores as a guide. Then choose a tire that matches your driving. If your vehicle takes an H-rated tire, consider the top-scoring Goodyear Eagle Ultra Grip GW-2, $132, Dunlop SP Winter Sport M2, $126, Pirelli Winter 210 SnowSport, $155, and Bridgestone Blizzak LM-22, $130. For less snowy areas, choose the Dunlop, Pirelli, or Bridgestone. The H-rated Nokian Hakkapeliitta NRW All Weather Plus, $157, excelled in snow-traction but not in our wet-weather braking and cornering tests. Within the Q-rated category, top scores in a variety of conditions helped put the Kumho I'zen Stud KW-11, $50, and Michelin Arctic Alpin, $85, out in front. Consider the Q-rated Dunlop Graspic DS-1, $55, for more-severe winter driving. While it involves some compromises, it's a good choice for snow-belt areas. The Nokian Hakkapeliitta Q, $85, is the obvious choice where winters include lots of snow and rain.

Overall Ratings — In performance order

Legend: Excellent ● | Very good ◕ | Good ○ | Fair ◓ | Poor ●

Ratings key: E = Excellent, VG = Very good, G = Good, F = Fair, P = Poor

KEY NO	BRAND & MODEL	PRICE	OVERALL SCORE	SNOW TRACTION	BRAKING — ICE	BRAKING — DRY	BRAKING — WET	HANDLING	HYDRO-PLANING
	H-RATED WINTER TIRES								
1	**Goodyear** Eagle Ultra Grip GW-2	$132		VG	VG	E	E	VG	VG
2	**Dunlop** SP Winter Sport M2	126		VG	E	E	VG	E	VG
3	**Pirelli** Winter 210 SnowSport	155		VG	VG	VG	VG	E	VG
4	**Bridgestone** Blizzak LM-22	130		VG	VG	E	VG	E	G
5	**Nokian** Hakkapeliitta NRW	157		E	VG	VG	G	VG	G
6	**Michelin** Pilot Alpin	116		G	G	VG	G	E	G
	Q-RATED WINTER TIRES								
7	**Kumho** I'zen Stud KW-11	50		G	VG	E	E	VG	VG
8	**Michelin** Arctic Alpin	85		G	VG	VG	E	E	G
9	**Dunlop** Graspic DS-1	55		E	E	VG	VG	G	G
10	**Gislaved** NordFrost II	75		G	VG	VG	VG	G	G
11	**Nokian** Hakkapeliitta Q	85		VG	VG	VG	VG	VG	E
12	**BFGoodrich** Winter Slalom	60		VG	G	VG	E	VG	VG
13	**Goodyear** Ultra Grip Ice	77		E	G	G	E	F	E
14	**Bridgestone** Blizzak WS-50	72		VG	VG	VG	VG	G	G
15	**Yokohama** Guardex F720	75		G	E	VG	G	VG	F
16	**Firestone** Winterfire	53		VG	F	VG	E	VG	VG
17	**Cooper** Weather-Master XGR	52		G	VG	F	E	G	G

See report, page 65. Based on tests published in Consumer Reports in November 2002.

The tests behind the Ratings

Overall score is based on 14 tests, with braking, emergency handling, hydroplaning, and winter performance weighted most heavily. **Snow traction** reflects how far the test vehicle had to travel to accelerate from 5 to 20 mph on flat, moderately packed snow. **Ice braking** is done from 10 mph on an ice rink. **Dry braking** is done from 60 mph, and wet braking, from 40 mph. Most braking scores shown are with the antilock brake system (ABS) engaged (ABS was disengaged for touring-performance ice braking); instances where turning ABS off significantly affected the score are noted above. **Handling** includes how well tires did in an avoidance maneuver that involved a swerve to the left, right, then left again, as well as wet and dry cornering performance and steering feel. **Hydroplaning** reflects the speed tires reached before they began to skim over water on our course. We also judged tire noise and ride comfort on the road, and measured rolling resistance for touring-performance tires with a dynamometer. **Price** is approximate retail for sizes tested. Most winter tires are Q- and H-rated; others are noted above.

Recommendations and notes

H-RATED WINTER TIRES

1> **GOODYEAR** Eagle Ultra Grip GW-2 **An excellent all-around choice.** Best dry and wet braking among H-rated tires. Best ice braking without ABS.

2> **DUNLOP** SP Winter Sport M2 **An excellent all-around choice, with responsive handling.**

3> **PIRELLI** Winter 210 SnowSport **An excellent all-around choice, but pricey.** Best dry cornering.

4> **BRIDGESTONE** Blizzak LM-22 **An excellent all-around choice.** Best emergency handling.

5> **NOKIAN** Hakkapeliitta NRW **A fine choice for snow, though not ideal for wet weather.** Least capable in wet cornering.

6> **MICHELIN** Pilot Alpin **Best suited to areas where snow is less severe.** Quiet ride.

Q-RATED WINTER TIRES

7> **KUMHO** I'zen Stud KW-11 **An excellent choice where snow is less severe.** Best dry and wet braking among this group. Studdable. T-rated in size tested.

8> **MICHELIN** Arctic Alpin **An excellent choice where snow is less severe.** Excellent cornering.

9> **DUNLOP** Graspic DS-1 **A top winter performer, although only fair emergency handling.**

10> **GISLAVED** NordFrost II **A very good choice where snow is less severe.** Studdable.

11> **NOKIAN** Hakkapeliitta Q **A very good all-around tire.**

12> **BF GOODRICH** Winter Slalom **A very good all-around tire, though slightly less capable than the Nokian in winter driving.** Studdable.

13> **GOODYEAR** Ultra Grip Ice **A fine choice for snow and wet weather, but only fair handling.**

14> **BRIDGESTONE** Blizzak WS-50 **A very good all-around tire, though less capable in emergency handling than top-rated models.** Stiff ride.

15> **YOKOHAMA** Guardex F720 **Most susceptible to hydroplaning.**

16> **FIRESTONE** Winterfire **Unimpressive ice braking compromises an otherwise fine, economical choice.** Studdable. S-rated in size tested.

17> **COOPER** Weather-Master XGR **Long dry stops and only fair emergency handling.**

Guide to the Profiles

On the pages that follow you'll find capsule reviews of more than 250 cars, SUVs, mini-vans, and pickup trucks from the model years 1995 through 2002. Each profile sums up performance and reliability information, and gives crash-test results and the model years for key redesigns and the adoption of major safety equipment. You'll also find a rough guide to retail prices.

KEY TO THE INFORMATION

The profiles of used cars are presented alphabetically. We've included major models sold between the 1995 and 2002 model years. For each, we include the following information:

CAR TYPE. This can help you find competing models.

PHOTO. We've chosen one representative year, as indicated. A model that performed well in CONSUMER REPORTS tests over the years and has proven to be better than average in overall reliability is labeled a "CR Good Bet."

OVERVIEW. CONSUMER REPORTS' assessment based on testing and research through the years covered.

RELATED MODELS. To cover more marketing niches with minimal investment, many car manufacturers sell essentially the same car under different nameplates. Or they may sell another manufacturer's car under their own name. We note any such relationships.

MAJOR REDESIGN. Here we note the model year or years that the vehicle received significant design changes.

SAFETY EQUIPMENT. We note here the availability of air bags and antilock brakes for each vehicle. For the growing number of cars that have them, we also note the presence of pre-tensioning front safety belts. In the past few years manufacturers have realized that safety equipment can help sell automobiles. Also, government regulations require all new cars and light trucks to have dual air bags and comply with a side-impact standard.

DRIVE WHEELS. Most vehicles these days have front-wheel drive. When there's a choice or there's been a change, we summarize the history.

RELIABILITY HISTORY. For each model, this chart details the problem rates in 14 trouble spots. Compare the individual Reliability History with the chart below, which is an average of the reliability ratings of all the vehicles in our survey. The Reliability Verdict sums up the overall reliability of each model year. Check whether any years of this model are on the "reliable" used car list or "used cars to avoid" lists on pages 32-34. For more on using reliability information to assess a car, see Chapter 2.

PRICES. Prices are an estimate of the "retail" price for the years this model was available.

CRASH-TEST RESULTS. Where available, crash-test results are listed for the eight model-years covered. We include frontal- and side-crash results from the National Highway Traffic Safety Administration and offset-frontal crash results from the Insurance Institute for Highway Safety. The IIHS uses a four-point scale: Good, Acceptable, Marginal, and Poor.

WHAT THE TROUBLE SPOTS INCLUDE

Use this guide to interpret the Reliability History chart that accompanies each model profile.

◆ **Engine.** Pistons, rings, valves, block, heads, bearings, camshafts, gaskets, supercharger, turbocharger, cam belts and chains, oil pump.

◆ **Cooling.** Radiator, heater core, water pump, thermostat, hoses, intercooler, plumbing.

◆ **Fuel.** Fuel injection, computer and sensors, fuel pump, tank, emissions controls, check-engine light.

◆ **Ignition.** Spark plugs, coil, distributor, electronic ignition, sensors and modules, timing.

◆ **Transmission.** Transaxle, gear selector and linkage, coolers and lines. We no longer provide separate data for manual transmissions, since survey responses in this area are few.

◆ **Electrical.** Starter, alternator, battery, horn, gauges, lights, wiring, wiper motor.

◆ **Air conditioning.** Compressor, condenser, evaporator, expansion valves, hoses, dryer, fans, electronics.

◆ **Suspension.** Steering linkage, power-steering gear, pump, coolers and lines, alignment and balance, springs or torsion bars, ball joints, bushings, shocks and struts, electronic or air suspension.

◆ **Brakes.** Hydraulic system, linings, rotors or drums, power boost, antilock system, parking brake and linkage.

◆ **Exhaust.** Manifold, muffler, catalytic converter, pipes.

◆ **Paint/trim/rust.** Fading, discoloring, chalking, peeling, cracking; loose exterior trim, moldings, rust.

◆ **Body integrity.** Seals, weather stripping, air and water leaks, wind noise, rattles and squeaks.

◆ **Power equipment.** Electronically operated accessories such as mirrors, sunroof, windows, door locks, and seats; audio system, navigational system.

◆ **Body hardware.** Manual mirrors, sunroof, window, door, seat mechanisms; locks, safety belts, loose interior trim, sunroof, glass defects.

Reliability History

TROUBLE SPOTS	The Average Model							
	95	96	97	98	99	00	01	02
Engine	○	○	●	●	●	●	●	●
Cooling	○	○	●	●	●	●	●	●
Fuel	○	○	○	●	●	●	●	●
Ignition	●	○	●	●	●	●	●	●
Transmission	○	○	●	●	●	●	●	●
Electrical	●	○	●	○	●	●	●	●
Air conditioning	●	○	○	●	●	●	●	●
Suspension	○	○	○	●	●	●	●	●
Brakes	●	○	●	○	●	●	●	●
Exhaust	●	●	●	●	●	●	●	●
Paint/trim/rust	○	●	●	●	●	●	●	●
Body Integrity	○	○	○	○	○	○	●	◐
Power equipment	○	◐	○	○	○	○	◐	●
Body hardware	○	○	○	○	○	○	○	◐
RELIABILITY VERDICT	✔	✔	✔	✔	✔	✔	✔	✔

KEY TO PROBLEM RATES
- ● 2.0% or less
- ◕ 2.0% to 5.0%
- ○ 5.0% to 9.3%
- ◐ 9.3% to 14.8%
- ● More than 14.8%

KEY TO RELIABILITY VERDICTS
- ✔ **Red check** Better-than-average overall reliability for that year.
- ✔ **Black check** Average overall reliability for that year.
- **Blank** Worse-than-average overall reliability for that year.

Note: Make and model Unless otherwise stated, includes all body, engine, and drive types. **Blank column** The model wasn't made this year. **Insufficient data** We didn't receive enough responses to evaluate this year's model. Scores for the individual trouble spots represent the percentage of respondents to our survey who reported problems occurring in the 12 months from April 1, 2001 through March 31, 2002 that they deemed serious on account of cost, failure, compromised safety, or downtime.

KEY FOR NHTSA CRASH-PROTECTION JUDGMENTS
- ● Probably no injury or a minor injury
- ◕ Moderate injury likely
- ○ Certain injury, possibly severe
- ◐ Severe or fatal injury highly likely
- ● Severe or fatal injury virtually certain

COUPE
Acura CL

1997 model shown

Based on the two-door Honda Accord, the CL debuted in 1997. The 2.2CL model came with a 2.2-liter, 145-hp four-cylinder engine. In 1998, the Four grew to 2.3 liters, and the car was renamed the 2.3CL. The 3.0CL model comes with a smooth 200-hp V6 and an automatic. The driving experience is similar to that of the Accord, with good handling and a comfortable ride. As with most coupes, the rear seat is a little tight and a bit hard to get in and out of. A redesigned model called the 3.2 CL (basically a two-door Acura TL) was launched for 2001, equipped with more powerful versions of the V6 engine.

MAJOR REDESIGN: 1997, 2001. **SAFETY EQUIPMENT:** Dual front air bags standard. Side air bags standard from 2001. ABS standard. Safety-belt pretensioners standard. **DRIVE WHEELS:** Front.

Reliability history

TROUBLE SPOTS	Acura CL							
	95	96	97	98	99	00	01	02
Engine			●	●	●		●	●
Cooling			●	●	●		●	●
Fuel			◕	●	●		●	●
Ignition			●	◕	●		●	●
Transmission			●	◑	●		●	◑
Electrical			○	◑	◑		●	●
Air-conditioning			○	●	●		●	●
Suspension			●	◕	●		●	●
Brakes			○	◑	○		◑	●
Exhaust			◕	●	●		●	●
Paint/trim/rust			◕	●	◕		●	●
Body integrity			◕	●	○		○	●
Power equipment			◑	○	●		◑	●
Body hardware			○	◕	◕		◑	●
RELIABILITY VERDICT			✓	✓	✓		✓	✓

Prices

1995	–
1996	–
1997	$12,000-$14,000
1998	$14,000-$16,000
1999	$18,000-$20,000
2000	–
2001	$22,000-$24,000
2002	$26,000-$28,000

Crash-test results

Model Years	Offset	Full frontal	Side
1995	–	–	–
1996	–	–	–
1997	NT	NT	NT
1998	NT	NT	NT
1999	NT	NT	NT
2000	–	–	–
2001	NT	NT	NT
2002	NT	NT	NT

SMALL CAR
Acura Integra, RSX

2002 model shown

Consistently rated as one of the best used cars, the Integra served as the entry-level model in Acura's vehicle lineup. In 1994, the third-generation Integra was introduced with better performance and good fuel economy. Available as a coupe or sedan, it was offered with two main engines, a base 142-hp and an uplevel 172-hp in the GS-R. The sporty 2000-2001 Type R Coupe made 195 hp. Interior space is OK in the front; the rear is cramped. The seats are too firm for some. An all-new replacement, the RSX, arrived for 2002. A two-door coupe only, it's quick but noisy inside and rides stiffly.

MAJOR REDESIGN: 1994, 2002. **SAFETY EQUIPMENT:** Dual front air bags standard. Side air bags standard from 2002. ABS available; standard from 1999. Safety-belt pretensioners standard from 2002. **DRIVE WHEELS:** Front.

Reliability history

TROUBLE SPOTS	Acura Integra, RSX							
	95	96	97	98	99	00	01	02
Engine	◕	●	●	●	●	◕		●
Cooling	○	○	◕	●	●	●		●
Fuel	●	●	●	●	●	◕		●
Ignition	●	●	●	●	●	●		●
Transmission	●	●	●	●	●	●		●
Electrical	◕	●	●	●	●	◑		●
Air-conditioning	●	●	●	●	●	◕		●
Suspension	●	●	●	●	●	◕		●
Brakes	◑	◑	●	●	◕	◑		●
Exhaust	○	◑	●	●	●	◕		●
Paint/trim/rust	○	◕	●	●	●	◑		●
Body integrity	○	◕	◕	◕	●	◑		●
Power equipment	○	◕	○	●	●	◕		●
Body hardware	●	●	●	●	◑	●		●
RELIABILITY VERDICT	✓	✓	✓	✓	✓	✓	Insufficient data	✓

Prices

1995	$8,000-$10,000
1996	$10,000-$12,000
1997	$10,000-$12,000
1998	$12,000-$14,000
1999	$14,000-$16,000
2000	$16,000-$18,000
2001	$18,000-$20,000
2002	$20,000-$22,000

Crash-test results

Model Years	Offset	Full frontal	Side
1995	NT	◕/○	NT
1996	NT	◕/○	NT
1997	NT	◕/○	NT
1998	NT	◕/○	NT
1999	NT	◕/○	NT
2000	NT	◕/○	NT
2001	NT	◕/○	NT
2002	NT	◕/◕	◕/NA

Acura Legend, RL

1999 model shown

Originally available in coupe and sedan forms, the Legend was the first flagship of Honda's luxury-car line. Acceleration was impressive in our tests, and the ride was both supple and well controlled. Inside, seating is comfortable for four, but tight for five. Controls and displays are excellent. The Legend was replaced in 1996 by the 3.5RL. While quiet, spacious, and refined, the front-drive RL trails its German competitors in performance and safety features. Overall, we've found the RL's cabin roomy, its ride comfortable, its handling sound, and its braking exceptional.

MAJOR REDESIGN: 1996. **SAFETY EQUIPMENT:** Dual front air bags standard. Side air bags standard from 1999. ABS standard. Safety-belt pretensioners standard. **DRIVE WHEELS:** Front.

Reliability history

TROUBLE SPOTS	Acura Legend, RL							
	95	96	97	98	99	00	01	02
Engine	◉	◉	◉	◉	◉	◉		◉
Cooling	◒	◉	◉	◉	◉	◉		◉
Fuel	◉	◉	◒	◒	◉	◉		◉
Ignition	◉	◉	◉	◒	◉	◉		◉
Transmission	◒	◉	◒	◒	◒	◉		◉
Electrical	○	◒	◒	◒	◒	◒		◉
Air conditioning	◒	◉	◉	◒	◒	◉		◉
Suspension	◒	◒	◉	◒	◒	◒	Insufficient data	◉
Brakes	○	●	○	○	◒	◉		◉
Exhaust	◉	◉	◉	◉	◉	◉		◉
Paint/trim/rust	◉	◒	◉	◉	◒	◉		◉
Body integrity	○	◒	◒	◒	◒	◉		◉
Power equipment	○	◐	◒	◒	◒	◉		◉
Body hardware	○	○	○	◒	○	◉		◉
RELIABILITY VERDICT	✓	✓	✓	✓	✓	✓		

Prices

1995	$14,000-$16,000
1996	$14,000-$16,000
1997	$18,000-$20,000
1998	$20,000-$22,000
1999	$24,000-$26,000
2000	$28,000-$30,000
2001	More than $30,000
2002	More than $30,000

Crash-test results

Model years	Offset	Full-frontal	Side
1995	NT	○/◒	NT
1996	NT	NT	NT
1997	NT	NT	NT
1998	NT	NT	NT
1999	NT	◒/◒	NT
2000	NT	◒/◒	NT
2001	NT	◒/◒	NT
2002	NT	◒/◒	NT

Acura MDX

2001 model shown

This luxurious, car-derived SUV is Acura's answer to the Lexus RX300. Based loosely on mechanicals from the Honda Odyssey minivan, the MDX features a strong 3.5-liter V6, independent suspension, and standard AWD. The 50/50 split folding third-row seat folds away into the floor when not in use. Other pluses include a firm but pleasant ride and responsive handling, though the MDX can get a bit twitchy in emergency maneuvers. The cabin is well appointed and quiet, though it does admit more road noise than does the RX300's. Overall, we rated the MDX slightly ahead of the Lexus, in part for its superior room and flexibility.

MAJOR REDESIGN: 2001. **SAFETY EQUIPMENT:** Dual front and side air bags standard. ABS standard. Safety-belt pretensioners standard. **DRIVE WHEELS:** AWD.

Reliability history

TROUBLE SPOTS	Acura MDX							
	95	96	97	98	99	00	01	02
Engine							◉	◉
Cooling							◉	◉
Fuel							◉	◉
Ignition							◉	◉
Transmission							◉	◉
Electrical							◒	◉
Air conditioning							◉	◒
Suspension							◒	◉
Brakes							◉	◉
Exhaust							◉	◉
Paint/trim/rust							◒	◉
Body integrity							◒	◉
Power equipment							◒	◉
Body hardware							◒	◉
RELIABILITY VERDICT							✓	✓

Prices

1995	–
1996	–
1997	–
1998	–
1999	–
2000	–
2001	More than $30,000
2002	More than $30,000

Crash-test results

Model years	Offset	Full-frontal	Side
1995	–	–	–
1996	–	–	–
1997	–	–	–
1998	–	–	–
1999	–	–	–
2000	–	–	–
2001	Good	NT	NT
2002	Good	◒/◒	◒/◒

Acura SLX

Acura TL

1996 model shown

1999 model shown

I ntroduced in 1996, the Acura SLX is essentially a rebadged Isuzu Trooper with hardly any cosmetic disguise. Offered initially with a basic part-time 4WD system, the SLX switched to a selectable full-time system for 1998. A tall vehicle, the SLX offers a roomy interior, but only a so-so ride. We rated the 1996 and 1997 SLX and the similar 1995 to 1997 Isuzu Trooper "Not Acceptable" because of their pronounced tendency to roll over in one of our emergency-handling tests. The SLX was dropped after 1999, clearing the way for Honda/Acura's own SUV, the MDX. **Related model:** Isuzu Trooper.

MAJOR REDESIGN: 1996. **SAFETY EQUIPMENT:** Dual front air bags standard. ABS standard. **DRIVE WHEELS:** Part-time 4WD 1996-1997; selectable 4WD from 1998.

T he Acura Vigor offered nimble handling and good braking, but its ride was rather stiff. Room is plentiful up front, but access is awkward and three-across rear seating is crowded. In 1996, the Vigor was replaced by the more luxury-oriented TL. It was offered in two model configurations—the 2.5 and 3.2—which used a 176-hp five-cylinder and a 200-hp V6 engine, respectively. The TL's ride is supple, and fit and finish are exceptional, but body roll is more pronounced than in the Vigor. Redesigned for 1999, the TL's engine was the 3.2-liter V6. The current TL is nicely finished, accelerates quickly, and rides fairly comfortably.

MAJOR REDESIGN: 1996, 1999. **SAFETY EQUIPMENT:** Dual front air bags standard. Side air bags standard from 2000. ABS standard. Safety-belt pretensioners standard from 2001. **DRIVE WHEELS:** Front.

Acura SLX

Reliability history

TROUBLE SPOTS	95 96 97 98 99 00 01 02
Engine	
Cooling	
Fuel	
Ignition	NOT
Transmission	
Electrical	ENOUGH
Air-conditioning	
Suspension	DATA
Brakes	
Exhaust	TO
Paint/trim/rust	
Body integrity	RATE
Power equipment	
Body hardware	
RELIABILITY VERDICT	

Prices

1995	–
1996	$10,000-$12,000
1997	$12,000-$14,000
1998	$16,000-$18,000
1999	$18,000-$20,000
2000	–
2001	–
2002	–

Crash-test results

Model Years	Offset	Full frontal	Side
1995	–	–	–
1996	NT	O/O	NT
1997	NT	O/O	NT
1998	NT	NT	NT
1999	NT	NT	NT
2000	–	–	–
2001	–	–	–
2002	–	–	–

Acura TL

Reliability history

TROUBLE SPOTS	Acura TL							
	95	96	97	98	99	00	01	02
Engine		●			●	●	●	●
Cooling		◐			●	●	●	●
Fuel		●			●	●	●	●
Ignition		◐			●	●	●	●
Transmission		●			●	●	●	●
Electrical		◐	Insufficient data	Insufficient data	◐	◐	●	●
Air-conditioning		◐			●	●	●	●
Suspension		●			◐	●	●	●
Brakes		◐			○	◐	●	●
Exhaust		◐			●	●	●	●
Paint/trim/rust		◐			●	●	●	●
Body integrity		◐			○	○	●	●
Power equipment		◐			●	●	●	●
Body hardware		◐			●	●	●	●
RELIABILITY VERDICT		✓			✓	✓	✓	✓

Prices

1995	–
1996	$12,000-$14,000
1997	$14,000-$16,000
1998	$18,000-$20,000
1999	$20,000-$22,000
2000	$22,000-$24,000
2001	$24,000-$26,000
2002	$28,000-$30,000

Crash-test results

Model Years	Offset	Full frontal	Side
1995	–	–	–
1996	NT	◐/◐	NT
1997	NT	◐/◐	NT
1998	NT	◐/◐	NT
1999	Good	NT	NT
2000	Good	NT	NT
2001	Good	◐/◐	◐/●
2002	Good	◐/◐	◐/●

CR Good Bet

Audi 90, A4

1996 model shown

Redesigned in 1993, the Audi 90 was offered as a sedan or, starting in 1994, as a convertible. The V6 engine provided ample, though not energetic, acceleration, and could be coupled with AWD. Unfortunately, the 90 didn't handle as well as many of its competitors. In 1996, it was superseded by the significantly better A4. The A4's automatic transmission blunted performance until a new five-speed version appeared in 1997, alongside a more powerful V6 and a turbocharged four-cylinder. A wagon version, called the Avant, debuted for 1998. AWD can be found on all models, which were redesigned for 2002.

MAJOR REDESIGN: 1993, 1996, 2002. **SAFETY EQUIPMENT:** Dual front air bags standard. Side air bags standard from 1997. Head protection air bags from 2000. ABS and safety-belt pretensioners standard. **DRIVE WHEELS:** Front or AWD.

Reliability history

TROUBLE SPOTS	Audi A4							
	95	96	97	98	99	00	01	02
Engine								
Cooling								
Fuel								
Ignition								
Transmission								
Electrical								
Air conditioning								
Suspension								
Brakes								
Exhaust								
Paint/trim/rust								
Body integrity								
Power equipment								
Body hardware								
RELIABILITY VERDICT		✓		✓	✓		✓	

Prices

1995	$10,000-$12,000
1996	$12,000-$14,000
1997	$14,000-$16,000
1998	$16,000-$18,000
1999	$20,000-$22,000
2000	$22,000-$24,000
2001	$26,000-$28,000
2002	$28,000-$30,000

Crash-test results

Model years	Offset	Full-frontal	Side
1995	NT	NT	NT
1996	NT	◐/●	NT
1997	NT	◐/●	NT
1998	NT	◐/●	NT
1999	NT	◐/●	NT
2000	NT	◐/●	NT
2001	NT	◐/●	NT
2002	Good	NT	●/◐

Audi A6

1998 model shown

The midlevel Audi 100 was equipped with a five-cylinder engine and available in sedan and wagon forms. As with other Audi lines, full-time AWD was offered on both versions. In 1995, the 100 was renamed the A6. A 1998 redesign brought major improvements, including a 200-hp V6. An A6 Avant wagon was added in 1999. We find the current A6 sedan and wagon stylish, comfortable, and refined. A turbocharged 2.7-liter V6 and a 4.2-liter V8 were added for 2000, and 2001 saw the debut of the Allroad wagon, which features an adjustable-height suspension and SUV-like styling cues.

MAJOR REDESIGN: 1995, 1998. **SAFETY EQUIPMENT:** Dual front air bags standard. Front side air bags standard from 1998, rear and head protection air bags from 2000. ABS and safety-belt pretensioners standard. **DRIVE WHEELS:** Front or AWD.

Reliability history

TROUBLE SPOTS	Audi A6 V6							
	95	96	97	98	99	00	01	02
Engine								
Cooling								
Fuel								
Ignition								
Transmission								
Electrical	Insufficient data	Insufficient data	Insufficient data					Insufficient data
Air conditioning								
Suspension								
Brakes								
Exhaust								
Paint/trim/rust								
Body integrity								
Power equipment								
Body hardware								
RELIABILITY VERDICT						✓	✓	

Prices

1995	$12,000-$14,000
1996	$14,000-$16,000
1997	$16,000-$18,000
1998	$22,000-$24,000
1999	$24,000-$26,000
2000	More than $30,000
2001	More than $30,000
2002	More than $30,000

Crash-test results

Model years	Offset	Full-frontal	Side
1995	NT	◐/◐	NT
1996	NT	◐/◐	NT
1997	NT	◐/◐	NT
1998	Accept.	NT	NT
1999	Accept.	NT	NT
2000	Accept.	NT	NT
2001	Accept.	NT	NT
2002	Accept.	NT	NT

LUXURY CAR
Audi A8

1997 model shown

In 1997 Audi introduced the A8, an aluminum-bodied, full-sized luxury sedan intended to compete with the best cars from BMW, Jaguar, Lexus, and Mercedes-Benz. Two V8 engines were available, with AWD standard on the top-of-the-line trim level. For 2000, numerous safety features were added to the standard-equipment list, including multiple airbags and a stability-control system. The stronger V8 engine and AWD also became standard. A high-performance, 360-hp S8 model joined the line for 2001.

MAJOR REDESIGN: 1997. **SAFETY EQUIPMENT:** Dual front air bags standard. Side air bags standard in front and available in rear. Head protection air bags standard from 2000. ABS standard. Safety-belt pretensioners standard. **DRIVE WHEELS:** Front or AWD until 1999, AWD only from 2000.

Reliability history	
TROUBLE SPOTS	
	95 96 97 98 99 00 01 02
Engine	
Cooling	
Fuel	
Ignition	NOT
Transmission	
Electrical	ENOUGH
Air-conditioning	
Suspension	DATA
Brakes	
Exhaust	TO
Paint/trim/rust	
Body integrity	
Power equipment	RATE
Body hardware	
RELIABILITY VERDICT	

Prices	
1995	–
1996	–
1997	$26,000-$28,000
1998	More than $30,000
1999	More than $30,000
2000	More than $30,000
2001	More than $30,000
2002	More than $30,000

Crash-test results			
Model Years	Offset	Full frontal	Side
1995	–	–	–
1996	–	–	–
1997	NT	NT	NT
1998	NT	⊙/⊙	NT
1999	NT	⊙/⊙	NT
2000	NT	⊙/⊙	NT
2001	NT	⊙/⊙	NT
2002	NT	⊙/⊙	NT

SPORTS/SPORTY CAR
Audi TT

2000 model shown

The TT coupe offers artful styling inside and out. Offered in front-wheel drive form initially, with Quattro AWD later added. The standard engine is a noisy 180-hp turbo Four matched with a five-speed manual transmission. Stability control was added in mid 2000. In 2001 a convertible model became available. AWD-equipped models got a gutsier but still noisy 225-hp engine and six-speed manual transmission. Handling is not as sporty as, say, the Porsche Boxster or Honda S2000 and the shifter doesn't feel crisp. The ride is very stiff, and visibility is poor.

MAJOR REDESIGN: 2000. **SAFETY EQUIPMENT:** Dual front and side air bags standard. Safety-belt pretensioners standard. ABS standard. **DRIVE WHEELS:** Front or AWD.

Reliability history	Audi TT		
TROUBLE SPOTS			
	95 96 97 98 99 00	01	02
Engine	⊙		
Cooling	⊙		
Fuel	◗		
Ignition	⊙		
Transmission	⊙		
Electrical	◗	Insufficient data	Insufficient data
Air-conditioning	⊙		
Suspension	⊙		
Brakes	⊙		
Exhaust	⊙		
Paint/trim/rust	⊙		
Body integrity	◗		
Power equipment	◗		
Body hardware	◗		
RELIABILITY VERDICT			

Prices	
1995	–
1996	–
1997	–
1998	–
1999	–
2000	$24,000-$26,000
2001	More than $30,000
2002	More than $30,000

Crash-test results			
Model Years	Offset	Full frontal	Side
1995	–	–	–
1996	–	–	–
1997	–	–	–
1998	–	–	–
1999	–	–	–
2000	NT	NT	NT
2001	NT	NT	⊙/NA
2002	NT	NT	⊙/NA

UPSCALE CAR

BMW 3-Series

1999 model shown

BMW's 3-Series cars have been exemplary in almost all respects, save for a tight rear seat. Sedan, coupe, wagon, convertible, and even hatchback models exist, though the hatchback 318ti was dropped for 2000. These cars exhibited excellent handling and braking in our tests. Model designations—from the 318ti to the 330xi —vary over the years, based on engine, body style, and drive wheels. Performance enthusiasts can also opt for the sport-tuned M3. A 1999 redesign brought safety improvements and a roomier cabin, and inline-six-cylinder engines have been used across the line since.

MAJOR REDESIGN: 1999. **SAFETY EQUIPMENT:** Dual front air bags standard. Side air bags available in 1997, standard from 1998. Head protection air bags standard from 2000. ABS standard. Safety-belt pretensioners standard. **DRIVE WHEELS:** Rear. AWD available from 2001.

Reliability history	
TROUBLE SPOTS	**BMW 3-Series**
	95 96 97 98 99 00 01 02
Engine	
Cooling	
Fuel	
Ignition	
Transmission	
Electrical	
Air conditioning	
Suspension	
Brakes	
Exhaust	
Paint/trim/rust	
Body integrity	
Power equipment	
Body hardware	
RELIABILITY VERDICT	✓ ✓ ✓ ✓ ✓ ✓

Prices	
1995	$14,000-$16,000
1996	$16,000-$18,000
1997	$18,000-$20,000
1998	$22,000-$24,000
1999	$22,000-$24,000
2000	$26,000-$28,000
2001	More than $30,000
2002	More than $30,000

Crash-test results			
Model years	Offset	Full-frontal	Side
1995	NT	◒/◒	NT
1996	NT	◒/◒	NT
1997	NT	◒/◒	NT
1998	NT	NT	NT
1999	NT	NT	NT
2000	Good	NT	NT
2001	Good	NT	NT
2002	Good	◒/●	NT

LUXURY CAR

BMW 5-Series

1998 model shown

Occupying the slot in BMW's lineup between the compact 3-Series and the large 7-Series, the mid-sized 5-Series models are superbly designed luxury sports sedans. With nimble handling, supple and controlled suspensions, and lively engines, the 5-Series cars are controllable, quiet, plush, and fun to drive. The inline-six-cylinder and V8 engines feel invigorating. The 5-Series wagons, known as Touring models, feel as sporty as the sedans. The V8-powered 540i sedan offers particularly vigorous performance. The high-performance M5 has topped the line since 2000.

MAJOR REDESIGN: 1997. **SAFETY EQUIPMENT:** Dual front air bags standard. Side air bags standard from 1997. Head protection air bags standard from 2000. ABS standard. Safety-belt pretensioners standard. **DRIVE WHEELS:** Rear.

Reliability history	
TROUBLE SPOTS	**BMW 5-Series**
	95 96 97 98 99 00 01 02
Engine	
Cooling	
Fuel	
Ignition	
Transmission	
Electrical	
Air conditioning	
Suspension	
Brakes	
Exhaust	
Paint/trim/rust	
Body integrity	
Power equipment	
Body hardware	
RELIABILITY VERDICT	✓ ✓ ✓ ✓ ✓

Prices	
1995	$14,000-$16,000
1996	–
1997	$22,000-$24,000
1998	$26,000-$28,000
1999	More than $30,000
2000	More than $30,000
2001	More than $30,000
2002	More than $30,000

Crash-test results			
Model years	Offset	Full-frontal	Side
1995	NT	NT	NT
1996	–	–	–
1997	Good	NT	NT
1998	Good	NT	NT
1999	Good	NT	NT
2000	Good	NT	NT
2001	Good	NT	NT
2002	Good	NT	NT

BMW 7-Series

1996 model shown

The 7-Series has been BMW's top-of-the-line sedan for years. A strong 4.0-liter V8 was the standard engine from 1993 through 1995. A 1995 redesign made the 7-Series quieter but less sporty than its predecessor. For 1996, the V8's displacement swelled to 4.4 liters. The slightly longer 740iL and 750iL provide more room for rear passengers. Accommodations are first class, with comfortable seats and abundant power features. These models have exceptional acceleration—particularly the V12-powered 750iL—and superior handling. The 2002 redesign brought a very hard-to-learn control layout.

MAJOR REDESIGN: 1995, 2002. **SAFETY EQUIPMENT:** Dual front air bags standard. Front side air bags standard from 1997, available in rear from 1999. Head protection air bags standard from 2000. ABS standard. Safety-belt pretensioners standard. **DRIVE WHEELS:** Rear.

BMW 8-Series

1996 model shown

The V12-powered 850i coupe made its debut in 1991. Ostensibly a replacement for the discontinued 635CSi, the 8-Series was more luxurious and technologically advanced than its predecessor. Unfortunately, a portly two-ton curb weight dulled the 850's performance. In 1994, BMW unveiled two new 8-Series models, the V8-powered 840i and the top-of-the-line 850CSi. With its 5.6-liter V12, six-speed manual transmission, and stiffened suspension, the 850CSi performed with considerably more verve than its 8-Series siblings. It disappeared after a brief two-year model run, with the rest of the 8-Series line following suit at the end of 1997.

MAJOR REDESIGN: 1991. **SAFETY EQUIPMENT:** Dual front air bags standard. ABS standard. **DRIVE WHEELS:** Rear.

BMW 7-Series

Reliability history — BMW 7-Series

TROUBLE SPOTS	95	96	97	98	99	00	01	02
Engine				◑			●	
Cooling				◐			●	
Fuel				◑			●	
Ignition				●			●	
Transmission				●			●	
Electrical	Insufficient data	Insufficient data	Insufficient data	○	Insufficient data	Insufficient data	◑	Insufficient data
Air-conditioning				◑			●	
Suspension				○			●	
Brakes				◐			●	
Exhaust				◑			●	
Paint/trim/rust				◐			●	
Body integrity				◑			◑	
Power equipment				○			◑	
Body hardware				◐			○	
RELIABILITY VERDICT				✓			✓	

Prices

Year	Price
1995	$20,000-$22,000
1996	$24,000-$26,000
1997	$26,000-$28,000
1998	More than $30,000
1999	More than $30,000
2000	More than $30,000
2001	More than $30,000
2002	More than $30,000

Crash-test results

Model Years	Offset	Full frontal	Side
1995	NT	NT	NT
1996	NT	NT	NT
1997	NT	NT	NT
1998	NT	NT	NT
1999	NT	NT	NT
2000	NT	NT	NT
2001	NT	NT	NT
2002	NT	NT	NT

BMW 8-Series

Reliability history

TROUBLE SPOTS	95	96	97	98	99	00	01	02
Engine								
Cooling								
Fuel								
Ignition	NOT							
Transmission								
Electrical	ENOUGH							
Air-conditioning								
Suspension	DATA							
Brakes								
Exhaust								
Paint/trim/rust	TO							
Body integrity								
Power equipment	RATE							
Body hardware								
RELIABILITY VERDICT								

Prices

Year	Price
1995	More than $30,000
1996	More than $30,000
1997	More than $30,000
1998	–
1999	–
2000	–
2001	–
2002	–

Crash-test results

Model Years	Offset	Full frontal	Side
1995	NT	NT	NT
1996	NT	NT	NT
1997	NT	NT	NT
1998	–	–	–
1999	–	–	–
2000	–	–	–
2001	–	–	–
2002	–	–	–

BMW X5

BMW Z3

2000 model shown

1996 model shown

The car-based X5 debuted for 2000 with an emphasis on sport over utility. It features unibody construction, fully independent suspension, and all-wheel drive. The V8-equipped 4.4i model accelerated like a sports car in our tests, and its handling and braking were outstanding. However, we found the ride firm and both cargo space and rear-seat room to be modest. The 3.0-liter six-cylinder model is less expensive but still provides good performance. Though the X5 lacks low-range gearing, an electronic hill-descent feature controls the vehicle's speed when descending steep off-road grades.

MAJOR REDESIGN: 2000. **SAFETY EQUIPMENT:** Dual front, side, and head protection air bags standard; rear side available. Safety-belt pretensioners standard. ABS standard. **DRIVE WHEELS:** AWD.

This American-built roadster debuted for 1996. The Z3's interior is cramped, and storage space is limited. Our tests showed handling to be good, but tricky at the limits until the car received stability control for 1997. Even then, the Z3's manners continued to trail those of the 3-Series BMWs. The first engine offered was a 1.9-liter Four, with 2.8- and 2.3-liter inline Sixes arriving for 1997 and 1999, respectively. In 1998, the high-performance M Coupe and M Roadster debuted, armed with more power and tire grip. The Sixes were replaced by larger, more powerful versions in 2001.

MAJOR REDESIGN: 1996. **SAFETY EQUIPMENT:** Dual front air bags standard. Side air bags standard from 1999. ABS standard. Safety-belt pretensioners standard. **DRIVE WHEELS:** Rear.

BMW X5

Reliability history

TROUBLE SPOTS	95	96	97	98	99	00	01	02
Engine							●	●
Cooling						○	●	●
Fuel							●	●
Ignition							●	●
Transmission							●	●
Electrical			Insufficient data			●	◐	●
Air conditioning						○	●	●
Suspension						●	●	●
Brakes							●	●
Exhaust							●	●
Paint/trim/rust							●	●
Body integrity						○	●	●
Power equipment							○	○
Body hardware							◐	◐
RELIABILITY VERDICT								

Prices

1995	–
1996	–
1997	–
1998	–
1999	–
2000	More than $30,000
2001	More than $30,000
2002	More than $30,000

Crash-test results

Model years	Offset	Full-frontal	Side
1995	–	–	–
1996	–	–	–
1997	–	–	–
1998	–	–	–
1999	–	–	–
2000	NT	NT	NT
2001	Good	NT	NT
2002	Good	NT	NT

BMW Z3

Reliability history

TROUBLE SPOTS	95	96	97	98	99	00	01	02
Engine		○	●		●	●		
Cooling		○	●		●	○		
Fuel		○	●		●	○		
Ignition		●	●		●	○		
Transmission		●	●		●	●		
Electrical	Insufficient data	○	●	Insufficient data	○	○	Insufficient data	
Air conditioning		○	●		●	○		
Suspension		●	●		●	●		
Brakes		○	○		●	●		
Exhaust		●	●		●	●		
Paint/trim/rust		●	●		●	●		
Body integrity		●	●		●	○		
Power equipment		●	●		○	○		
Body hardware		○	○		○	○		
RELIABILITY VERDICT			✔	✔		✔	✔	

Prices

1995	–
1996	$16,000-$18,000
1997	$18,000-$20,000
1998	$20,000-$22,000
1999	$24,000-$26,000
2000	$28,000-$30,000
2001	More than $30,000
2002	More than $30,000

Crash-test results

Model years	Offset	Full-frontal	Side
1995	–	–	–
1996	NT	NT	NT
1997	NT	NT	NT
1998	NT	NT	NT
1999	NT	NT	NT
2000	NT	NT	NT
2001	NT	NT	NT
2002	NT	NT	NT

FAMILY CAR
Buick Century

1998 model shown

The Century has felt out-of-date for ten years or more, despite redesigns. The ride was spongy on smooth pavement, and hopped and wallowed on bumpy roads. Though it looks big on the outside, the car is cramped inside, especially in the rear. Four- and six-cylinder engines were offered, and a wagon model was available through 1996. The Century was redesigned in 1997, but still has unresponsive handling, mediocre brakes, and a merely adequate 3.1-liter V6. A smooth, quiet ride at low speeds is its major virtue. Front and rear bench seats are roomy, but too soft. The trunk is spacious. **Related model:** Oldsmobile Cutlass Ciera.

MAJOR REDESIGN: 1997. **SAFETY EQUIPMENT:** Driver air bag standard; passenger air bag standard from 1997. Side air bags available from 2001. ABS standard. **DRIVE WHEELS:** Front.

Reliability history

TROUBLE SPOTS	Buick Century
	95 96 97 98 99 00 01 02
Engine	
Cooling	
Fuel	
Ignition	
Transmission	
Electrical	
Air-conditioning	
Suspension	
Brakes	
Exhaust	
Paint/trim/rust	
Body integrity	
Power equipment	
Body hardware	
RELIABILITY VERDICT	✓ ✓ ✓ ✓ ✓ ✓

Prices

Year	Price
1995	$4,000–$6,000
1996	$4,000–$6,000
1997	$8,000–$10,000
1998	$8,000–$10,000
1999	$10,000–$12,000
2000	$12,000–$14,000
2001	$14,000–$16,000
2002	$16,000–$18,000

Crash-test results

Model Years	Offset	Full frontal	Side
1995	NT	◑/◑	NT
1996	NT	◑/◑	NT
1997	Accept.	NT	NT
1998	Accept.	NT	○/○
1999	Accept.	◑/○	○/○
2000	Accept.	◑/○	○/○
2001	Accept.	◑/○	○/○
2002	Accept.	◑/○	○/○

LARGE CAR
Buick LeSabre

1998 model shown

The Buick LeSabre is a classic domestic freeway cruiser, with a soft ride, quiet interior, and pretty good reliability. In 1992 to 1999 models, the interior is roomy and the ride is quiet, but the seats are too soft and unsupportive. Updated significantly for 2000, the LeSabre got more comfortable seats, improved brakes and suspension, and side air bags. Our testing showed that handling was much improved, as well, especially with the Gran Touring suspension. The 3.8-liter V6 is not overly refined but delivers strong power. **Related models:** Oldsmobile Eighty-Eight, Pontiac Bonneville.

MAJOR REDESIGN: 1992, 2000. **SAFETY EQUIPMENT:** Dual front air bags standard. Side air bags standard from 2000. ABS standard. **DRIVE WHEELS:** Front.

Reliability history

TROUBLE SPOTS	Buick LeSabre
	95 96 97 98 99 00 01 02
Engine	
Cooling	
Fuel	
Ignition	
Transmission	
Electrical	
Air-conditioning	
Suspension	
Brakes	
Exhaust	
Paint/trim/rust	
Body integrity	
Power equipment	
Body hardware	
RELIABILITY VERDICT	✓ ✓ ✓ ✓ ✓ ✓ ✓

Prices

Year	Price
1995	$6,000–$8,000
1996	$8,000–$10,000
1997	$8,000–$10,000
1998	$10,000–$12,000
1999	$12,000–$14,000
2000	$14,000–$16,000
2001	$16,000–$18,000
2002	$20,000–$22,000

Crash-test results

Model Years	Offset	Full frontal	Side
1995	NT	◑/○	NT
1996	NT	◑/○	NT
1997	NT	◑/◑	NT
1998	NT	◑/◑	○/○
1999	NT	◑/◑	○/○
2000	Good	◑/◑	◑/◑
2001	Good	◑/◑	◑/◑
2002	Good	◑/◑	◑/◑

LARGE CAR
Buick Park Avenue

1998 model shown

A traditional American highway cruiser, Buick's top-of-the-line Park Avenue offers expansive seating, a cavernous trunk, and a soft, quiet ride. Cars equipped with the optional Gran Touring package have a firmer suspension and, consequently, better handling and ride control. The Park Avenue was redesigned and much improved for 1997 and has stayed much the same since. It's offered in base and Ultra versions, and features many conveniences. The base car comes standard with a 3.8-liter, 205-hp V6. The Ultra model uses a 240-hp supercharged version of that engine, which endows the car with effortless acceleration. **Related model:** Oldsmobile Ninety-Eight.

MAJOR REDESIGN: 1991, 1997. **SAFETY EQUIPMENT:** Dual front air bags standard. Side air bags standard from 2000. ABS standard. **DRIVE WHEELS:** Front.

Reliability history

TROUBLE SPOTS	Buick Park Avenue							
	95	96	97	98	99	00	01	02
Engine								
Cooling								
Fuel								
Ignition								
Transmission								
Electrical								
Air conditioning								
Suspension								
Brakes								
Exhaust								
Paint/trim/rust								
Body integrity								
Power equipment								
Body hardware								
RELIABILITY VERDICT	✔	✔			✔	✔		

Prices

1995	$8,000–$10,000
1996	$10,000–$12,000
1997	$12,000–$14,000
1998	$14,000–$16,000
1999	$16,000–$18,000
2000	$18,000–$20,000
2001	$20,000–$22,000
2002	$24,000–$26,000

Crash-test results

Model years	Offset	Full-frontal	Side
1995	NT	NT	NT
1996	NT	NT	NT
1997	Good	NT	NT
1998	Good	NT	NT
1999	Good	NT	NT
2000	Good	NT	NT
2001	Good	⊖/○	⊖/○
2002	Good	⊖/○	⊖/○

FAMILY CAR
Buick Regal

1998 model shown

This sedan provided a smooth ride and responsive routine handling in our tests in the early 1990s, but was not very competent in emergency maneuvers. Regals of this vintage have a split-bench front seat and an uncomfortable rear seat. The car was redesigned for 1997, but retained an old-fashioned floaty ride and rubbery steering. Handling is improved somewhat with the Gran Touring suspension package. Acceleration is good with the base 3.8-liter, 200-hp V6, and quicker with the supercharged version, which pumps out 240 horses, and makes the Regal quick but not sporty. **Related models:** Oldsmobile Cutlass Supreme, Pontiac Grand Prix.

MAJOR REDESIGN: 1997. **SAFETY EQUIPMENT:** Dual front air bags standard. Side air bags available from 2000. ABS standard. **DRIVE WHEELS:** Front.

Reliability history

TROUBLE SPOTS	Buick Regal							
	95	96	97	98	99	00	01	02
Engine								
Cooling								
Fuel								
Ignition								
Transmission								
Electrical								
Air conditioning								
Suspension								
Brakes								
Exhaust								
Paint/trim/rust								
Body integrity								
Power equipment								
Body hardware								
RELIABILITY VERDICT	✔	✔	✔	✔	✔	✔	✔	✔

Prices

1995	$6,000–$8,000
1996	$8,000–$10,000
1997	$10,000–$12,000
1998	$12,000–$14,000
1999	$14,000–$16,000
2000	$16,000–$18,000
2001	$18,000–$20,000
2002	$20,000–$22,000

Crash-test results

Model years	Offset	Full-frontal	Side
1995	NT	NT	NT
1996	NT	⊖/○	NT
1997	Accept.	NT	NT
1998	Accept.	NT	○/○
1999	Accept.	⊖/○	○/○
2000	Accept.	⊖/○	○/○
2001	Accept.	⊖/○	○/○
2002	Accept.	⊖/○	○/○

Buick Rendezvous

Buick Riviera

2002 model shown

1995 model shown

The Rendezvous is a plausible attempt at combining the better elements of a minivan and an SUV. The second seating row consists of either two captain's chairs or a bench, and the optional third-row seat folds into the floor when not in use. Front- and all-wheel-drive versions are offered. The Rendezvous' old-tech 3.4-liter pushrod V6—from GM's minivans—is over-taxed in all-wheel-drive versions, and acceleration is notably weak. Handling is secure, however, and the ride is fairly comfortable. The interior is made of cheap-looking materials, and the gray-on-gray gauges can be hard to read.

MAJOR REDESIGN: 2002. **SAFETY EQUIPMENT:** Dual front air bags standard. Side air bags standard. ABS and safety-belt pretension-ers standard. **DRIVE WHEELS:** Front or AWD.

After a brief absence, the classic Riviera moniker returned on a large "personal luxury coupe" for 1995. Based on the Oldsmobile Aurora platform, the Riviera had a pleasant and quiet ride on expressways, but was ponderous on country roads. The heavy, front-drive Riviera is powered by a 3.8-liter V6 in standard or supercharged form. The control layout includes awk-ward displays and hard-to-reach switches. Tall drivers need more front headroom, and short ones must sit too close to the wheel. Rear-seat access is difficult, and rear headroom is limited. The Riviera was discontinued after the 1999 model year.

MAJOR REDESIGN: 1995. **SAFETY EQUIPMENT:** Dual front air bags standard. ABS standard. **DRIVE WHEELS:** Front.

Buick Rendezvous

Reliability history

TROUBLE SPOTS	Buick Rendezvous							
	95	96	97	98	99	00	01	02
Engine								●
Cooling								●
Fuel								●
Ignition								●
Transmission								●
Electrical								◐
Air-conditioning								●
Suspension								◐
Brakes								◐
Exhaust								●
Paint/trim/rust								●
Body integrity								◐
Power equipment								○
Body hardware								◐
RELIABILITY VERDICT								

Prices

1995	–
1996	–
1997	–
1998	–
1999	–
2000	–
2001	–
2002	$24,000-$26,000

Crash-test results

Model Years	Offset	Full frontal	Side
1995	–	–	–
1996	–	–	–
1997	–	–	–
1998	–	–	–
1999	–	–	–
2000	–	–	–
2001	–	–	–
2002	Accept.	○/○	◑/○

Buick Riviera

Reliability history

TROUBLE SPOTS	Buick Riviera							
	95	96	97	98	99	00	01	02
Engine	○							
Cooling	○							
Fuel	○							
Ignition	○							
Transmission	○							
Electrical	◐	Insufficient data	Insufficient data	Insufficient data	Insufficient data	Insufficient data		
Air-conditioning	○							
Suspension	○							
Brakes	●							
Exhaust	◐							
Paint/trim/rust	◐							
Body integrity	○							
Power equipment	●							
Body hardware	◐							
RELIABILITY VERDICT								

Prices

1995	$6,000-$8,000
1996	$8,000-$10,000
1997	$10,000-$12,000
1998	$12,000-$14,000
1999	$16,000-$18,000
2000	–
2001	–
2002	–

Crash-test results

Model Years	Offset	Full frontal	Side
1995	NT	NT	NT
1996	NT	NT	NT
1997	NT	NT	NT
1998	NT	NT	NT
1999	NT	NT	NT
2000	–	–	–
2001	–	–	–
2002	–	–	–

Buick Roadmaster

1995 model shown

This massive, rear-wheel-drive model was produced from 1991 to 1996 in both sedan and wagon versions. Like classic full-sized American cars before it, the Roadmaster can fit three across in both the front and rear seats. A large-displacement V8 provides enough power to tow modest trailers, but gobbles fuel. The ride is exceptionally smooth and quiet, although handling is ponderous and sluggish. Wide rear roof pillars limit visibility, and the long hood can make it difficult to judge the exact location of the front bumper. The Roadmaster was one of the last big, full-frame American cars.
Related models: Cadillac Fleetwood, Chevrolet Caprice.

MAJOR REDESIGN: 1991. **SAFETY EQUIPMENT:** Dual front air bags standard. ABS standard. **DRIVE WHEELS:** Rear.

Reliability history

TROUBLE SPOTS	Buick Roadmaster	
	95 96 97 98 99 00 01 02	
Engine	○ ○	
Cooling	◑ ●	
Fuel	◑ ●	
Ignition	◑ ○	
Transmission	◑ ○	
Electrical	● ◑	
Air conditioning	○ ○	
Suspension	◑ ◑	
Brakes	○ ◑	
Exhaust	● ●	
Paint/trim/rust	● ◑	
Body integrity	○ ○	
Power equipment	● ◑	
Body hardware	● ◑	
RELIABILITY VERDICT		

Prices

Year	Price
1995	$8,000-$10,000
1996	$10,000-$12,000
1997	–
1998	–
1999	–
2000	–
2001	–
2002	–

Crash-test results

Model years	Offset	Full-frontal	Side
1995	NT	◑/◐	NT
1996	NT	◑/◐	NT
1997	–	–	–
1998	–	–	–
1999	–	–	–
2000	–	–	–
2001	–	–	–
2002	–	–	–

Buick Skylark

1995 model shown

Buick redesigned the Skylark for 1992, along with its cousins the Oldsmobile Achieva and Pontiac Grand Am. Handling was merely adequate, even with the optional Gran Sport package. The base engine was a noisy Four, but the stronger 3.1-liter V6 was both better and more widespread. The Skylark's front seats are satisfactory, but the rear is uncomfortable. The controls and displays needed improvement. In 1996, Buick updated the dash, along with other interior elements, and gave the front end a facelift. The Skylark was dropped after 1998. **Related models:** Oldsmobile Achieva, Pontiac Grand Am.

MAJOR REDESIGN: 1992. **SAFETY EQUIPMENT:** Driver air bag standard; passenger air bag standard from 1996. ABS available. **DRIVE WHEELS:** Front.

Reliability history

TROUBLE SPOTS	
	95 96 97 98 99 00 01 02
Engine	
Cooling	
Fuel	
Ignition	**NOT**
Transmission	
Electrical	**ENOUGH**
Air conditioning	
Suspension	**DATA**
Brakes	
Exhaust	**TO**
Paint/trim/rust	
Body integrity	
Power equipment	**RATE**
Body hardware	
RELIABILITY VERDICT	

Prices

Year	Price
1995	$4,000-$6,000
1996	$4,000-$6,000
1997	$6,000-$8,000
1998	$6,000-$8,000
1999	–
2000	–
2001	–
2002	–

Crash-test results

Model years	Offset	Full-frontal	Side
1995	NT	◑/○	NT
1996	NT	◑/○	NT
1997	NT	◐/◑	●/○
1998	NT	◐/◑	●/○
1999	–	–	–
2000	–	–	–
2001	–	–	–
2002	–	–	–

Cadillac Catera

1997 model shown

Introduced for 1997, Cadillac's entry-level Catera was built in Germany and derived from the European Opel Omega. Equipped with a 3.0-liter V6, this rear-drive sports sedan accelerates smoothly and handles with agility. The ride is firm, yet well controlled and supple. An effective traction-control system was standard. The Catera has a roomy interior, with large, supportive front seats and a spacious rear seat. Luxury features are abundant, and include automatic climate control as well as heated seats front and rear. It was a good car, plagued from the start with reliability problems. Replaced by the CTS in 2002.

MAJOR REDESIGN: 1997. **SAFETY EQUIPMENT:** Dual front air bags standard. Side air bags standard from 2000. ABS standard. Safety-belt pretensioners standard. **DRIVE WHEELS:** Rear.

Reliability history

TROUBLE SPOTS	Cadillac Catera							
	95	96	97	98	99	00	01	02
Engine			●	○				
Cooling			●	●				
Fuel			○	○				
Ignition			○	○	○			
Transmission			◐	○		●		
Electrical			●	●	◐			
Air-conditioning			○	◐	◐			
Suspension			○	◐				
Brakes			◐	◐	○			
Exhaust			●	○	○			
Paint/trim/rust			○	○		●		
Body integrity			○	○		●		
Power equipment			◐	●		○		
Body hardware			●	●		◐		
RELIABILITY VERDICT								

(00, 01, 02: Insufficient data)

Prices

1995	–
1996	–
1997	$10,000–$12,000
1998	$12,000–$14,000
1999	$16,000–$18,000
2000	$20,000–$22,000
2001	$22,000–$24,000
2002	–

Crash-test results

Model Years	Offset	Full frontal	Side
1995	–	–	–
1996	–	–	–
1997	Good	NT	NT
1998	Good	NT	NT
1999	Good	NT	NT
2000	Good	NT	NT
2001	Good	NT	NT
2002	–	–	–

Cadillac DeVille

1997 model shown

The DeVille is big, plush, quiet, and roomy. Despite its size, the DeVille rides and handles relatively well. Cadillac's superb aluminum Northstar V8 became standard on all models in 1996. Significant updates in 1997 included a facelift, a new dash, standard side air bags, and a stability-control system. The Concours trim line features individual front seats, while other DeVilles have a traditional bench. A complete redesign for 2000 brought new styling, more efficient interior packaging, and the introduction of GM's Night Vision technology. **Related model:** Oldsmobile Ninety-Eight.

MAJOR REDESIGN: 1994, 2000. **SAFETY EQUIPMENT:** Dual front air bags standard. Front side air bags standard from 1997; rear available from 2000. Safety-belt pretensioners standard from 2000. ABS standard. **DRIVE WHEELS:** Front.

Reliability history

TROUBLE SPOTS	Cadillac DeVille							
	95	96	97	98	99	00	01	02
Engine	○	◐	○	◐	◐	◐	◐	●
Cooling	○	◐	◐	◐	◐	◐	◐	●
Fuel	◐	●	○	○	○	○	◐	●
Ignition	○	○	◐	◐	◐	◐	◐	●
Transmission	○	○	◐	●	○	◐	◐	●
Electrical	◐	●	●	◐	◐	◐	○	◐
Air-conditioning	●	●	◐	◐	◐	○	◐	◐
Suspension	◐	○	○	○	○	○	◐	◐
Brakes	●	◐	○	●	◐	○	◐	◐
Exhaust	◐	◐	◐	◐	◐	○	◐	◐
Paint/trim/rust	◐	◐	◐	◐	◐	◐	◐	○
Body integrity	◐	◐	◐	◐	◐	◐	◐	◐
Power equipment	◐	◐	◐	◐	○	○	◐	◐
Body hardware	○	○	○	◐	◐	◐	●	○
RELIABILITY VERDICT				✓		✓		

Prices

1995	$10,000–$12,000
1996	$12,000–$14,000
1997	$14,000–$16,000
1998	$18,000–$20,000
1999	$22,000–$24,000
2000	$24,000–$26,000
2001	$28,000–$30,000
2002	More than $30,000

Crash-test results

Model Years	Offset	Full frontal	Side
1995	NT	NT	NT
1996	NT	○/●	NT
1997	NT	○/◐	◐/○
1998	NT	○/◐	◐/○
1999	NT	○/◐	◐/○
2000	NT	○/◐	◐/○
2001	NT	○/◐	◐/○
2002	NT	○/◐	◐/○

Cadillac Eldorado

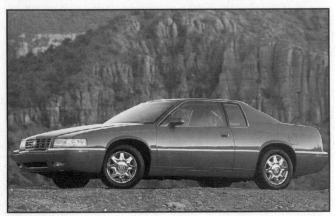

1998 model shown

The last version of the long-running Eldorado coupe was introduced in 1992, but it wasn't until the following year that Cadillac's strong Northstar V8 engine was added to top models. An array of luxury features was standard. The Eldorado's ride is good on smooth surfaces, but bumps tend to unsettle it. Handling is cumbersome. The front seat is roomy, and there is adequate room for two adults in the rear, though access is very awkward. Stability control was added in 1997, to complement the car's traction-control system. The Eldorado was the last survivior of the breed of big, bulky domestic luxury coupes when it ceased production in 2002.

MAJOR REDESIGN: 1992. **SAFETY EQUIPMENT:** Dual front air bags standard. ABS standard. **DRIVE WHEELS:** Front.

Reliability history	
TROUBLE SPOTS	
	95 96 97 98 99 00 01 02
Engine	
Cooling	
Fuel	
Ignition	NOT
Transmission	
Electrical	ENOUGH
Air conditioning	
Suspension	DATA
Brakes	
Exhaust	TO
Paint/trim/rust	
Body integrity	
Power equipment	RATE
Body hardware	
RELIABILITY VERDICT	

Prices	
1995	$12,000-$14,000
1996	$14,000-$16,000
1997	$16,000-$18,000
1998	$18,000-$20,000
1999	$22,000-$24,000
2000	$26,000-$28,000
2001	More than $30,000
2002	More than $30,000

Crash-test results			
Model years	Offset	Full-frontal	Side
1995	NT	NT	NT
1996	NT	NT	NT
1997	NT	NT	NT
1998	NT	NT	NT
1999	NT	NT	NT
2000	NT	NT	NT
2001	NT	NT	NT
2002	NT	NT	NT

Cadillac Escalade, Escalade EXT

2002 model shown

The first Escalade was rushed to market in 1999 to compete with the popular Lincoln Navigator. It was marketed as a new luxury SUV, but it was really a rebadged Chevrolet Tahoe/GMC Yukon with leather upholstery, wood trim, a cushier ride, and an inflated price tag. There was no 2001 Escalade, though a redesigned version based on GM's current full-sized truck chassis bowed as an early 2002 model. The EXT, Cadillac's first pickup, is essentially a plusher version of the Chevrolet Avalanche. **Related models:** Chevrolet Tahoe, GMC Yukon, Chevrolet Avalanche.

MAJOR REDESIGN: 1999, 2002. **SAFETY EQUIPMENT:** Dual front air bags standard. Side air bags standard. ABS standard. **DRIVE WHEELS:** Selectable 4WD; rear or AWD.

Reliability history	
TROUBLE SPOTS	Cadillac Escalade
	95 96 97 98 99 00 01 02
Engine	●
Cooling	●
Fuel	●
Ignition	●
Transmission	●
Electrical	◐
Air conditioning	●
Suspension	●
Brakes	●
Exhaust	●
Paint/trim/rust	◐
Body integrity	○
Power equipment	○
Body hardware	○
RELIABILITY VERDICT	

(Insufficient data columns noted for 2000 and 2001)

Prices	
1995	–
1996	–
1997	–
1998	–
1999	$28,000-$30,000
2000	More than $30,000
2001	–
2002	More than $30,000

Crash-test results			
Model years	Offset	Full-frontal	Side
1995	–	–	–
1996	–	–	–
1997	–	–	–
1998	–	–	–
1999	NT	○/◐	NT
2000	NT	○/◐	NT
2001	–	–	–
2002	NT	○/◐	NT

Cadillac Fleetwood

Cadillac Seville

1995 model shown

1998 model shown

Once known as the Brougham, this old-style Cadillac was redesigned and renamed Fleetwood for 1993. Built with full-frame construction and rear-wheel drive, the Fleetwood is a long, large car powered by a 5.7-liter V8. It maintained the traditional characteristics of large domestic sedans: a soft ride, a quiet and plush interior, and a powerful engine. The passenger compartment offers plenty of room, and the trunk is spacious. Unfortunately, the Fleetwood's bulk exacted a penalty in the areas of handling and fuel economy. Like the similar Buick Roadmaster and Chevrolet Caprice, the Fleetwood was dropped after the 1996 model year. **Related models:** Buick Roadmaster, Chevrolet Caprice.

MAJOR REDESIGN: 1993. **SAFETY EQUIPMENT:** Dual front air bags standard. ABS standard. **DRIVE WHEELS:** Rear.

Cadillac tried to position the Seville as an alternative to BMWs, Lexuses, and Mercedes-Benzes. It never really measured up to those, though. It came equipped with a strong 4.6-liter Northstar V8 engine, traction control, and an active suspension system. The STS version accelerated faster than many performance cars, and even carved relatively crisp corners, but didn't ride particularly well. Though redesigned for 1998, the Seville still didn't hold its own against most European and Japanese competitors. While it has an excellent powertrain and a quiet cabin, its ride and handling are just OK, and the rear seat is cramped.

MAJOR REDESIGN: 1992, 1998. **SAFETY EQUIPMENT:** Dual front air bags standard. Side air bags and safety-belt pretensioners standard from 1998. ABS standard. **DRIVE WHEELS:** Front.

Cadillac Fleetwood

Reliability history

TROUBLE SPOTS	95 96 97 98 99 00 01 02
Engine	
Cooling	
Fuel	
Ignition	NOT
Transmission	
Electrical	ENOUGH
Air-conditioning	
Suspension	DATA
Brakes	
Exhaust	TO
Paint/trim/rust	
Body integrity	RATE
Power equipment	
Body hardware	
RELIABILITY VERDICT	

Prices

1995	$12,000-$14,000
1996	$14,000-$16,000
1997	–
1998	–
1999	–
2000	–
2001	–
2002	–

Crash-test results

Model Years	Offset	Full frontal	Side
1995	NT	⊖/⊖	NT
1996	NT	⊖/⊖	NT
1997	–	–	–
1998	–	–	–
1999	–	–	–
2000	–	–	–
2001	–	–	–
2002	–	–	–

Cadillac Seville

Reliability history

TROUBLE SPOTS	Cadillac Seville 95 96 97 98 99 00 01 02	
Engine		
Cooling		
Fuel		
Ignition		
Transmission		
Electrical		
Air-conditioning		
Suspension		Insufficient data
Brakes		
Exhaust		
Paint/trim/rust		
Body integrity		
Power equipment		
Body hardware		
RELIABILITY VERDICT		

Prices

1995	$12,000-$14,000
1996	$14,000-$16,000
1997	$18,000-$20,000
1998	$20,000-$22,000
1999	$24,000-$26,000
2000	$28,000-$30,000
2001	More than $30,000
2002	More than $30,000

Crash-test results

Model Years	Offset	Full frontal	Side
1995	Poor	NT	NT
1996	Poor	NT	NT
1997	Poor	NT	NT
1998	NT	NT	NT
1999	NT	NT	NT
2000	Good	NT	NT
2001	Good	NT	NT
2002	Good	NT	NT

Chevrolet Astro

1999 model shown

The rear-drive Chevrolet Astro has always been better at hauling payload than at transporting people. Tall and squarish, it offers commodious cargo space, especially in extended-length versions. (As of 1995, all Astros were extended-length.) Its large-displacement V6 makes it better at towing a trailer than most minivans, and the Astro has been available with AWD for most of its long life. But on the road, the old-tech Astro suffers from clumsy handling and a harsh ride. Front-seat occupants also have far too little foot room. In 1996, the Astro received an improved instrument panel. **Related model:** GMC Safari.

MAJOR REDESIGN: 1985. **SAFETY EQUIPMENT:** Driver air bag standard; passenger air bag standard from 1996. ABS standard. **DRIVE WHEELS:** Rear or AWD.

Reliability history

TROUBLE SPOTS	Chevrolet Astro
	95 96 97 98 99 00 01 02
Engine	
Cooling	
Fuel	
Ignition	
Transmission	
Electrical	
Air conditioning	
Suspension	
Brakes	
Exhaust	
Paint/trim/rust	
Body integrity	
Power equipment	
Body hardware	
RELIABILITY VERDICT	

Prices

Year	Price
1995	$6,000-$8,000
1996	$8,000-$10,000
1997	$10,000-$12,000
1998	$10,000-$12,000
1999	$12,000-$14,000
2000	$14,000-$16,000
2001	$16,000-$18,000
2002	$18,000-$20,000

Crash-test results

Model years	Offset	Full-frontal	Side
1995	NT	NT	NT
1996	Poor	O/O	NT
1997	Poor	O/O	NT
1998	Poor	O/O	NT
1999	Poor	O/◐	NT
2000	Poor	O/◐	NT
2001	Poor	O/◐	NT
2002	Poor	O/◐	NT

Chevrolet Avalanche

2002 model shown

The Chevrolet Avalanche is basically a full-sized crew-cab truck with a unified bed and cab. An innovative "midgate" panel between the bed and passenger compartment can be folded down to make room for longer cargo items. This feature allows the Avalanche to be configured to accommodate a variety of different passenger and cargo loads. Fussing with all these pieces, however, can be a chore. Based on the Suburban it uses the same 5.3-liter V8 which provides impressive acceleration but isn't terribly economical. The ride is commendably comfortable and quiet for a truck. **Related model:** Cadillac Escalade EXT.

MAJOR REDESIGN: 2002. **SAFETY EQUIPMENT:** Dual front and side air bags standard. ABS standard. **DRIVE WHEELS:** Rear or selectable 4WD.

Reliability history

TROUBLE SPOTS	Chevrolet Avalanche
	95 96 97 98 99 00 01 02
Engine	
Cooling	
Fuel	
Ignition	
Transmission	
Electrical	
Air conditioning	
Suspension	
Brakes	
Exhaust	
Paint/trim/rust	
Body integrity	
Power equipment	
Body hardware	
RELIABILITY VERDICT	✓

Prices

Year	Price
1995	–
1996	–
1997	–
1998	–
1999	–
2000	–
2001	–
2002	$28,000-$30,000

Crash-test results

Model years	Offset	Full-frontal	Side
1995	–	–	–
1996	–	–	–
1997	–	–	–
1998	–	–	–
1999	–	–	–
2000	–	–	–
2001	–	–	–
2002	NT	O/◐	NT

SPORT-UTILITY VEHICLE
Chevrolet Blazer

1998 model shown

A 1995 redesign eliminated most of the previous version's crudities. Power was increased and ergonomics improved, but CONSUMER REPORTS testing showed that the brakes remained inferior and the body leaned a lot in hard cornering. The 1998 models received better brakes, but still had cumbersome handling, a so-so ride, and sloppy fit and finish. It also received a "Poor" rating in an IIHS offset-frontal crash test. **Related models:** GMC Jimmy, Oldsmobile Bravada. The newer TrailBlazer, which essentially replaced the Blazer, arrived in 2001 as a 2002 model.

MAJOR REDESIGN: 1995. **SAFETY EQUIPMENT:** Driver air bag standard; passenger air bag standard from 1998. ABS standard. **DRIVE WHEELS:** Rear or part-time 4WD; AWD available from 1995-1997; selectable 4WD available from 1999.

Reliability history

TROUBLE SPOTS	Chevrolet Blazer							
	95	96	97	98	99	00	01	02
Engine								
Cooling								
Fuel								
Ignition								
Transmission								
Electrical								
Air-conditioning								
Suspension								
Brakes								
Exhaust								
Paint/trim/rust								
Body integrity								
Power equipment								
Body hardware								
RELIABILITY VERDICT								

Prices

1995	$8,000-$10,000
1996	$8,000-$10,000
1997	$10,000-$12,000
1998	$12,000-$14,000
1999	$14,000-$16,000
2000	$16,000-$18,000
2001	$18,000-$20,000
2002	$20,000-$22,000

Crash-test results

Model Years	Offset	Full frontal	Side
1995	Poor	○/●	NT
1996	Poor	○/●	NT
1997	Poor	○/●	NT
1998	Poor	●/○	NT
1999	Poor	○/○	●/○
2000	Poor	○/○	●/○
2001	Poor	○/○	●/○
2002	Poor	○/○	●/○

PICKUP TRUCK
Chevrolet C/K1500, Silverado

1999 model shown

The full-sized C/K1500 pickup ("C" is used for 2WD versions, "K" for 4WD) was fundamentally unchanged from 1991 through 1998, though upgraded powertrains and an optional third door for extended-cab models were added in 1996. If this truck appeals to you, look for 1999 or later versions, when the truck was renamed Silverado. The Silverado is much improved over the dated C/K, and has powerful, efficient engines, a more inviting interior, and better braking and handling. Extended-cab models received a fourth door for 2000. **Related model:** GMC Sierra C/K1500.

MAJOR REDESIGN: 1999. **SAFETY EQUIPMENT:** Driver air bag available in 1995, standard from 1996; passenger air bag standard from 1997. ABS standard. **DRIVE WHEELS:** Rear or part-time 4WD; selectable 4WD available from 1999.

Reliability history

TROUBLE SPOTS	Chevrolet C1500, Silverado 2WD							
	95	96	97	98	99	00	01	02
Engine								
Cooling								
Fuel								
Ignition								
Transmission								
Electrical								
Air-conditioning								
Suspension								
Brakes								
Exhaust								
Paint/trim/rust								
Body integrity								
Power equipment								
Body hardware								
RELIABILITY VERDICT	✓		✓	✓	✓	✓	✓	

Prices

1995	$12,000-$14,000
1996	$12,000-$14,000
1997	$14,000-$16,000
1998	$16,000-$18,000
1999	$18,000-$20,000
2000	$20,000-$22,000
2001	$22,000-$24,000
2002	$26,000-$28,000

Crash-test results

Model Years	Offset	Full frontal	Side
1995	NT	●/○	NT
1996	NT	●/○	NT
1997	NT	●/○	NT
1998	NT	●/○	NT
1999	Marg.	NT	NT
2000	Marg.	○/●	NT
2001	Marg.	○/●	NT
2002	Marg.	○/●	NT

SPORTS/SPORTY CAR

Chevrolet Camaro

1998 model shown

The fourth generation of this American muscle car was introduced for 1993 and the nameplate ran through 2002. Initially, this rear-drive coupe was powered by either a 160-hp V6 or a 275-hp V8, though the larger engine was uprated to 285 horses for 1996. The V8 models provide good acceleration, handling, and braking. The anemic V6, clumsy access, a stiff ride, and a minuscule luggage area are low points. Updates over the years include a convertible model (1994), and a high-performance SS model (1996). Be aware that muscle cars can be hideously expensive to insure, particularly if there's a young male driver in the family. **Related model:** Pontiac Firebird.

MAJOR REDESIGN: 1993. **SAFETY EQUIPMENT:** Dual front air bags standard. ABS standard. **DRIVE WHEELS:** Rear.

LARGE CAR

Chevrolet Caprice

1995 model shown

The Chevrolet Caprice is a large rear-wheel-drive car with full-frame construction and a big V8 engine. Its most alluring feature was a pillow-smooth ride. It was available in sedan and wagon forms. In CR's tests, the Caprice handled steadily in normal driving, but was sluggish and vague in emergency maneuvers. Although available with a front bench, the interior was roomy enough for five, not six. The last few production years saw a sporty Impala SS model, with suspension upgrades that improved the handling. 1996 was its last year. **Related models:** Buick Roadmaster, Cadillac Fleetwood.

MAJOR REDESIGN: 1991. **SAFETY EQUIPMENT:** Dual front air bags standard. ABS standard. **DRIVE WHEELS:** Rear.

Reliability history — Chevrolet Camaro

TROUBLE SPOTS	95	96	97	98	99	00	01	02
Engine							Insufficient data	Insufficient data
Cooling								
Fuel								
Ignition								
Transmission								
Electrical								
Air conditioning								
Suspension								
Brakes								
Exhaust								
Paint/trim/rust								
Body integrity								
Power equipment								
Body hardware								
RELIABILITY VERDICT	✓							

Prices — Camaro

Year	Price
1995	$8,000–$10,000
1996	$10,000–$12,000
1997	$12,000–$14,000
1998	$14,000–$16,000
1999	$16,000–$18,000
2000	$18,000–$20,000
2001	$20,000–$22,000
2002	$22,000–$24,000

Crash-test results — Camaro

Model years	Offset	Full-frontal	Side
1995	NT	●/●	NT
1996	NT	●/●	NT
1997	NT	●/●	○/◐
1998	NT	◐/●	○/◐
1999	NT	◐/●	○/◐
2000	NT	◐/●	○/◐
2001	NT	◐/●	○/◐
2002	NT	◐/●	○/◐

Reliability history — Chevrolet Caprice

TROUBLE SPOTS	95	96	97	98	99	00	01	02
Engine								
Cooling								
Fuel								
Ignition								
Transmission								
Electrical								
Air conditioning								
Suspension								
Brakes								
Exhaust								
Paint/trim/rust								
Body integrity								
Power equipment								
Body hardware								
RELIABILITY VERDICT	✓							

Prices — Caprice

1995	$6,000–$8,000
1996	$8,000–$10,000
1997	–
1998	–
1999	–
2000	–
2001	–
2002	–

Crash-test results — Caprice

Model years	Offset	Full-frontal	Side
1995	NT	◐/○	NT
1996	NT	◐/○	NT
1997	–	–	–
1998	–	–	–
1999	–	–	–
2000	–	–	–
2001	–	–	–
2002	–	–	–

Chevrolet Cavalier

Chevrolet Corsica/Beretta

1997 model shown

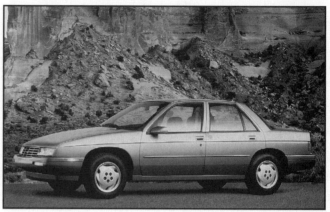

1995 model shown

The Cavalier was available in coupe, sedan, wagon, and convertible versions through 1994. Chevrolet redesigned it for 1995, dropping the wagon in the process. This version stacked up well initially, but lost a lot of ground to more-refined competition through the years. Two four-cylinder engines are available, coupled with either an inefficient three-speed or smooth four-speed automatic or a sloppy five-speed manual. The base 2.2-liter four-cylinder engine is weak and buzzy; the larger optional Four provides quick acceleration but is even less refined. Both engines were replaced by a more modern 2.2-liter Four in 2002. **Related model:** Pontiac Sunfire.

MAJOR REDESIGN: 1995. **SAFETY EQUIPMENT:** Dual front air bags standard. ABS standard. **DRIVE WHEELS:** Front.

The Corsica four-door sedan and the pseudo-sporty Beretta two-door coupe are largely unremarkable cars that changed little during their production run from 1987 to 1996. Little more than basic transportation, these models offer no surprises, good or bad. The 3.1-liter V6 is a better engine choice than the weak and noisy 2.2-liter Four. The steering feels vague, and the cars lean sharply in turns. The front seats are bearable, but the rear seats are not, especially for three passengers. Although the displays are clear, the controls are awkwardly placed and the climate-control system is weak. Both models were discontinued after 1996.

MAJOR REDESIGN: 1987. **SAFETY EQUIPMENT:** Driver air bag standard. ABS standard. **DRIVE WHEELS:** Front.

Reliability history — Chevrolet Cavalier

TROUBLE SPOTS	95	96	97	98	99	00	01	02
Engine	◐	○	○	◐	○	○	●	◐
Cooling	◐	◐	◐	○	◐	◐	●	◐
Fuel	◐	○	○	◐	◐	◐	◐	◐
Ignition	○	○	○	◐	○	◐	●	◐
Transmission	○	◐	◐	◐	●	◐	●	◐
Electrical	●	●	●	◐	◐	◐	◐	◐
Air-conditioning	◐	◐	○	◐	◐	◐	◐	◐
Suspension	◐	○	○	◐	○	◐	○	◐
Brakes	◐	◐	◐	●	◐	◐	○	◐
Exhaust	●	◐	●	◐	◐	◐	◐	●
Paint/trim/rust	◐	○	○	◐	○	◐	◐	◐
Body integrity	◐	◐	◐	◐	◐	◐	○	◐
Power equipment	◐	◐	◐	◐	◐	◐	◐	●
Body hardware	◐	◐	◐	◐	○	○	●	◐
RELIABILITY VERDICT	✔			✔	✔	✔	✔	

Prices — Chevrolet Cavalier

Year	Price
1995	$4,000–$6,000
1996	$4,000–$6,000
1997	$4,000–$6,000
1998	$6,000–$8,000
1999	$6,000–$8,000
2000	$8,000–$10,000
2001	$10,000–$12,000
2002	$10,000–$12,000

Crash-test results — Chevrolet Cavalier

Model Years	Offset	Full frontal	Side
1995	Poor	○/○	NT
1996	Poor	○/○	NT
1997	Poor	◐/○	NT
1998	Poor	◐/◐	●/○
1999	Poor	◐/◐	●/○
2000	Poor	◐/◐	●/○
2001	Poor	◐/◐	●/○
2002	Poor	◐/◐	●/○

Reliability history — Chevrolet Corsica, Beretta

TROUBLE SPOTS	95	96	97	98	99	00	01	02
Engine	●	○						
Cooling	●	◐						
Fuel	○	○						
Ignition	◐	◐						
Transmission	◐	◐						
Electrical	●	●						
Air-conditioning	●	○						
Suspension	○	○						
Brakes	●	●						
Exhaust	◐	◐						
Paint/trim/rust	○	●						
Body integrity	◐	◐						
Power equipment	◐	◐						
Body hardware	○	○						
RELIABILITY VERDICT		✔						

Prices — Chevrolet Corsica/Beretta

Year	Price
1995	$2,000–$4,000
1996	$4,000–$6,000
1997	–
1998	–
1999	–
2000	–
2001	–
2002	–

Crash-test results — Chevrolet Corsica/Beretta

Model Years	Offset	Full frontal	Side
1995	NT	○/◐	NT
1996	NT	○/◐	NT
1997	–	–	–
1998	–	–	–
1999	–	–	–
2000	–	–	–
2001	–	–	–
2002	–	–	–

SPORTS/SPORTY CAR

Chevrolet Corvette

1998 model shown

The fourth-generation Corvette was introduced in 1984 and received many refinements over the years, increasing performance and sophistication. The base model boasted 300 hp from 1992 through 1996, though a higher-performance ZR-1 reached 405 hp before fading away in 1995. In our tests, the steering was quick, but the Corvette felt too bulky to be nimble. The car was completely redesigned for 1997, gaining handling finesse and power. A convertible model of this version was added in 1998, with a fixed hardtop following in 1999. A 385-hp Z06 model joined the line in 2001, and grew to 405 hp for 2002.

MAJOR REDESIGN: 1984, 1997. **SAFETY EQUIPMENT:** Dual front air bags standard. ABS standard. **DRIVE WHEELS:** Rear.

FAMILY CAR

Chevrolet Impala

2000 model shown

The Impala was introduced for 2000 as Chevrolet's new flagship sedan, reviving a name that once graced a much larger, rear-drive car. It is a family sedan that essentially replaced the smaller Lumina. In tests, we found its performance to be just average overall. The Impala's ride and handling are sound. And while its V6 gets the job done, it isn't as smooth or refined as the V6s found in the Honda Accord, Nissan Maxima, or Toyota Camry. Head room and leg room are generous up front, and the front seats are reasonably comfortable. The rear is spacious, but the uncomfortable bench seat is too low and short. **Related model:** Chevrolet Monte Carlo.

MAJOR REDESIGN: 2000. **SAFETY EQUIPMENT:** Dual front air bags standard. Driver-only side air bag available. ABS available. **DRIVE WHEELS:** Front.

Chevrolet Corvette

Reliability history

TROUBLE SPOTS	95	96	97	98	99	00	01	02
Engine				◑	◑	○	◑	◑
Cooling				◑	◑	○	◑	◑
Fuel				◑	◑	○	◑	◑
Ignition	Insufficient data	Insufficient data	Insufficient data	◑	◑	○	◑	◑
Transmission				◑	◑	○	◑	◑
Electrical				●	◑	○	◑	◑
Air conditioning				◑	◑	○	◑	◑
Suspension				◑	◑	○	◑	◑
Brakes				◑	◑	◑	◑	◑
Exhaust				◑	◑	◑	◑	◑
Paint/trim/rust				◑	◑	◑	◑	◑
Body integrity				◑	◑	◑	◑	◑
Power equipment				◑	◑	○	◑	◑
Body hardware				◑	◑	◑	○	◑
RELIABILITY VERDICT				✓	✓			✓

Prices

1995	$18,000-$20,000
1996	$18,000-$20,000
1997	$26,000-$28,000
1998	$28,000-$30,000
1999	More than $30,000
2000	More than $30,000
2001	More than $30,000
2002	More than $30,000

Crash-test results

Model years	Offset	Full-frontal	Side
1995	NT	NT	NT
1996	NT	NT	NT
1997	NT	NT	NT
1998	NT	NT	NT
1999	NT	NT	NT
2000	NT	NT	NT
2001	NT	NT	NT
2002	NT	NT	NT

Chevrolet Impala

Reliability history

TROUBLE SPOTS	95	96	97	98	99	00	01	02
Engine						◑	◑	●
Cooling						◑	◑	●
Fuel						◑	◑	●
Ignition						◑	◑	●
Transmission						◑	◑	●
Electrical						○	◑	●
Air conditioning						◑	◑	●
Suspension						○	◑	●
Brakes						○	◑	●
Exhaust						●	●	●
Paint/trim/rust						◑	●	●
Body integrity						○	◑	●
Power equipment						◑	◑	●
Body hardware						◑	◑	◑
RELIABILITY VERDICT						✓	✓	✓

Prices

1995	–
1996	–
1997	–
1998	–
1999	–
2000	$12,000-$14,000
2001	$14,000-$16,000
2002	$16,000-$18,000

Crash-test results

Model years	Offset	Full-frontal	Side
1995	–	–	–
1996	–	–	–
1997	–	–	–
1998	–	–	–
1999	–	–	–
2000	Good	◑/◑	◑/◑
2001	Good	◑/◑	◑/◑
2002	Good	◑/◑	◑/◑

FAMILY CAR
Chevrolet Lumina

1997 model shown

Redesigned for 1995, the Lumina became a nicely equipped family sedan that performed competently, but not outstandingly, in CR's tests. It has a good ride and a smooth powertrain, and is very quiet and fairly roomy inside. The seats, however, are mediocre. Most Luminas you'll see were equipped with a 160-hp 3.1-liter V6. A few came with the upgrade 3.4-liter 215-hp version. The Lumina was discontinued after 2000, replaced by the significantly better Impala. **Related model:** Chevrolet Monte Carlo.

MAJOR REDESIGN: 1995. **SAFETY EQUIPMENT:** Dual front air bags standard. ABS available. **DRIVE WHEELS:** Front.

MINIVAN
Chevrolet Lumina, Venture

1997 model shown

Introduced for 1990, the early Lumina APVs were competent minivans, with distinctive styling and innovative plastic body panels. A mild 1994 redesign brought a handy optional electric sliding side door, and the "APV" label was dropped. The Lumina van was replaced for 1997 by the Chevrolet Venture, available in standard- and extended-wheelbase versions. Though generally competent, the Venture scored poorly in an insurance-industry offset-crash test, and its reliability has been subpar. **Related models:** Oldsmobile Silhouette, Pontiac Trans Sport/Montana.

MAJOR REDESIGN: 1994, 1997. **SAFETY EQUIPMENT:** Driver air bag standard; passenger air bag standard from 1997. Side air bags standard from 1999. ABS standard. Safety-belt pretensioners standard from 1999. **DRIVE WHEELS:** Front. AWD available from 2002.

Reliability history — Chevrolet Lumina

Trouble spots (model years 95 96 97 98 99 00 01 02): Engine, Cooling, Fuel, Ignition, Transmission, Electrical, Air-conditioning, Suspension, Brakes, Exhaust, Paint/trim/rust, Body integrity, Power equipment, Body hardware. Insufficient data for 00 01 02.

RELIABILITY VERDICT: ✓ 95, ✓ 96, ✓ 97, ✓ 98, ✓ 99

Prices — Chevrolet Lumina

Year	Price
1995	$4,000-$6,000
1996	$4,000-$6,000
1997	$6,000-$8,000
1998	$8,000-$10,000
1999	$8,000-$10,000
2000	$10,000-$12,000
2001	–
2002	–

Crash-test results — Chevrolet Lumina

Model Years	Offset	Full frontal	Side
1995	Good	◕/○	NT
1996	Good	◕/○	NT
1997	Good	◕/○	◕/○
1998	Good	○/◕	◕/○
1999	Good	◕/○	◕/○
2000	Good	◕/○	◕/○
2001	–	–	–
2002	–	–	–

Reliability history — Chevrolet Lumina Van, Venture (reg.)

Trouble spots (model years 95 96 97 98 99 00 01 02): Engine, Cooling, Fuel, Ignition, Transmission, Electrical, Air-conditioning, Suspension, Brakes, Exhaust, Paint/trim/rust, Body integrity, Power equipment, Body hardware. Insufficient data for 01 02.

RELIABILITY VERDICT: ✓ 96, ✓ 97, ✓ 98, ✓ 00

Prices — Chevrolet Lumina, Venture

Year	Price
1995	$4,000-$6,000
1996	$6,000-$8,000
1997	$8,000-$10,000
1998	$10,000-$12,000
1999	$12,000-$14,000
2000	$14,000-$16,000
2001	$14,000-$16,000
2002	$18,000-$20,000

Crash-test results — Chevrolet Lumina, Venture

Model Years	Offset	Full frontal	Side
1995	NT	◕/○	NT
1996	NT	◕/○	NT
1997	Poor	◕/○	NT
1998	Poor	◕/○	NT
1999	Poor	◕/○	◕/○
2000	Poor	◕/○	◕/○
2001	Poor	◕/○	◕/○
2002	Poor	◕/○	◕/○

FAMILY CAR
Chevrolet Malibu

1997 model shown

The Malibu is a good deal less refined than its mainstream Japanese competition, but it is not without some basic strengths. It has a roomy interior, with well-placed controls and displays, though many interior fittings feel insubstantial and cheap. The trunk is large, and the rear seatback folds down to expand it further. The Malibu delivers sound handling and a firm, controlled ride. A noisy 2.4-liter four-cylinder served as the base engine through 1999, at which time the previously optional 3.1-liter V6 became the sole powerplant. **Related model:** Oldsmobile Cutlass.

MAJOR REDESIGN: 1997. **SAFETY EQUIPMENT:** Dual front air bags standard. ABS standard. **DRIVE WHEELS:** Front.

COUPE
Chevrolet Monte Carlo

2000 model shown

Chevrolet resurrected the Monte Carlo nameplate for 1995 as the name for the coupe version of the redesigned Lumina sedan. The Z34 version's "sporty" suspension is too stiff on small bumps and too soft on big ones; the LS version rides better. Handling is sloppy and the ride is bounding on rough roads. The Monte Carlo offers generous space up front, but the rear seat barely accommodates two tall people. A 2000 redesign was based on that year's Impala. Acceleration is strong with the 3.8-liter V6, but road noise is prominent. Overall, these cars provide an underwhelming driving experience. **Related models:** Chevrolet Lumina, Chevrolet Impala.

MAJOR REDESIGN: 1995, 2000. **SAFETY EQUIPMENT:** Dual front air bags standard. Driver-only side air bag available from 2001. ABS standard. **DRIVE WHEELS:** Front.

Chevrolet Malibu

Reliability history

TROUBLE SPOTS	95	96	97	98	99	00	01	02
Engine			○	●	●	◐	◐	●
Cooling			◐	◐	●	◐	●	●
Fuel			○	●	◐	○	◐	●
Ignition			●	●	●	◐	◐	●
Transmission			●	●	●	◐	●	●
Electrical			●	●	●	○	○	◐
Air conditioning			○	◐	●	◐	◐	●
Suspension			○	○	◐	◐	●	●
Brakes			●	●	●	●	○	○
Exhaust			●	◐	●	●	◐	●
Paint/trim/rust			◐	●	◐	◐	○	●
Body integrity			○	◐	○	○	○	●
Power equipment			◐	○	◐	○	●	●
Body hardware			○	○	○	◐	○	●
RELIABILITY VERDICT							✓	✓

Prices

1995	–
1996	–
1997	$6,000-$8,000
1998	$6,000-$8,000
1999	$8,000-$10,000
2000	$10,000-$12,000
2001	$12,000-$14,000
2002	$14,000-$16,000

Crash-test results

Model years	Offset	Full-frontal	Side
1995	–	–	–
1996	–	–	–
1997	Accept.	◐/◑	●/○
1998	Accept.	◐/◑	●/○
1999	Accept.	◐/◑	●/○
2000	Accept.	◐/◑	◐/○
2001	Accept.	◐/◑	○/○
2002	Accept.	◐/◑	○/◐

Chevrolet Monte Carlo

Reliability history

TROUBLE SPOTS	95	96	97	98	99	00	01	02
Engine	●					◐	●	●
Cooling	○					◐	●	●
Fuel	◐				○	◐	●	●
Ignition	◐					◐	●	●
Transmission	○				◐	●	●	●
Electrical	●	Insufficient data	Insufficient data	Insufficient data	○	○	○	Insufficient data
Air conditioning	◐				●	◐	●	
Suspension	○				◐	◐	●	
Brakes	◐				◐	○	●	
Exhaust	◐				●	◐	●	
Paint/trim/rust	●				●	◐	●	
Body integrity	◐				○	◐	●	
Power equipment	◐				◐	◐	●	
Body hardware	●				○	○	○	
RELIABILITY VERDICT					✓	✓	✓	

Prices

1995	$4,000-$6,000
1996	$6,000-$8,000
1997	$6,000-$8,000
1998	$8,000-$10,000
1999	$10,000-$12,000
2000	$14,000-$16,000
2001	$14,000-$16,000
2002	$16,000-$18,000

Crash-test results

Model years	Offset	Full-frontal	Side
1995	NT	◑/◑	NT
1996	NT	◑/◑	NT
1997	NT	◑/◑	NT
1998	NT	◑/◑	NT
1999	NT	◑/◑	NT
2000	NT	NT	NT
2001	NT	◐/◑	○/◑
2002	NT	◐/◑	○/◐

Chevrolet S-10

Chevrolet Suburban

1998 model shown

2000 model shown

The compact S-Series trucks are available in a variety of bed and cab configurations. Handling is predictably trucklike, with the S-10 exhibiting a surplus of body lean in corners. The steering is heavy and vague, and the brakes provided subpar stopping power in our tests. The S-10 rides stiffly without a load, but smooths out considerably when fully laden. In 1997, extended-cab versions gained a driver-side third door useful for loading cargo. A four-door crew-cab model followed in 2001. Subpar crash-test results detract from the package. **Related models:** GMC Sonoma, Isuzu Hombre.

MAJOR REDESIGN: 1994. SAFETY EQUIPMENT: Driver air bag standard; passenger air bag standard from 1998. Four-wheel ABS available from 1995, standard from 1996. DRIVE WHEELS: Rear or part-time 4WD.

GM's largest SUV, the Suburban emphasizes "utility." It seats up to nine people, and hauls massive cargo loads. Available in 2WD and 4WD, the Suburban shares its basic platform and V8 powertrain lineup with GM's pickups. In our tests, power was strong, but the brakes were awful. The big SUV was redesigned for 2000 and a 2001 model would be the preferred choice. This updated version rides better, handles commendably, and brakes well. Motivation is provided by a powerful-but-thirsty 5.3-liter V8, allied with a smooth automatic. **Related models:** GMC Suburban, GMC Yukon XL.

MAJOR REDESIGN: 2000. SAFETY EQUIPMENT: Driver air bag standard; passenger air bag standard from 1997. Side air bags standard from 2000. ABS standard. DRIVE WHEELS: Rear or part-time 4WD through 1997; rear or selectable 4WD from 1998.

Reliability history — Chevrolet S-10 V6 2WD

TROUBLE SPOTS	95	96	97	98	99	00	01	02
Engine								
Cooling								
Fuel								
Ignition								
Transmission								
Electrical								
Air-conditioning								
Suspension								
Brakes								
Exhaust								
Paint/trim/rust								
Body integrity								
Power equipment								
Body hardware								
RELIABILITY VERDICT	✓							✓

(Insufficient data)

Prices

Year	Price
1995	$6,000-$8,000
1996	$6,000-$8,000
1997	$8,000-$10,000
1998	$8,000-$10,000
1999	$10,000-$12,000
2000	$10,000-$12,000
2001	$12,000-$14,000
2002	$14,000-$16,000

Crash-test results

Model Years	Offset	Full frontal	Side
1995	NT	○/●	NT
1996	NT	○/●	NT
1997	NT	○/◖	NT
1998	Marg.	◖/◖	NT
1999	Marg.	◖/○	○/NA
2000	Marg.	◖/○	○/NA
2001	Marg.	◖/○	○/NA
2002	Marg.	◖/○	○/NA

Reliability history — Chevrolet Suburban

TROUBLE SPOTS	95	96	97	98	99	00	01	02
Engine								
Cooling								
Fuel								
Ignition								
Transmission								
Electrical								
Air-conditioning								
Suspension								
Brakes								
Exhaust								
Paint/trim/rust								
Body integrity								
Power equipment								
Body hardware								
RELIABILITY VERDICT	✓					✓	✓	

Prices

Year	Price
1995	$14,000-$16,000
1996	$14,000-$16,000
1997	$16,000-$18,000
1998	$18,000-$20,000
1999	$20,000-$22,000
2000	$26,000-$28,000
2001	$28,000-$30,000
2002	More than $30,000

Crash-test results

Model Years	Offset	Full frontal	Side
1995	NT	NT	NT
1996	NT	NT	NT
1997	NT	NT	NT
1998	NT	◖/◖	NT
1999	NT	◖/◖	NT
2000	NT	NT	NT
2001	NT	◖/◖	NT
2002	NT	◖/◖	NT

Chevrolet Tahoe

2000 model shown

This full-sized SUV was once known as the K Blazer but in 1995 it was renamed Tahoe and became a four-door as well as a two-door. Although shorter than the Suburban, the Tahoe still has a cavernous cargo bay. In our tests, we found that the Tahoe rode and handled quite well, but braking was mediocre, and fuel economy was dismal. Redesigned for 2000, the Tahoe improved all around, gaining strong, efficient new engines, better handling, and a superior ride. Optional third-row seating provides room for up to nine. **Related models:** GMC Yukon, Cadillac Escalade.

MAJOR REDESIGN: 1995, 2000. **SAFETY EQUIPMENT:** Driver air bag standard; passenger air bag standard from 1997. Side air bags standard from 2000. ABS standard. **DRIVE WHEELS:** Rear or part-time 4WD through 1997; rear or selectable 4WD from 1998.

Reliability history

TROUBLE SPOTS	Chevrolet Tahoe 95 96 97 98 99 00 01 02
Engine	○ ○ ○ ○ ○ ● ● ●
Cooling	◐ ○ ○ ○ ○ ● ● ●
Fuel	● ◐ ◐ ○ ○ ○ ● ●
Ignition	○ ◐ ● ● ◐ ● ● ●
Transmission	◐ ◐ ◐ ○ ○ ● ● ○
Electrical	● ● ● ○ ○ ○ ◐ ◐
Air conditioning	◐ ◐ ○ ◐ ◐ ● ● ●
Suspension	○ ○ ○ ○ ◐ ● ● ●
Brakes	● ● ● ● ● ○ ◐ ●
Exhaust	○ ● ● ● ● ● ● ●
Paint/trim/rust	○ ◐ ● ◐ ● ● ● ○
Body integrity	○ ○ ◐ ◐ ● ◐ ○ ○
Power equipment	○ ○ ◐ ● ◐ ● ◐ ●
Body hardware	● ○ ○ ◐ ○ ◐ ◐ ○
RELIABILITY VERDICT	✓ ✓ ✓ ✓ ✓

Prices

1995	$12,000-$14,000
1996	$14,000-$16,000
1997	$16,000-$18,000
1998	$18,000-$20,000
1999	$20,000-$22,000
2000	$26,000-$28,000
2001	$26,000-$28,000
2002	More than $30,000

Crash-test results

Model years	Offset	Full-frontal	Side
1995	NT	NT	NT
1996	NT	◐/○	NT
1997	NT	◐/◐	NT
1998	NT	◐/◐	NT
1999	NT	◐/◐	NT
2000	NT	○/◐	NT
2001	NT	○/◐	NT
2002	NT	○/◐	NT

Chevrolet TrailBlazer

2002 model shown

This midsized SUV was introduced in spring 2001 as a 2002 model. The TrailBlazer accelerates enthusiastically and offers a compliant, if slightly jiggly, ride. Its handling, however, is ungainly, with excessive body lean and slow steering. A stability-control system might help tame the twitchy rear end, but none is offered. Braking is also unimpressive. The TrailBlazer's interior is mostly quiet, but wind noise is pronounced. Front-seat comfort is only mediocre, and the seat-mounted front safety belts are a nuisance. First-year reliability was poor. **Related models:** GMC Envoy, Oldsmobile Bravada.

MAJOR REDESIGN: 2002. **SAFETY EQUIPMENT:** Dual front and side air bags standard. ABS standard. **DRIVE WHEELS:** Rear or selectable 4WD.

Reliability history

TROUBLE SPOTS	Chevrolet TrailBlazer 95 96 97 98 99 00 01 02
Engine	●
Cooling	●
Fuel	●
Ignition	●
Transmission	●
Electrical	●
Air conditioning	●
Suspension	○
Brakes	●
Exhaust	●
Paint/trim/rust	●
Body integrity	○
Power equipment	●
Body hardware	●
RELIABILITY VERDICT	

Prices

1995	–
1996	–
1997	–
1998	–
1999	–
2000	–
2001	–
2002	$28,000-$30,000

Crash-test results

Model years	Offset	Full-frontal	Side
1995	–	–	–
1996	–	–	–
1997	–	–	–
1998	–	–	–
1999	–	–	–
2000	–	–	–
2001	–	–	–
2002	Marg.	○/○	●/○

SMALL CAR
Chevrolet/Geo Metro

1998 model shown

The diminutive Metro, built by Suzuki, is more at home as an around-town runabout than on the interstates. The gutless three-cylinder engine and cramped interior are fatiguing on long trips. The Metro became a little roomier with its 1995 redesign, but it remained one of the smallest cars on the road. A more powerful four-cylinder engine became available for the 1995 sedan, while the hatchback continued to use the 1.0-liter Three. The ride remained choppy and noisy. When the Geo line was discontinued after 1997, the Metro was rebadged as a Chevrolet. The Metro was dropped after the 2000 model year. **Related model:** Suzuki Swift.

MAJOR REDESIGN: 1995. **SAFETY EQUIPMENT:** Dual front air bags standard. ABS available. **DRIVE WHEELS:** Front.

Reliability history

TROUBLE SPOTS	Chevrolet/Geo Metro							
	95	96	97	98	99	00	01	02
Engine	◓							
Cooling	◓							
Fuel	●							
Ignition	◓							
Transmission	◓	Insufficient data	Insufficient data	Insufficient data	Insufficient data	Insufficient data		
Electrical	○							
Air-conditioning	●							
Suspension	●							
Brakes	○							
Exhaust	○							
Paint/trim/rust	○							
Body integrity	○							
Power equipment	●							
Body hardware	○							
RELIABILITY VERDICT	✔							

Prices

1995	$2,000-$4,000
1996	$2,000-$4,000
1997	$4,000-$6,000
1998	$4,000-$6,000
1999	$6,000-$8,000
2000	$6,000-$8,000
2001	–
2002	–

Crash-test results

Model Years	Offset	Full frontal	Side
1995	NT	⊖/⊖	NT
1996	NT	⊖/⊖	NT
1997	NT	⊖/⊖	NT
1998	NT	⊖/⊖	NT
1999	NT	⊖/⊖	NT
2000	NT	⊖/⊖	NT
2001	–	–	–
2002	–	–	–

SMALL CAR
Chevrolet/Geo Prizm

1998 model shown

The Chevrolet/Geo Prizm is essentially a California-built Toyota Corolla. The Prizm is a good sedan that depreciated faster than its Corolla cousin. Redesigned and badged a Chevrolet in 1998, the Prizm grew more refined. It rides quite comfortably and quietly, accelerates with reasonable urgency, and gets good fuel economy. Suspension changes for 1999 improved the tricky emergency handling we found when testing the 1998 model. The Prizm's exemplary reliability record is a major advantage, but the interior isn't as well trimmed as the Corolla's. The Prizm was dropped after the 2002 model year. **Related model:** Toyota Corolla.

MAJOR REDESIGN: 1993, 1998. **SAFETY EQUIPMENT:** Dual front air bags standard. Side air bags available from 1998. Safety-belt pretensioners standard from 1998. ABS available. **DRIVE WHEELS:** Front.

Reliability history

TROUBLE SPOTS	Chevrolet/Geo Prizm							
	95	96	97	98	99	00	01	02
Engine	●	●	●	●	●	●	●	●
Cooling	●	●	●	●	●	●	●	●
Fuel	●	●	●	◓	◓	●	●	●
Ignition	◓	●	●	●	●	●	●	●
Transmission	●	●	◓	●	●	●	●	●
Electrical	●	○	○	●	◓	●	●	●
Air-conditioning	◓	●	●	●	●	●	●	●
Suspension	◓	◓	◓	●	●	◓	●	●
Brakes	○	○	◓	●	●	●	●	●
Exhaust	●	●	●	●	●	●	●	●
Paint/trim/rust	◓	○	●	●	●	●	●	●
Body integrity	●	●	●	●	●	●	●	●
Power equipment	●	●	●	●	◓	●	●	●
Body hardware	○	◓	◓	●	●	◓	●	●
RELIABILITY VERDICT	✔	✔	✔	✔	✔	✔	✔	✔

Prices

1995	$4,000-$6,000
1996	$4,000-$6,000
1997	$6,000-$8,000
1998	$6,000-$8,000
1999	$8,000-$10,000
2000	$8,000-$10,000
2001	$10,000-$12,000
2002	$12,000-$14,000

Crash-test results

Model Years	Offset	Full frontal	Side
1995	NT	⊖/⊖	NT
1996	NT	⊖/⊖	NT
1997	NT	⊖/⊖	○/○
1998	Accept.	⊖/⊖	○/○
1999	Accept.	⊖/⊖	○/○
2000	Accept.	⊖/⊖	○/○
2001	Accept.	⊖/⊖	○/○
2002	Accept.	⊖/⊖	○/○

Chevrolet/Geo Tracker

Chrysler 300M

1998 model shown

1999 model shown

This small and uncomfortable SUV is built by Suzuki, with pre-'99 models using parts from the Suzuki Sidekick. The four-cylinder engine provided just adequate power in our tests, and the ride was punishing. Initially, the Tracker was available as a two-door hardtop or a convertible, but a four-door version was added for 1996. When GM abandoned the Geo brand in 1998, the Tracker migrated to the Chevrolet line. Redesigned for 1999 (as a rebadged Suzuki Vitara), the Tracker remains relatively basic and trucklike compared to most modern competitors. A 2.5-liter V6 was new for 2001. **Related models:** Suzuki Sidekick, Suzuki Vitara.

MAJOR REDESIGN: 1999. **SAFETY EQUIPMENT:** Dual front air bags standard from 1996. Rear-wheel ABS standard; four-wheel ABS available from 1996. **DRIVE WHEELS:** Rear or part-time 4WD.

In 1999, Chrysler resurrected the 300-letter-series badging—last used in the 1960s—as a name for this upscale sibling of the roomy Dodge Intrepid and Chrysler Concorde. The 300M was intended to appeal to "near luxury" car buyers who might otherwise have considered an Acura 3.2TL or a Lexus ES300. It distinguishes itself with a strong 3.5-liter V6 and an optional suspension system tuned for more responsive handling. On the downside, road noise is pronounced, the brake pedal is spongy, and the interior appointments lack a high-quality feel. **Related models:** Chrysler Concorde, Chrysler LHS, Dodge Intrepid.

MAJOR REDESIGN: 1999. **SAFETY EQUIPMENT:** Dual front air bags standard. Side air bags available from 2001. ABS standard. **DRIVE WHEELS:** Front.

Reliability history — Chevrolet/Geo Tracker

TROUBLE SPOTS (model years 95 96 97 98 99 00 01 02):
Engine, Cooling, Fuel, Ignition, Transmission, Electrical, Air conditioning, Suspension, Brakes, Exhaust, Paint/trim/rust, Body integrity, Power equipment, Body hardware. (Insufficient data for model years 97, 98, 99, and 02.) RELIABILITY VERDICT: ✓ recommended 95, 96, 00.

Prices — Chevrolet/Geo Tracker

Year	Price
1995	$4,000-$6,000
1996	$4,000-$6,000
1997	$6,000-$8,000
1998	$6,000-$8,000
1999	$10,000-$12,000
2000	$10,000-$12,000
2001	$12,000-$14,000
2002	$14,000-$16,000

Crash-test results — Chevrolet/Geo Tracker

Model years	Offset	Full-frontal	Side
1995	NT	◐/○	NT
1996	NT	◐/○	NT
1997	NT	◐/○	NT
1998	NT	NT	NT
1999	Accept.	NT	NT
2000	Accept.	NT	NT
2001	Accept.	◐/◐	◐/○
2002	Accept.	◐/◐	◐/○

Reliability history — Chrysler 300M

TROUBLE SPOTS (model years 95 96 97 98 99 00 01 02):
Engine, Cooling, Fuel, Ignition, Transmission, Electrical, Air conditioning, Suspension, Brakes, Exhaust, Paint/trim/rust, Body integrity, Power equipment, Body hardware. (Data begins 1999.) RELIABILITY VERDICT: ✓ recommended 00, 01.

Prices — Chrysler 300M

Year	Price
1995	–
1996	–
1997	–
1998	–
1999	$16,000-$18,000
2000	$20,000-$22,000
2001	$22,000-$24,000
2002	$26,000-$28,000

Crash-test results — Chrysler 300M

Model years	Offset	Full-frontal	Side
1995	–	–	–
1996	–	–	–
1997	–	–	–
1998	–	–	–
1999	Poor	NT	NT
2000	Poor	○/◐	NT
2001	Accept.	○/◐	NT
2002	Accept.	○/◐	◐/○

Chrysler Cirrus

1998 model shown

This midsized sedan was introduced for 1995. The interior is relatively spacious and offers roomy seating. The displays are also first-rate. The base engine is a noisy 2.4-liter, 150-hp four-cylinder cadged from the Neon parts bin. The optional 2.5-liter, 168-hp V6 accelerates nicely and is much more refined. In some model years, only the V6 was available. In our tests, the Cirrus suffered from subpar braking and an unresponsive automatic transmission. The ride feels jittery, but handling is secure. The Cirrus received a revised suspension for 1999, and was replaced by a reborn Sebring for 2001. **Related models:** Dodge Stratus, Plymouth Breeze.

MAJOR REDESIGN: 1995. **SAFETY EQUIPMENT:** Dual front air bags standard. ABS available. **DRIVE WHEELS:** Front.

Reliability history

TROUBLE SPOTS — Chrysler Cirrus V6 (95 96 97 98 99 00 01 02)

- Engine
- Cooling
- Fuel
- Ignition
- Transmission
- Electrical
- Air-conditioning
- Suspension
- Brakes
- Exhaust
- Paint/trim/rust
- Body integrity
- Power equipment
- Body hardware
- RELIABILITY VERDICT

Prices

Year	Price
1995	$4,000-$6,000
1996	$6,000-$8,000
1997	$6,000-$8,000
1998	$8,000-$10,000
1999	$10,000-$12,000
2000	$12,000-$14,000
2001	–
2002	–

Crash-test results

Model Years	Offset	Full frontal	Side
1995	Poor	O/NA	NT
1996	Poor	O/NA	NT
1997	Poor	O/NA	O/●
1998	Poor	O/●	O/●
1999	Poor	O/●	O/●
2000	Poor	O/●	O/●
2001	–		
2002	–		

Chrysler Concorde

1998 model shown

The Concorde was introduced as a 1993 model, serving as the most upscale of Chrysler's three large "LH" sedans. It handled surprisingly nimbly for a big car and offered a fairly placid ride. The interior is well laid out, with seating for five and generous trunk space. Despite the positives, this car doesn't age well and reliability is subpar, and its V6 engine is too noisy when revved. The current version, introduced for 1998, is roomy and nimble, but very noisy inside. The 3.2-liter V6 lacks refinement, and the standard 2.7-liter V6 is even worse. **Related models:** Chrysler 300M, Chrysler LHS/New Yorker, Dodge Intrepid, Eagle Vision.

MAJOR REDESIGN: 1993, 1998. **SAFETY EQUIPMENT:** Dual front air bags standard. Side air bags available from 2001. ABS standard through 1996; available from 1997. **DRIVE WHEELS:** Front.

Reliability history

TROUBLE SPOTS — Chrysler Concorde (95 96 97 98 99 00 01 02)

- Engine
- Cooling
- Fuel
- Ignition
- Transmission
- Electrical
- Air-conditioning
- Suspension
- Brakes
- Exhaust
- Paint/trim/rust
- Body integrity
- Power equipment
- Body hardware
- RELIABILITY VERDICT

Prices

Year	Price
1995	$6,000-$8,000
1996	$6,000-$8,000
1997	$8,000-$10,000
1998	$10,000-$12,000
1999	$12,000-$14,000
2000	$14,000-$16,000
2001	$16,000-$18,000
2002	$18,000-$20,000

Crash-test results

Model Years	Offset	Full frontal	Side
1995	NT	●/●	NT
1996	NT	●/●	NT
1997	NT	●/●	●/○
1998	NT	NT	NT
1999	NT	●/●	NT
2000	Marg.	●/●	●/○
2001	Accept.	●/●	●/○
2002	Accept.	●/●	●/○

Chrysler New Yorker/LHS

1999 model shown

Introduced in 1994, these models are five inches longer than the Chrysler "LH" cars on which they are based. The LHS, with individual front seats, can accommodate five very comfortably. The virtually identical New Yorker has a front bench and can seat six. These models handle nimbly and ride comfortably, though they prove noisy. The New Yorker was discontinued after 1995. Redesigned for 1999, the well-equipped LHS is a luxury cruiser. The standard 3.5-liter, 253-hp V6 is powerful but unrefined. **Related models:** Chrysler 300M, Chrysler Concorde, Dodge Intrepid, Eagle Vision.

MAJOR REDESIGN: 1994, 1999. **SAFETY EQUIPMENT:** Dual front air bags standard. Side air bags available from 2001. ABS standard. **DRIVE WHEELS:** Front.

Chrysler PT Cruiser

2001 model shown

Introduced for the 2001 model year, the PT Cruiser is a tall front-drive wagon dressed in modish retro-rod sheet metal. Strengths include a versatile interior, easy access, and secure, predictable handling. The brakes also work very well. Acceleration is disappointing, however, especially in models equipped with an automatic transmission, and the Cruiser's wide turning circle hinders maneuverability. The ride is also a bit stiff, and the cabin rather noisy. Mediocre fuel economy is another concern. The 2001 Cruiser did poorly in a government frontal-crash test, but had improved by its second go at the test a year or so later. Reliability has been very good so far.

MAJOR REDESIGN: 2001. **SAFETY EQUIPMENT:** Dual front air bags standard. Side air bags and ABS available. Safety-belt pretensioners standard. **DRIVE WHEELS:** Front.

Chrysler New Yorker/LHS

Reliability history

TROUBLE SPOTS	95	96	97	98	99	00	01	02
Engine	○	◗	○		◑	●		
Cooling	●	●	●		◑	●		
Fuel	◗	○	○		◑	●		
Ignition	○	○	◑		◑	◑		
Transmission	●	◗	◑		◑	●		
Electrical	◗	○	○		◑	●		
Air conditioning	●	●	●		◑	●		
Suspension	●	●	◗		◑	●		
Brakes	●	◑	◗		◑	◑		
Exhaust	◑	◑	◗		◑	●		
Paint/trim/rust	◗	○	○		◑	○		
Body integrity	◗	○	◑		◑	○		
Power equipment	○	○	◑		◑	○		
Body hardware	○	○	○		◑	○		
RELIABILITY VERDICT						✓		

Insufficient data (98, 01, 02)

Prices

1995	$6,000-$8,000
1996	$8,000-$10,000
1997	$10,000-$12,000
1998	–
1999	$14,000-$16,000
2000	$18,000-$20,000
2001	$20,000-$22,000
2002	–

Crash-test results

Model years	Offset	Full-frontal	Side
1995	NT	◑/○	NT
1996	NT	◑/○	NT
1997	NT	◑/○	NT
1998	–	–	–
1999	Poor	NT	NT
2000	Poor	○/◑	◑/○
2001	Accept.	○/◑	◑/○
2002	–	–	–

Chrysler PT Cruiser

Reliability history

TROUBLE SPOTS	95	96	97	98	99	00	01	02
Engine							◑	●
Cooling							◑	●
Fuel							◑	●
Ignition							◑	●
Transmission							◑	●
Electrical							◗	●
Air conditioning							◑	●
Suspension							◑	●
Brakes							◗	●
Exhaust							◑	●
Paint/trim/rust							◑	●
Body integrity							◑	●
Power equipment							◑	●
Body hardware							◗	●
RELIABILITY VERDICT							✓	✓

Prices

1995	–
1996	–
1997	–
1998	–
1999	–
2000	–
2001	$16,000-$18,000
2002	$20,000-$22,000

Crash-test results

Model years	Offset	Full-frontal	Side
1995	–	–	–
1996	–	–	–
1997	–	–	–
1998	–	–	–
1999	–	–	–
2000	–	–	–
2001	NT	○/◑	◑/○
2002	NT	◑/○	◑/○

Chrysler Sebring

2001 model shown

The Sebring debuted for 1995 as a two-door coupe. Handling is competent and predictable. Look for a model equipped with the 2.5-liter V6 instead of the 2.0-liter Four. A 2001 redesign has the sedan and convertible sharing a platform with the Dodge Stratus sedan, and the Sebring coupe using parts from the Mitsubishi Eclipse. The V6-powered LX sedan we tested accelerated quickly and handled securely, but its ride was stiff, and access was difficult. **Related models:** Dodge Avenger, Dodge Stratus from 2001.

MAJOR REDESIGN: 1995, 2001. **SAFETY EQUIPMENT:** Dual front air bags standard. Head protection air bags available from 2001. Safety-belt pretensioners standard from 2001. ABS standard in 1995 and 1996; available from 1997. **DRIVE WHEELS:** Front.

Reliability history

TROUBLE SPOTS	Chrysler Sebring V6							
	95	96	97	98	99	00	01	02
Engine							●	●
Cooling							●	●
Fuel							●	●
Ignition							●	●
Transmission							●	●
Electrical	Insufficient data	Insufficient data	Insufficient data	Insufficient data	Insufficient data	Insufficient data	○	●
Air-conditioning							●	●
Suspension							●	●
Brakes							●	●
Exhaust							●	●
Paint/trim/rust							●	●
Body integrity							○	●
Power equipment							●	●
Body hardware							●	●
RELIABILITY VERDICT								✔

Prices

1995	$6,000-$8,000
1996	$6,000-$8,000
1997	$8,000-$10,000
1998	$10,000-$12,000
1999	$10,000-$12,000
2000	$12,000-$14,000
2001	$12,000-$14,000
2002	$14,000-$16,000

Crash-test results

Model Years	Offset	Full frontal	Side
1995	NT	○/●	NT
1996	NT	○/●	NT
1997	NT	○/●	NT
1998	NT	○/●	NT
1999	NT	○/●	NT
2000	NT	○/●	NT
2001	Accept.	○/●	○/○
2002	Accept.	○/●	○/○

Chrysler Sebring Convertible

1996 model shown

Although it shares its name with the Sebring coupe, the first iteration of this convertible has more in common with the Chrysler Cirrus sedan. Introduced for 1996, it offers fairly good accommodations, including front safety belts that retract into the seatbacks, easing rear access. The Sebring convertible is among the largest modern droptops, with a fairly roomy rear seat. As with the Sebring coupe, the V6 is a better engine choice than the Four. The ride is jittery, and handling is predictable but not crisp. For 2001, the Sebring convertible moved to the new Sebring/Stratus sedan platform, and a 2.7-liter V6 became standard.

MAJOR REDESIGN: 1996, 2001. **SAFETY EQUIPMENT:** Dual front air bags standard. ABS available. **DRIVE WHEELS:** Front.

Reliability history

TROUBLE SPOTS	Chrysler Sebring Convertible							
	95	96	97	98	99	00	01	02
Engine		○	◐	●	●	●	●	●
Cooling		◐	◐	●	●	●	●	●
Fuel		●	○	○	◐	●	●	●
Ignition		○	◐	◐	●	◐	●	●
Transmission		○	◐	●	◐	●	●	●
Electrical		◐	●	●	◐	○	○	○
Air-conditioning		○	○	○	◐	●	●	●
Suspension		◐	○	◐	◐	●	●	●
Brakes		●	●	○	◐	◐	●	●
Exhaust		◐	●	◐	●	●	●	●
Paint/trim/rust		○	○	○	◐	●	●	●
Body integrity		●	◐	◐	●	◐	●	○
Power equipment		◐	◐	○	◐	●	●	●
Body hardware		○	◐	○	○	○	○	●
RELIABILITY VERDICT		✔	✔		✔		✔	

Prices

1995	–
1996	$8,000-$10,000
1997	$8,000-$10,000
1998	$10,000-$12,000
1999	$14,000-$16,000
2000	$14,000-$16,000
2001	$18,000-$20,000
2002	$20,000-$22,000

Crash-test results

Model Years	Offset	Full frontal	Side
1995	–	–	–
1996	NT	○/●	NT
1997	NT	○/●	NT
1998	NT	○/●	NT
1999	NT	○/●	NT
2000	NT	○/●	NT
2001	NT	○/○	○/○
2002	NT	○/○	○/○

MINIVAN
Chrysler Town & Country

1998 model shown

A more luxurious version of the Dodge Grand Caravan, it offers seating for seven and optional AWD. After a 1996 redesign, a regular-length Town & Country briefly joined the lineup. These models ride quietly, handle relatively nimbly, and convert easily from people-carriers to roomy cargo-haulers. A second, left-side sliding door is a handy feature, and the middle and rear seats, while heavy, can be removed. The standard 3.3-liter V6 provides lackluster acceleration and unimpressive fuel economy. A stronger 3.8-liter V6 is also available. A 2001 redesign improved it. **Related models:** Dodge Grand Caravan, Plymouth Grand Voyager.

MAJOR REDESIGN: 1996, 2001. **SAFETY EQUIPMENT:** Dual front air bags standard. Side air bags available from 2001. Safety-belt pretensioners standard from 2001. ABS standard. **DRIVE WHEELS:** Front or AWD.

SMALL CAR
Daewoo Lanos

1999 model shown

The Lanos is the smallest of Daewoo's three U.S. cars. Introduced in 1999, it was available as either a three-door hatchback or four-door sedan. The Lanos is about the size of a Hyundai Accent, but CR found it to be much cruder, less nimble, and more cramped than its fellow South Korean. The engine is a weak 1.6-liter Four. Although the Lanos came well equipped, the market is crowded with better-performing and more-refined competitors. The demise of Daewoo's tiny U.S. dealer network is another concern.

MAJOR REDESIGN: 1999. **SAFETY EQUIPMENT:** Dual front air bags standard. ABS available from 1999 to 2000. Safety-belt pretensioners standard from 2000. **DRIVE WHEELS:** Front.

Chrysler Town & Country — Reliability history

TROUBLE SPOTS	Chrysler Town & Country 2WD
	95 96 97 98 99 00 01 02
Engine	○ ● ● ○ ○ ○ ● ●
Cooling	○ ● ● ● ● ● ● ●
Fuel	○ ● ● ● ● ● ● ●
Ignition	● ● ● ○ ○ ● ● ●
Transmission	● ● ○ ○ ○ ● ● ●
Electrical	● ● ● ○ ○ ○ ● ●
Air conditioning	● ● ● ● ○ ○ ● ●
Suspension	○ ○ ○ ○ ○ ○ ● ●
Brakes	○ ● ● ○ ● ● ○ ●
Exhaust	● ● ● ● ● ● ● ●
Paint/trim/rust	● ○ ○ ● ● ● ● ●
Body integrity	● ● ● ○ ○ ● ● ●
Power equipment	● ● ● ○ ○ ○ ● ●
Body hardware	● ● ● ○ ○ ○ ● ●
RELIABILITY VERDICT	✓ ✓ ✓

Chrysler — Prices

1995	$8,000-$10,000
1996	$8,000-$10,000
1997	$12,000-$14,000
1998	$14,000-$16,000
1999	$16,000-$18,000
2000	$18,000-$20,000
2001	$20,000-$22,000
2002	$22,000-$24,000

Chrysler — Crash-test results

Model years	Offset	Full-frontal	Side
1995	NT	●/○	NT
1996	Marg.	○/●	NT
1997	Marg.	○/●	NT
1998	Marg.	○/○	NT
1999	Marg.	●/●	●/○
2000	Marg.	●/●	●/○
2001	Poor	●/●	●/●
2002	Marg.	●/●	●/●

Daewoo Lanos — Reliability history

TROUBLE SPOTS	95 96 97 98 99 00 01 02
Engine	
Cooling	
Fuel	
Ignition	NOT
Transmission	
Electrical	ENOUGH
Air conditioning	
Suspension	DATA
Brakes	
Exhaust	TO
Paint/trim/rust	
Body integrity	
Power equipment	RATE
Body hardware	
RELIABILITY VERDICT	

Daewoo — Prices

Year	Price
1995	–
1996	–
1997	–
1998	–
1999	$4,000-$6,000
2000	$4,000-$6,000
2001	$6,000-$8,000
2002	$6,000-$8,000

Daewoo — Crash-test results

Model years	Offset	Full-frontal	Side
1995	–	–	–
1996	–	–	–
1997	–	–	–
1998	–	–	–
1999	NT	NT	NT
2000	NT	NT	NT
2001	NT	NT	NT
2002	NT	NT	NT

FAMILY CAR

Daewoo Leganza

1999 model shown

The Leganza's many standard features can't make up for this car's inherent mediocrity. Though marketed as a less expensive alternative to the Toyota Camry and Honda Accord, the Leganza actually competes—albeit poorly—with more prosaic models like the Pontiac Grand Am. The Leganza's ride is sloppy and queasy, and its handling is ponderous. The 2.2-liter Four sounds gruff but provides adequate acceleration. The automatic transmission also lacks polish. The rear seat is roomy enough for three adults, but it's not comfortable. Parts and service may also be hard to come by, given the demise of Daewoo dealerships.

MAJOR REDESIGN: 1999. **SAFETY EQUIPMENT:** Dual front air bags standard. ABS available. Safety-belt pretensioners standard. **DRIVE WHEELS:** Front.

Reliability history

TROUBLE SPOTS	95 96 97 98 99 00 01 02
Engine	
Cooling	
Fuel	
Ignition	NOT
Transmission	
Electrical	ENOUGH
Air-conditioning	
Suspension	DATA
Brakes	
Exhaust	TO
Paint/trim/rust	
Body integrity	
Power equipment	RATE
Body hardware	
RELIABILITY VERDICT	

Prices

1995	–
1996	–
1997	–
1998	–
1999	$6,000-$8,000
2000	$8,000-$10,000
2001	$8,000-$10,000
2002	$10,000-$12,000

Crash-test results

Model Years	Offset	Full frontal	Side
1995	–	–	–
1996	–	–	–
1997	–	–	–
1998	–	–	–
1999	Poor	NT	NT
2000	Poor	NT	NT
2001	Poor	O/O	◑/O
2002	Poor	O/O	◑/O

SMALL CAR

Daewoo Nubira

1999 model shown

Of the three Daewoos introduced for 1999, the Nubira seemed to possess the most potential. The sedan had more equipment than competitors like the Nissan Sentra and Toyota Corolla. It also had a responsive (if whiny) engine, a smooth-shifting automatic transmission. The Nubira's ride, handling, and fuel economy, however, are unremarkable. Some of CR's testers also had trouble getting comfortable behind the wheel because it's too far away. A wagon version is also available. The collapse of Daewoo's dealer network bodes ill for parts and service.

MAJOR REDESIGN: 1999. **SAFETY EQUIPMENT:** Dual front air bags standard. ABS available from 1999 to 2001. Safety-belt pretensioners standard. **DRIVE WHEELS:** Front.

Reliability history

TROUBLE SPOTS	95 96 97 98 99 00 01 02
Engine	
Cooling	
Fuel	
Ignition	NOT
Transmission	
Electrical	ENOUGH
Air-conditioning	
Suspension	DATA
Brakes	
Exhaust	
Paint/trim/rust	TO
Body integrity	
Power equipment	RATE
Body hardware	
RELIABILITY VERDICT	

Prices

1995	–
1996	–
1997	–
1998	–
1999	$6,000-$8,000
2000	$6,000-$8,000
2001	$8,000-$10,000
2002	$8,000-$10,000

Crash-test results

Model Years	Offset	Full frontal	Side
1995	–	–	–
1996	–	–	–
1997	–	–	–
1998	–	–	–
1999	NT	NT	NT
2000	NT	NT	NT
2001	NT	NT	NT
2002	NT	◑/◑	NT

Dodge Avenger

1995 model shown

This sporty coupe, designed by Chrysler and built in Illinois by Mitsubishi, debuted for the 1995 model year. The front seats provide good support except for the lower back. The rear seat is roomier than those of most sporty coupes and can hold two tall adults in only moderate discomfort; three are a tight squeeze. Look for a model equipped with the 2.5-liter, 163-hp V6 instead of the 2.0-liter four-cylinder engine. Handling was competent and predictable in our tests. The suspension absorbed big bumps well, but little pavement flaws transmitted firm kicks. The Avenger was replaced by the new Stratus coupe for 2001. **Related model:** Chrysler Sebring until 2000.

MAJOR REDESIGN: 1995. **SAFETY EQUIPMENT:** Dual front air bags standard. ABS available. **DRIVE WHEELS:** Front.

Reliability history								
TROUBLE SPOTS	95	96	97	98	99	00	01	02
Engine								
Cooling								
Fuel								
Ignition				NOT				
Transmission								
Electrical				ENOUGH				
Air conditioning								
Suspension				DATA				
Brakes								
Exhaust				TO				
Paint/trim/rust								
Body integrity				RATE				
Power equipment								
Body hardware								
RELIABILITY VERDICT								

Prices	
1995	$6,000-$8,000
1996	$6,000-$8,000
1997	$8,000-$10,000
1998	$10,000-$12,000
1999	$10,000-$12,000
2000	$14,000-$16,000
2001	–
2002	–

Crash-test results			
Model years	Offset	Full-frontal	Side
1995	NT	●/●	NT
1996	NT	●/●	NT
1997	NT	●/●	NT
1998	NT	●/●	NT
1999	NT	●/●	NT
2000	NT	●/●	NT
2001	–	–	–
2002	–	–	–

Dodge Caravan/Grand Caravan

2001 model shown

Early-90's versions of the Caravan and the extended-length Grand Caravan handled clumsily and unsteadily. A complete 1996 redesign brought substantial improvements, including a more refined chassis, an optional second sliding door, and a well-conceived interior. The removable rear seats unhitch easily but are heavy, making them difficult to drag in and out. The 2001 model year brought a redesigned interior, additional refinement, and available side air bags, but the engines remained a bit thirsty. **Related models:** Chrysler Town & Country, Plymouth Voyager/Grand Voyager.

MAJOR REDESIGN: 1996, 2001. **SAFETY EQUIPMENT:** Dual front air bags standard. Side air bags available from 2001. Safety-belt pretensioners standard from 2001. ABS available. **DRIVE WHEELS:** Front or AWD.

Reliability history								
TROUBLE SPOTS	Dodge Grand Caravan V6 2WD							
	95	96	97	98	99	00	01	02
Engine	○	○	○	○	●	●	○	●
Cooling	◐	◐	◐	●	●	●	●	●
Fuel	○	●	◐	●	●	●	●	●
Ignition	◐	◐	◐	●	●	●	●	●
Transmission	●	◐	◐	●	●	●	○	●
Electrical	●	◐	◐	◐	◐	○	○	●
Air conditioning	●	◐	◐	○	●	●	○	●
Suspension	○	○	○	◐	●	●	○	●
Brakes	●	◐	◐	●	●	●	○	●
Exhaust	●	●	◐	●	●	●	●	●
Paint/trim/rust	◐	○	●	●	●	●	●	●
Body integrity	●	◐	◐	●	●	●	◐	●
Power equipment	●	◐	○	◐	●	●	○	●
Body hardware	◐	●	○	○	◐	◐	◐	◐
RELIABILITY VERDICT			✔	✔		✔		✔

Prices	
1995	$4,000-$6,000
1996	$6,000-$8,000
1997	$8,000-$10,000
1998	$10,000-$12,000
1999	$12,000-$14,000
2000	$14,000-$16,000
2001	$14,000-$16,000
2002	$16,000-$18,000

Crash-test results			
Model years	Offset	Full-frontal	Side
1995	NT	○/●	NT
1996	Marg.	○/●	NT
1997	Marg.	●/●	NT
1998	Marg.	○/●	NT
1999	Marg.	●/●	●/○
2000	Marg.	●/●	●/○
2001	Poor	●/●	●/○
2002	Marg.	●/●	●/○

PICKUP TRUCK
Dodge Dakota

1998 model shown

Since its introduction, the Dakota has been marketed as a "midsized" pickup—larger than a typical compact truck, but smaller than full-sized models. A wide powertrain range includes four-, six-, and eight-cylinder engines, although only the thirsty V8s could be considered strong. Handling is ponderous, and the ride is stiff and boundy. The redesigned 1997 Dakota was nicely executed. Handling was much improved, but the ride remained a little choppy, especially with no load in the bed. In 2000, a four-door Quad Cab model was introduced, along with a refined 4.7-liter V8.

MAJOR REDESIGN: 1997. **SAFETY EQUIPMENT:** Driver air bag standard; passenger air bag standard from 1997. ABS available. Safety-belt pretensioners available from 2001. **DRIVE WHEELS:** Rear or part-time 4WD; permanent 4WD available from 2000.

SPORT-UTILITY VEHICLE
Dodge Durango

1998 model shown

Introduced for 1998, the midsized Durango SUV is derived from the Dakota pickup truck. Larger than the Chevrolet Blazer and Ford Explorer, the Durango boasts three-row seating and two available V8 engines. In our tests, the optional 5.2-liter V8 guzzled gas and didn't give the heavy Durango the oomph it needed. The brakes were mediocre, and the ride stiff. The front seats are reasonably comfortable. The third-row bench is flat and too firm, but easy to fold and erect. Full-time 4WD is available on later models. A 4.7-liter V8 arrived for 2000, improving performance and refinement.

MAJOR REDESIGN: 1998. **SAFETY EQUIPMENT:** Dual front air bags standard. Head protection air bags available from 2002. ABS available. Safety-belt pretensioners standard from 2001. **DRIVE WHEELS:** Rear, part-time or permanent 4WD.

Dodge Dakota

Reliability history — Dodge Dakota 2WD

TROUBLE SPOTS	95	96	97	98	99	00	01	02
Engine								
Cooling								
Fuel								
Ignition								
Transmission								
Electrical								
Air-conditioning								
Suspension								
Brakes								
Exhaust								
Paint/trim/rust								
Body integrity								
Power equipment								
Body hardware								
RELIABILITY VERDICT	✓	✓	✓			✓	✓	

Prices

Year	Price
1995	$8,000–$10,000
1996	$8,000–$10,000
1997	$12,000–$14,000
1998	$12,000–$14,000
1999	$14,000–$16,000
2000	$16,000–$18,000
2001	$18,000–$20,000
2002	$20,000–$22,000

Crash-test results

Model Years	Offset	Full frontal	Side
1995	NT	●/○	NT
1996	NT	●/○	NT
1997	Poor	○/●	NT
1998	Poor	○/●	NT
1999	Poor	○/●	●/NA
2000	Poor	○/●	●/NA
2001	Poor	○/●	●/○
2002	Poor	○/●	●/NA

Dodge Durango

Reliability history — Dodge Durango

TROUBLE SPOTS	95	96	97	98	99	00	01	02
Engine								
Cooling								
Fuel								
Ignition								
Transmission								
Electrical								
Air-conditioning								
Suspension								
Brakes								
Exhaust								
Paint/trim/rust								
Body integrity								
Power equipment								
Body hardware								
RELIABILITY VERDICT								

Prices

Year	Price
1995	–
1996	–
1997	–
1998	$16,000–$18,000
1999	$18,000–$20,000
2000	$20,000–$22,000
2001	$22,000–$24,000
2002	$26,000–$28,000

Crash-test results

Model Years	Offset	Full frontal	Side
1995	–	–	–
1996	–	–	–
1997	–	–	–
1998	Accept.	●/○	NT
1999	Accept.	●/○	NT
2000	Accept.	●/○	NT
2001	Accept.	●/○	NT
2002	Accept.	●/○	NT

Dodge Intrepid

Dodge Ram

1998 model shown

1996 model shown

The front-drive Intrepid sedan was introduced as a 1993 model. It performed well in our tests, with surprisingly nimble handling for a big car. The "touring" suspension gives the best combination of ride and handling. Seating is comfortable for five. The Intrepid was redesigned for 1998. Ride and handling are still very good, but the engines are unrefined and the cabin is noisy. The interior is roomy, though access is compromised by the swooping roof design. A sporty R/T version, with a stronger 3.5-liter V6, became available in 2000. **Related models:** Chrysler 300M, Chrysler Concorde, Chrysler LHS/New Yorker, Eagle Vision.

MAJOR REDESIGN: 1993, 1998. **SAFETY EQUIPMENT:** Dual front air bags standard. Side air bags available from 2001. ABS available. **DRIVE WHEELS:** Front.

The Ram's cabin is roomy and the cargo bed voluminous, but ponderous handling, poor fuel economy, and subpar braking performance limit the Ram's appeal. Engines include a hopelessly overmatched V6, an inline-6 turbodiesel, two V8s, and a powerful V10. The popular 5.2-liter V8 is weak and thirsty. A new-for-1998 four-door Quad Cab model offers improved rear access on extended-cab trucks. The extended-cab Ram was discontinued with the 2002 redesign, replaced by a crew cab.

MAJOR REDESIGN: 1994, 2002. **SAFETY EQUIPMENT:** Driver air bag standard; passenger air bag standard from 1998. Head protection air bags available from 2002. Safety-belt pretensioners standard from 2002. ABS available. **DRIVE WHEELS:** Rear or part-time 4WD. Permanent 4WD available from 2002.

Reliability history — Dodge Intrepid

TROUBLE SPOTS	95	96	97	98	99	00	01	02
Engine								
Cooling								
Fuel								
Ignition								
Transmission								
Electrical								
Air conditioning								
Suspension								
Brakes								
Exhaust								
Paint/trim/rust								
Body integrity								
Power equipment								
Body hardware								
RELIABILITY VERDICT						✔	✔	✔

Prices

1995	$6,000-$8,000
1996	$6,000-$8,000
1997	$8,000-$10,000
1998	$10,000-$12,000
1999	$12,000-$14,000
2000	$14,000-$16,000
2001	$14,000-$16,000
2002	$18,000-$20,000

Crash-test results

Model years	Offset	Full-frontal	Side
1995	NT	⊖/⊖	NT
1996	NT	⊖/⊖	NT
1997	NT	⊖/⊖	⊖/○
1998	NT	NT	NT
1999	NT	⊖/⊖	⊖/○
2000	Marg.	⊖/⊖	⊖/○
2001	Accept.	⊖/⊖	⊖/○
2002	Accept.	⊖/⊖	⊖/○

Reliability history — Dodge Ram 1500 4WD

TROUBLE SPOTS	95	96	97	98	99	00	01	02
Engine								
Cooling								
Fuel								
Ignition								
Transmission								
Electrical								
Air conditioning								
Suspension								
Brakes								
Exhaust								
Paint/trim/rust								
Body integrity								
Power equipment								
Body hardware								
RELIABILITY VERDICT	✔						✔	

Prices

1995	$10,000-$12,000
1996	$10,000-$12,000
1997	$12,000-$14,000
1998	$12,000-$14,000
1999	$14,000-$16,000
2000	$14,000-$16,000
2001	$16,000-$18,000
2002	$20,000-$22,000

Crash-test results

Model years	Offset	Full-frontal	Side
1995	NT	⊖/NA	NT
1996	NT	⊖/NA	NT
1997	NT	⊖/○	NT
1998	Poor	⊖/⊖	NT
1999	Poor	⊖/⊖	NT
2000	Poor	⊖/⊖	NT
2001	Poor	⊖/⊖	NT
2002	Good	⊖/●	NT

SPORTS/SPORTY CAR

Dodge Stealth

1995 model shown

In their sportiest forms, the Dodge Stealth and the mechanically identical Mitsubishi 3000GT are loaded with gadgets. The Stealth lineup ranged from a V6-powered base version with front-wheel drive on up to the high-tech R/T Turbo, with twin turbochargers, four-wheel steering, and all-wheel drive. The 300-hp R/T Turbo we tested offered quick steering and strong tire grip, short stops, and blazing acceleration. Overall, though, it somehow wasn't that much fun to drive. The front seats are comfortable and supportive, but the rear seat is quite compact. 1994 brought a six-speed manual and an additional 20 hp for the R/T Turbo. The Stealth was discontinued early in 1996. **Related model:** Mitsubishi 3000GT.

MAJOR REDESIGN: 1991. **SAFETY EQUIPMENT:** Dual front air bags standard. ABS standard. **DRIVE WHEELS:** Front or AWD.

Reliability history	
TROUBLE SPOTS	95 96 97 98 99 00 01 02
Engine	
Cooling	
Fuel	
Ignition	**NOT**
Transmission	
Electrical	**ENOUGH**
Air-conditioning	
Suspension	**DATA**
Brakes	
Exhaust	**TO**
Paint/trim/rust	
Body integrity	
Power equipment	**RATE**
Body hardware	
RELIABILITY VERDICT	

Prices	
1995	$10,000-$12,000
1996	$10,000-$12,000
1997	–
1998	–
1999	–
2000	–
2001	–
2002	–

Crash-test results			
Model Years	Offset	Full frontal	Side
1995	NT	NT	NT
1996	NT	NT	NT
1997	–	–	–
1998	–	–	–
1999	–	–	–
2000	–	–	–
2001	–	–	–
2002	–	–	–

FAMILY CAR

Dodge Stratus

1998 model shown

The Stratus was introduced for 1995. The interior feels fairly spacious, and seating is quite roomy. The base model uses a noisy four-cylinder engine, shared with the Neon, but the more refined 2.5-liter, 168-hp V6 engine accelerates nicely. In our tests, the Stratus and the similar Chrysler Cirrus exhibited subpar braking and an unresponsive automatic transmission. The ride feels jittery, but handling is secure. For 2001, the Stratus was redesigned and a new coupe model added to the line. **Related models:** Chrysler Cirrus, Plymouth Breeze, Chrysler Sebring starting in 2001.

MAJOR REDESIGN: 1995, 2001. **SAFETY EQUIPMENT:** Dual front air bags standard. Head protection air bags available from 2001. Safety-belt pretensioners standard from 2001. ABS available. **DRIVE WHEELS:** Front.

Reliability history								
TROUBLE SPOTS	____ Dodge Stratus V6 ____							
	95	96	97	98	99	00	01	02
Engine	○	○	●	●	●	●	●	●
Cooling	○	◐	●	●	●	●	●	●
Fuel	○	◐	○	◐	○	○	●	●
Ignition	○	◐	●	●	●	●	●	●
Transmission	◐	○	●	◐	●	●	○	●
Electrical	○	○	◐	●	◐	●	●	○
Air-conditioning	●	◐	○	◐	●	●	●	●
Suspension	◐	●	◐	○	●	◐	●	●
Brakes	●	●	●	◐	○	○	●	●
Exhaust	●	◐	●	●	●	●	●	●
Paint/trim/rust	●	◐	●	◐	●	◐	●	●
Body integrity	○	◐	●	●	◐	●	◐	●
Power equipment	●	○	◐	◐	●	●	●	●
Body hardware	○	●	●	◐	●	●	◐	●
RELIABILITY VERDICT	✔	✔	✔	✔		✔		✔

Prices	
1995	$4,000-$6,000
1996	$4,000-$6,000
1997	$6,000-$8,000
1998	$6,000-$8,000
1999	$10,000-$12,000
2000	$12,000-$14,000
2001	$14,000-$16,000
2002	$16,000-$18,000

Crash-test results			
Model Years	Offset	Full frontal	Side
1995	Poor	○/NA	NT
1996	Poor	○/NA	NT
1997	Poor	○/NA	○/○
1998	Poor	○/●	○/○
1999	Poor	○/●	○/○
2000	Poor	○/●	○/○
2001	Accept.	●/●	○/○
2002	Accept.	●/●	○/○

Dodge Viper

1996 model shown

Early Vipers emphasized raw power over comfort and convenience, with plastic curtains in place of side windows, a snap-on canvas top, and doors that lacked exterior handles. The 1996 model year brought added civility and even more performance in the form of the GTS coupe. Along with a 50-hp boost for the engine, the GTS got power windows, outside door latches, and a handful of other refinements. The RT/10 convertible adopted the upgraded engine and most of the GTS's other enhancements for 1998, and a removable hardtop became standard. Even so, the Viper remained a thinly disguised race car best appreciated on a track.

MAJOR REDESIGN: 1992, 1996. **SAFETY EQUIPMENT:** Dual front air bags available from 1996, standard from 1997. ABS standard from 2001. **DRIVE WHEELS:** Rear.

Reliability history	
TROUBLE SPOTS	95 96 97 98 99 00 01 02
Engine	
Cooling	
Fuel	
Ignition	NOT
Transmission	
Electrical	ENOUGH
Air conditioning	
Suspension	DATA
Brakes	
Exhaust	TO
Paint/trim/rust	
Body integrity	RATE
Power equipment	
Body hardware	
RELIABILITY VERDICT	

Prices	
1995	More than $30,000
1996	More than $30,000
1997	More than $30,000
1998	More than $30,000
1999	More than $30,000
2000	More than $30,000
2001	More than $30,000
2002	More than $30,000

Crash-test results			
Model years	Offset	Full-frontal	Side
1995	NT	NT	NT
1996	NT	NT	NT
1997	NT	NT	NT
1998	NT	NT	NT
1999	NT	NT	NT
2000	NT	NT	NT
2001	NT	NT	NT
2002	NT	NT	NT

Dodge/Plymouth Neon

2000 model shown

Introduced for 1995, the Dodge and Plymouth Neon twins boast a relatively roomy interior and a choice of two four-cylinder engines. Neons equipped with the manual transmission are difficult to drive smoothly, and the three-speed automatic steals a lot of power. Both 2.0-liter engines sound harsh, and fuel economy is unimpressive. The ride is jittery and stiff. Three adults can, however, fit in the rear seat. A sporty R/T version debuted for 1998. The Neon was redesigned for 2000, when the coupe was discontinued. This new version provides secure handling and excellent braking. But a noisy cabin and uncomfortable ride detract from the driving experience.

MAJOR REDESIGN: 1995, 2000. **SAFETY EQUIPMENT:** Dual front air bags standard. Side air bags available from 2001. ABS available. **DRIVE WHEELS:** Front.

Reliability history	Dodge Neon
TROUBLE SPOTS	95 96 97 98 99 00 01 02
Engine	
Cooling	
Fuel	
Ignition	
Transmission	
Electrical	
Air conditioning	
Suspension	
Brakes	
Exhaust	
Paint/trim/rust	
Body integrity	
Power equipment	
Body hardware	
RELIABILITY VERDICT	Insufficient data (01, 02)

Prices	
1995	$2,000-$4,000
1996	$4,000-$6,000
1997	$4,000-$6,000
1998	$4,000-$6,000
1999	$6,000-$8,000
2000	$8,000-$10,000
2001	$8,000-$10,000
2002	$10,000-$12,000

Crash-test results			
Model years	Offset	Full-frontal	Side
1995	Poor	◒/◒	NT
1996	Poor	◒/◒	NT
1997	Poor	◒/◒	NT
1998	Poor	○/◒	◒/○
1999	Poor	○/◒	◒/○
2000	Marg.	◒/◒	○/○
2001	Marg.	◒/◒	○/○
2002	Marg.	◒/◒	○/○

Eagle Summit

Eagle Talon

1995 model shown

1997 model shown

Built by Mitsubishi, the Summit was a worthy small car for its time, with good handling but an awful ride. The front seats are satisfactory, but the rear is tight. Major controls are easy to see and grasp, and the climate-control system works quickly. Later models were short on feature equipment. Antilock brakes were hard to find and the conventional brakes were pretty poor. The Summit Wagon was a different vehicle altogether, available from 1992 to 1996. It had a high seating position and a single sliding rear door and lots of cargo space. The engine of choice, a 2.4-liter Four, felt lively in CR tests. The ride was good, handling was so-so. **Related model:** Mitsubishi Mirage.

MAJOR REDESIGN: 1993. **SAFETY EQUIPMENT:** Dual front air bags standard. ABS available. **DRIVE WHEELS:** Front.

This sporty coupe was built in Illinois by Mitsubishi, and is a mechanical twin of the Mitsubishi Eclipse and Plymouth Laser. The Talon line ranged from base versions with a four-cylinder engine and front-wheel drive to higher-performance turbocharged, all-wheel-drive models. The TSi we tested handled well, and had excellent braking and a decent ride. As with many sport coupes, the rear seat is very tight, and luggage space is skimpy. A major redesign for 1995 brought fresh sheet metal and a slightly roomier interior. The Talon was discontinued—along with the entire Eagle brand—in early 1998. **Related model:** Mitsubishi Eclipse.

MAJOR REDESIGN: 1995. **SAFETY EQUIPMENT:** Dual front air bags standard. ABS available. **DRIVE WHEELS:** Front or AWD.

Reliability history

TROUBLE SPOTS	95 96 97 98 99 00 01 02
Engine	
Cooling	
Fuel	
Ignition	NOT
Transmission	
Electrical	ENOUGH
Air-conditioning	
Suspension	DATA
Brakes	
Exhaust	TO
Paint/trim/rust	
Body integrity	
Power equipment	RATE
Body hardware	
RELIABILITY VERDICT	

Prices

1995	$2,000-$4,000
1996	$4,000-$6,000
1997	–
1998	–
1999	–
2000	–
2001	–
2002	–

Crash-test results

Model Years	Offset	Full frontal	Side
1995	NT	NT	NT
1996	NT	○/○	NT
1997	–	–	–
1998	–	–	–
1999	–	–	–
2000	–	–	–
2001	–	–	–
2002	–	–	–

Reliability history

TROUBLE SPOTS	95 96 97 98 99 00 01 02
Engine	
Cooling	
Fuel	
Ignition	NOT
Transmission	
Electrical	ENOUGH
Air-conditioning	
Suspension	DATA
Brakes	
Exhaust	
Paint/trim/rust	TO
Body integrity	
Power equipment	RATE
Body hardware	
RELIABILITY VERDICT	

Prices

1995	$6,000-$8,000
1996	$8,000-$10,000
1997	$8,000-$10,000
1998	$10,000-$12,000
1999	–
2000	–
2001	–
2002	–

Crash-test results

Model Years	Offset	Full frontal	Side
1995	NT	○/○	NT
1996	NT	○/○	NT
1997	NT	○/○	NT
1998	NT	NT	●/NA
1999	–	–	–
2000	–	–	–
2001	–	–	–
2002	–	–	–

Eagle Vision

Ford Aerostar

1995 model shown

1995 model shown

One of Chrysler's big LH sedans, the Eagle Vision was introduced as a 1993 model. It performed well in our tests, with the 3.3-liter V6 accelerating strongly and the 3.5-liter V6 delivering a bit more punch. The automatic transmission shifted smoothly enough. The Vision is surprisingly nimble for a big car, with the TSi version providing the sportiest handling, but also the stiffest ride. Seating is comfortable for five. For 1996, Chrysler's AutoStick system was added to the automatic, permitting the transmission to be shifted like a manual. The Vision was retired at the end of the 1997 model year. **Related models:** Chrysler Concorde, Chrysler LHS/New Yorker, Dodge Intrepid.

MAJOR REDESIGN: 1993. **SAFETY EQUIPMENT:** Dual front air bags standard. ABS available. **DRIVE WHEELS:** Front.

The Ford Aerostar was available in rear-drive and all-wheel-drive versions. The base engine was a 3.0-liter V6, with a stronger 4.0-liter offered as an option. This latter V6 is well suited to towing a trailer. The AWD model handles more surefootedly than the ponderous rear-wheel-drive model. Both configurations provide an acceptable ride. Offered in two lengths, either can hold six or seven people, thanks to a roomy interior. Integrated child-safety seats, which folded out from the middle bench, became available in 1993. A five-speed automatic transmission became available in 1997, the Aerostar's final year.

MAJOR REDESIGN: 1986. **SAFETY EQUIPMENT:** Driver air bag standard. Rear-wheel ABS standard. **DRIVE WHEELS:** Rear or AWD.

Reliability history

TROUBLE SPOTS	95 96 97 98 99 00 01 02
Engine	
Cooling	
Fuel	
Ignition	NOT
Transmission	
Electrical	ENOUGH
Air conditioning	
Suspension	DATA
Brakes	
Exhaust	TO
Paint/trim/rust	
Body integrity	RATE
Power equipment	
Body hardware	
RELIABILITY VERDICT	

Prices

1995	$4,000-$6,000
1996	$6,000-$8,000
1997	$6,000-$8,000
1998	–
1999	–
2000	–
2001	–
2002	–

Crash-test results

Model years	Offset	Full-frontal	Side
1995	NT	◒/◐	NT
1996	NT	◒/◐	NT
1997	NT	◒/◐	◒/○
1998	–	–	–
1999	–	–	–
2000	–	–	–
2001	–	–	–
2002	–	–	–

Reliability history

TROUBLE SPOTS	Ford Aerostar
	95 96 97 98 99 00 01 02
Engine	● ● ○
Cooling	○ ○ ○
Fuel	● ○ ◐
Ignition	● ○ ○
Transmission	○ ○ ○
Electrical	● ◐ ◐
Air conditioning	○ ○ ●
Suspension	◐ ○ ○
Brakes	● ◐ ◐
Exhaust	○ ● ●
Paint/trim/rust	○ ◐ ◐
Body integrity	◐ ◐ ◐
Power equipment	○ ○ ●
Body hardware	◐ ○ ○
RELIABILITY VERDICT	✓ ✓ ✓

Prices

1995	$6,000-$8,000
1996	$6,000-$8,000
1997	$6,000-$8,000
1998	–
1999	–
2000	–
2001	–
2002	–

Crash-test results

Model years	Offset	Full-frontal	Side
1995	Poor	◒/○	NT
1996	Poor	◒/○	NT
1997	Poor	◒/○	NT
1998	–	–	–
1999	–	–	–
2000	–	–	–
2001	–	–	–
2002	–	–	–

SMALL CAR

Ford Aspire

1996 model shown

Made by South Korean automaker Kia, this small economy car replaced the Ford Festiva for 1994. Powered by a 1.3-liter four-cylinder engine, the Aspire is fuel efficient but painfully slow. Even with a five-speed manual transmission, we found that frequent shifting was required to maintain speed on inclines. In our tests, the Aspire handled clumsily, and the ride was both busy and stiff. The Aspire has plenty of head room, but leg room comes up short. Forward visibility is quite good, and the front seats provide good support. The rear seat can hold only two passengers. The Aspire expired after 1997, handing the entry-level mantle back to the Escort.

MAJOR REDESIGN: 1994. **SAFETY EQUIPMENT:** Dual front air bags standard. ABS available. **DRIVE WHEELS:** Front.

Reliability history	
TROUBLE SPOTS	95 96 97 98 99 00 01 02
Engine	
Cooling	
Fuel	
Ignition	NOT
Transmission	
Electrical	ENOUGH
Air-conditioning	
Suspension	DATA
Brakes	
Exhaust	TO
Paint/trim/rust	
Body integrity	
Power equipment	RATE
Body hardware	
RELIABILITY VERDICT	

Prices	
1995	$2,000-$4,000
1996	$2,000-$4,000
1997	$4,000-$6,000
1998	–
1999	–
2000	–
2001	–
2002	–

Crash-test results			
Model Years	Offset	Full frontal	Side
1995	NT	⊙/⊙	NT
1996	NT	⊙/⊙	NT
1997	NT	⊙/⊙	NT
1998	–	–	–
1999	–	–	–
2000	–	–	–
2001	–	–	–
2002	–	–	–

SPORT-UTILITY VEHICLE

Ford Bronco

1995 model shown

The bulky, full-sized two-door Bronco was based on Ford's F-Series pickup trucks and was one of the early pioneers of the sport-utility segment. The Bronco is a pure truck from its ladder frame outward, even though it was available with various levels of interior luxury appointments. Designed for people who needed to haul a lot of gear or tow a heavy trailer, it excels at these work chores more than as an everyday passenger vehicle. A choice of two thirsty V8 engines was available. The Bronco was finally discontinued at the end of the 1996 model year, clearing the way for the larger and more competent four-door Expedition.

MAJOR REDESIGN: 1988. **SAFETY EQUIPMENT:** Driver air bag standard. ABS standard. **DRIVE WHEELS:** Rear or part-time 4WD.

Reliability history	
TROUBLE SPOTS	95 96 97 98 99 00 01 02
Engine	
Cooling	
Fuel	
Ignition	NOT
Transmission	
Electrical	ENOUGH
Air-conditioning	
Suspension	DATA
Brakes	
Exhaust	TO
Paint/trim/rust	
Body integrity	
Power equipment	RATE
Body hardware	
RELIABILITY VERDICT	

Prices	
1995	$10,000-$12,000
1996	$10,000-$12,000
1997	–
1998	–
1999	–
2000	–
2001	–
2002	–

Crash-test results			
Model Years	Offset	Full frontal	Side
1995	NT	⊙/⊙	NT
1996	NT	⊙/⊙	NT
1997	–	–	–
1998	–	–	–
1999	–	–	–
2000	–	–	–
2001	–	–	–
2002	–	–	–

Ford Contour

1998 model shown

Introduced to the U.S. in 1995, the Contour slotted into Ford's lineup between the Escort and Taurus. Handling was nimble, especially with the "sport" suspension and performance tires. The softer base suspension gave a slightly better ride. Road noise was pronounced. The standard four-cylinder engine was adequately powerful but fairly noisy; look for a model equipped with the strong V6. The front seats are roomy and comfortable, but the rear seat is cramped. An extra inch of rear leg room in the 1996 model helped somewhat. The very sporty SVT model, introduced for 1998, was an excellent-driving car. 2000 was the Contour's final run. **Related model:** Mercury Mystique.

MAJOR REDESIGN: 1995. **SAFETY EQUIPMENT:** Dual front air bags standard. ABS available. **DRIVE WHEELS:** Front.

Reliability history

Ford Contour 4 cyl.

TROUBLE SPOTS	95	96	97	98	99	00	01	02
Engine								
Cooling								
Fuel								
Ignition								
Transmission								
Electrical								
Air conditioning								
Suspension								
Brakes								
Exhaust								
Paint/trim/rust								
Body integrity								
Power equipment								
Body hardware								
RELIABILITY VERDICT			✓	✓	✓			

Prices

1995	$4,000-$6,000
1996	$4,000-$6,000
1997	$4,000-$6,000
1998	$6,000-$8,000
1999	$8,000-$10,000
2000	$10,000-$12,000
2001	–
2002	–

Crash-test results

Model years	Offset	Full-frontal	Side
1995	Poor	●/◐	NT
1996	Poor	●/◐	NT
1997	Poor	●/◐	○/◐
1998	Poor	●/◐	○/◐
1999	Poor	●/◐	○/◐
2000	Poor	●/◐	○/◐
2001			
2002			

Ford Crown Victoria

1997 model shown

The Crown Victoria is among the last big, full-frame American cars with a V8 and rear-wheel drive. A 4.6-liter SOHC engine provides good acceleration and fuel economy with substantial trailer-towing capability. It offers an absorbent ride. An available performance-and-handling package provides improved handling and ride control. The Crown Victoria also boasts three-across seating front and rear, as well as a huge trunk. Still, the rear seat isn't as roomy as one might expect. A 1998 freshening brought a number of suspension tweaks. **Related model:** Mercury Grand Marquis.

MAJOR REDESIGN: 1992, 1998. **SAFETY EQUIPMENT:** Dual front air bags standard. Safety-belt pretensioners standard from 2001. ABS available. **DRIVE WHEELS:** Rear.

Reliability history

Ford Crown Victoria

TROUBLE SPOTS	95	96	97	98	99	00	01	02
Engine								
Cooling								
Fuel								
Ignition								
Transmission								
Electrical								
Air conditioning								
Suspension								
Brakes								
Exhaust								
Paint/trim/rust								
Body integrity								
Power equipment								
Body hardware								
RELIABILITY VERDICT	✓	✓	✓	✓	✓	✓	✓	✓

Prices

1995	$6,000-$8,000
1996	$8,000-$10,000
1997	$8,000-$10,000
1998	$10,000-$12,000
1999	$12,000-$14,000
2000	$14,000-$16,000
2001	$16,000-$18,000
2002	$20,000-$22,000

Crash-test results

Model years	Offset	Full-frontal	Side
1995	NT	○/◐	NT
1996	NT	○/◐	NT
1997	NT	●/◐	○/◐
1998	NT	●/◐	○/◐
1999	NT	●/◐	○/◐
2000	NT	●/◐	○/◐
2001	NT	●/◐	○/◐
2002	NT	●/◐	○/◐

SPORT-UTILITY VEHICLE

Ford Escape

2001 model shown

The product of a joint venture between Ford and Mazda, the Escape is mechanically similar to the Mazda Tribute. Both are car-based SUVs, with unibody chassis and fully independent suspensions. An available AWD system powers only the front wheels until slippage is sensed, then re-routes torque aft as needed to regain traction. Engine choices include an adequate 2.0-liter four-cylinder and a lively 3.0-liter, 201-hp V6. Virtues like nimble handling, excellent braking, impressive cabin space, and class-leading acceleration (in V6 models) are offset by a noisy interior, stiff ride, and sub-par reliability. **Related model:** Mazda Tribute.

MAJOR REDESIGN: 2001. **SAFETY EQUIPMENT:** Dual front air bags standard. Side air bags available. Safety-belt pretensioners standard. ABS available. **DRIVE WHEELS:** Front or AWD.

Reliability history

TROUBLE SPOTS	Ford Escape V6
	95 96 97 98 99 00 01 02
Engine	● ●
Cooling	● ●
Fuel	○ ●
Ignition	● ●
Transmission	● ●
Electrical	○ ●
Air-conditioning	● ●
Suspension	● ●
Brakes	● ●
Exhaust	● ●
Paint/trim/rust	● ●
Body integrity	● ○
Power equipment	● ●
Body hardware	○ ●
RELIABILITY VERDICT	

Prices

1995	–
1996	–
1997	–
1998	–
1999	–
2000	–
2001	$18,000-$20,000
2002	$22,000-$24,000

Crash-test results

Model Years	Offset	Full frontal	Side
1995	–	–	–
1996	–	–	–
1997	–	–	–
1998	–	–	–
1999	–	–	–
2000	–	–	–
2001	Marg.	●/◐	●/◐
2002	Marg.	●/◐	●/◐

SMALL CAR

Ford Escort

1998 model shown

From 1991 to 1996, the Escort was based on a shared Mazda platform and available as a hatchback, sedan, or wagon. In CR's tests the Escort was twitchy in emergency maneuvers, and its 1.9-liter four-cylinder engine was a throbbing dullard. The GT model, available until 1996, offered a far-sprightlier 1.8-liter Four. Without ABS (available only on the GT), the Escort stops poorly. A significant redesign for 1997 produced a much-improved sedan and wagon, followed by the sportier ZX2 coupe. Power climbed to 130 hp and vehicle dynamics improved. The Escort was sold mainly to fleets from 2000 on, when the much better Focus arrived. **Related model:** Mercury Tracer.

MAJOR REDESIGN: 1997. **SAFETY EQUIPMENT:** Dual front air bags standard. ABS available. **DRIVE WHEELS:** Front.

Reliability history

TROUBLE SPOTS	Ford Escort							
	95	96	97	98	99	00	01	02
Engine	○	◐	◐	◐	●	●		
Cooling	◐	●	○	◐	●	●		
Fuel	◐	◐	●	●	●	●		
Ignition	●	◐	●	●	●	●		
Transmission	●	◐	●	●	●	●		
Electrical	○	◐	◐	○	◐	●		
Air-conditioning	○	○	◐	◐	●	●		
Suspension	○	○	○	○	◐	◐		
Brakes	◐	○	○	○	○	◐		
Exhaust	●	◐	●	◐	●	●		
Paint/trim/rust	○	○	◐	●	●	●		
Body integrity	○	○	◐	○	●	●		
Power equipment	●	◐	●	●	●	●		
Body hardware	◐	○	●	◐	◐	◐		
RELIABILITY VERDICT	✔	✔	✔	✔	✔	✔		

(Insufficient data for 01 and 02 columns)

Prices

1995	$4,000-$6,000
1996	$4,000-$6,000
1997	$4,000-$6,000
1998	$4,000-$6,000
1999	$6,000-$8,000
2000	$6,000-$8,000
2001	$8,000-$10,000
2002	$10,000-$12,000

Crash-test results

Model Years	Offset	Full frontal	Side
1995	NT	◐/○	NT
1996	NT	◐/○	NT
1997	Accept.	○/○	○/○
1998	Accept.	○/○	○/○
1999	Accept.	○/○	○/○
2000	Accept.	○/○	○/○
2001	Accept.	○/○	○/○
2002	Accept.	○/○	○/○

SPORT-UTILITY VEHICLE	SPORT-UTILITY VEHICLE

Ford Excursion

2000 model shown

Ford Expedition

1997 model shown

Currently the largest SUV on the market, the Excursion was introduced for 2000. Derived from the Ford "SuperDuty" pickup-truck chassis, the Excursion offers V8, V8 turbodiesel, and V10 engines. The V10 we tested delivered just adequate oomph, but it slurped down more than a gallon of fuel while covering just 10 miles of mixed-road driving. The ride is stiff, bouncy, and uncomfortable. The Excursion's vast bulk makes it difficult to hold in a traffic lane, and its slow and vague steering demands constant attention. The brakes are inferior. A huge interior, a commanding view out, roomy three-row seating, and tremendous towing capacity are among this model's few virtues.

MAJOR REDESIGN: 2000. **SAFETY EQUIPMENT:** Dual front air bags standard. ABS standard. **DRIVE WHEELS:** Rear or part-time 4WD.

The huge Expedition debuted for 1997, based on the F-150 pickup truck. We tested the Expedition with the standard 4.6-liter V8, which performed well enough but slurped fuel. Also available is a more powerful 5.4-liter V8. This full-sized, seven-passenger SUV rides fairly well and corners capably for its heft. Parking this behemoth and maneuvering it around town can be trying. The Expedition's seating was roomy and quite comfortable, except for the optional third-row bench. Climbing in and out takes athletic ability. For 1999, full-time 4WD became available. **Related model:** Lincoln Navigator.

MAJOR REDESIGN: 1997. **SAFETY EQUIPMENT:** Dual front air bags standard. Side air bags available from 2001. ABS standard. **DRIVE WHEELS:** Rear or selectable 4WD through 1998; rear or permanent 4WD from 1999.

Ford Excursion

Reliability history

TROUBLE SPOTS	Ford Excursion V10
	95 96 97 98 99 00 01 02
Engine	00
Cooling	00
Fuel	00
Ignition	00
Transmission	00
Electrical	00
Air conditioning	00
Suspension	00
Brakes	00
Exhaust	00
Paint/trim/rust	00
Body integrity	00
Power equipment	00
Body hardware	00
RELIABILITY VERDICT	✓

(01 and 02 columns: Insufficient data)

Prices

1995	–
1996	–
1997	–
1998	–
1999	–
2000	$26,000-$28,000
2001	$28,000-$30,000
2002	More than $30,000

Crash-test results

Model years	Offset	Full-frontal	Side
1995	–	–	–
1996	–	–	–
1997	–	–	–
1998	–	–	–
1999	–	–	–
2000	NT	NT	NT
2001	NT	NT	NT
2002	NT	NT	NT

Ford Expedition

Reliability history

TROUBLE SPOTS	Ford Expedition 4WD
	95 96 97 98 99 00 01 02
Engine	97 98 99 00 01 02
Cooling	97 98 99 00 01 02
Fuel	97 98 99 00 01 02
Ignition	97 98 99 00 01 02
Transmission	97 98 99 00 01 02
Electrical	97 98 99 00 01 02
Air conditioning	97 98 99 00 01 02
Suspension	97 98 99 00 01 02
Brakes	97 98 99 00 01 02
Exhaust	97 98 99 00 01 02
Paint/trim/rust	97 98 99 00 01 02
Body integrity	97 98 99 00 01 02
Power equipment	97 98 99 00 01 02
Body hardware	97 98 99 00 01 02
RELIABILITY VERDICT	✓ ✓ ✓ ✓ ✓

Prices

1995	–
1996	–
1997	$16,000-$18,000
1998	$18,000-$20,000
1999	$20,000-$22,000
2000	$22,000-$24,000
2001	$24,000-$26,000
2002	$28,000-$30,000

Crash-test results

Model years	Offset	Full-frontal	Side
1995	–	–	–
1996	–	–	–
1997	NT	◐/◐	NT
1998	NT	◐/◐	NT
1999	NT	◐/◐	NT
2000	NT	◐/◐	NT
2001	NT	◐/◐	NT
2002	NT	◐/◐	NT

Ford Explorer

1996 model shown

A 1995 redesign of the Explorer brought a more tolerable ride, though now it was stiff and choppy instead of soft and bouncy. It also brought improved handling, braking, and controls. A 5.0-liter V8 was added in 1996, and a more refined SOHC 4.0-liter V6/five-speed automatic combo was introduced for 1997. This is the best model to find. Front side air bags and a reverse sensing system were added to the options list in 1999. The Explorer was redesigned and improved for 2002. **Related models:** Mercury Mountaineer, Ford Explorer Sport Trac.

MAJOR REDESIGN: 1995, 2002. **SAFETY EQUIPMENT:** Dual front air bags standard. Side air bags available from 1999-2001. Head protection air bags available from 2002. Safety-belt pretensioners standard from 2002. ABS standard. **DRIVE WHEELS:** Rear; full-time 4WD and AWD available.

Ford Explorer Sport Trac

2001 model shown

Though marketed as a crossbreed truck/SUV, the Sport Trac is essentially a crew-cab Ranger pickup. It mates a five-passenger cabin based on the pre-2002 Explorer SUV to a short cargo bed. Handling is secure and relatively responsive, but the ride is stiff, choppy, and uncomfortable. The 4.0-liter, 210-hp V6 engine is unrefined but provides adequate acceleration. The cargo box is big enough to handle small-to-moderate loads, and its dimensions can be stretched if necessary using an optional bed extender. Clever convenience features include a power-operated rear window that improves ventilation. **Related models:** Ford Ranger, Ford Explorer.

MAJOR REDESIGN: 2001. **SAFETY EQUIPMENT:** Dual front air bags standard. ABS standard. **DRIVE WHEELS:** Rear or part-time 4WD.

Reliability history — Ford Explorer 4WD

TROUBLE SPOTS	95	96	97	98	99	00	01	02
Engine	◐	◐	○	○	◐	◐	●	●
Cooling	○	◐	○	◐	◐	◐	●	●
Fuel	○	○	○	○	○	◐	○	●
Ignition	◐	◐	◐	◐	◐	●	◐	●
Transmission	◐	○	○	○	◐	◐	◐	●
Electrical	◐	○	○	◐	◐	◐	◐	●
Air-conditioning	○	○	◐	◐	●	●	●	●
Suspension	○	○	○	◐	◐	●	●	●
Brakes	●	◐	●	○	○	○	◐	●
Exhaust	●	◐	◐	●	◐	◐	◐	●
Paint/trim/rust	●	●	●	◐	●	●	◐	●
Body integrity	○	○	◐	○	○	○	◐	◐
Power equipment	○	○	●	◐	○	○	◐	●
Body hardware	○	○	○	○	○	○	○	◐
RELIABILITY VERDICT	✔	✔	✔					

Prices — Ford Explorer

1995	$8,000-$10,000
1996	$10,000-$12,000
1997	$12,000-$14,000
1998	$14,000-$16,000
1999	$16,000-$18,000
2000	$18,000-$20,000
2001	$20,000-$22,000
2002	$24,000-$26,000

Crash-test results — Ford Explorer

Model Years	Offset	Full frontal	Side
1995	Accept.	◐/◐	NT
1996	Accept.	◐/◐	NT
1997	Accept.	◐/◐	NT
1998	Accept.	◐/◐	NT
1999	Accept.	◐/◐	●/◐
2000	Accept.	◐/◐	●/◐
2001	Accept.	◐/◐	●/◐
2002	Good	◐/●	NT

Reliability history — Ford Explorer Sport Trac

TROUBLE SPOTS	95	96	97	98	99	00	01	02
Engine							◐	●
Cooling							◐	●
Fuel							◐	○
Ignition							◐	●
Transmission							◐	●
Electrical							○	●
Air-conditioning							◐	●
Suspension							◐	●
Brakes							◐	●
Exhaust							◐	●
Paint/trim/rust							◐	◐
Body integrity							◐	◐
Power equipment							◐	●
Body hardware							○	○
RELIABILITY VERDICT								

Prices — Ford Explorer Sport Trac

Year	Price
1995	–
1996	–
1997	–
1998	–
1999	–
2000	–
2001	$20,000-$22,000
2002	$24,000-$26,000

Crash-test results — Ford Explorer Sport Trac

Model Years	Offset	Full frontal	Side
1995	–	–	–
1996	–	–	–
1997	–	–	–
1998	–	–	–
1999	–	–	–
2000	–	–	–
2001	NT	NT	NT
2002	NT	NT	NT

Ford F-150

1997 model shown

The F-150 is the half-ton version of Ford's best-selling F-Series pickup line. During CR's tests, the boxy pre-1997 F-150 rode relatively well. Its ride and braking improved with a full load. We found the seats erect, but roomy. Ford completely redesigned the F-150 for 1997, improving comfort, handling, and refinement. An optional third door on extended-cab models became available in 1997, and a fourth door was offered in 1999. The supercharged SVT Lightning is very quick. A four-door crew-cab was introduced for 2001. A poor offset-crash showing raises some concern.

MAJOR REDESIGN: 1997. **SAFETY EQUIPMENT:** Driver air bag standard; passenger air bag standard from 1997. Rear-wheel ABS standard; ABS available from 1997, standard from 2001. **DRIVE WHEELS:** Rear or part-time 4WD.

Reliability history

TROUBLE SPOTS	Ford F-150 2WD							
	95	96	97	98	99	00	01	02
Engine	◑	◑	●	◑	●	●	●	●
Cooling	○	◑	◑	●	●	●	●	●
Fuel	◑	○	◑	◑	◑	◑	●	●
Ignition	◑	◑	◑	●	●	●	●	●
Transmission	○	◑	◑	◑	●	●	◑	●
Electrical	○	○	○	○	◑	◑	◑	●
Air conditioning	◑	◑	◑	◑	◑	◑	◑	●
Suspension	◑	○	○	◑	◑	●	◑	●
Brakes	◑	◑	○	◑	◑	◑	●	●
Exhaust	●	◑	◑	●	●	●	●	●
Paint/trim/rust	●	◑	◑	◑	●	◑	◑	●
Body integrity	○	○	○	○	○	◑	◑	●
Power equipment	◑	○	○	◑	◑	◑	●	●
Body hardware	◑	◑	◑	◑	○	○	◑	●
RELIABILITY VERDICT	✓	✓	✓	✓	✓	✓	✓	✓

Prices

1995	$10,000-$12,000
1996	$10,000-$12,000
1997	$14,000-$16,000
1998	$16,000-$18,000
1999	$16,000-$18,000
2000	$18,000-$20,000
2001	$20,000-$22,000
2002	$22,000-$24,000

Crash-test results

Model years	Offset	Full-frontal	Side
1995	NT	◑/◑	NT
1996	NT	◑/◑	NT
1997	Poor	◑/◑	NT
1998	Poor	◑/◑	NT
1999	Poor	◑/◑	◑/NA
2000	Poor	◑/◑	◑/NA
2001	Poor	◑/◑	◑/◑
2002	Poor	◑/◑	◑/◑

Ford Focus

2000 model shown

Introduced in the U.S. for 2000, the Focus is one of the best-performing small cars. Originally designed and sold in Europe, the Focus is nimble and fun to drive, with quick and communicative steering and a comfortable ride. It also uses clever interior packaging to create lots of interior room, and is easy to get in and out of. The weak link is the powertrain: It's not so polished and serves up only average acceleration and fuel economy. The model range includes a sedan, a roomy wagon, a hatchback, and a sporty SVT. Reliability has been below average.

MAJOR REDESIGN: 2000. **SAFETY EQUIPMENT:** Dual front air bags standard. Side air bags and ABS available. Safety-belt pretensioners standard. **DRIVE WHEELS:** Front.

Reliability history

TROUBLE SPOTS	Ford Focus							
	95	96	97	98	99	00	01	02
Engine						◑	◑	●
Cooling						◑	◑	●
Fuel						○	◑	●
Ignition						◑	◑	●
Transmission						◑	◑	●
Electrical						○	○	●
Air conditioning						◑	◑	●
Suspension						○	◑	●
Brakes						●	○	●
Exhaust						◑	◑	●
Paint/trim/rust						◑	◑	●
Body integrity						○	○	●
Power equipment						○	◑	●
Body hardware						●	○	●
RELIABILITY VERDICT								✓

Prices

1995	–
1996	–
1997	–
1998	–
1999	–
2000	$10,000-$12,000
2001	$12,000-$14,000
2002	$12,000-$14,000

Crash-test results

Model years	Offset	Full-frontal	Side
1995	–	–	–
1996	–	–	–
1997	–	–	–
1998	–	–	–
1999	–	–	–
2000	Good	◑/◑	○/◑
2001	Good	◑/◑	○/◑
2002	Good	◑/◑	○/◑

SPORTS/SPORTY CAR

Ford Mustang

2000 model shown

Ford's popular "pony car," the Mustang, was redesigned for 1994 with a more rigid construction and new exterior and interior styling. Available as a coupe or convertible, this rear-wheel-drive car handles steadily on smooth roads, but bounces and steps to the side on bumpy ones. The V6 model feels sluggish; the V8 has more punch. The car's nose dives severely during hard braking. The Mustang was updated for 1999 with fresh styling, more power for both the V6 and V8, and a stiffer structure for the convertible. The more powerful Cobra model also received an upgraded independent rear suspension.

MAJOR REDESIGN: 1994. **SAFETY EQUIPMENT:** Dual front air bags standard. Safety-belt pretensioners standard from 2002. ABS available. **DRIVE WHEELS:** Rear.

SPORTS/SPORTY CAR

Ford Probe

1995 model shown

The Probe hatchback and the related Mazda MX-6 coupe were made in the same Michigan plant and share many powertrain parts. Redesigned for 1993, the Probe has excellent handling and responsive steering. The optional 2.5-liter V6 provides smooth, authoritative acceleration, though the automatic transmission shifts roughly. There's lots of luggage room under the Probe's hatchback, and the rear seatbacks can be folded to increase space further. A typical victim of the fickle sporty-coupe-segment cycle, the Probe was dropped after 1997. **Related model:** Mazda MX-6.

MAJOR REDESIGN: 1993. **SAFETY EQUIPMENT:** Dual front air bags standard. ABS available. **DRIVE WHEELS:** Front.

Ford Mustang

Reliability history

TROUBLE SPOTS	95	96	97	98	99	00	01	02
Engine	●	○	◐	◐	●	●	◐	◐
Cooling	●	◐	○	◐	●	●	◐	◐
Fuel	○	◐	◐	○	○	●	●	◐
Ignition	●	◐	●	◐	●	●	◐	●
Transmission	○	○	◐	◐	◐	◐	●	◐
Electrical	○	◐	○	○	◐	◐	◐	◐
Air-conditioning	○	○	◐	◐	◐	◐	◐	◐
Suspension	◐	○	◐	◐	◐	◐	◐	◐
Brakes	◐	○	○	◐	◐	◐	◐	◐
Exhaust	●	●	◐	◐	●	◐	●	◐
Paint/trim/rust	○	○	○	◐	◐	◐	○	○
Body integrity	●	○	◐	◐	●	○	◐	○
Power equipment	○	◐	◐	◐	◐	●	●	●
Body hardware	●	◐	◐	◐	○	○	○	◐
RELIABILITY VERDICT	✓	✓	✓	✓	✓	✓		

Prices

1995	$8,000-$10,000
1996	$8,000-$10,000
1997	$10,000-$12,000
1998	$12,000-$14,000
1999	$14,000-$16,000
2000	$14,000-$16,000
2001	$16,000-$18,000
2002	$20,000-$22,000

Crash-test results

Model Years	Offset	Full frontal	Side
1995	NT	◐/◐	NT
1996	NT	◐/◐	NT
1997	NT	◐/◐	NT
1998	NT	●/◐	○/○
1999	NT	◐/◐	○/○
2000	NT	◐/◐	○/○
2001	NT	●/◐	○/○
2002	NT	●/◐	○/○

Ford Probe

Reliability history

TROUBLE SPOTS	95	96	97	98	99	00	01	02
Engine	◐							
Cooling	◐							
Fuel	○							
Ignition	●							
Transmission	◐							
Electrical	◐	Insufficient data	Insufficient data					
Air-conditioning	○							
Suspension	◐							
Brakes	○							
Exhaust	○							
Paint/trim/rust	●							
Body integrity	●							
Power equipment	○							
Body hardware	◐							
RELIABILITY VERDICT								

Prices

1995	$4,000-$6,000
1996	$4,000-$6,000
1997	$6,000-$8,000
1998	–
1999	–
2000	–
2001	–
2002	–

Crash-test results

Model Years	Offset	Full frontal	Side
1995	NT	◐/◐	NT
1996	NT	◐/◐	NT
1997	NT	◐/◐	NT
1998	–	–	–
1999	–	–	–
2000	–	–	–
2001	–	–	–
2002	–	–	–

PICKUP TRUCK
Ford Ranger

1998 model shown

As is the case with most trucks, the Ranger's ride is stiff and choppy but the steering is relatively responsive. An extended cab is a worthwhile option, providing extra interior room for luggage; however, even children won't be happy in the small jump seats. The Ranger was redesigned for 1998, when a four-door extended-cab model was added. Handling is relatively good but the ride remains stiff. The Ranger remains one of the better choices in compact pickups. **Related models:** Mazda B-Series, Ford Explorer Sport Trac.

MAJOR REDESIGN: 1998. **SAFETY EQUIPMENT:** Driver air bag standard; passenger side from 1998. Safety-belt pretensioners standard from 2001. ABS available, standard from 2001. **DRIVE WHEELS:** Rear or part-time 4WD.

FAMILY CAR
Ford Taurus

2000 model shown

Available as a sedan or wagon, even the first Taurus provided good handling and comfortable seats for its time. A significant redesign for 1996 brought the Taurus line back up to date, with crisper handling and a firm ride. CR found this version roomy, comfortable, and quiet. A higher-performance SHO version was available through 1999. The Taurus was treated to a style freshening for 2000, when it also picked up such safety equipment as side air bags, adjustable pedals, and an emergency trunk release. The uplevel V6 is powerful, but not terribly refined. **Related model:** Mercury Sable.

MAJOR REDESIGN: 1996, 2000. **SAFETY EQUIPMENT:** Dual front air bags standard. Side air bags available from 2000. Safety-belt pretensioners standard from 2000. ABS available. **DRIVE WHEELS:** Front.

Ford Ranger

Reliability history — Ford Ranger 2WD

TROUBLE SPOTS	95	96	97	98	99	00	01	02
Engine								
Cooling								
Fuel								
Ignition								
Transmission								
Electrical								
Air conditioning								
Suspension								
Brakes								
Exhaust								
Paint/trim/rust								
Body integrity								
Power equipment								
Body hardware								
RELIABILITY VERDICT	✓	✓	✓	✓	✓	✓	✓	

Prices

Year	Price
1995	$6,000-$8,000
1996	$6,000-$8,000
1997	$6,000-$8,000
1998	$6,000-$8,000
1999	$8,000-$10,000
2000	$10,000-$12,000
2001	$12,000-$14,000
2002	$12,000-$14,000

Crash-test results

Model years	Offset	Full-frontal	Side
1995	NT	⊖/⊖	NT
1996	NT	⊖/⊖	NT
1997	NT	⊖/⊖	NT
1998	Accept.	⊖/⊖	NT
1999	Accept.	⊖/⊖	●/NA
2000	Accept.	⊖/⊖	⊖/NA
2001	Accept.	⊖/⊖	⊖/NA
2002	Accept.	⊖/⊖	⊖/NA

Ford Taurus

Reliability history — Ford Taurus

TROUBLE SPOTS	95	96	97	98	99	00	01	02
Engine								
Cooling								
Fuel								
Ignition								
Transmission								
Electrical								
Air conditioning								
Suspension								
Brakes								
Exhaust								
Paint/trim/rust								
Body integrity								
Power equipment								
Body hardware								
RELIABILITY VERDICT		✓	✓	✓	✓	✓	✓	✓

Prices

Year	Price
1995	$4,000-$6,000
1996	$6,000-$8,000
1997	$6,000-$8,000
1998	$6,000-$8,000
1999	$8,000-$10,000
2000	$10,000-$12,000
2001	$12,000-$14,000
2002	$14,000-$16,000

Crash-test results

Model years	Offset	Full-frontal	Side
1995	Good	⊖/⊖	NT
1996	Good	⊖/⊖	NT
1997	Good	⊖/⊖	○/○
1998	Good	⊖/⊖	○/○
1999	Good	●/●	○/○
2000	Good	●/●	○/○
2001	Good	●/●	○/○
2002	Good	●/●	○/○

126 • CONSUMER REPORTS USED CAR BUYING GUIDE 2003

Ford Thunderbird

Ford Windstar

1995 model shown

1998 model shown

A large luxury coupe, the Ford Thunderbird underwent a freshening in 1994. A more refined, fuel-efficient 4.6-liter V8 was introduced. A 3.8-liter V6 was also available, in both standard and supercharged forms. An updated interior further improved the driving experience. The seats aren't very supportive or, in the rear, roomy. 1997 was the last year for this version. The T-Bird reappeared for 2002 as a brand-new roadster, unrelated to the previous car, based on the Lincoln LS and Jaguar S-Type platform. **Related model:** Mercury Cougar till 1997.

MAJOR REDESIGN: 1994, 2002. **SAFETY EQUIPMENT:** Dual front air bags standard. Side air bags and safety-belt pretensioners standard from 2002. ABS available, standard from 2002. **DRIVE WHEELS:** Rear.

New for 1995, this front-wheel-drive model was one of the most refined minivans when it reached the market. Compared to the truck-based Aerostar, the Windstar's ride is comfortable and carlike. The interior is big and quiet, but not as roomy as the extended-length Chrysler minivans. The third seat is heavy and cumbersome to remove, but the low floor makes loading cargo easy. A wider driver's door was new for 1998. The 1999 model received a face-lift, a second sliding side door, and improved controls. Stability control and adjustable pedals became available in 2001. The Windstar's poor reliability is its major weakness.

MAJOR REDESIGN: 1995, 1999. **SAFETY EQUIPMENT:** Dual front air bags standard. Side air bags available from 1999. Safety-belt pretensioners standard from 2001. ABS standard. **DRIVE WHEELS:** Front.

Ford Thunderbird

Reliability history

TROUBLE SPOTS	95	96	97	98	99	00	01	02
Engine	○	○	○					
Cooling	○	●	◐					
Fuel	◐	○	○					
Ignition	◐	◐	◐					
Transmission	●	○	○					
Electrical	◐	○	○					
Air-conditioning	○	◐	○					
Suspension	◐	◐	◐					
Brakes	◐	◐	◐					
Exhaust	●	●	○					
Paint/trim/rust	◐	◐	◐					
Body integrity	◐	○	○					
Power equipment	○	◐	◐					
Body hardware	◐	◐	○					
RELIABILITY VERDICT	✓	✓	✓					

Insufficient data

Prices

1995	$6,000-$8,000
1996	$6,000-$8,000
1997	$8,000-$10,000
1998	–
1999	–
2000	–
2001	–
2002	More than $30,000

Crash-test results

Model Years	Offset	Full frontal	Side
1995	NT	◐/◐	NT
1996	NT	◐/◐	NT
1997	NT	◐/◐	○/●
1998	–	–	–
1999	–	–	–
2000	–	–	–
2001	–	–	–
2002	NT	◐/◐	●/NA

Ford Windstar

Reliability history

TROUBLE SPOTS	95	96	97	98	99	00	01	02
Engine	●	◐	○	◐	◐	◐	◐	◐
Cooling	◐	○	◐	◐	●	◐	◐	◐
Fuel	○	◐	○	◐	◐	◐	◐	◐
Ignition	○	○	◐	◐	◐	◐	◐	●
Transmission	●	○	○	○	◐	○	◐	●
Electrical	●	●	●	●	●	◐	●	◐
Air-conditioning	○	○	◐	◐	◐	◐	●	◐
Suspension	○	◐	◐	◐	●	◐	●	◐
Brakes	●	●	●	◐	◐	◐	◐	◐
Exhaust	◐	◐	◐	◐	◐	◐	◐	●
Paint/trim/rust	◐	◐	◐	○	○	◐	◐	●
Body integrity	◐	○	○	◐	◐	◐	◐	○
Power equipment	◐	◐	◐	◐	◐	○	○	◐
Body hardware	◐	◐	◐	◐	◐	◐	◐	◐
RELIABILITY VERDICT								

Prices

1995	$6,000-$8,000
1996	$6,000-$8,000
1997	$8,000-$10,000
1998	$10,000-$12,000
1999	$12,000-$14,000
2000	$14,000-$16,000
2001	$16,000-$18,000
2002	$20,000-$22,000

Crash-test results

Model Years	Offset	Full frontal	Side
1995	Good	◐/◐	NT
1996	Good	◐/◐	NT
1997	Good	◐/◐	NT
1998	Good	◐/◐	NT
1999	Good	◐/◐	◐/◐
2000	Good	◐/◐	◐/◐
2001	Good	◐/◐	◐/◐
2002	Good	◐/◐	◐/◐

GMC Envoy

2002 model shown

This body-on-frame SUV shares its platform with the Chevrolet TrailBlazer. Strengths include a compliant, if slightly jiggly, ride and a powerful inline Six engine. The Envoy corners clumsily, with slow, vague steering and lots of body lean. A stability-control system might have improved the twitchy emergency handling CR found in its tests, but none is offered. Braking is mediocre. The interior is quiet for the most part, but some wind noise intrudes. The front seats aren't particularly comfortable, and the seat-mounted safety belts are annoying. First-year reliability was poor. **Related models:** Chevrolet TrailBlazer, Oldsmobile Bravada.

MAJOR REDESIGN: 2002. **SAFETY EQUIPMENT:** Dual front and side air bags standard. ABS standard. **DRIVE WHEELS:** Rear or selectable 4WD.

Reliability history

TROUBLE SPOTS	GMC Envoy
	95 96 97 98 99 00 01 02
Engine	●
Cooling	●
Fuel	●
Ignition	●
Transmission	◐
Electrical	◐
Air conditioning	◐
Suspension	◐
Brakes	●
Exhaust	●
Paint/trim/rust	◐
Body integrity	○
Power equipment	◐
Body hardware	◐
RELIABILITY VERDICT	

Prices

1995	–
1996	–
1997	–
1998	–
1999	–
2000	–
2001	–
2002	More than $30,000

Crash-test results

Model years	Offset	Full-frontal	Side
1995	–	–	–
1996	–	–	–
1997	–	–	–
1998	–	–	–
1999	–	–	–
2000	–	–	–
2001	–	–	–
2002	Marg.	○/○	●/◐

GMC Jimmy

1997 model shown

Available in two- and four-door models. Pre-1995 models have a trucklike ride and fairly ungainly handling. A significant redesign for 1995 eliminated many crudities, but the Jimmy still leaned a lot in turns, the brakes were inferior, and fit and finish were subpar. Strengths include a strong 4.3-liter V6 and a smooth-shifting automatic transmission. The 1998 models received marginally better brakes, and a selectable 4WD system was added a year later. Reliability and crash-test results are both concerns. 2001 was the Jimmy's last year. **Related models:** Chevrolet Blazer, Oldsmobile Bravada.

MAJOR REDESIGN: 1995. **SAFETY EQUIPMENT:** Driver air bag standard; passenger side from 1998. ABS standard. **DRIVE WHEELS:** Rear or part-time 4WD; AWD available from 1995 to 1997; selectable 4WD available from 1999.

Reliability history

TROUBLE SPOTS	GMC Jimmy
	95 96 97 98 99 00 01 02
Engine	○ ● ○ ◐ ● ○ ○ ◐
Cooling	○ ● ◐ ○ ● ● ◐
Fuel	● ● ◐ ◐ ◐ ○ ●
Ignition	○ ◐ ● ◐ ○ ● ●
Transmission	○ ○ ◐ ● ◐ ● ◐
Electrical	● ● ● ◐ ● ◐ ◐
Air conditioning	○ ◐ ● ◐ ○ ◐ ◐
Suspension	○ ◐ ● ◐ ○ ● ◐
Brakes	● ● ◐ ○ ○ ● ◐
Exhaust	○ ◐ ● ◐ ● ● ●
Paint/trim/rust	○ ○ ◐ ◐ ◐ ◐ ●
Body integrity	○ ◐ ○ ○ ◐ ◐ ◐
Power equipment	○ ◐ ● ○ ○ ◐ ◐
Body hardware	○ ○ ◐ ● ● ○ ○
RELIABILITY VERDICT	

Prices

1995	$6,000-$8,000
1996	$8,000-$10,000
1997	$8,000-$10,000
1998	$10,000-$12,000
1999	$12,000-$14,000
2000	$14,000-$16,000
2001	$16,000-$18,000
2002	–

Crash-test results

Model years	Offset	Full-frontal	Side
1995	Poor	○/●	NT
1996	Poor	○/●	NT
1997	Poor	○/●	NT
1998	Poor	◐/◐	NT
1999	Poor	○/◐	●/○
2000	Poor	○/◐	●/○
2001	Poor	○/◐	●/○
2002	–	–	–

GMC Safari

1999 model shown

The rear-drive GMC Safari has always been better at hauling cargo than people. Tall and squarish, it offers commodious cargo space, especially in extended-length versions. (As of 1995, all Safaris were extended-length.) Its large-displacement V6 makes it better at towing a trailer than most other minivans, and it has been available in AWD for most of its long life. But on the road, the Safari's clumsy handling and harsh, truck-like ride reveal its outdated underpinnings. Front-seat occupants also have too little foot room. In 1996, the Safari received an improved instrument panel and dual air bags. **Related model:** Chevrolet Astro.

MAJOR REDESIGN: 1985. **SAFETY EQUIPMENT:** Driver air bag standard; passenger side from 1996. ABS standard. **DRIVE WHEELS:** Rear or AWD.

GMC Sierra C/K1500

1998 model shown

This full-sized half-ton pickup ("C" is used for 2WD versions, "K" for 4WD) was fundamentally unchanged from 1991 through 1998, though upgraded powertrains and an optional third door for extended-cab models were added in 1996. A complete redesign for 1999 brought powerful, more efficient engines and friendlier interior packaging. Braking and handling were also significantly improved. Extended-cab models received a fourth door for 2000, and the pricey, AWD C3 model joined the line in 2001, later called Denali. **Related models:** Chevrolet C/K1500, Chevrolet Silverado.

MAJOR REDESIGN: 1999. **SAFETY EQUIPMENT:** Driver air bag standard from 1996; passenger side from 1997. ABS standard. **DRIVE WHEELS:** Rear or part-time 4WD; selectable 4WD available from 1999, AWD available from 2001.

GMC Safari

Reliability history

TROUBLE SPOTS	95	96	97	98	99	00	01	02
Engine	○	○	○	○	◐	●	●	
Cooling	○	◐	○	◐	◐	●	◐	
Fuel	◐	●	●	○	○	○	◐	
Ignition	◐	●	●	◐	◐	●	●	
Transmission	○	◐	●	◐	○	○	◐	
Electrical	●	●	●	◐	◐	○	○	
Air-conditioning	●	◐	●	○	○	◐	●	
Suspension	◐	●	◐	◐	◐	◐	○	
Brakes	●	◐	●	◐	◐	◐	●	
Exhaust	◐	○	◐	◐	◐	●	●	
Paint/trim/rust	○	○	◐	◐	●	●	●	
Body integrity	◐	●	●	◐	●	◐	●	
Power equipment	◐	◐	●	◐	○	○	◐	
Body hardware	◐	●	●	●	●	●	○	
RELIABILITY VERDICT								

Insufficient data

Prices

Year	Price
1995	$6,000-$8,000
1996	$8,000-$10,000
1997	$10,000-$12,000
1998	$10,000-$12,000
1999	$12,000-$14,000
2000	$14,000-$16,000
2001	$16,000-$18,000
2002	$18,000-$20,000

Crash-test results

Model Years	Offset	Full frontal	Side
1995	NT	NT	NT
1996	Poor	○/○	NT
1997	Poor	○/○	NT
1998	Poor	○/○	NT
1999	Poor	○/◐	NT
2000	Poor	○/◐	NT
2001	Poor	○/◐	NT
2002	Poor	○/◐	NT

GMC Sierra 1500 4WD

Reliability history

TROUBLE SPOTS	95	96	97	98	99	00	01	02
Engine	○	○	○	○	◐	●	●	●
Cooling	◐	◐	◐	○	◐	●	●	●
Fuel	●	◐	●	○	○	◐	●	●
Ignition	◐	●	●	◐	◐	●	●	●
Transmission	○	○	◐	◐	○	◐	●	●
Electrical	●	●	●	◐	◐	◐	●	●
Air-conditioning	○	○	○	◐	●	●	●	●
Suspension	◐	○	○	◐	◐	◐	●	●
Brakes	◐	◐	◐	◐	○	◐	●	●
Exhaust	○	◐	●	●	◐	●	●	●
Paint/trim/rust	○	○	◐	●	●	◐	●	●
Body integrity	○	○	◐	◐	●	○	○	●
Power equipment	●	●	◐	○	◐	◐	●	●
Body hardware	○	○	○	◐	●	○	●	●
RELIABILITY VERDICT	✓							

Prices

Year	Price
1995	$10,000-$12,000
1996	$10,000-$12,000
1997	$12,000-$14,000
1998	$12,000-$14,000
1999	$14,000-$16,000
2000	$16,000-$18,000
2001	$18,000-$20,000
2002	$20,000-$22,000

Crash-test results

Model Years	Offset	Full frontal	Side
1995	NT	●/○	NT
1996	NT	●/○	NT
1997	NT	●/○	NT
1998	NT	◐/○	NT
1999	Marg.	NT	NT
2000	Marg.	○/◐	NT
2001	Marg.	○/◐	NT
2002	Marg.	○/◐	NT

GMC Sonoma

GMC Suburban, Yukon XL

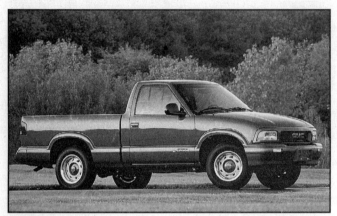

1997 model shown

2000 model shown

Redesigned in 1994, the compact Sonoma and mechanically identical Chevrolet S-10 offer a strong 4.3-liter V6 and a quiet, roomy cabin. Handling is quite trucklike, however, with a surplus of body lean in corners. The steering feels both vague and heavy, the ride is stiff, and the brakes are inferior. The Sonoma's reliability record and crash-test results are also subpar. In 1997, extended-cab versions gained a driver-side third door useful for loading cargo. A four-door crew-cab model was new for 2001. **Related models:** Chevrolet S-10, Isuzu Hombre.

MAJOR REDESIGN: 1994. **SAFETY EQUIPMENT:** Driver air bag standard; passenger side from 1998. ABS available; standard from 1996. **DRIVE WHEELS:** Rear or part-time 4WD.

GMC's largest SUV, the Suburban emphasizes "utility" with its ability to seat up to nine people, haul massive cargo loads, or tow a 10,000-lb. trailer. Available in 2WD and 4WD versions, the Suburban shares its powertrain lineup with GM's full-sized pickups. If you're looking for a used Suburban, look for a 2001 model, which is after a major redesign and is reliable enough. The renamed, updated, and upgraded Yukon XL handles commendably and its brakes work well. It also has a well-controlled ride and an improved 4WD system. **Related model:** Chevrolet Suburban.

MAJOR REDESIGN: 2000. **SAFETY EQUIPMENT:** Driver air bag standard; passenger side from 1997. Side air bags standard from 2000. ABS standard. **DRIVE WHEELS:** Rear or part-time 4WD through 1997; rear or selectable 4WD from 1998; AWD available from 2001.

Reliability history — GMC S-15 Sonoma V6 4WD

TROUBLE SPOTS	95	96	97	98	99	00	01	02
Engine						●	●	
Cooling						●	●	
Fuel						●	●	
Ignition						●	●	
Transmission						●	●	
Electrical	Insufficient data	Insufficient data	Insufficient data	Insufficient data	Insufficient data	●	◐	Insufficient data
Air conditioning						●	◐	
Suspension						●	◐	
Brakes						○	◐	
Exhaust						●	●	
Paint/trim/rust						◐	◐	
Body integrity						○	○	
Power equipment						●	●	
Body hardware						●	◐	
RELIABILITY VERDICT								

Prices

1995	$4,000-$6,000
1996	$4,000-$6,000
1997	$6,000-$8,000
1998	$6,000-$8,000
1999	$8,000-$10,000
2000	$8,000-$10,000
2001	$10,000-$12,000
2002	$10,000-$12,000

Crash-test results

Model years	Offset	Full-frontal	Side
1995	NT	○/●	NT
1996	NT	○/●	NT
1997	NT	○/◐	NT
1998	Marg.	●/◐	NT
1999	Marg.	◐/○	○/NA
2000	Marg.	◐/○	○/NA
2001	Marg.	◐/○	○/NA
2002	Marg.	◐/○	○/NA

Reliability history — GMC Suburban, Yukon XL

TROUBLE SPOTS	95	96	97	98	99	00	01	02
Engine	◐	○	○	◐	○	◐	●	●
Cooling	○	●	◐	◐	◐	◐	●	◐
Fuel	○	◐	◐	◐	◐	◐	●	●
Ignition	◐	◐	●	●	●	●	●	●
Transmission	○	○	○	◐	◐	◐	●	◐
Electrical	●	●	●	●	●	◐	◐	○
Air conditioning	●	◐	○	○	◐	●	◐	○
Suspension	○	○	◐	◐	◐	◐	◐	○
Brakes	●	●	●	●	●	●	◐	◐
Exhaust	◐	◐	●	◐	◐	◐	●	◐
Paint/trim/rust	○	◐	◐	●	●	●	●	◐
Body integrity	○	○	○	○	○	◐	◐	◐
Power equipment	○	○	○	◐	◐	◐	●	◐
Body hardware	●	○	○	○	○	●	◐	◐
RELIABILITY VERDICT	✓				✓	✓		

Prices

1995	$14,000-$16,000
1996	$14,000-$16,000
1997	$16,000-$18,000
1998	$18,000-$20,000
1999	$20,000-$22,000
2000	$28,000-$30,000
2001	More than $30,000
2002	More than $30,000

Crash-test results

Model years	Offset	Full-frontal	Side
1995	NT	NT	NT
1996	NT	NT	NT
1997	NT	NT	NT
1998	NT	◐/○	NT
1999	NT	◐/○	NT
2000	NT	NT	NT
2001	NT	◐/○	NT
2002	NT	◐/○	NT

GMC Yukon

2000 model shown

Based on GM's full-sized pickup, the Yukon line expanded in 1995, when a four-door model was introduced. The cabin is quiet, the cargo bay is commodious, and the Yukon rides and handles reasonably well for such a big vehicle. The Yukon got better all around in 2000, when it moved to a new platform shared with the Sierra and other full-sized GM trucks, gaining engines that are stronger and more economical, better brakes and handling, and a more comfortable ride. **Related models:** Chevrolet Tahoe, Cadillac Escalade.

MAJOR REDESIGN: 1995, 2000. **SAFETY EQUIPMENT:** Driver air bag standard; passenger side from 1997. Side air bags standard from 2000. ABS standard. **DRIVE WHEELS:** Rear or part-time 4WD through 1997; rear or selectable 4WD from 1998; AWD available from 2001.

Honda Accord

CR Good Bet

1998 model shown

The Accord has been one of our top-rated sedans for years. A 1994 redesign gave the car a quieter ride and a slightly larger interior. A 2.7-liter V6 became available in 1995, though only with an automatic transmission. While smoother and quieter than the standard 2.2-liter Four, the larger engine made the car more front-heavy and less nimble. Interior space is fine for four, tight for five. A wagon model was available through 1997. The redesigned 1998 Accord is larger and quieter but similar overall. It is very refined for the class, especially when equipped with the 3.0-liter V6 engine.

MAJOR REDESIGN: 1994, 1998. **SAFETY EQUIPMENT:** Dual front air bags standard. Side air bags available from 2000. Safety-belt pretensioners standard from 2000. ABS available. **DRIVE WHEELS:** Front.

GMC Yukon — Reliability history

TROUBLE SPOTS	95	96	97	98	99	00	01	02
Engine								
Cooling								
Fuel								
Ignition								
Transmission								
Electrical								
Air-conditioning								
Suspension								
Brakes								
Exhaust								
Paint/trim/rust								
Body integrity								
Power equipment								
Body hardware								
RELIABILITY VERDICT	✓			✓		✓		✓

GMC Yukon — Prices

Year	Price
1995	$12,000-$14,000
1996	$14,000-$16,000
1997	$16,000-$18,000
1998	$18,000-$20,000
1999	$20,000-$22,000
2000	$28,000-$30,000
2001	More than $30,000
2002	More than $30,000

GMC Yukon — Crash-test results

Model Years	Offset	Full frontal	Side
1995	NT	NT	NT
1996	NT	○/◐	NT
1997	NT	○/◐	NT
1998	NT	○/◐	NT
1999	NT	○/◐	NT
2000	NT	○/◐	NT
2001	NT	○/◐	NT
2002	NT	○/◐	NT

Honda Accord — Reliability history

TROUBLE SPOTS	95	96	97	98	99	00	01	02
Engine								
Cooling								
Fuel								
Ignition								
Transmission								
Electrical								
Air-conditioning								
Suspension								
Brakes								
Exhaust								
Paint/trim/rust								
Body integrity								
Power equipment								
Body hardware								
RELIABILITY VERDICT	✓	✓	✓	✓	✓	✓	✓	✓

Honda Accord — Prices

1995	$8,000-$10,000
1996	$10,000-$12,000
1997	$12,000-$14,000
1998	$12,000-$14,000
1999	$14,000-$16,000
2000	$16,000-$18,000
2001	$18,000-$20,000
2002	$20,000-$22,000

Honda Accord — Crash-test results

Model Years	Offset	Full frontal	Side
1995	Accept.	◐/○	NT
1996	Accept.	◐/○	NT
1997	Accept.	◐/○	○/◐
1998	Accept.	◐/○	◐/◐
1999	Accept.	◐/○	◐/◐
2000	Accept.	◐/○	◐/◐
2001	Accept.	◐/◐	◐/◐
2002	Accept.	◐/◐	◐/◐

Honda Civic

1996 model shown

CR Good Bet

Long a CONSUMER REPORTS recommended model, the Civic has come in a series of coupe, sedan, and hatchback versions through the years. The 1992-1995 models have noisy but efficient high-revving four-cylinder engines. Braking is capable, but handling can be twitchy in abrupt maneuvers. A 1996 redesign improved the handling and added refinement throughout. The engines also grew quieter. Redesigned for 2001, the current Civic offers a bit more cabin space, despite a slight exterior downsizing. The new model's ride is less supple than its predecessor's, however, and road noise is pronounced. ABS is standard on the uplevel EX, unavailable on other versions.

MAJOR REDESIGN: 1996, 2001. **SAFETY EQUIPMENT:** Dual front air bags standard. Side air bags available from 2001. Safety-belt pretensioners standard from 2001. ABS available. **DRIVE WHEELS:** Front.

Honda Civic del Sol

1995 model shown

The Civic del Sol is a two-seater with a removable roof panel that makes it a pseudo convertible. Despite its roadsterlike configuration, handling is nothing special, and the del Sol doesn't feel sporty to drive. The ride is busy, and the flexing body creaks on most roads. It was offered with a range of four-cylinder engines, with the high-revving 160-hp VTEC version providing the most power. The shifter works smoothly and front legroom is quite generous. The trunk has lots of room, too, even with the roof panel stowed inside. The del Sol was dropped after 1997.

MAJOR REDESIGN: 1993. **SAFETY EQUIPMENT:** Dual front air bags standard. ABS standard on VTEC model. **DRIVE WHEELS:** Front.

Honda Civic

Reliability history

TROUBLE SPOTS	95	96	97	98	99	00	01	02
Engine	●	●	●	●	●	●	●	●
Cooling	●	●	●	●	●	●	●	●
Fuel	●	●	●	●	●	●	●	●
Ignition	●	●	●	●	●	●	●	●
Transmission	●	●	●	●	●	●	●	●
Electrical	◐	●	●	●	●	●	●	●
Air conditioning	○	◐	●	●	●	●	●	●
Suspension	◐	●	●	●	●	●	◐	●
Brakes	◐	◐	◐	●	●	●	●	●
Exhaust	○	○	○	●	●	●	●	●
Paint/trim/rust	◐	◐	◐	●	●	◐	●	◐
Body integrity	◐	○	◐	◐	●	◐	◐	◐
Power equipment	●	◐	◐	●	●	●	◐	●
Body hardware	◐	○	◐	●	●	◐	○	◐
RELIABILITY VERDICT	✓	✓	✓	✓	✓	✓	✓	✓

Prices

1995	$6,000-$8,000
1996	$6,000-$8,000
1997	$8,000-$10,000
1998	$10,000-$12,000
1999	$10,000-$12,000
2000	$12,000-$14,000
2001	$12,000-$14,000
2002	$14,000-$16,000

Crash-test results

Model years	Offset	Full-frontal	Side
1995	NT	○/○	NT
1996	Accept.	◐/●	NT
1997	Accept.	◐/●	○/○
1998	Accept.	◐/●	○/○
1999	Accept.	◐/●	○/○
2000	Accept.	◐/●	○/○
2001	Good	●/●	◐/●
2002	Good	●/●	◐/●

Honda Civic del Sol

Reliability history

TROUBLE SPOTS	95	96	97	98	99	00	01	02
Engine								
Cooling								
Fuel								
Ignition	NOT							
Transmission								
Electrical	ENOUGH							
Air conditioning								
Suspension	DATA							
Brakes								
Exhaust	TO							
Paint/trim/rust								
Body integrity								
Power equipment	RATE							
Body hardware								
RELIABILITY VERDICT								

Prices

1995	$6,000-$8,000
1996	$8,000-$10,000
1997	$8,000-$10,000
1998	–
1999	–
2000	–
2001	–
2002	–

Crash-test results

Model years	Offset	Full-frontal	Side
1995	NT	NT	NT
1996	NT	NT	NT
1997	NT	NT	NT
1998	–		
1999	–		
2000	–		
2001	–		
2002	–		

Honda CR-V

1997 model shown

The CR-V, new for 1997, was Honda's first foray into the small sport-utility market. Derived from Civic mechanicals, the CR-V resembles a high station wagon more than a traditional SUV. Initially, it was available with AWD only. The ride is compliant and carlike, but handling is fairly clumsy. The four-cylinder engine is noisy, and acceleration is less than sizzling. The driving position was awkward and the rear gate a nuisance to use. A front-wheel-drive version and a five-speed manual transmission were added for 1998, and 1999 brought 20 more horsepower—a modest improvement. The 2002 redesign improved the CR-V dramatically.

MAJOR REDESIGN: 1997, 2002. **SAFETY EQUIPMENT:** Dual front air bags standard. Side air bags available from 2002. ABS available. Safety-belt pretensioners standard from 1998. **DRIVE WHEELS:** Front or AWD.

Reliability history — Honda CR-V

TROUBLE SPOTS	95	96	97	98	99	00	01	02
Engine			●	●	●	●	●	●
Cooling			●	●	●	●	●	●
Fuel			●	●	●	●	●	◐
Ignition			●	●	●	●	●	●
Transmission			●	●	●	●	●	●
Electrical			●	●	●	●	●	●
Air-conditioning			●	●	●	●	●	●
Suspension			◐	●	●	●	●	●
Brakes			●	●	●	●	●	●
Exhaust			●	●	●	●	●	●
Paint/trim/rust			◐	◐	●	●	●	●
Body integrity			●	●	◐	●	●	◐
Power equipment			●	◐	●	●	●	●
Body hardware			◐	●	●	●	◐	●
RELIABILITY VERDICT			✓	✓	✓	✓	✓	✓

Prices

1995	–
1996	–
1997	$12,000-$14,000
1998	$12,000-$14,000
1999	$14,000-$16,000
2000	$16,000-$18,000
2001	$18,000-$20,000
2002	$20,000-$22,000

Crash-test results

Model Years	Offset	Full frontal	Side
1995	–	–	–
1996	–	–	–
1997	Marg.	NT	NT
1998	Marg.	◐/●	NT
1999	Marg.	◐/●	◐/●
2000	Marg.	◐/●	◐/●
2001	Marg.	◐/●	◐/●
2002	Good	◐/●	◐/●

Honda Insight

2000 model shown

The gas/electric hybrid Insight is a small two-seater that debuted as a 2000 model. The novel powertrain consists of a small three-cylinder gasoline engine and a 13-hp electric motor. Fuel economy is outstanding—51 mpg overall in our tests—but the good news ends there. Acceleration is reasonable, but it takes a lot of shifting to keep up with highway traffic. A continuously variable transmission became available in 2001. The interior is cramped, hard-riding, noisy, and uncomfortable. It doesn't corner eagerly, and trunk space is largely usurped by the battery pack. Among hybrids, both the Toyota Prius and the '03 Honda Civic Hybrid are better cars.

MAJOR REDESIGN: 2000. **SAFETY EQUIPMENT:** Dual front air bags standard. ABS standard. Safety-belt pretensioners standard. **DRIVE WHEELS:** Front.

Reliability history

TROUBLE SPOTS	95	96	97	98	99	00	01	02
Engine								
Cooling								
Fuel								
Ignition				NOT				
Transmission								
Electrical				ENOUGH				
Air-conditioning								
Suspension				DATA				
Brakes								
Exhaust				TO				
Paint/trim/rust								
Body integrity				RATE				
Power equipment								
Body hardware								
RELIABILITY VERDICT								

Prices

1995	–
1996	–
1997	–
1998	–
1999	–
2000	$14,000-$16,000
2001	$16,000-$18,000
2002	$16,000-$18,000

Crash-test results

Model Years	Offset	Full frontal	Side
1995	–	–	–
1996	–	–	–
1997	–	–	–
1998	–	–	–
1999	–	–	–
2000	NT	◐/●	NT
2001	NT	◐/●	◐/NA
2002	NT	◐/●	◐/NA

MINIVAN
Honda Odyssey

CR Good Bet

1999 model shown

The original Odyssey, introduced in 1995, was derived from the Accord and shares the car's good handling and supple ride. It also has four swing-out doors instead of a typical minivan's sliding doors. The third-row bench seat cleverly folds and stows flush with the floor. The vehicle's chief weakness is its overworked four-cylinder engine. The Odyssey was reinvented as a traditional minivan for 1999, complete with sliding doors and a smooth 3.5-liter V6. Traction control became standard for 2001. That second-generation Odyssey is a top pick, because of its agile handling and large, flexible interior. **Related model:** Isuzu Oasis up to 1998.

MAJOR REDESIGN: 1995, 1999. **SAFETY EQUIPMENT:** Dual front air bags standard. Side air bags standard from 2002. Safety-belt pretensioners standard from 2000. ABS standard. **DRIVE WHEELS:** Front.

Reliability history — Honda Odyssey

TROUBLE SPOTS	95	96	97	98	99	00	01	02
Engine								
Cooling								
Fuel								
Ignition								
Transmission								
Electrical								
Air conditioning								
Suspension								
Brakes								
Exhaust								
Paint/trim/rust								
Body integrity								
Power equipment								
Body hardware								
RELIABILITY VERDICT	✔	✔	✔	✔	✔	✔	✔	✔

Prices

1995	$10,000-$12,000
1996	$12,000-$14,000
1997	$14,000-$16,000
1998	$16,000-$18,000
1999	$20,000-$22,000
2000	$24,000-$26,000
2001	$26,000-$28,000
2002	$28,000-$30,000

Crash-test results

Model years	Offset	Full-frontal	Side
1995	Marg.	◐/○	NT
1996	Marg.	◐/○	NT
1997	Marg.	◐/○	NT
1998	Marg.	◐	NT
1999	Good	◐/◐	NT
2000	Good	◐/◐	◐/◐
2001	Good	◐/◐	◐/◐
2002	Good	◐/◐	◐/◐

SPORT-UTILITY VEHICLE
Honda Passport

1998 model shown

Honda took a shortcut into the sport-utility market for 1994 by rebadging the Isuzu Rodeo. The Passport's handling felt clumsy in our tests, the steering was slow, the body leaned heavily in turns, and the ride was stiff. Space is generous for passengers, modest for cargo. The smooth 3.2-liter V6 is a better choice than the Four (which was dropped for 1997). For 1996, the Passport received more power for the V6 and an improved dashboard. A significant 1998 redesign updated the exterior and interior and brought more power, but the ride remained stiff and bouncy. **Related model:** Isuzu Rodeo.

MAJOR REDESIGN: 1994, 1998. **SAFETY EQUIPMENT:** Dual front air bags standard from 1996. Rear-wheel ABS standard through 1997; four-wheel ABS standard from 1998. **DRIVE WHEELS:** Rear or part-time 4WD.

Reliability history — Honda Passport

TROUBLE SPOTS	95	96	97	98	99	00	01	02
Engine								
Cooling								
Fuel								
Ignition								
Transmission								
Electrical		Insufficient data	Insufficient data					Insufficient data
Air conditioning								
Suspension								
Brakes								
Exhaust								
Paint/trim/rust								
Body integrity								
Power equipment								
Body hardware								
RELIABILITY VERDICT	✔		✔					

Prices

1995	$10,000-$12,000
1996	$10,000-$12,000
1997	$12,000-$14,000
1998	$14,000-$16,000
1999	$18,000-$20,000
2000	$20,000-$22,000
2001	$22,000-$24,000
2002	$26,000-$28,000

Crash-test results

Model years	Offset	Full-frontal	Side
1995	NT	○/○	NT
1996	Poor	◐/○	NT
1997	Poor	◐/○	NT
1998	Poor	○/◐	NT
1999	Poor	○/◐	◐/◐
2000	Poor	◐/◐	◐/◐
2001	Poor	◐/◐	◐/◐
2002	Marg.	○/◐	◐/◐

Honda Prelude

1998 model shown

The Prelude is very quick and nimble. The steering feels well weighted and responsive. Four-wheel steering was available on Si 4WS models until 1994. A high-performance VTEC engine was added as an option for 1993. The Prelude's interior is quiet for a sporty car, with firm front seats, a tight rear seat, and a dazzling, semi-digital instrument display. A 1997 redesign improved the line with a more traditional dash, standard VTEC engines, and an automatic transmission that could be manually shifted. The Prelude was discontinued after the 2001 model year.

MAJOR REDESIGN: 1997. **SAFETY EQUIPMENT:** Dual front air bags standard. ABS standard from 1997. **DRIVE WHEELS:** Front.

Reliability history

TROUBLE SPOTS	95 96 97 98 99 00 01 02
Engine	
Cooling	
Fuel	
Ignition	NOT
Transmission	
Electrical	ENOUGH
Air-conditioning	
Suspension	DATA
Brakes	
Exhaust	TO
Paint/trim/rust	
Body integrity	RATE
Power equipment	
Body hardware	
RELIABILITY VERDICT	

Prices

1995	$10,000-$12,000
1996	$10,000-$12,000
1997	$12,000-$14,000
1998	$14,000-$16,000
1999	$16,000-$18,000
2000	$18,000-$20,000
2001	$20,000-$22,000
2002	–

Crash-test results

Model Years	Offset	Full frontal	Side
1995	NT	NT	NT
1996	NT	NT	NT
1997	NT	NT	NT
1998	NT	NT	NT
1999	NT	NT	NT
2000	NT	NT	NT
2001	NT	NT	NT
2002	–	–	–

Honda S2000

2000 model shown

The rear-drive S2000 debuted for the 2000 model year as a pure, uncompromising sports car. It's quick, agile, and has tenacious tire grip, but it's also noisy and harsh-riding. The S2000's 2.0-liter Four easily revs to 9,000 RPM and develops 240 hp without turbo- or super-charging. But stirring performance is only available between 6,000 revs and the screaming redline. Otherwise, power delivery is less urgent and makes the car feel ordinary in everyday driving. The six-speed manual transmission is crisp and precise. This car is fun to drive fast, but as a commuter car it's cramped and frenetically noisy inside.

MAJOR REDESIGN: 2000. **SAFETY EQUIPMENT:** Dual front air bags standard. Safety-belt pretensioners and ABS standard. **DRIVE WHEELS:** Rear.

Reliability history

TROUBLE SPOTS	Honda S2000 95 96 97 98 99 00 01 02
Engine	◕ ◕
Cooling	◕ ◕
Fuel	◕ ◕
Ignition	◕ ◕
Transmission	◕ ◕ (Insufficient data)
Electrical	◕ ◕
Air-conditioning	◕ ◕
Suspension	◔ ◕
Brakes	◕ ◕
Exhaust	◕ ◕
Paint/trim/rust	◖ ◕
Body integrity	◕ ◕
Power equipment	○ ◔
Body hardware	◕ ◕
RELIABILITY VERDICT	✓ ✓

Prices

1995	–
1996	–
1997	–
1998	–
1999	–
2000	$28,000-$30,000
2001	More than $30,000
2002	More than $30,000

Crash-test results

Model Years	Offset	Full frontal	Side
1995	–	–	–
1996	–	–	–
1997	–	–	–
1998	–	–	–
1999	–	–	–
2000	NT	NT	NT
2001	NT	NT	NT
2002	NT	NT	NT

Hyundai Accent

2000 model shown

The small 1995 Hyundai Accent was a marked improvement over the unreliable, poor-performing Excel it replaced. With its freshened interior and styling, the entry-level Accent competed well with its peers, the Geo Metro and Toyota Tercel. The 1.5-liter, 92-hp Four accelerates adequately. The ride is choppy and noisy. As expected for such a small car, the rear seat is tight for tall people. Look for a model that is equipped with the optional power steering—it's a must. A 2000 redesign brought a roomier interior and updated styling, and a stronger, 1.6-liter engine became available a year later. Accents equipped with ABS are hard to find.

MAJOR REDESIGN: 1995, 2000. **SAFETY EQUIPMENT:** Dual front air bags standard. Safety-belt pretensioners standard from 2000. ABS available until 2000. **DRIVE WHEELS:** Front.

Reliability history

TROUBLE SPOTS	Hyundai Accent							
	95	96	97	98	99	00	01	02
Engine							●	
Cooling							●	
Fuel							○	
Ignition							●	
Transmission							◒	
Electrical	Insufficient data	Insufficient data	Insufficient data	Insufficient data	Insufficient data	Insufficient data	◒	Insufficient data
Air conditioning							◒	
Suspension							●	
Brakes							●	
Exhaust							●	
Paint/trim/rust							●	
Body integrity							◒	
Power equipment							●	
Body hardware							○	
RELIABILITY VERDICT							✓	

Prices

1995	$2,000-$4,000
1996	$2,000-$4,000
1997	$4,000-$6,000
1998	$4,000-$6,000
1999	$4,000-$6,000
2000	$6,000-$8,000
2001	$8,000-$10,000
2002	$8,000-$10,000

Crash-test results

Model years	Offset	Full-frontal	Side
1995	NT	NT	NT
1996	NT	○/◒	NT
1997	NT	○/◒	NT
1998	NT	○/◒	NT
1999	NT	○/◒	NT
2000	NT	NT	NT
2001	NT	NT	○/◒
2002	NT	◒/◒	○/◒

Hyundai Elantra

2001 model shown

Early Elantras handle well enough on smooth roads, but pavement imperfections elicit unseemly jolts. The Elantra was redesigned for 1996, and a wagon was added to the lineup. The interior is nicely appointed, handling is agile, and power is acceptable, but ride comfort is wanting. A 2.0-liter, 140-hp Four became standard for 1999. The Elantra was again redesigned for 2001, and the wagon was dropped. This version features a refined powertrain, a spacious cabin, and a quiet, comfortable ride. A GT hatchback joined the line for 2002.

MAJOR REDESIGN: 1996, 2001. **SAFETY EQUIPMENT:** Driver air bag standard; passenger air bag standard from 1996. Side air bags standard from 2001. ABS available. Safety-belt pretensioners standard from 1999. **DRIVE WHEELS:** Front.

Reliability history

TROUBLE SPOTS	Hyundai Elantra							
	95	96	97	98	99	00	01	02
Engine						●	●	●
Cooling						●	●	●
Fuel						◒	●	◒
Ignition						◒	●	◒
Transmission						○	◒	●
Electrical	Insufficient data	Insufficient data	Insufficient data	Insufficient data	Insufficient data	○	◒	●
Air conditioning						●	●	●
Suspension						●	◒	●
Brakes						●	●	◒
Exhaust						●	●	●
Paint/trim/rust						●	●	◒
Body integrity						●	○	◒
Power equipment						○	●	●
Body hardware						○	◒	●
RELIABILITY VERDICT						✓	✓	✓

Prices

1995	$2,000-$4,000
1996	$4,000-$6,000
1997	$4,000-$6,000
1998	$6,000-$8,000
1999	$8,000-$10,000
2000	$8,000-$10,000
2001	$10,000-$12,000
2002	$12,000-$14,000

Crash-test results

Model years	Offset	Full-frontal	Side
1995	NT	◒/●	NT
1996	Accept.	○/○	NT
1997	Accept.	○/○	NT
1998	Accept.	○/○	○/●
1999	Accept.	○/○	○/●
2000	Accept.	●/○	○/●
2001	Poor	◒/◒	●/◒
2002	Poor	◒/◒	●/◒

SPORT-UTILITY VEHICLE
Hyundai Santa Fe

FAMILY CAR
Hyundai Sonata

2001 model shown

1999 model shown

Introduced for 2001, the Santa Fe is a car-based SUV derived from the Sonata sedan. It features unibody construction, four-wheel independent suspension, and available full-time AWD. Front-drive versions come with a 2.4-liter Four or a refined 2.7-liter V6, while AWD editions offer only the larger engine. Fit and finish are good, and controls are logically placed. Handling is sound and secure, though not very agile, and the ride is supple and quiet. The AWD system works transparently, and models with ABS also get traction control. Unfortunately, the Santa Fe's weight takes a toll on acceleration and fuel economy.

MAJOR REDESIGN: 2001. **SAFETY EQUIPMENT:** Dual front air bags standard. ABS available. Safety-belt pretensioners standard. **DRIVE WHEELS:** Front or AWD.

The first-generation Sonata had a roomy interior, a poor reliability record, and technology that was dated even then. Redesigned in 1995, the Sonata grew larger and benefited from a much-improved interior design. The standard 2.0-liter Four got more power, and a 3.0-liter V6 was optional. This version's ride is jittery, but handling is secure. The Sonata was redesigned again for 1999, gaining a more refined V6 and a quieter interior. It has a decent ride and secure, if not very nimble, handling. 2002 brought a facelift and a larger V6. **Related model:** Kia Optima.

MAJOR REDESIGN: 1995, 1999. **SAFETY EQUIPMENT:** Dual front air bags standard. Side air bags and safety-belt pretensioners standard from 1999. ABS available. **DRIVE WHEELS:** Front.

Hyundai Santa Fe — Reliability history

TROUBLE SPOTS	95	96	97	98	99	00	01	02
Engine							◐	●
Cooling							◐	●
Fuel							○	●
Ignition							◐	●
Transmission							◐	●
Electrical							◐	●
Air-conditioning							◐	●
Suspension							◐	●
Brakes							◐	●
Exhaust							◐	●
Paint/trim/rust							◐	●
Body integrity							○	●
Power equipment							◐	●
Body hardware							◐	●
RELIABILITY VERDICT							✓	✓

Prices

1995	–
1996	–
1997	–
1998	–
1999	–
2000	–
2001	$18,000-$20,000
2002	$20,000-$22,000

Crash-test results

Model Years	Offset	Full frontal	Side
1995	–	–	–
1996	–	–	–
1997	–	–	–
1998	–	–	–
1999	–	–	–
2000	–	–	–
2001	Good	NT	NT
2002	Good	NT	●/NA

Hyundai Sonata — Reliability history

TROUBLE SPOTS	95	96	97	98	99	00	01	02
Engine	Insufficient data	Insufficient data	Insufficient data	Insufficient data	Insufficient data	◐	●	●
Cooling						◐	●	●
Fuel						◐	●	●
Ignition						◐	●	●
Transmission						○	●	●
Electrical						◐	◐	●
Air-conditioning						◐	●	●
Suspension						◐	●	●
Brakes						◐	●	●
Exhaust						◐	●	●
Paint/trim/rust						○	●	●
Body integrity						◐	●	●
Power equipment						◐	●	●
Body hardware						◐	●	●
RELIABILITY VERDICT						✓	✓	✓

Prices

1995	$4,000-$6,000
1996	$4,000-$6,000
1997	$6,000-$8,000
1998	$6,000-$8,000
1999	$10,000-$12,000
2000	$10,000-$12,000
2001	$12,000-$14,000
2002	$14,000-$16,000

Crash-test results

Model Years	Offset	Full frontal	Side
1995	Poor	○/◐	NT
1996	Poor	○/◐	NT
1997	Poor	○/◐	●/◐
1998	Poor	○/◐	●/◐
1999	Accept.	NT	NT
2000	Accept.	NT	◐/◐
2001	Accept.	NT	◐/◐
2002	Accept.	◐/◐	◐/◐

Hyundai Tiburon

Hyundai XG300, XG350

1997 model shown

2001 model shown

The Tiburon was introduced in 1997, filling a void in Hyundai's lineup created by the departure of the Scoupe two years earlier. Even though it's based on the pedestrian Elantra sedan, the Tiburon is fun to drive, with crisp handling, responsive steering, and lively acceleration. The 2.0-liter four-cylinder engine lacks refinement, however, and the shifting is a bit sloppy. As is typical of a small sporty coupe, the ride is hard and noisy and the rear seat is tight. The front seats are reasonably well shaped, but very firm and mounted low. There is little head room. For 2000, the Tiburon received freshened exterior styling and some new interior details.

MAJOR REDESIGN: 1997. **SAFETY EQUIPMENT:** Dual front air bags standard. Safety-belt pretensioners standard from 2000. ABS available. **DRIVE WHEELS:** Front.

Introduced for 2001, Hyundai's flagship sedan is intended to compete with cars like the V6-powered Honda Accord, Nissan Maxima, and Toyota Camry. The XG300 is equipped with a smooth and refined 3.0-liter V6 coupled with a five-speed automatic transmission. It features a quiet, roomy interior jammed with amenities like automatic climate control and heated, powered leather seats. Traction control, ABS, and side air bags are also standard. Handling is short on agility, however, and the ride, while compliant at low speeds, gets buoyant on the highway. A larger (3.5-liter) V6 introduced in 2002 prompted the name change to XG350.

MAJOR REDESIGN: 2001. **SAFETY EQUIPMENT:** Dual front and side air bags standard. ABS standard. Safety-belt pretensioners standard. **DRIVE WHEELS:** Front.

Reliability history

TROUBLE SPOTS	95 96 97 98 99 00 01 02
Engine	
Cooling	
Fuel	
Ignition	NOT
Transmission	
Electrical	ENOUGH
Air conditioning	
Suspension	DATA
Brakes	
Exhaust	TO
Paint/trim/rust	
Body integrity	
Power equipment	RATE
Body hardware	
RELIABILITY VERDICT	

Prices

1995	–
1996	–
1997	$6,000-$8,000
1998	$6,000-$8,000
1999	$8,000-$10,000
2000	$12,000-$14,000
2001	$12,000-$14,000
2002	

Crash-test results

Model years	Offset	Full-frontal	Side
1995	–	–	–
1996	–	–	–
1997	NT	NT	NT
1998	NT	NT	NT
1999	NT	NT	NT
2000	NT	NT	NT
2001	NT	NT	NT
2002	–	–	–

Reliability history

TROUBLE SPOTS	Hyundai XG300, XG350 95 96 97 98 99 00 01 02	
Engine		◒
Cooling		◒
Fuel		◔
Ignition		◒
Transmission		◒
Electrical		◔
Air conditioning		◒
Suspension		◔
Brakes		◒
Exhaust		◒
Paint/trim/rust		◔
Body integrity		○
Power equipment		◒
Body hardware		○
RELIABILITY VERDICT		✓

Insufficient data

Prices

1995	–
1996	–
1997	–
1998	–
1999	–
2000	–
2001	$18,000-$20,000
2002	$22,000-$24,000

Crash-test results

Model years	Offset	Full-frontal	Side
1995	–	–	–
1996	–	–	–
1997	–	–	–
1998	–	–	–
1999	–	–	–
2000	–	–	–
2001	Good	NT	NT
2002	Good	NT	NT

Infiniti G20

Infiniti I30, I35

1999 model shown

2000 model shown

Introduced in 1991, the first-generation G20 felt like a good European sports sedan—nimble and supple. It also packed lots of standard equipment, and its 2.0-liter four-cylinder engine was responsive and economical. The G20t (for "touring") arrived for 1994, adding a limited-slip differential and a fold-down rear seatback. The original G20 was discontinued after 1996, but the model line was redesigned and reintroduced for 1999. This later version didn't handle as well as its predecessor, though, and had a cramped interior, noisy engine, and an automatic transmission that robbed power. It was dropped after 2002.

New for 1996, the I30 sedan was a rebadged Nissan Maxima with extra sound-deadening material, a plusher interior, and subtle exterior trim differences. Nissan's zesty and silky-smooth 3.0-liter V6 is the I30's best feature. The interior is roomy, with generous rear accommodations. The I30 was redesigned and moderately improved for 2000. The powertrain, which gained more power, remains top-notch, and fit and finish are impressive. Handling is secure but not very agile, and ride comfort is not its forte either. It became the I35 for 2002 to reflect the larger engine. **Related model:** Nissan Maxima.

MAJOR REDESIGN: 1999. **SAFETY EQUIPMENT:** Dual front air bags standard. Side air bags standard from 1999. ABS standard. Safety-belt pretensioners standard. **DRIVE WHEELS:** Front.

MAJOR REDESIGN: 1996, 2000. **SAFETY EQUIPMENT:** Dual front air bags standard. Side air bags standard from 1998. Safety-belt pretensioners standard from 2000. ABS standard. **DRIVE WHEELS:** Front.

Reliability history — Infiniti G20

TROUBLE SPOTS	95	96	97	98	99	00	01	02
Engine	◐	◐			●			
Cooling	◐	●			●			
Fuel	◐	◐			●			
Ignition	●	●			●			
Transmission	◐	●			●			
Electrical	○	○			◐	Insufficient data	Insufficient data	Insufficient data
Air-conditioning	○	○			◐			
Suspension	◐	○			◐			
Brakes	◐	○			◐			
Exhaust	○	●			◐			
Paint/trim/rust	●	●			◐			
Body integrity	○	◐			●			
Power equipment	◐	◐			●			
Body hardware	◐	◐			●			
RELIABILITY VERDICT	✓	✓			✓			

Prices

1995	$8,000-$10,000
1996	$8,000-$10,000
1997	–
1998	–
1999	$14,000-$16,000
2000	$18,000-$20,000
2001	$18,000-$20,000
2002	$20,000-$22,000

Crash-test results

Model Years	Offset	Full frontal	Side
1995	NT	NT	NT
1996	NT	NT	NT
1997	–	–	–
1998	–	–	–
1999	NT	NT	NT
2000	NT	NT	NT
2001	NT	NT	NT
2002	NT	NT	NT

Reliability history — Infiniti I30, I35

TROUBLE SPOTS	95	96	97	98	99	00	01	02
Engine	●	●	●	●	●	●	●	
Cooling	●	●	●	●	●	●	●	
Fuel	○	●	●	●	◐	●	●	
Ignition	◐	●	●	●	●	◐	●	
Transmission	◐	●	●	●	●	●	◐	
Electrical	○	◐	●	●	●	◐	◐	
Air-conditioning	●	●	●	●	●	●	●	
Suspension	●	●	●	●	●	●	●	
Brakes	◐	◐	○	◐	◐	●	◐	
Exhaust	●	●	●	●	●	●	●	
Paint/trim/rust	◐	◐	◐	●	●	●	●	
Body integrity	◐	●	○	●	●	●	●	
Power equipment	◐	◐	◐	◐	●	●	●	
Body hardware	●	●	●	●	●	●	●	
RELIABILITY VERDICT	✓	✓	✓	✓	✓	✓	✓	

Prices

1995	–
1996	$10,000-$12,000
1997	$12,000-$14,000
1998	$16,000-$18,000
1999	$18,000-$20,000
2000	$22,000-$24,000
2001	$24,000-$26,000
2002	$26,000-$28,000

Crash-test results

Model Years	Offset	Full frontal	Side
1995	–	–	–
1996	Poor	◐/○	NT
1997	Accept.	◐/○	◐/○
1998	Accept.	◐/●	◐/○
1999	Accept.	◐/●	◐/○
2000	Accept.	◐/●	◐/●
2001	Accept.	◐/●	◐/●
2002	Accept.	◐/●	◐/●

Infiniti J30

Infiniti Q45

1995 model shown

1997 model shown

Introduced for 1993, Infiniti's midlevel J30 is a car for people who value near-absolute isolation from the road. The front seats are comfortable, but with its cramped rear and small trunk, the J30 feels more like a plush coupe than a near-luxury sedan. Strengths include a quiet cabin, a responsive 3.0-liter V6 engine, and a smooth automatic transmission. The ride is placid and quiet over all kinds of road surfaces. The J30t "touring" model has a firmer suspension and four-wheel steering, a feature dropped after 1994. The J30 was discontinued after 1997, leaving the I30 to fill the midlevel Infiniti slot.

MAJOR REDESIGN: 1993. **SAFETY EQUIPMENT:** Dual front air bags standard. ABS standard. Safety-belt pretensioners standard. **DRIVE WHEELS:** Rear.

The flagship of the Infiniti line, the Q45 boasts a powerful V8 and strong acceleration, though it is too big to be agile. The Q45a features a hydraulically operated "active" suspension; the ride is fine even without it. The Q45t has a stiffer suspension for sportier handling. The Q45 was redesigned for 1997, trading in its sporty personality for more of a luxury-cruiser feel. Nevertheless it lacked the rear-seat roominess and rich cabin materials found on direct competitors. It was redesigned for 2002, when it picked up 340-hp and a wealth of safety equipment and high-tech gadgets.

MAJOR REDESIGN: 1997, 2002. **SAFETY EQUIPMENT:** Dual front air bags standard. Side air bags standard from 1998. Head protection air bags standard from 2002. ABS standard. Safety-belt pretensioners standard. **DRIVE WHEELS:** Rear.

J30

Reliability history								
TROUBLE SPOTS								
	95	96	97	98	99	00	01	02
Engine								
Cooling								
Fuel								
Ignition				NOT				
Transmission								
Electrical				ENOUGH				
Air conditioning								
Suspension				DATA				
Brakes								
Exhaust				TO				
Paint/trim/rust								
Body integrity				RATE				
Power equipment								
Body hardware								
RELIABILITY VERDICT								

Prices	
1995	$10,000-$12,000
1996	$12,000-$14,000
1997	$14,000-$16,000
1998	–
1999	–
2000	–
2001	–
2002	–

Crash-test results			
Model years	Offset	Full-frontal	Side
1995	NT	◐/◐	NT
1996	NT	◐/◐	NT
1997	NT	◐/◐	NT
1998	–	–	–
1999	–	–	–
2000	–	–	–
2001	–	–	–
2002	–	–	–

Q45

Reliability history								
TROUBLE SPOTS								
	95	96	97	98	99	00	01	02
Engine								
Cooling								
Fuel								
Ignition				NOT				
Transmission								
Electrical				ENOUGH				
Air conditioning								
Suspension				DATA				
Brakes								
Exhaust				TO				
Paint/trim/rust								
Body integrity				RATE				
Power equipment								
Body hardware								
RELIABILITY VERDICT								

Prices	
1995	$12,000-$14,000
1996	$14,000-$16,000
1997	$18,000-$20,000
1998	$22,000-$24,000
1999	$26,000-$28,000
2000	More than $30,000
2001	More than $30,000
2002	More than $30,000

Crash-test results			
Model years	Offset	Full-frontal	Side
1995	NT	NT	NT
1996	NT	NT	NT
1997	Marg.	NT	NT
1998	Marg.	NT	NT
1999	Marg.	NT	NT
2000	Marg.	NT	NT
2001	Marg.	NT	NT
2002	NT	NT	NT

Infiniti QX4

1997 model shown

This SUV, an upscale version of the Nissan Pathfinder, debuted for 1997. The QX4 has a relatively comfortable ride, good front seats, and predictable handling. Somewhat small for its class, the QX4 has a relatively modest load capacity and scant cargo space. Significant updates for 2000 included a more powerful engine, stronger brakes, and better-placed controls. Except for the QX4's selectable full-time 4WD system (which became available on the Pathfinder LE for 2001), there is little reason to choose it over the less costly Nissan. **Related model:** Nissan Pathfinder.

MAJOR REDESIGN: 1997. **SAFETY EQUIPMENT:** Dual front air bags standard. Side air bags and safety-belt pretensioners standard from 1999. ABS standard. **DRIVE WHEELS:** Selectable 4WD. Rear available starting in 2001.

Reliability history

TROUBLE SPOTS	Infiniti QX4							
	95	96	97	98	99	00	01	02
Engine							◉	
Cooling							◉	
Fuel							◉	
Ignition							◉	
Transmission							◉	
Electrical	Insufficient data	Insufficient data	Insufficient data	Insufficient data	Insufficient data		◉	Insufficient data
Air-conditioning							◉	
Suspension							◉	
Brakes							◉	
Exhaust							◉	
Paint/trim/rust							◉	
Body integrity							◐	
Power equipment							◐	
Body hardware							◐	
RELIABILITY VERDICT							✓	

Prices

1995	–
1996	–
1997	$16,000-$18,000
1998	$18,000-$20,000
1999	$20,000-$22,000
2000	$24,000-$26,000
2001	$28,000-$30,000
2002	More than $30,000

Crash-test results

Model Years	Offset	Full frontal	Side
1995	–	–	–
1996	–	–	–
1997	Marg.	○/○	NT
1998	Marg.	○/○	NT
1999	Marg.	◐/◉	◉/◉
2000	Marg.	◐/◉	◉/◉
2001	Marg.	◐/◉	◉/◉
2002	Marg.	◐/◉	◉/◉

Isuzu Amigo, Rodeo Sport

1998 model shown

The Amigo is a semi-convertible two-door with a canvas top that covers only the rear seat and cargo area. Two four-cylinder engines are available, with the larger 2.6-liter Four being the preferred one. The Amigo was reintroduced for 1998, now spun off the redesigned Rodeo, with both four- and six-cylinder engines. Still based on a truck chassis, the Amigo trails car-based SUV competitors in ride and handling refinement. A hardtop model joined the lineup for 1999. In 2001, the Amigo was rechristened the Rodeo Sport.

MAJOR REDESIGN: 1998. **SAFETY EQUIPMENT:** Dual front air bags standard from 1998. ABS standard from 1998. **DRIVE WHEELS:** Rear or part-time 4WD.

Reliability history

TROUBLE SPOTS								
	95	96	97	98	99	00	01	02
Engine								
Cooling								
Fuel								
Ignition				NOT				
Transmission								
Electrical				ENOUGH				
Air-conditioning								
Suspension				DATA				
Brakes								
Exhaust				TO				
Paint/trim/rust								
Body integrity				RATE				
Power equipment								
Body hardware								
RELIABILITY VERDICT								

Prices

1995	–
1996	–
1997	–
1998	$8,000-$10,000
1999	$12,000-$14,000
2000	$14,000-$16,000
2001	$16,000-$18,000
2002	$18,000-$20,000

Crash-test results

Model Years	Offset	Full frontal	Side
1995	–	–	–
1996	–	–	–
1997	–	–	–
1998	Poor	NT	NT
1999	Poor	NT	NT
2000	NT	NT	NT
2001	NT	NT	NT
2002	NT	NT	NT

Isuzu Axiom

Isuzu Hombre

2002 model shown

1999 model shown

The four-door Axiom bowed as a 2002 model last spring. Billed by Isuzu as a "Sportwagon," the futuristic-looking Axiom is in fact based on the trucky Rodeo, with body-on-frame construction and a solid rear axle. While promoted as an alternative to car-based SUVs like the 2003 Honda Pilot and Toyota Highlander, the Axiom lacks the mechanical refinement and overall ability of those models. Highlights include a lively and competent 3.5-liter, 230-hp aluminum V6, also used in the Trooper, and a selectable full-time four-wheel-drive system. The Axiom also features a "semi-active" suspension that automatically adjusts shock-absorber damping to match road conditions.

MAJOR REDESIGN: 2002. **SAFETY EQUIPMENT:** Dual front air bags standard. ABS standard. **DRIVE WHEELS:** Rear or selectable 4WD.

In 1996, this compact pickup—essentially a Chevrolet S-10 standard-cab model with different sheetmetal—replaced Isuzu's own pickup model. Initially, the only engine for the Hombre was Chevrolet's base 2.2-liter Four, which was barely adequate. Additions for 1997 included more features and options, such as an extended-cab version and a strong 4.3-liter V6. The S-10's subpar reliability, reflected in our surveys, has us concerned about the reliability of the Hombre. Likewise, the S-10's poor showing in government crash tests doesn't inspire confidence. The Hombre was dropped after 2000. **Related models:** Chevrolet S-10, GMC Sonoma.

MAJOR REDESIGN: 1996. **SAFETY EQUIPMENT:** Driver air bag standard; passenger side from 1998. ABS not available in 1996-1997; standard from 1998. **DRIVE WHEELS:** Rear or part-time 4WD.

Isuzu Axiom

Reliability history		
TROUBLE SPOTS		
	95 96 97 98 99 00 01 02	
Engine		
Cooling		
Fuel		
Ignition	NOT	
Transmission		
Electrical	ENOUGH	
Air conditioning		
Suspension	DATA	
Brakes		
Exhaust	TO	
Paint/trim/rust		
Body integrity		
Power equipment	RATE	
Body hardware		
RELIABILITY VERDICT		

Prices	
1995	–
1996	–
1997	–
1998	–
1999	–
2000	–
2001	–
2002	$26,000-$28,000

Crash-test results			
Model years	Offset	Full-frontal	Side
1995	–	–	–
1996	–	–	–
1997	–	–	–
1998	–	–	–
1999	–	–	–
2000	–	–	–
2001	–	–	–
2002	Accept.	◐/◐	◑/◐

Isuzu Hombre

Reliability history		
TROUBLE SPOTS		
	95 96 97 98 99 00 01 02	
Engine		
Cooling		
Fuel		
Ignition	NOT	
Transmission		
Electrical	ENOUGH	
Air conditioning		
Suspension	DATA	
Brakes		
Exhaust	TO	
Paint/trim/rust		
Body integrity		
Power equipment	RATE	
Body hardware		
RELIABILITY VERDICT		

Prices	
1995	–
1996	$4,000-$6,000
1997	$4,000-$6,000
1998	$6,000-$8,000
1999	$6,000-$8,000
2000	$8,000-$10,000
2001	–
2002	–

Crash-test results			
Model years	Offset	Full-frontal	Side
1995	–	–	–
1996	NT	○/●	NT
1997	NT	○/●	NT
1998	Marg.	○/○	NT
1999	Marg.	○/○	◒/NA
2000	Marg.	○/○	◒/NA
2001	–	–	–
2002	–	–	–

Isuzu Oasis

Isuzu Rodeo

1996 model shown

1998 model shown

The Oasis minivan is a rebadged version of Honda's pre-'99 Odyssey. It provides a supple, well-controlled ride, good handling, an efficient powertrain, and an easy-to-use control layout. People who dislike sliding doors may appreciate the four conventional doors. The four-cylinder engine is noisy and overworked, but it provides acceptable acceleration when the vehicle is unladen. Leg room is a little tight for tall people, but the seats are comfortable. The rearmost bench seat cleverly folds flush with the floor, making the most of the modest cargo space behind the middle seats. The Oasis was discontinued after 1999. **Related model:** Honda Odyssey.

MAJOR REDESIGN: 1996. **SAFETY EQUIPMENT:** Dual front air bags standard. ABS standard. **DRIVE WHEELS:** Front.

Early Rodeo models offer generous passenger room but limited cargo space. These SUVs deliver disappointing performance, with sloppy handling, a stiff ride, and considerable body lean. In 1996, the Rodeo's part-time 4WD system was upgraded to a shift-on-the-fly design, and the engine gained more horsepower. Redesigned for 1998, the Rodeo improved in nearly every way, with more power and increased interior comfort. The ride, however, remains stiff and bouncy. **Related model:** Honda Passport.

MAJOR REDESIGN: 1998. **SAFETY EQUIPMENT:** Dual front air bags standard. ABS available from 1998, standard from 1999. **DRIVE WHEELS:** Rear or part-time 4WD.

Reliability history — Isuzu Oasis

TROUBLE SPOTS	95	96	97	98	99	00	01	02
Engine		○	●	●				
Cooling		●	●	●				
Fuel		●	●	◐				
Ignition		●	●	●				
Transmission		●	●	◐				
Electrical		◐	◐	●		Insufficient data		
Air-conditioning		◐	●	●				
Suspension		●	◐	●				
Brakes		◐	○	○				
Exhaust		◐	●	◐				
Paint/trim/rust		◐	●	◐				
Body integrity		◐	◐	◐				
Power equipment		◐	●	●				
Body hardware		◐	◐	●				
RELIABILITY VERDICT		✔	✔	✔				

Prices — Isuzu Oasis

Year	Price
1995	–
1996	$10,000–$12,000
1997	$12,000–$14,000
1998	$14,000–$16,000
1999	$14,000–$16,000
2000	–
2001	–
2002	–

Crash-test results — Isuzu Oasis

Model Years	Offset	Full frontal	Side
1995	–	–	–
1996	Marg.	◐/○	NT
1997	Marg.	◐/○	NT
1998	Marg.	◐/○	NT
1999	Marg.	◐/○	NT
2000	–	–	–
2001	–	–	–
2002	–	–	–

Reliability history — Isuzu Rodeo

TROUBLE SPOTS	95	96	97	98	99	00	01	02
Engine	●			○	◐	◐	●	
Cooling	◐			●	◐	◐	◐	
Fuel	◐			○	○	○	◐	
Ignition	○			◐	◐	●	●	
Transmission	◐			●	◐	●	◐	
Electrical	●	Insufficient data	Insufficient data	◐	○	○	◐	Insufficient data
Air-conditioning	○			◐	◐	◐	●	
Suspension	◐			◐	◐	○	◐	
Brakes	◐			◐	●	○	◐	
Exhaust	◐			◐	◐	◐	◐	
Paint/trim/rust	○			◐	●	●	◐	
Body integrity	◐			◐	●	●	◐	
Power equipment	●			◐	◐	◐	●	
Body hardware	●			○	○	○	○	
RELIABILITY VERDICT	✔			✔				

Prices — Isuzu Rodeo

Year	Price
1995	$8,000–$10,000
1996	$8,000–$10,000
1997	$10,000–$12,000
1998	$12,000–$14,000
1999	$12,000–$14,000
2000	$14,000–$16,000
2001	$16,000–$18,000
2002	$20,000–$22,000

Crash-test results — Isuzu Rodeo

Model Years	Offset	Full frontal	Side
1995	NT	◐/○	NT
1996	Poor	◐/○	NT
1997	Poor	◐/○	NT
1998	Poor	○/◐	NT
1999	Poor	○/◐	◐/○
2000	Poor	◐/○	◐/○
2001	Poor	◐/○	◐/○
2002	Marg.	○/◐	◐/○

Isuzu Trooper

1999 model shown

The tall, boxy Isuzu Trooper last underwent a complete redesign for 1992. After our 1996 tests, we judged the 1995 to 1997 Trooper (and the similar 1996 and 1997 Acura SLX) Not Acceptable because of a pronounced tendency to roll over in our emergency-handling tests. The 1998 model received a full-time 4WD system, a revised transmission, and a more powerful 3.5-liter V6 engine. CR didn't test the later models, so we couldn't say whether the changes affected their handling. A two-wheel-drive version debuted for 2000. The Trooper was discontinued after 2002. **Related model:** Acura SLX.

MAJOR REDESIGN: 1992, 1998. **SAFETY EQUIPMENT:** Dual front air bags standard. ABS available, standard from 1997. **DRIVE WHEELS:** Part-time 4WD through 1997; selectable 4WD from 1998; rear available from 2000.

Reliability history	
TROUBLE SPOTS	95 96 97 98 99 00 01 02
Engine	
Cooling	
Fuel	
Ignition	NOT
Transmission	
Electrical	ENOUGH
Air conditioning	
Suspension	DATA
Brakes	
Exhaust	TO
Paint/trim/rust	
Body integrity	RATE
Power equipment	
Body hardware	
RELIABILITY VERDICT	

Prices	
1995	$8,000-$10,000
1996	$10,000-$12,000
1997	$12,000-$14,000
1998	$12,000-$14,000
1999	$14,000-$16,000
2000	$18,000-$20,000
2001	$20,000-$22,000
2002	$22,000-$24,000

Crash-test results			
Model years	Offset	Full-frontal	Side
1995	NT	O/O	NT
1996	NT	O/O	NT
1997	NT	O/O	NT
1998	NT	NT	NT
1999	NT	NT	NT
2000	Marg.	NT	NT
2001	Marg.	NT	NT
2002	Marg.	NT	NT

Jaguar S-Type

2000 model shown

Jaguar's mid-level model, the S-Type was introduced for 2000 to compete against cars such as the Audi A6, BMW 5-Series, and Mercedes-Benz E-Class. As a member of the Ford family, the S-Type shares its rear-drive platform with the Lincoln LS and current Ford Thunderbird. Handling is fairly nimble, and the ride is supple and controlled. The optional V8 is both strong and smooth, the V6 much less so. The interior is a bit cramped inside and the trunk is tiny. Among its features is an optional and pricey voice-control system for the audio, climate-control, and phone functions—a gadget that CR found worked with only limited success.

MAJOR REDESIGN: 2000. **SAFETY EQUIPMENT:** Dual front and side air bags standard. Head protection air bags standard from 2002. ABS standard. Safety-belt pretensioners standard. **DRIVE WHEELS:** Rear.

Reliability history	
TROUBLE SPOTS	Jaguar S-Type
	95 96 97 98 99 00 01 02
Engine	● ● ●
Cooling	● ○ ●
Fuel	● ● ●
Ignition	● ● ●
Transmission	○ ○
Electrical	○ ○
Air conditioning	● ○
Suspension	○ ○
Brakes	● ○
Exhaust	● ● ●
Paint/trim/rust	● ●
Body integrity	○ ○
Power equipment	○ ●
Body hardware	○ ○
RELIABILITY VERDICT	

(Insufficient data)

Prices	
1995	–
1996	–
1997	–
1998	–
1999	–
2000	More than $30,000
2001	More than $30,000
2002	More than $30,000

Crash-test results			
Model years	Offset	Full-frontal	Side
1995	–	–	–
1996	–	–	–
1997	–	–	–
1998	–	–	–
1999	–	–	–
2000	NT	NT	NT
2001	NT	NT	NT
2002	NT	NT	NT

UPSCALE CAR
Jaguar X-Type

2002 model shown

Introduced for 2002, the X-Type serves as Jaguar's entry-level model. It's derived from the same underpinnings as the discontinued Ford Contour. AWD and numerous safety features are standard. The X-Type's uplevel 3.0-liter V6 is a lively performer, and the optional five-speed automatic shifts smoothly. (A five-speed manual is standard.) Handling is balanced at the limits but not all that agile in normal driving. The ride is comfortable, and braking performance is excellent. On the downside, the cabin is a bit tight, road noise is pronounced, and cheap-feeling switchgear reveals the car's proletarian origins. First year reliability has been much worse than average.

MAJOR REDESIGN: 2002. **SAFETY EQUIPMENT:** Dual front, side, and head protection air bags standard. Safety-belt pretensioners and ABS standard. **DRIVE WHEELS:** AWD.

Reliability history

TROUBLE SPOTS	Jaguar X-Type
	95 96 97 98 99 00 01 02
Engine	◑
Cooling	◑
Fuel	◐
Ignition	◑
Transmission	◐
Electrical	◑
Air-conditioning	◑
Suspension	◑
Brakes	◑
Exhaust	◑
Paint/trim/rust	◑
Body integrity	◐
Power equipment	◐
Body hardware	○
RELIABILITY VERDICT	

Prices

1995	–
1996	–
1997	–
1998	–
1999	–
2000	–
2001	–
2002	$26,000-$28,000

Crash-test results

Model Years	Offset	Full frontal	Side
1995	–	–	–
1996	–	–	–
1997	–	–	–
1998	–	–	–
1999	–	–	–
2000	–	–	–
2001	–	–	–
2002	Good	NT	NT

LUXURY CAR
Jaguar XJ6, XJ8

1998 model shown

For years Jaguar has been polishing an antiquated design by adding technological updates rather than starting anew. Low and long, the XJ's interior is a bit snug for a car in this class. The front seats are nicely shaped, but cramped. Long-wheelbase models comfortably hold three in the rear seat. The XJ received significant updates in 1998. Beyond exterior upgrades, the most notable change is the stronger 290-hp V8 that replaced the relatively smooth six-cylinder, forcing a name change to XJ8. Jaguar also added a muscular, supercharged XJR model.

MAJOR REDESIGN: 1995. **SAFETY EQUIPMENT:** Dual front air bags standard. Side air bags standard from 1998. ABS standard. Safety-belt pretensioners standard from 1998. **DRIVE WHEELS:** Rear.

Reliability history

TROUBLE SPOTS	
	95 96 97 98 99 00 01 02
Engine	
Cooling	
Fuel	
Ignition	NOT
Transmission	
Electrical	ENOUGH
Air-conditioning	
Suspension	DATA
Brakes	
Exhaust	TO
Paint/trim/rust	
Body integrity	
Power equipment	RATE
Body hardware	
RELIABILITY VERDICT	

Prices

1995	$14,000-$16,000
1996	$18,000-$20,000
1997	$22,000-$24,000
1998	$26,000-$28,000
1999	More than $30,000
2000	More than $30,000
2001	More than $30,000
2002	More than $30,000

Crash-test results

Model Years	Offset	Full frontal	Side
1995	NT	NT	NT
1996	NT	NT	NT
1997	NT	NT	NT
1998	NT	NT	NT
1999	NT	NT	NT
2000	NT	NT	NT
2001	NT	NT	NT
2002	NT	NT	NT

Jeep Cherokee

Jeep Grand Cherokee

1999 model shown

1998 model shown

Introduced in 1984, the Jeep Cherokee continued little changed until its partial 1997 redesign. The boxy sport-utility sold well with its off-road reputation, but it is a harsh-riding, noisy vehicle with limited cargo space. The 4.0-liter inline six-cylinder engine is a better choice than the snarling 2.5-liter Four. The 1997 freshening brought a more modern interior, a passenger air bag, and a slight exterior update. It's hard to reach the tight rear seat. Handling is secure though clumsy, and the ride remains choppy. Road, wind, and engine noise fill the cabin. Look for a model equipped with Selec-Trac, a full-time 4WD system you can use on dry pavement.

MAJOR REDESIGN: 1984, 1997. **SAFETY EQUIPMENT:** Driver air bag standard; passenger side from 1997. ABS available. **DRIVE WHEELS:** Rear, selectable, or part-time 4WD.

Launched in 1992, the Grand Cherokee offered a larger, better-equipped, more refined alternative to the basic Cherokee. It is available in 2WD and 4WD versions. Handling has been secure and stable in our tests. The ride is absorbent but on bumpy roads the Grand Cherokee rocks annoyingly from side to side. The 4.0-liter is noisy and slow. The 5.2 V8 was strong but thirsty. It was redesigned for 1999, but other than the addition of a powerful 4.7-liter V8, the improvement was modest. Handling continues to be secure, but ride quality, rear seat room, and cargo space remain subpar.

MAJOR REDESIGN: 1993, 1999. **SAFETY EQUIPMENT:** Driver air bag standard; passenger side from 1996. Head protection air bags available from 2002. Safety-belt pretensioners standard from 2002. ABS standard. **DRIVE WHEELS:** Rear, selectable, or permanent 4WD.

Jeep Cherokee

Reliability history

TROUBLE SPOTS	95	96	97	98	99	00	01	02
Engine								
Cooling								
Fuel								
Ignition								
Transmission								
Electrical								
Air conditioning								
Suspension								
Brakes								
Exhaust								
Paint/trim/rust								
Body integrity								
Power equipment								
Body hardware								
RELIABILITY VERDICT	✓	✓	✓	✓	✓			

Prices

1995	$6,000-$8,000
1996	$8,000-$10,000
1997	$8,000-$10,000
1998	$10,000-$12,000
1999	$12,000-$14,000
2000	$14,000-$16,000
2001	$16,000-$18,000
2002	–

Crash-test results

Model years	Offset	Full-frontal	Side
1995	NT	○/◓	NT
1996	NT	○/◓	NT
1997	Marg.	○/○	NT
1998	Marg.	NT	NT
1999	Marg.	○/○	○/◒
2000	Marg.	○/○	○/◒
2001	Marg.	○/○	○/◒
2002	–	–	–

Jeep Grand Cherokee

Reliability history

TROUBLE SPOTS	95	96	97	98	99	00	01	02
Engine								
Cooling								
Fuel								
Ignition								
Transmission								
Electrical								
Air conditioning								
Suspension								
Brakes								
Exhaust								
Paint/trim/rust								
Body integrity								
Power equipment								
Body hardware								
RELIABILITY VERDICT								

Prices

1995	$8,000-$10,000
1996	$10,000-$12,000
1997	$10,000-$12,000
1998	$12,000-$14,000
1999	$16,000-$18,000
2000	$18,000-$20,000
2001	$22,000-$24,000
2002	$24,000-$26,000

Crash-test results

Model years	Offset	Full-frontal	Side
1995	NT	○/○	NT
1996	Marg.	○/○	NT
1997	Marg.	○/○	NT
1998	Marg.	○/○	NT
1999	Marg.	○/○	○/◒
2000	Marg.	○/○	○/◒
2001	Marg.	○/○	○/◒
2002	Marg.	○/○	○/◒

SPORT-UTILITY VEHICLE
Jeep Liberty

2002 model shown

Introduced for 2002, the Liberty replaced the primeval Cherokee as Jeep's midlevel SUV offering. Although it boasts modern features such as an independent front suspension (a first on a four-wheel-drive Jeep) and a rack-and-pinion steering setup, the Liberty is less well rounded than class leaders such as the Toyota RAV4 and Honda CR-V. The ride is jittery, even on smooth roads, and the narrow cockpit can be difficult to access. The popular 3.7-liter V6 is smoother than the Cherokee's growling 4.0-liter inline Six, but thirsty. In keeping with Jeep tradition, the Liberty acquits itself well in virtually any off-road situation.

MAJOR REDESIGN: 2002. **SAFETY EQUIPMENT:** Dual front air bags standard. Head protection air bags and ABS available. Safety-belt pretensioners standard. **DRIVE WHEELS:** Rear, part-time, or selectable 4WD.

Reliability history

TROUBLE SPOTS	Jeep Liberty V6
	95 96 97 98 99 00 01 02
Engine	02: ●
Cooling	02: ●
Fuel	02: ●
Ignition	02: ●
Transmission	02: ●
Electrical	02: ◑
Air-conditioning	02: ◑
Suspension	02: ◑
Brakes	02: ●
Exhaust	02: ●
Paint/trim/rust	02: ●
Body integrity	02: ◑
Power equipment	02: ◑
Body hardware	02: ◑
RELIABILITY VERDICT	✓

Prices

Year	Price
1995	–
1996	–
1997	–
1998	–
1999	–
2000	–
2001	–
2002	$18,000–$20,000

Crash-test results

Model Years	Offset	Full frontal	Side
1995	–	–	–
1996	–	–	–
1997	–	–	–
1998	–	–	–
1999	–	–	–
2000	–	–	–
2001	–	–	–
2002	Marg.	●/◑	●/◑

SPORT-UTILITY VEHICLE
Jeep Wrangler

1997 model shown

Touting a legacy that spans back to World War II, the Wrangler is Jeep's smallest, least expensive, and crudest model. It's changed little since its 1986 introduction. Better off-road than on, it has abrupt, numb, routine handling, tricky emergency handling, and a very noisy, punishing ride. Revamped for the 1997 model year, the Wrangler regained round headlamps and received an improved interior. Otherwise, the basic formula continues, with cramped quarters, a dreadful ride, and vague, imprecise steering. The 2001 model features a quieter, better-padded convertible top.

MAJOR REDESIGN: 1997. **SAFETY EQUIPMENT:** Dual front air bags standard from 1997. ABS available. **DRIVE WHEELS:** Part-time 4WD.

Reliability history

TROUBLE SPOTS	Jeep Wrangler
	95 96 97 98 99 00 01 02
Engine	(Insufficient data 95–96) ● ◑ ● ● (Insufficient data 01–02)
Cooling	○ ○ ● ●
Fuel	◑ ● ● ●
Ignition	◑ ● ◑ ◑
Transmission	○ ◑ ◑ ◑
Electrical	○ ◑ ◑ ○
Air-conditioning	○ ◑ ◑ ●
Suspension	○ ◑ ◑ ◑
Brakes	○ ◑ ◑ ◑
Exhaust	○ ○ ● ◑
Paint/trim/rust	◑ ○ ○ ○
Body integrity	◑ ◑ ○ ○
Power equipment	● ● ● ●
Body hardware	◑ ○ ○ ◑
RELIABILITY VERDICT	

Prices

Year	Price
1995	$8,000–$10,000
1996	–
1997	$10,000–$12,000
1998	$12,000–$14,000
1999	$14,000–$16,000
2000	$16,000–$18,000
2001	$18,000–$20,000
2002	$20,000–$22,000

Crash-test results

Model Years	Offset	Full frontal	Side
1995	NT	◑/◑	NT
1996	–	–	–
1997	Accept.	◑/◑	NT
1998	Accept.	◑/◑	NT
1999	Accept.	◑/◑	NT
2000	Accept.	◑/◑	NT
2001	Accept.	◑/◑	NT
2002	Accept.	◑/◑	NT

Kia Optima

2001 model shown

Introduced for 2001, the midsized Optima is essentially a rebadged Hyundai Sonata sedan with a chrome-intensive external makeover. Like the Sonata, it is available in two trim levels and with a choice of two engines: a 2.4-liter Four or a 2.5-liter V6 that grew to 2.7 in 2002. V6 models are only available with an automatic transmission, but a five-speed manual can be had with the Four. Four-cylinder models come reasonably well equipped, though antilock brakes aren't offered. As in the Sonata, the interior is fairly spacious and quiet, and the V6 powertrain reasonably refined. **Related model:** Hyundai Sonata.

MAJOR REDESIGN: 2001. **SAFETY EQUIPMENT:** Dual front and side air bags standard. ABS available. Safety-belt pretensioners standard. **DRIVE WHEELS:** Front.

Kia Rio

2001 model shown

The new-for-2001 Rio sedan is based on the unimpressive Ford Aspire, which was made for Ford by Kia for a few years in the mid-1990s. It offers a tall body for extra head room and a rounded-off roof. A 1.5-liter, 96-hp four-cylinder engine—the only available powertrain—can be coupled with either a five-speed manual or a four-speed automatic transmission. The Rio competes with low-end economy cars as well as midpriced used cars. Expect to get what you pay for. A wagon called Cinco was added for 2001.

MAJOR REDESIGN: 2001. **SAFETY EQUIPMENT:** Dual front air bags standard. ABS available. **DRIVE WHEELS:** Front.

Kia Optima

Reliability history

TROUBLE SPOTS	95 96 97 98 99 00 01 02
Engine	
Cooling	
Fuel	
Ignition	NOT
Transmission	
Electrical	ENOUGH
Air conditioning	
Suspension	DATA
Brakes	
Exhaust	TO
Paint/trim/rust	
Body integrity	
Power equipment	RATE
Body hardware	
RELIABILITY VERDICT	

Prices

Year	Price
1995	–
1996	–
1997	–
1998	–
1999	–
2000	–
2001	$14,000-$16,000
2002	$16,000-$18,000

Crash-test results

Model years	Offset	Full-frontal	Side
1995	–	–	–
1996	–	–	–
1997	–	–	–
1998	–	–	–
1999	–	–	–
2000	–	–	–
2001	Accept.	NT	NT
2002	Accept.	NT	NT

Kia Rio

Reliability history

TROUBLE SPOTS	95 96 97 98 99 00 01 02
Engine	
Cooling	
Fuel	
Ignition	NOT
Transmission	
Electrical	ENOUGH
Air conditioning	
Suspension	DATA
Brakes	
Exhaust	TO
Paint/trim/rust	
Body integrity	
Power equipment	RATE
Body hardware	
RELIABILITY VERDICT	

Prices

Year	Price
1995	–
1996	–
1997	–
1998	–
1999	–
2000	–
2001	$6,000-$8,000
2002	$8,000-$10,000

Crash-test results

Model years	Offset	Full-frontal	Side
1995	–	–	
1996	–	–	
1997	–	–	
1998	–	–	
1999	–	–	
2000	–	–	
2001	NT	NT	O/O
2002	NT	O/O	O/O

MINIVAN
Kia Sedona

2002 model shown

Introduced for 2002, the Sedona marks the first incursion by a Korean automaker into the nearly saturated U.S. minivan market. It uses a refined 3.5-liter V6, developed by corporate parent Hyundai for use in the XG350 sedan, mated to a five-speed automatic transmission. The Sedona's interior shows commendable attention to detail, with lots of storage bins. Convenience features include dual sliding doors and either a second-row bench seat (in the LX model) or a pair of captain's chairs (in the EX). The third-row seat is a split 50/50 bench. Unfortunately, the Sedona's hefty curb weight takes a toll on both acceleration and handling.

MAJOR REDESIGN: 2002. **SAFETY EQUIPMENT:** Dual front air bags standard. ABS available. **DRIVE WHEELS:** Front.

SMALL CAR
Kia Sephia/Spectra

1998 model shown

The small Kia Sephia sedan was originally based on the Mazda 323, but has used a Kia platform since its 1998 redesign. This newer version is slightly larger than the original. New platform notwithstanding, the Sephia remains crude, noisy, uncomfortable, and shoddily built. The Mazda-derived 1.8-liter four-cylinder provides adequate acceleration, but the automatic transmission shifts abruptly and often. High depreciation means that used models are attractively priced, but the Sephia is not the best choice in transportation. The Spectra, new in 2001, is merely a lightly restyled four-door hatchback version. In 2002 the Sephia and Spectra names merged to just Spectra.

MAJOR REDESIGN: 1994, 1998, 2001. **SAFETY EQUIPMENT:** Dual front air bags standard. ABS available. **DRIVE WHEELS:** Front.

Reliability history — Kia Sedona

TROUBLE SPOTS	95 96 97 98 99 00 01 02
Engine	⊕
Cooling	⊕
Fuel	⊖
Ignition	⊕
Transmission	⊕
Electrical	⊕
Air-conditioning	⊕
Suspension	⊕
Brakes	⊕
Exhaust	⊕
Paint/trim/rust	⊕
Body integrity	⊖
Power equipment	○
Body hardware	⊖
RELIABILITY VERDICT	✓

Prices

1995	–
1996	–
1997	–
1998	–
1999	–
2000	–
2001	–
2002	$20,000-$22,000

Crash-test results

Model Years	Offset	Full frontal	Side
1995	–	–	–
1996	–	–	–
1997	–	–	–
1998	–	–	–
1999	–	–	–
2000	–	–	–
2001	–	–	–
2002	Accept.	⊕/⊕	⊕/⊕

Reliability history — Kia Sephia/Spectra

TROUBLE SPOTS	95 96 97 98 99 00 01 02
Engine	
Cooling	
Fuel	
Ignition	NOT
Transmission	
Electrical	ENOUGH
Air-conditioning	
Suspension	DATA
Brakes	
Exhaust	TO
Paint/trim/rust	
Body integrity	
Power equipment	RATE
Body hardware	
RELIABILITY VERDICT	

Prices

1995	$2,000-$4,000
1996	$2,000-$4,000
1997	$2,000-$4,000
1998	$4,000-$6,000
1999	$6,000-$8,000
2000	$6,000-$8,000
2001	$8,000-$10,000
2002	$8,000-$10,000

Crash-test results

Model Years	Offset	Full frontal	Side
1995	NT	○/⊕	NT
1996	Poor	NT	NT
1997	Poor	⊕/⊕	⊖/●
1998	Poor	NT	NT
1999	Poor	NT	NT
2000	Poor	NT	NT
2001	Poor	⊕/⊕	○/○
2002	Poor	⊕/⊕	○/○

Kia Sportage

Land Rover Discovery

1998 model shown

1999 model shown

Kia got a toehold in the growing small-SUV segment when it introduced its trucklike Sportage in 1995. The Sportage is made in the mold of the Geo Tracker and Suzuki Sidekick, with a body-on-frame chassis instead of the carlike unibody construction that's become common on small SUVs. A shorter-wheelbase, two-door soft-top model expanded the model range in 1998. The Sportage has an uncomfortable ride, clumsy handling, and a noisy, unrefined powertrain. It offers only a part-time 4WD system that can't be used on dry roads. Overall it's not nearly as good as the Toyota RAV4 or Honda CR-V. Kia treated the Sportage to mild restyling for 2001.

MAJOR REDESIGN: 1995. **SAFETY EQUIPMENT:** Dual front air bags standard. ABS available. Safety-belt pretensioners standard from 2002. **DRIVE WHEELS:** Rear or part-time 4WD.

Introduced in the U.S. in 1994, the original Discovery was well suited for off-road excursions, but came up short in everyday driving. The ride suffers from considerable side-to-side jostling, and fuel economy was dismal in our tests. Headroom is ample, but tall drivers have little legroom. Redesigned for 1999, the Discovery gained some cargo room but unintuitive controls and difficult access remained. It also boasted such advanced electronics systems as an Active Cornering Enhancement (ACE) system and a Hill Descent Control system. In CR's tests, the ACE helped keep the vehicle fairly flat in normal cornering, but emergency handling was poor.

MAJOR REDESIGN: 1994, 1999. **SAFETY EQUIPMENT:** Dual front air bags standard. ABS standard. Safety-belt pretensioners standard from 1999. **DRIVE WHEELS:** Permanent 4WD.

Kia Sportage

Reliability history

TROUBLE SPOTS	95 96 97 98 99 00 01 02
Engine	
Cooling	
Fuel	
Ignition	NOT
Transmission	
Electrical	ENOUGH
Air conditioning	
Suspension	DATA
Brakes	
Exhaust	
Paint/trim/rust	TO
Body integrity	
Power equipment	RATE
Body hardware	
RELIABILITY VERDICT	

Prices

1995	$4,000-$6,000
1996	$6,000-$8,000
1997	$6,000-$8,000
1998	$8,000-$10,000
1999	$8,000-$10,000
2000	$10,000-$12,000
2001	$12,000-$14,000
2002	$14,000-$16,000

Crash-test results

Model years	Offset	Full-frontal	Side
1995	NT	NT	NT
1996	NT	NT	NT
1997	NT	O/O	NT
1998	Marg.	NT	NT
1999	Marg.	NT	NT
2000	Marg.	NT	NT
2001	Marg.	NT	NT
2002	Marg.	NT	NT

Land Rover Discovery

Reliability history

TROUBLE SPOTS	95 96 97 98 99 00 01 02
Engine	
Cooling	
Fuel	
Ignition	NOT
Transmission	
Electrical	ENOUGH
Air conditioning	
Suspension	DATA
Brakes	
Exhaust	
Paint/trim/rust	TO
Body integrity	
Power equipment	RATE
Body hardware	
RELIABILITY VERDICT	

Prices

1995	$10,000-$12,000
1996	$14,000-$16,000
1997	$16,000-$18,000
1998	$18,000-$20,000
1999	$20,000-$22,000
2000	$26,000-$28,000
2001	More than $30,000
2002	More than $30,000

Crash-test results

Model years	Offset	Full-frontal	Side
1995	Accept.	NT	NT
1996	Accept.	O/O	NT
1997	Accept.	NT	NT
1998	Accept.	NT	NT
1999	Accept.	NT	NT
2000	Accept.	NT	NT
2001	Accept.	NT	NT
2002	Accept.	O/O	NT

Land Rover Freelander

Land Rover Range Rover

2002 model shown

1996 model shown

New in the U.S. in 2002, the Freelander departs from Land Rover convention with its four-wheel independent suspension and lack of a low range. The powertrain uses a thirsty, underachieving 2.5-liter V6 and a rough-shifting five-speed automatic. Ride, handling, and brakes are quite good. Road noise is pronounced at highway speeds. The seats are comfortable but the controls are awkward. Besides its all-wheel drive, it has four-wheel traction control and a hill-descent system that controls vehicle speed on precipitous downhill grades. As such, it is the first car-based SUV capable of tackling on- and off-road duties with equal aplomb.

MAJOR REDESIGN: 2002. **SAFETY EQUIPMENT:** Dual front air bags standard. ABS standard. Safety-belt pretensioners standard. **DRIVE WHEELS:** AWD.

Launched in the U.S. in 1987, the Range Rover has been upgraded over the years, with the 4.0 SE debuting in 1995 and the 4.6 HSE in 1996. In any version, this upscale SUV comes with a long list of luxury-car amenities. Some models feature a height-adjusting air suspension that allows the vehicle to be raised or lowered to accommodate different on- and off-road conditions. The Range Rover rides comfortably for an SUV and handles adequately, though it doesn't accelerate briskly, even with its husky, uplevel V8. Also, don't expect much in the way of fuel economy.

MAJOR REDESIGN: 1995. **SAFETY EQUIPMENT:** Dual front air bags standard. Side air bags and safety-belt pretensioners standard from 1999. ABS standard. **DRIVE WHEELS:** Permanent 4WD.

Reliability history

TROUBLE SPOTS	95 96 97 98 99 00 01 02
Engine	
Cooling	
Fuel	
Ignition	NOT
Transmission	
Electrical	ENOUGH
Air-conditioning	
Suspension	DATA
Brakes	
Exhaust	TO
Paint/trim/rust	
Body integrity	
Power equipment	RATE
Body hardware	
RELIABILITY VERDICT	

Prices

1995	–
1996	–
1997	–
1998	–
1999	–
2000	–
2001	–
2002	$26,000-$28,000

Crash-test results

Model Years	Offset	Full frontal	Side
1995	–	–	–
1996	–	–	–
1997	–	–	–
1998	–	–	–
1999	–	–	–
2000	–	–	–
2001	–	–	–
2002	Accept.	NT	NT

Reliability history

TROUBLE SPOTS	95 96 97 98 99 00 01 02
Engine	
Cooling	
Fuel	
Ignition	NOT
Transmission	
Electrical	ENOUGH
Air-conditioning	
Suspension	DATA
Brakes	
Exhaust	TO
Paint/trim/rust	
Body integrity	
Power equipment	RATE
Body hardware	
RELIABILITY VERDICT	

Prices

1995	$18,000-$20,000
1996	$20,000-$22,000
1997	$22,000-$24,000
1998	$26,000-$28,000
1999	More than $30,000
2000	More than $30,000
2001	More than $30,000
2002	More than $30,000

Crash-test results

Model Years	Offset	Full frontal	Side
1995	NT	NT	NT
1996	NT	NT	NT
1997	NT	NT	NT
1998	NT	NT	NT
1999	NT	NT	NT
2000	NT	NT	NT
2001	NT	NT	NT
2002	NT	NT	NT

Lexus ES300

1997 model shown

The ES300 shares its engine, driveline, and chassis with the V6 version of the Toyota Camry. The ES300 did just about everything well in our tests. The V6 provides powerful acceleration, the transmission shifts flawlessly, and the ride is isolated and composed. The cabin is exceptionally quiet. A 1997 redesign made a good car even better. The front seats are amply supportive, and the rear is fine for two adults, with three being crowded. Acceleration is brisk and handling is predictable. As in most other Lexus models, reliability has been outstanding. **Related model:** Toyota Camry.

MAJOR REDESIGN: 1997, 2002. **SAFETY EQUIPMENT:** Dual front air bags standard. Side air bags standard from 1998. Head protection air bags standard from 2002. ABS standard. Safety-belt pretensioners standard from 1997. **DRIVE WHEELS:** Front.

Reliability history

TROUBLE SPOTS	Lexus ES300							
	95	96	97	98	99	00	01	02
Engine	○	◐	◐	●	●	●	●	●
Cooling	●	●	●	●	●	●	●	●
Fuel	●	●	◐	●	◐	●	●	●
Ignition	●	●	●	●	●	●	●	●
Transmission	●	●	●	●	●	●	●	◐
Electrical	○	●	●	●	●	●	●	●
Air conditioning	○	●	●	●	◐	●	●	●
Suspension	○	○	◐	○	●	●	●	●
Brakes	◐	○	●	●	●	●	●	●
Exhaust	●	●	●	●	●	●	●	●
Paint/trim/rust	●	●	◐	●	●	●	●	●
Body integrity	●	●	◐	●	●	●	●	●
Power equipment	○	●	●	●	●	●	●	●
Body hardware	◐	●	●	◐	●	●	●	●
RELIABILITY VERDICT	✓	✓	✓	✓	✓	✓	✓	✓

Prices

1995	$12,000-$14,000
1996	$14,000-$16,000
1997	$18,000-$20,000
1998	$20,000-$22,000
1999	$22,000-$24,000
2000	$26,000-$28,000
2001	$28,000-$30,000
2002	More than $30,000

Crash-test results

Model years	Offset	Full-frontal	Side
1995	NT	NT	NT
1996	NT	●/○	NT
1997	NT	NT	NT
1998	NT	●/○	●/○
1999	NT	●/○	●/○
2000	NT	●/○	●/○
2001	NT	●/○	●/○
2002	Good	●/○	●/○

Lexus GS430, GS300/GS400

1999 model shown

This rear-drive sedan is sized and priced between Lexus' entry-level ES300 and its flagship LS400. The GS lacks the balanced handling of the BMW 5-Series and Mercedes-Benz E-Class. A five-speed automatic was new for 1996. The GS was redesigned for 1998, getting more aggressive styling and better drivetrains. A more powerful 3.0-liter inline Six powered the GS300; the top-of-the-line GS400 used a 4.0-liter V8. For 2001, the V8 was upgraded to 4.3 liters, making the GS430 very quick. Handling is competent but unexceptional. The brakes are excellent and the transmissions super smooth.

MAJOR REDESIGN: 1993, 1998. **SAFETY EQUIPMENT:** Dual front air bags standard. Side air bags standard from 1998. Head protection air bags standard from 2001. ABS standard. Safety-belt pretensioners standard. **DRIVE WHEELS:** Rear.

Reliability history

TROUBLE SPOTS	Lexus GS300/GS400, GS430							
	95	96	97	98	99	00	01	02
Engine	Insufficient data	Insufficient data	Insufficient data	●	●	●	●	●
Cooling				●	●	●	●	●
Fuel				●	●	●	●	●
Ignition				●	●	●	●	●
Transmission				●	●	●	●	●
Electrical				○	●	●	●	●
Air conditioning				●	●	●	●	●
Suspension				●	●	●	●	●
Brakes				◐	●	●	●	●
Exhaust				●	●	●	●	●
Paint/trim/rust				●	●	●	●	●
Body integrity				○	●	●	●	●
Power equipment				●	●	●	●	●
Body hardware				◐	●	●	◐	●
RELIABILITY VERDICT				✓	✓	✓	✓	

Prices

1995	$18,000-$20,000
1996	$20,000-$22,000
1997	$22,000-$24,000
1998	$24,000-$26,000
1999	$28,000-$30,000
2000	More than $30,000
2001	More than $30,000
2002	More than $30,000

Crash-test results

Model years	Offset	Full-frontal	Side
1995	NT	○/○	NT
1996	NT	○/○	NT
1997	NT	○/○	NT
1998	NT	~ NT	NT
1999	Good	NT	NT
2000	Good	NT	NT
2001	Good	NT	NT
2002	Good	NT	NT

Lexus IS300

2001 model shown

The rear-wheel-drive IS300 joined Lexus's model line-up for 2001 to compete with cars like the BMW 3-Series and Mercedes-Benz C-Class. Power comes from a silky-smooth 215-hp inline Six mated to a five-speed automatic transmission. The ride is quite stiff and a bit jittery, and lacks the compliance found in the aforementioned German models. The brakes are excellent. Handling is very capable but falls a bit short of the 3-Series benchmark. The IS300's interior is quite snug, and the interior ambience is not everyone's taste. Tire noise is noticeable but not unbearable. The rear seat is tight for two adults, and trunk space is meager.

MAJOR REDESIGN: 2001. **SAFETY EQUIPMENT:** Dual front and side air bags standard. Head protection air bags standard from 2002. ABS standard. Safety-belt pretensioners standard. **DRIVE WHEELS:** Rear.

Reliability history

TROUBLE SPOTS	Lexus IS300							
	95	96	97	98	99	00	01	02
Engine							●	
Cooling							●	
Fuel							●	
Ignition							●	
Transmission							◐	
Electrical							●	
Air-conditioning							●	
Suspension							●	
Brakes							●	
Exhaust							●	
Paint/trim/rust							●	
Body integrity							◐	
Power equipment							●	
Body hardware							◐	
RELIABILITY VERDICT							✓	

(Insufficient data for 02)

Prices

1995	–
1996	–
1997	–
1998	–
1999	–
2000	–
2001	$28,000-$30,000
2002	$28,000-$30,000

Crash-test results

Model Years	Offset	Full frontal	Side
1995	–	–	–
1996	–	–	–
1997	–	–	–
1998	–	–	–
1999	–	–	–
2000	–	–	–
2001	NT	◐/◐	◐/◐
2002	Good	◐/◐	◐/◐

Lexus LS400, LS430

CR Good Bet

1997 model shown

Introduced in 1990, the flagship LS400 is one of the world's finest luxury sedans. It is superquiet, glides comfortably over bumps, and is filled with luxury features. A 1995 redesign left the outside looking similar, but a longer wheelbase provided more interior room. Acceleration and steering feel improved. The LS400 continued to emphasize quietness and road isolation with a long list of comfort and convenience features. Stability control was made standard for 1999. 2001 saw the V8's displacement swell to 4.3 liters, and the car was renamed the LS430.

MAJOR REDESIGN: 1995, 2001. **SAFETY EQUIPMENT:** Dual front air bags standard. Side air bags standard from 1997. Head protection air bags standard from 2001. ABS standard. Safety-belt pretensioners standard. **DRIVE WHEELS:** Rear.

Reliability history

TROUBLE SPOTS	Lexus LS400, LS430							
	95	96	97	98	99	00	01	02
Engine	●	●	●	●	●	●	●	●
Cooling	●	●	●	●	●	●	●	●
Fuel	●	●	●	●	◐	●	●	●
Ignition	●	●	●	●	●	●	●	●
Transmission	◐	●	●	◐	●	●	●	●
Electrical	○	◐	◐	●	●	○	●	●
Air-conditioning	●	◐	●	●	●	●	●	●
Suspension	○	◐	○	●	●	◐	●	●
Brakes	○	○	◐	●	●	●	●	●
Exhaust	●	●	●	●	●	●	●	●
Paint/trim/rust	●	●	◐	●	●	●	●	●
Body integrity	●	◐	●	◐	●	●	●	●
Power equipment	○	◐	●	●	◐	○	○	●
Body hardware	●	◐	●	●	◐	●	●	●
RELIABILITY VERDICT	✓	✓	✓	✓	✓	✓	✓	

Prices

1995	$18,000-$20,000
1996	$22,000-$24,000
1997	$26,000-$28,000
1998	More than $30,000
1999	More than $30,000
2000	More than $30,000
2001	More than $30,000
2002	More than $30,000

Crash-test results

Model Years	Offset	Full frontal	Side
1995	Good	NT	NT
1996	Good	NT	NT
1997	Good	NT	NT
1998	Good	NT	NT
1999	Good	NT	NT
2000	Good	NT	NT
2001	Good	NT	NT
2002	Good	NT	NT

Lexus LX450, LX470

1996 model shown

Lexus made its first foray into the world of SUVs in 1996 with the upscale LX450, essentially a Toyota Land Cruiser with a slightly softer suspension, more features, and a richer interior. Both of these big, imposing vehicles competed at the high end of the market. Five adults can fit quite comfortably, and cargo space is generous. Acceleration from the inline Six is leisurely, and the ride is too jiggly. Full-time 4WD assures good traction. The 1998 model, renamed the LX470, received an extensive redesign and a larger, more powerful V8 engine. Stability control became standard for 2000. **Related model:** Toyota Land Cruiser.

MAJOR REDESIGN: 1996, 1998. **SAFETY EQUIPMENT:** Dual front air bags standard. ABS standard. Safety-belt pretensioners standard from 1998. **DRIVE WHEELS:** Permanent 4WD.

Reliability history

TROUBLE SPOTS	95 96 97 98 99 00 01 02
Engine	
Cooling	
Fuel	
Ignition	NOT
Transmission	
Electrical	ENOUGH
Air conditioning	
Suspension	DATA
Brakes	
Exhaust	TO
Paint/trim/rust	
Body integrity	
Power equipment	RATE
Body hardware	
RELIABILITY VERDICT	

Prices

1995	–
1996	$22,000-$24,000
1997	$24,000-$26,000
1998	More than $30,000
1999	More than $30,000
2000	More than $30,000
2001	More than $30,000
2002	More than $30,000

Crash-test results

Model years	Offset	Full-frontal	Side
1995	–	–	–
1996	NT	NT	NT
1997	NT	NT	NT
1998	NT	NT	NT
1999	NT	NT	NT
2000	NT	NT	NT
2001	NT	NT	NT
2002	NT	NT	NT

Lexus RX300

CR Good Bet

1999 model shown

Launched in 1999 as the first car-based luxury SUV, the RX300 was derived from the Toyota Camry platform. In our tests, we found the mild-mannered RX300 pleasant to drive. It handles soundly, and the 3.0-liter, 220-hp V6 performs well. The AWD RX300 lacks a low range, making it better for adverse weather conditions and moderate off-pavement use than for heavy-duty off-roading. The front seats are firm and supportive. Three adults can fit in the rear, but the seat is too low. Cargo volume is modest. A long roster of standard equipment and typical Lexus refinement add to the RX's appeal. Stability control was made standard for 2001.

MAJOR REDESIGN: 1999. **SAFETY EQUIPMENT:** Dual front air bags standard. Side air bags and safety-belt pretensioners standard. ABS standard. **DRIVE WHEELS:** Front or AWD.

Reliability history

TROUBLE SPOTS	Lexus RX300 95 96 97 98 99 00 01 02
Engine	● ● ● ●
Cooling	● ● ● ●
Fuel	◐ ● ● ●
Ignition	● ● ● ●
Transmission	● ● ● ●
Electrical	◐ ● ● ●
Air conditioning	● ● ● ●
Suspension	● ● ● ●
Brakes	◐ ● ● ●
Exhaust	● ● ● ●
Paint/trim/rust	● ● ● ●
Body integrity	◐ ● ◐ ●
Power equipment	◐ ● ◐ ●
Body hardware	○ ● ● ●
RELIABILITY VERDICT	✓ ✓ ✓

Prices

1995	–
1996	–
1997	–
1998	–
1999	$26,000-$28,000
2000	More than $30,000
2001	More than $30,000
2002	More than $30,000

Crash-test results

Model years	Offset	Full-frontal	Side
1995	–	–	–
1996	–	–	–
1997	–	–	–
1998	–	–	–
1999	Good	NT	NT
2000	Good	NT	NT
2001	Good	◐/●	◐/●
2002	Good	◐/●	◐/●

Lexus SC300/SC400, SC430

1999 model shown

The original SC coupes were introduced for 1992. The six-cylinder SC300 cost thousands less than the V8-powered SC400 and still delivered good performance, though at the expense of some engine smoothness. The SC300 offered a five-speed manual transmission, but the SC400 was only available with an automatic. These cars handled nimbly in our tests, and their suspensions soaked up bumps without fuss. The front seats offer fine accommodation, but the rear is tight. The trunk is also small. Both cars were dropped following the 2000 model year. A successor, a convertible with a retractable hard top, bowed in 2002.

MAJOR REDESIGN: 1992, 2002. **SAFETY EQUIPMENT:** Dual front air bags standard. Side air bags standard from 2002. ABS standard. Safety-belt pretensioners standard from 1996. **DRIVE WHEELS:** Rear.

Reliability history

TROUBLE SPOTS	Lexus SC300/SC400, SC430							
	95	96	97	98	99	00	01	02
Engine	◒							●
Cooling	●							●
Fuel	●							●
Ignition	●							●
Transmission	●							●
Electrical	○	*Insufficient data*	*Insufficient data*	*Insufficient data*	*Insufficient data*	*Insufficient data*	*Insufficient data*	◒
Air-conditioning	◒							●
Suspension	○							●
Brakes	●							●
Exhaust	●							●
Paint/trim/rust	●							◒
Body integrity	◒							◒
Power equipment	○							●
Body hardware	◒							◒
RELIABILITY VERDICT	✓							✓

Prices

1995	$18,000–$20,000
1996	$20,000–$22,000
1997	$24,000–$26,000
1998	$28,000–$30,000
1999	More than $30,000
2000	More than $30,000
2001	–
2002	More than $30,000

Crash-test results

Model Years	Offset	Full frontal	Side
1995	NT	NT	NT
1996	NT	NT	NT
1997	NT	NT	NT
1998	NT	NT	NT
1999	NT	NT	NT
2000	NT	NT	NT
2001	–	–	–
2002	NT	NT	NT

Lincoln Continental

1997 model shown

Loosely based on the Ford Taurus since 1988, the Continental has long been big and roomy, with a host of amenities. In tests, handling was fine in routine driving, but sluggish and sloppy when pressed. Suspension modifications for 1994 improved handling somewhat. Redesigned for 1995, it received a modern, aluminum V8. The powertrain is outstanding, but the car is unimpressive in other respects. The spacious interior seats five with ease, but lacks the quality found in the Cadillac DeVille and Acura 3.5RL. The pillowy seats aren't very comfortable over time. Freshened for 1998, it was discontinued after 2002.

MAJOR REDESIGN: 1995. **SAFETY EQUIPMENT:** Dual front air bags standard. Side air bags standard from 1999. ABS standard. **DRIVE WHEELS:** Front.

Reliability history

TROUBLE SPOTS	Lincoln Continental							
	95	96	97	98	99	00	01	02
Engine	◒	◒	●	●	●	●	●	*Insufficient data*
Cooling	◒	◒	●	●	●	●	●	
Fuel	○	◒	●	●	○	●	◒	
Ignition	○	◒	○	●	●	●	●	
Transmission	○	◒	●	●	●	●	◒	
Electrical	●	◒	◒	○	○	◒	◒	
Air-conditioning	○	○	○	●	●	◒	◒	
Suspension	●	◒	●	○	○	●	◒	
Brakes	○	◒	◒	○	●	●	◒	
Exhaust	●	●	●	●	●	●	◒	
Paint/trim/rust	○	◒	●	◒	●	●	◒	
Body integrity	◒	○	◒	●	◒	◒	○	
Power equipment	●	○	◒	◒	○	○	○	
Body hardware	●	○	○	○	◒	○	◒	
RELIABILITY VERDICT	✓	✓	✓	✓	✓	✓	✓	

Prices

1995	$8,000–$10,000
1996	$10,000–$12,000
1997	$12,000–$14,000
1998	$14,000–$16,000
1999	$16,000–$18,000
2000	$20,000–$22,000
2001	$24,000–$26,000
2002	$28,000–$30,000

Crash-test results

Model Years	Offset	Full frontal	Side
1995	Accept.	NT	NT
1996	Accept.	NT	NT
1997	Accept.	NT	NT
1998	Accept.	NT	NT
1999	Accept.	NT	NT
2000	Accept.	NT	NT
2001	Accept.	NT	NT
2002	Accept.	NT	NT

UPSCALE CAR
Lincoln LS

2000 model shown

New for 2000, the LS is a sporty rear-wheel-drive sedan meant to breathe new life into the stodgy Lincoln line. By design, it rides and handles more like the European sports sedans it targets than a traditional Lincoln. In some respects, like ride quietness, it lacks the polish of imported luxury cars. The 3.0-liter V6 is not all that quick. The 3.9-liter V8 is stronger and the automatic is Ford's smoothest. Handling is agile, and the ride is firm and well controlled. The front seats are comfortable. The rear bench is comfortable enough, but knee room is tight. Sparse interior storage is one of the car's few drawbacks. 2001 brought standard traction control.

MAJOR REDESIGN: 2000. **SAFETY EQUIPMENT:** Dual front and side air bags standard. ABS standard. **DRIVE WHEELS:** Rear.

Reliability history

TROUBLE SPOTS	Lincoln LS							
	95	96	97	98	99	00	01	02
Engine						●	●	●
Cooling						●	●	●
Fuel						●	●	●
Ignition						●	●	●
Transmission						●	●	●
Electrical						○	○	●
Air conditioning						●	●	●
Suspension						●	●	●
Brakes						●	●	●
Exhaust						●	●	●
Paint/trim/rust						●	●	●
Body integrity						○	○	○
Power equipment						○	●	●
Body hardware						○	○	●
RELIABILITY VERDICT								

Prices

1995	–
1996	–
1997	–
1998	–
1999	–
2000	$24,000-$26,000
2001	$26,000-$28,000
2002	More than $30,000

Crash-test results

Model years	Offset	Full-frontal	Side
1995	–	–	–
1996	–	–	–
1997	–	–	–
1998	–	–	–
1999	–	–	–
2000	Good	NT	NT
2001	Good	◐/◑	◐/◑
2002	Good	◐/◑	◐/◑

COUPE
Lincoln Mark VIII

1995 model shown

The rear-wheel-drive Mark VIII luxury coupe competed primarily with the Cadillac Eldorado. It's powered by a muscular V8 and provides a smooth, comfortable ride. In our tests, the Mark VIII, employing an independent air-spring suspension, handled with surprising agility for such a large car. The front seats, each with power adjustments, offer good, firm support, but rear seating is cramped. The automatic climate-control system works well. The Mark VIII received a mild restyling for 1997. At its peak, power climbed to 290 horses in the top LSC model. The Mark VIII was discontinued after the 1998 model year.

MAJOR REDESIGN: 1993. **SAFETY EQUIPMENT:** Dual front air bags standard. ABS standard. **DRIVE WHEELS:** Rear.

Reliability history

TROUBLE SPOTS	Lincoln Mark VIII							
	95	96	97	98	99	00	01	02
Engine			●	●				
Cooling			●	●				
Fuel			○	●				
Ignition			○	●				
Transmission			○	●				
Electrical	Insufficient data	Insufficient data	●	●				
Air conditioning			●	○				
Suspension			●	○				
Brakes			○	●				
Exhaust			●	●				
Paint/trim/rust			○	●				
Body integrity			●	●				
Power equipment			○	○				
Body hardware			●	○				
RELIABILITY VERDICT			✔	✔				

Prices

1995	$8,000-$10,000
1996	$10,000-$12,000
1997	$14,000-$16,000
1998	$16,000-$18,000
1999	–
2000	–
2001	–
2002	–

Crash-test results

Model years	Offset	Full-frontal	Side
1995	NT	NT	NT
1996	NT	NT	NT
1997	NT	NT	NT
1998	NT	NT	NT
1999	–	–	–
2000	–	–	–
2001	–	–	–
2002	–	–	–

Lincoln Navigator

Lincoln Town Car

1998 model shown

1998 model shown

Introduced for 1998, the Navigator is basically an upgraded version of the Ford Expedition. It comes swathed in luxury items, such as leather and wood interior trim, and with a third-row seat it provides passenger capacity for seven. The selectable 4WD system can be left permanently engaged. The Navigator handled very clumsily in our tests and drank a lot of fuel. The ride was reasonably comfortable. Climbing in and out takes agility, and parking and maneuvering around town can be a challenge. Initially, the 5.4-liter V8 produced only 230 horsepower, but its output climbed to a more suitable 300 hp for 1999. **Related model:** Ford Expedition.

With its V8 and stately appearance, the Town Car maintains the tradition of domestic luxury turnpike cruisers. It comes with a full frame, rear-wheel drive, and a panoply of electronic and convenience features, especially in the Cartier and Signature trim lines. Expect a soft, quiet ride and seating for six. The optional Ride Control Package helps tame the previous-generation Town Car's tendency to wallow on bad roads. Redesigned for 1998, the Town Car carried over the same old-tech powertrain and suspension in a more contemporary package. The ride is smooth; the handling, relatively cumbersome.

MAJOR REDESIGN: 1998. **SAFETY EQUIPMENT:** Dual front air bags standard. Side air bags standard from 2000. ABS standard. **DRIVE WHEELS:** Rear or selectable 4WD.

MAJOR REDESIGN: 1998. **SAFETY EQUIPMENT:** Dual front air bags standard. Side air bags standard from 1999. ABS standard. **DRIVE WHEELS:** Rear.

Lincoln Navigator

Reliability history

TROUBLE SPOTS	95	96	97	98	99	00	01	02
Engine				◐		◐		
Cooling				◐		◐		
Fuel				○		◐		
Ignition				◐		◐		
Transmission				◐		◐		
Electrical				◐	Insufficient data	◐	Insufficient data	Insufficient data
Air-conditioning				◐		◐		
Suspension				◐		◐		
Brakes				◐		◐		
Exhaust				◐		◐		
Paint/trim/rust				○		◐		
Body integrity				○		○		
Power equipment				○		○		
Body hardware				○		○		
RELIABILITY VERDICT				✔		✔		

Prices

1995	–
1996	–
1997	–
1998	$24,000-$26,000
1999	$28,000-$30,000
2000	More than $30,000
2001	More than $30,000
2002	More than $30,000

Crash-test results

Model Years	Offset	Full frontal	Side
1995	–	–	–
1996	–	–	–
1997	–	–	–
1998	NT	◐/◐	NT
1999	NT	◐/◐	NT
2000	NT	◐/◐	NT
2001	NT	◐/◐	NT
2002	NT	◐/◐	NT

Lincoln Town Car

Reliability history

TROUBLE SPOTS	95	96	97	98	99	00	01	02
Engine	○	◐	◐	◐	◐	◐	◐	◐
Cooling	◐	◐	◐	◐	◐	◐	◐	◐
Fuel	○	○	○	◐	◐	◐	◐	◐
Ignition	○	○	○	◐	◐	◐	◐	◐
Transmission	○	○	○	◐	◐	◐	◐	◐
Electrical	◐	○	○	○	○	○	○	◐
Air-conditioning	○	○	○	◐	◐	◐	◐	◐
Suspension	◐	○	○	○	◐	◐	◐	◐
Brakes	●	◐	○	○	◐	◐	◐	◐
Exhaust	◐	◐	◐	◐	◐	◐	◐	◐
Paint/trim/rust	○	◐	◐	◐	◐	◐	◐	◐
Body integrity	○	○	○	○	○	○	○	◐
Power equipment	○	◐	◐	◐	○	◐	◐	◐
Body hardware	○	○	○	◐	○	○	○	◐
RELIABILITY VERDICT	✔	✔	✔	✔	✔	✔		✔

Prices

1995	$8,000-$10,000
1996	$12,000-$14,000
1997	$14,000-$16,000
1998	$16,000-$18,000
1999	$20,000-$22,000
2000	$24,000-$26,000
2001	$28,000-$30,000
2002	More than $30,000

Crash-test results

Model Years	Offset	Full frontal	Side
1995	NT	◐/NA	NT
1996	NT	◐/◐	NT
1997	NT	◐/◐	NT
1998	NT	NT	NT
1999	NT	NT	◐/◐
2000	NT	◐/◐	◐/◐
2001	NT	◐/◐	◐/◐
2002	NT	◐/◐	◐/◐

Mazda 626

1998 model shown

With its 1993 redesign the 626 took its place as a well-rounded and highly rated family sedan among its contemporary peers. The body leaned in turns, but the car's safe handling and good grip inspired confidence. The 626 came with an adequate 2.0-liter Four or a smooth 2.5-liter V6. With either engine, the automatic transmission is never quite smooth. The 1998 redesign did not improve it, leaving the 626 a step behind major competitors. Ride and handling were both mediocre. For 2000, Mazda made a few changes for the better. Handling is secure but the ride is fairly uncomfortable, access is tight, and road noise is pronounced.

MAJOR REDESIGN: 1993, 1998. **SAFETY EQUIPMENT:** Dual front air bags standard. Side air bags available from 2000. ABS available. **DRIVE WHEELS:** Front.

Mazda B-Series

1998 model shown

This compact pickup is a Ford Ranger with a Mazda nameplate and minor exterior differences. The ride is stiff and choppy but the steering is relatively responsive. An extended cab is a worthwhile option, providing extra interior room for luggage; however, even children won't be happy in the small jump seats. The 1998 redesign brought a four-door extended-cab model. Handling is relatively good but the ride hasn't changed. The B-Series remains one of the better choices in compact pickups. **Related model:** Ford Ranger.

MAJOR REDESIGN: 1994, 1998. **SAFETY EQUIPMENT:** Driver air bag standard; passenger side available in 1996-1997, standard from 1998. Safety-belt pretensioners standard from 2001. ABS available, standard from 2001. **DRIVE WHEELS:** Rear or part-time 4WD.

Mazda 626

Reliability history

TROUBLE SPOTS	95	96	97	98	99	00	01	02
Engine								
Cooling								
Fuel								
Ignition								
Transmission								
Electrical								
Air conditioning								
Suspension								
Brakes								
Exhaust								
Paint/trim/rust								
Body integrity								
Power equipment								
Body hardware								
RELIABILITY VERDICT	✓	✓	✓	✓	✓	✓	✓	

(Insufficient data)

Prices

1995	$6,000-$8,000
1996	$6,000-$8,000
1997	$8,000-$10,000
1998	$10,000-$12,000
1999	$10,000-$12,000
2000	$12,000-$14,000
2001	$14,000-$16,000
2002	$16,000-$18,000

Crash-test results

Model years	Offset	Full-frontal	Side
1995	NT	⊖/●	NT
1996	NT	⊖/●	NT
1997	NT	⊖/●	⊖/○
1998	Accept.	NT	○/○
1999	Accept.	⊖/●	○/○
2000	Accept.	⊖/●	○/○
2001	Accept.	⊖/●	○/○
2002	Accept.	⊖/●	○/○

Mazda B-Series 4WD

Reliability history

TROUBLE SPOTS	95	96	97	98	99	00	01	02
Engine								
Cooling								
Fuel								
Ignition								
Transmission								
Electrical								
Air conditioning								
Suspension								
Brakes								
Exhaust								
Paint/trim/rust								
Body integrity								
Power equipment								
Body hardware								
RELIABILITY VERDICT	✓	✓						

Prices

1995	$6,000-$8,000
1996	$6,000-$8,000
1997	$8,000-$10,000
1998	$8,000-$10,000
1999	$10,000-$12,000
2000	$10,000-$12,000
2001	$14,000-$16,000
2002	$14,000-$16,000

Crash-test results

Model years	Offset	Full-frontal	Side
1995	NT	NT	NT
1996	NT	⊖/○	NT
1997	NT	⊖/○	NT
1998	Accept.	⊖/○	NT
1999	Accept.	⊖/○	⊖/NA
2000	Accept.	⊖/○	⊖/NA
2001	Accept.	⊖/○	⊖/NA
2002	Accept.	⊖/○	⊖/NA

UPSCALE CAR

Mazda Millenia

CR Good Bet

1997 model shown

Good quality combined with steep depreciation makes this a good used-car value. The Millenia debuted for the 1995 model year, replacing the 929. It delivers a fine ride and adequate acceleration from its small V6. The high-line S version has a Miller-cycle V6 engine, which uses a form of supercharging to deliver effortless power, particularly in the mid-rpm range. The suspension soaks up ripples and ruts with aplomb. The front seats are very comfortable, but the cockpit is tight. The rear seat isn't all that roomy. The Millenia was dropped after 2002.

MAJOR REDESIGN: 1995. **SAFETY EQUIPMENT:** Dual front air bags standard. Side air bags standard from 2001. ABS standard. Safety-belt pretensioners standard from 2000. **DRIVE WHEELS:** Front.

MINIVAN

Mazda MPV

2000 model shown

The original MPV was a crude rear-drive minivan. It could seat up to seven although the raised rear floor and permanently attached third seat limited its versatility. Bucking the minivan standard, its one rear door was a swing-out instead of a slider. In 1996, Mazda added a fourth swing-out door. In CR's tests, the MPV felt sloppy during abrupt maneuvers and the ride was stiff and uncomfortable. An all-new, front-drive MPV debuted for 2000. It handles securely, is quiet, and has a third-row seat that folds flat. The engine was underpowered until a 2002 upgrade.

MAJOR REDESIGN: 2000. **SAFETY EQUIPMENT:** Driver air bag standard; passenger side from 1996. Side air bags available from 2000. ABS standard from 1996. **DRIVE WHEELS:** Rear or AWD up to 1998. Front starting in 2000.

Mazda Millenia — Reliability history

TROUBLE SPOTS	95	96	97	98	99	00	01	02
Engine	●	Insufficient data	Insufficient data	●	●	Insufficient data	Insufficient data	Insufficient data
Cooling	◐			●	●			
Fuel	○			◐	●			
Ignition	○			◐	●			
Transmission	◐			●	●			
Electrical	○			◐	●			
Air-conditioning	○			◐	●			
Suspension	◐			●	●			
Brakes	◐			●	●			
Exhaust	●			●	●			
Paint/trim/rust	○			◐	●			
Body integrity	◐			●	○			
Power equipment	○			○	◐			
Body hardware	○			◐	◐			
RELIABILITY VERDICT	✓			✓	✓			

Mazda Millenia — Prices

Year	Price
1995	$8,000-$10,000
1996	$10,000-$12,000
1997	$12,000-$14,000
1998	$14,000-$16,000
1999	$18,000-$20,000
2000	$20,000-$22,000
2001	$22,000-$24,000
2002	$22,000-$24,000

Mazda Millenia — Crash-test results

Model Years	Offset	Full frontal	Side
1995	Accept.	◐/○	NT
1996	Accept.	◐/○	NT
1997	Accept.	◐/○	NT
1998	Accept.	◐/○	NT
1999	Accept.	◐/○	NT
2000	Accept.	◐/○	NT
2001	Accept.	◐/●	◐/○
2002	Accept.	◐/●	◐/○

Mazda MPV — Reliability history

TROUBLE SPOTS	95	96	97	98	99	00	01	02
Engine	Insufficient data	Insufficient data	Insufficient data	Insufficient data	Insufficient data	◐	●	Insufficient data
Cooling						◐	●	
Fuel						◐	●	
Ignition						◐	●	
Transmission						◐	●	
Electrical						◐	●	
Air-conditioning						◐	●	
Suspension						●	○	
Brakes						●	●	
Exhaust						●	●	
Paint/trim/rust						◐	●	
Body integrity						◐	●	
Power equipment						◐	●	
Body hardware						○	○	
RELIABILITY VERDICT						✓	✓	

Mazda MPV — Prices

Year	Price
1995	$8,000-$10,000
1996	$10,000-$12,000
1997	$10,000-$12,000
1998	$12,000-$14,000
1999	–
2000	$16,000-$18,000
2001	$18,000-$20,000
2002	$20,000-$22,000

Mazda MPV — Crash-test results

Model Years	Offset	Full frontal	Side
1995	NT	◐/○	NT
1996	Marg.	◐/●	NT
1997	Marg.	◐/●	NT
1998	Marg.	◐/●	NT
1999	–	–	–
2000	Accept.	◐/●	●/○
2001	Accept.	◐/●	●/○
2002	Accept.	●/●	●/○

Mazda MX-5 Miata

Mazda MX-6

CR Good Bet

1999 model shown

1995 model shown

Mazda hit a home run when it introduced this two-seater for 1990. It is fun to drive, and unlike the 1950s British sports cars it imitates, the Miata is reliable and weathertight. Handling is responsive and direct, though the ride is firm. The five-speed manual transmission shifts crisply. A larger, more powerful 1.8-liter Four replaced the 1.6-liter engine for 1994. The Miata was redesigned for 1999, providing a more up-level look, a glass rear window, and a slight horsepower increase. Zesty performance, nimble handling, and precise steering continue to make this car fun. A six-speed manual and a light exterior restyling arrived in 2001.

MAJOR REDESIGN: 1990, 1999. **SAFETY EQUIPMENT:** Dual front air bags standard. Safety-belt pretensioners standard from 2001. ABS available. **DRIVE WHEELS:** Rear.

The Mazda MX-6 coupe and the related Ford Probe hatchback were completely redesigned for 1993. Both models handle predictably, though the MX-6 rides more comfortably than does the grippier Probe. A 2.0-liter four-cylinder engine was standard, with a stronger, smoother 2.5-liter V6 available optionally. Transmission choices include a five-speed manual and a rough-shifting automatic. The front seats are comfortable, but the rear seat is best reserved for packages. Of the two siblings, we prefer the MX-6's interior layout. Like the Probe, the MX-6 was retired after 1997. **Related model:** Ford Probe.

MAJOR REDESIGN: 1993 **SAFETY EQUIPMENT:** Dual front air bags standard. ABS available. **DRIVE WHEELS:** Front.

Mazda MX-5 Miata

Reliability history

TROUBLE SPOTS — Mazda MX-5 Miata (model years 95 96 97 98 99 00 01 02)

- Engine
- Cooling
- Fuel
- Ignition
- Transmission
- Electrical
- Air conditioning
- Suspension
- Brakes
- Exhaust
- Paint/trim/rust
- Body integrity
- Power equipment
- Body hardware
- RELIABILITY VERDICT: ✓ ✓ ✓ (98 insufficient data) ✓ ✓ ✓

Insufficient data (1998)

Prices

Year	Price
1995	$6,000-$8,000
1996	$8,000-$10,000
1997	$8,000-$10,000
1998	–
1999	$14,000-$16,000
2000	$16,000-$18,000
2001	$16,000-$18,000
2002	$18,000-$20,000

Crash-test results

Model years	Offset	Full-frontal	Side
1995	NT	NT	NT
1996	NT	●/○	NT
1997	NT	●/○	NT
1998	–	–	–
1999	NT	NT	NT
2000	NT	NT	NT
2001	NT	●/●	○/NA
2002	NT	●/●	○/NA

Mazda MX-6

Reliability history

TROUBLE SPOTS (model years 95 96 97 98 99 00 01 02)

- Engine
- Cooling
- Fuel
- Ignition
- Transmission
- Electrical
- Air conditioning
- Suspension
- Brakes
- Exhaust
- Paint/trim/rust
- Body integrity
- Power equipment
- Body hardware
- RELIABILITY VERDICT

NOT ENOUGH DATA TO RATE

Prices

Year	Price
1995	$6,000-$8,000
1996	$6,000-$8,000
1997	$8,000-$10,000
1998	–
1999	–
2000	–
2001	–
2002	–

Crash-test results

Model years	Offset	Full-frontal	Side
1995	NT	●/○	NT
1996	NT	●/○	NT
1997	NT	●/○	NT
1998	–	–	–
1999	–	–	–
2000			
2001			
2002			

Mazda Protegé

1999 model shown

The Protegé has long been one of CR's top choices among small sedans. A 1995 redesign made this car much better. The ride is a little better, and the handling is safe and forgiving. The front seats are hard but nicely shaped. The ES version, with its lively 1.8-liter engine, is the one to choose. A redesign came in 1999, marginally improving the car in most areas. A 130-hp 2.0-liter became standard, but a stiff ride and considerable road noise remained. The Protegé5 is a hatchback wagon that appeared in 2002, and the 2.0-liter became the standard engine.

MAJOR REDESIGN: 1995, 1999. **SAFETY EQUIPMENT:** Dual front air bags standard. Side air bags available from 2000. Safety-belt pretensioners standard from 2002. ABS available. **DRIVE WHEELS:** Front.

Mazda Tribute

2001 model shown

The product of a joint venture between Ford and Mazda, the Tribute is mechanically similar to the Ford Escape. Both are car-based SUVs, with unibody chassis and fully independent suspensions. Engine choices include an unimpressive 2.0-liter four-cylinder and a lively 3.0-liter, 200-hp V6. Major virtues include nimble handling, excellent brakes, commodious cabin space, and quick acceleration (in V6 models). Those are offset by a stiff ride, a noisy interior, flimsy plastic trim, and subpar reliability. **Related model:** Ford Escape.

MAJOR REDESIGN: 2001. **SAFETY EQUIPMENT:** Dual front air bags standard. Side air bags available. Safety-belt pretensioners standard. ABS available. **DRIVE WHEELS:** Front or AWD.

Mazda Protegé

Reliability history

TROUBLE SPOTS	Mazda Protegé							
	95	96	97	98	99	00	01	02
Engine								
Cooling								
Fuel								
Ignition								
Transmission								
Electrical								
Air-conditioning								
Suspension								
Brakes								
Exhaust								
Paint/trim/rust								
Body integrity								
Power equipment								
Body hardware								
RELIABILITY VERDICT	✓	✓	✓	✓	✓	✓	✓	✓

Prices

Year	Price
1995	$4,000-$6,000
1996	$4,000-$6,000
1997	$6,000-$8,000
1998	$6,000-$8,000
1999	$8,000-$10,000
2000	$8,000-$10,000
2001	$10,000-$12,000
2002	$12,000-$14,000

Crash-test results

Model Years	Offset	Full frontal	Side
1995	Accept.	○/NA	NT
1996	Accept.	○/NA	NT
1997	Accept.	○/NA	NT
1998	Accept.	○/NA	NT
1999	Accept.	◐/◐	○/◐
2000	Accept.	◐/◐	○/◐
2001	Accept.	●/◐	○/◐
2002	Accept.	●/◐	○/◐

Mazda Tribute

Reliability history

TROUBLE SPOTS	Mazda Tribute V6							
	95	96	97	98	99	00	01	02
Engine								
Cooling								
Fuel								
Ignition								
Transmission								
Electrical								
Air-conditioning								
Suspension								
Brakes								
Exhaust								
Paint/trim/rust								
Body integrity								
Power equipment								
Body hardware								
RELIABILITY VERDICT								

Prices

Year	Price
1995	–
1996	–
1997	–
1998	–
1999	–
2000	–
2001	$18,000-$20,000
2002	$20,000-$22,000

Crash-test results

Model Years	Offset	Full frontal	Side
1995	–	–	–
1996	–	–	–
1997	–	–	–
1998	–	–	–
1999	–	–	–
2000	–	–	–
2001	Marg.	●/◐	○/◐
2002	Marg.	●/◐	○/◐

Mercedes-Benz C-Class

Mercedes-Benz CLK

1999 model shown

1998 model shown

The C-Class debuted for 1994, replacing the entry-level 190E. The C-Class handles responsively and is easy to control in abrupt maneuvers. The ride is supple and quiet, and the firm front seats are very comfortable. A 2001 redesign brought bolder, less conservative styling and improved overall performance. The C320 sedan CR tested was smooth, quick, quiet, and comfortable, with agile handling and excellent steering and brakes. An unintuitive control layout is its one major shortcoming.

MAJOR REDESIGN: 1994, 2001. **SAFETY EQUIPMENT:** Dual front air bags standard. Front side air bags standard from 1998. Rear side and head protection air bags standard from 2001. ABS and safety-belt pretensioners standard. **DRIVE WHEELS:** Rear.

New for 1998, the Mercedes CLK was styled like the larger E-Class, but used C-Class underpinnings. The initial model was powered by a smooth-revving 3.2-liter V6, good for 215 horsepower. An optional 4.3-liter V8 was added in mid '98. Both engines are matched to a five-speed automatic. Informal testing indicates that the CLK handles well and is fast, frugal, and comfortable, though not as rewarding to drive as a BMW 3-Series coupe. The two rear seats are reasonably hospitable. A convertible model, new for 1999, features pop-up safety bars that deploy when a rollover is detected. The high-performance CLK55 AMG debuted in 2001.

MAJOR REDESIGN: 1998. **SAFETY EQUIPMENT:** Dual front and side air bags standard. ABS and safety-belt pretensioners standard. **DRIVE WHEELS:** Rear.

Reliability history — Mercedes-Benz C-Class

TROUBLE SPOTS	95	96	97	98	99	00	01	02
Engine								
Cooling								
Fuel								
Ignition								
Transmission								
Electrical								
Air conditioning								
Suspension								
Brakes								
Exhaust								
Paint/trim/rust								
Body integrity								
Power equipment								
Body hardware								
RELIABILITY VERDICT			✓	✓	✓	✓		✓

(96 column: Insufficient data)

Prices

Year	Price
1995	$16,000–$18,000
1996	$16,000–$18,000
1997	$18,000–$20,000
1998	$22,000–$24,000
1999	$24,000–$26,000
2000	$28,000–$30,000
2001	More than $30,000
2002	More than $30,000

Crash-test results

Model years	Offset	Full-frontal	Side
1995	NT	⊖/⊖	NT
1996	NT	⊖/⊖	NT
1997	NT	⊖/⊖	NT
1998	NT	⊖/⊖	○/⊖
1999	NT	⊖/⊖	○/⊖
2000	NT	⊖/⊖	○/⊖
2001	Good	NT	NT
2002	Good	NT	NT

Reliability history — Mercedes-Benz CLK

TROUBLE SPOTS	95	96	97	98	99	00	01	02
Engine								
Cooling								
Fuel								
Ignition								
Transmission								
Electrical								
Air conditioning								
Suspension								
Brakes								
Exhaust								
Paint/trim/rust								
Body integrity								
Power equipment								
Body hardware								
RELIABILITY VERDICT					✓			

(95–97 and 01–02 columns: Insufficient data)

Prices

Year	Price
1995	–
1996	–
1997	–
1998	More than $30,000
1999	More than $30,000
2000	More than $30,000
2001	More than $30,000
2002	More than $30,000

Crash-test results

Model years	Offset	Full-frontal	Side
1995	–	–	–
1996	–	–	–
1997	–	–	–
1998	NT	NT	NT
1999	NT	NT	NT
2000	NT	NT	NT
2001	NT	NT	NT
2002	NT	NT	NT

Mercedes-Benz E-Class

Mercedes-Benz M-Class

1997 model shown

1998 model shown

Redesigned for 1996, the E-Class sedan and wagon are among the best cars available. High points include precise handling, effortless performance, and an excellent ride. CR ranked the pricey E320 4Matic (AWD) wagon one of the best all-around vehicles ever tested. Acceleration is spirited and fuel economy respectable. The seats are very comfortable. Engine choices over the years have included a 3.2-liter inline-6 (V6 after 1997), 4.2- and 4.3-liter V8s, an inline-6 turbodiesel (until 1999), and a high-performance 5.5-liter V8. All are mated to a smooth five-speed automatic transmission.

MAJOR REDESIGN: 1996. **SAFETY EQUIPMENT:** Dual front air bags standard. Front side air bags standard from 1998. Rear side and head protection air bags standard from 2000. ABS and safety-belt pretensioners standard. **DRIVE WHEELS:** Rear; AWD optional from 1998.

Introduced for 1998, the M-Class is built in Alabama. The initial model was the ML320, powered by a 3.2-liter V6. The ML430 V8 debuted for 1999. The following year brought a high-performance ML55 and stability control across the board. It has a fully independent suspension and a full-time 4WD system. The ML320 CR tested in 1998 rode and handled well. It has roomy seating for five and lots of cargo room. The ML320's fuel economy is good for a vehicle of this size and weight. The V8s are stronger but thirsty and less comfortable. Reliability started out poor and has remained so.

MAJOR REDESIGN: 1998. **SAFETY EQUIPMENT:** Dual front air bags standard. Front and rear side air bags standard from 2000. Head protection air bags standard from 2002. ABS and safety-belt pretensioners standard. **DRIVE WHEELS:** Permanent 4WD.

Reliability history — Mercedes-Benz E-Class

TROUBLE SPOTS	95	96	97	98	99	00	01	02
Engine								
Cooling								
Fuel								
Ignition								
Transmission								
Electrical								
Air-conditioning								
Suspension								
Brakes								
Exhaust								
Paint/trim/rust								
Body integrity								
Power equipment								
Body hardware								
RELIABILITY VERDICT	✓	✓	✓		✓		✓	✓

Prices

Year	Price
1995	$18,000-$20,000
1996	$24,000-$26,000
1997	$26,000-$28,000
1998	More than $30,000
1999	More than $30,000
2000	More than $30,000
2001	More than $30,000
2002	More than $30,000

Crash-test results

Model Years	Offset	Full frontal	Side
1995	NT	NT	NT
1996	NT	NT	NT
1997	Accept.	NT	NT
1998	Accept.	NT	NT
1999	Accept.	NT	NT
2000	Accept.	NT	NT
2001	Good	NT	NT
2002	Good	NT	NT

Reliability history — Mercedes-Benz M-Class

TROUBLE SPOTS	95	96	97	98	99	00	01	02
Engine								
Cooling								
Fuel								
Ignition								
Transmission								
Electrical								
Air-conditioning								
Suspension								
Brakes								
Exhaust								
Paint/trim/rust								
Body integrity								
Power equipment								
Body hardware								
RELIABILITY VERDICT								

Prices

Year	Price
1995	–
1996	–
1997	–
1998	$24,000-$26,000
1999	$26,000-$28,000
2000	More than $30,000
2001	More than $30,000
2002	More than $30,000

Crash-test results

Model Years	Offset	Full frontal	Side
1995	–	–	–
1996	–	–	–
1997	–	–	–
1998	NT	◒/●	NT
1999	Good	◒/●	NT
2000	Good	◒/●	NT
2001	Good	◒/●	NT
2002	Good	◒/●	NT

Mercedes-Benz S-Class

2000 model shown

The S-Class has always ranked among the world's best and costliest luxury cars. Available in standard and long-wheelbase forms, it has a roomy interior and a large trunk. The ride is comfortable and quiet, and handling is commendable. Engine choices range from a strained inline Six to a more appropriate V8 and even a powerful V12. A new, more advanced S-Class was introduced for 2000. This iteration also handles well for its size, with excellent ride quality. The CL-Class coupes are essentially two-door S-Class models with altered styling.

MAJOR REDESIGN: 2000. **SAFETY EQUIPMENT:** Dual front air bags standard. Front side air bags standard from 1998. Rear side and head protection air bags standard from 2000. ABS and safety-belt pretensioners standard. **DRIVE WHEELS:** Rear.

Reliability history

TROUBLE SPOTS	Mercedes-Benz S-Class							
	95	96	97	98	99	00	01	02
Engine						●		
Cooling						◐		
Fuel						○		
Ignition						●		
Transmission						◐		
Electrical	Insufficient data	Insufficient data	Insufficient data	Insufficient data	Insufficient data	○	Insufficient data	Insufficient data
Air conditioning						○		
Suspension						◐		
Brakes						○		
Exhaust						◐		
Paint/trim/rust						◐		
Body integrity						◐		
Power equipment						●		
Body hardware						◐		
RELIABILITY VERDICT								

Prices

1995	$26,000-$28,000
1996	More than $30,000
1997	More than $30,000
1998	More than $30,000
1999	More than $30,000
2000	More than $30,000
2001	More than $30,000
2002	More than $30,000

Crash-test results

Model years	Offset	Full-frontal	Side
1995	NT	NT	NT
1996	NT	NT	NT
1997	NT	NT	NT
1998	NT	NT	NT
1999	NT	NT	NT
2000	NT	NT	NT
2001	NT	NT	NT
2002	NT	NT	NT

Mercedes-Benz SLK

1998 model shown

This two-seat convertible was introduced for 1998, boasting many innovative technical and safety features. Its major draw is an electrically retractable hardtop that folds and stows in the trunk at the touch of a button. With the roof up, this convertible feels almost as solid as a fixed-roof coupe, but overall the SLK isn't very sporty. The steering isn't quick or precise, and the supercharged, intercooled 2.3-liter Four lacks oomph. Interior space is tight. Model-line updates include a vague and rubbery five-speed manual transmission for 1999 and the V6-powered, six-speed SLK320 for 2001.

MAJOR REDESIGN: 1998. **SAFETY EQUIPMENT:** Dual front and side air bags standard. ABS and safety-belt pretensioners standard. **DRIVE WHEELS:** Rear.

Reliability history

TROUBLE SPOTS	Mercedes-Benz SLK							
	95	96	97	98	99	00	01	02
Engine				◐			◐	
Cooling				●			●	
Fuel				◐			○	
Ignition				●			●	
Transmission				●			◐	
Electrical				●	Insufficient data	Insufficient data	○	Insufficient data
Air conditioning				●			●	
Suspension				◐			○	
Brakes				○			○	
Exhaust				●			◐	
Paint/trim/rust				●			○	
Body integrity				○			◐	
Power equipment				○			●	
Body hardware				◐			○	
RELIABILITY VERDICT				✓				

Prices

1995	–
1996	–
1997	–
1998	$26,000-$28,000
1999	More than $30,000
2000	More than $30,000
2001	More than $30,000
2002	More than $30,000

Crash-test results

Model years	Offset	Full-frontal	Side
1995	–	–	–
1996	–	–	–
1997	–	–	–
1998	NT	NT	NT
1999	NT	NT	NT
2000	NT	NT	NT
2001	NT	NT	NT
2002	NT	NT	NT

Mercury Cougar

Mercury Grand Marquis

1999 model shown

1998 model shown

U ntil 1997, the Cougar was Mercury's twin to the Ford Thunderbird. This large rear-wheel-drive coupe was available with a V6 or V8 engine. In 1994, the Cougar received an updated interior and a new 4.6-liter V8. This version handles fairly decently but has a stiff ride. The seats provide insufficient support, and the rear is tight. The rear-drive Cougar was axed after 1997. In 1999, the Cougar was reborn as a smaller front-wheel-drive coupe with excellent handling but a stiff ride. A 2.5-liter V6 provides just-adequate acceleration, but the automatic transmission is occasionally reluctant to downshift. **Related model:** Ford Thunderbird up to 1997.

MAJOR REDESIGN: 1994, 1999. **SAFETY EQUIPMENT:** Dual front air bags standard. Side air bags available from 1999. ABS available. **DRIVE WHEELS:** Rear until 1997; front from 1999.

A classic highway cruiser, the rear-wheel-drive Grand Marquis is built on a full frame and is powered by a 4.6-liter V8. A compliant ride, huge trunk, and substantial trailer-towing capability are its major advantages. Handling is fairly clumsy and the steering feels light. The front seat is a bench. The rear seat is not as roomy as you might expect in a car of this size. This model was freshened for 1998 and also received some suspension tweaks. For 2001, the Grand Marquis picked up more power and optional adjustable pedals. **Related model:** Ford Crown Victoria.

MAJOR REDESIGN: 1992, 1998. **SAFETY EQUIPMENT:** Dual front air bags standard. Safety-belt pretensioners standard from 2001. ABS available, standard from 2002. **DRIVE WHEELS:** Rear.

Reliability history — Mercury Cougar

TROUBLE SPOTS	95	96	97	98	99	00	01	02
Engine							Insufficient data	Insufficient data
Cooling								
Fuel								
Ignition								
Transmission								
Electrical								
Air-conditioning								
Suspension								
Brakes								
Exhaust								
Paint/trim/rust								
Body integrity								
Power equipment								
Body hardware								
RELIABILITY VERDICT	✓	✓	✓		✓			

Prices — Mercury Cougar

Year	Price
1995	$6,000-$8,000
1996	$6,000-$8,000
1997	$8,000-$10,000
1998	–
1999	$10,000-$12,000
2000	$12,000-$14,000
2001	$14,000-$16,000
2002	$14,000-$16,000

Crash-test results — Mercury Cougar

Model Years	Offset	Full frontal	Side
1995	NT	◐/○	NT
1996	NT	◐/○	NT
1997	NT	◐/○	○/●
1998	–	–	–
1999	NT	NT	NT
2000	NT	NT	NT
2001	NT	NT	○/○
2002	NT	NT	○/○

Reliability history — Mercury Grand Marquis

TROUBLE SPOTS	95	96	97	98	99	00	01	02
Engine								
Cooling								
Fuel								
Ignition								
Transmission								
Electrical								
Air-conditioning								
Suspension								
Brakes								
Exhaust								
Paint/trim/rust								
Body integrity								
Power equipment								
Body hardware								
RELIABILITY VERDICT	✓	✓	✓	✓	✓	✓	✓	

Prices — Mercury Grand Marquis

Year	Price
1995	$6,000-$8,000
1996	$8,000-$10,000
1997	$10,000-$12,000
1998	$10,000-$12,000
1999	$12,000-$14,000
2000	$16,000-$18,000
2001	$18,000-$20,000
2002	$20,000-$22,000

Crash-test results — Mercury Grand Marquis

Model Years	Offset	Full frontal	Side
1995	NT	◐/○	NT
1996	NT	◐/○	NT
1997	NT	◐/○	◐/○
1998	NT	◐/○	◐/○
1999	NT	◐/○	◐/○
2000	NT	◐/○	◐/○
2001	NT	◐/○	◐/○
2002	NT	◐/○	◐/○

Mercury Mountaineer

Mercury Mystique

1997 model shown

1998 model shown

A rebadged Ford Explorer, the Mountaineer debuted for 1997. Initially, the single engine choice was a 5.0-liter, 210-hp V8. Ride and handling are stiff and choppy. The Mountaineer comes either as a rear-driver or with an AWD system that lacks the low-range gearing. For 1998, a 4.0-liter V6 became the standard engine and was mated to a smooth five-speed automatic transmission. The torquier V8 became optional. The Mountaineer's interior is roomy, and cargo space is generous. 2002 brought a complete redesign. **Related model:** Ford Explorer.

MAJOR REDESIGN: 1997, 2002. **SAFETY EQUIPMENT:** Dual front air bags standard. Side air bags available from 1999-2001. Head protection air bags available from 2002. Safety-belt pretensioners standard from 2002. ABS standard. **DRIVE WHEELS:** Rear, permanent 4WD, or AWD.

The Mystique is the Mercury version of Ford's Contour. Introduced in 1995, this modern compact sedan was slotted into Mercury's line between the Tracer and Sable. In CR tests, handling was nimble, especially with the "sport" suspension and performance tires. The softer base suspension gives a slightly better ride. The base four-cylinder engine was unimpressive and noisy; look for a model equipped with the stronger V6. The front seats are roomy and comfortable, but the rear seat is cramped. An extra inch of rear legroom in the 1996 model helped somewhat. The lineup received a style freshening for 1998, but was discontinued after 2000. **Related model:** Ford Contour.

MAJOR REDESIGN: 1995. **SAFETY EQUIPMENT:** Dual front air bags standard. ABS available. **DRIVE WHEELS:** Front.

Mercury Mountaineer

Reliability history — Mercury Mountaineer 2WD

TROUBLE SPOTS	95	96	97	98	99	00	01	02
Engine			○	○	○	○	●	●
Cooling			○	◐	◐	◐	●	●
Fuel			○	○	○	○	●	●
Ignition			●	◐	◐	◐	●	●
Transmission			●	◐	◐	○	●	●
Electrical			○	◐	●	◐	◐	●
Air conditioning			●	○	◐	○	◐	●
Suspension			○	◐	○	◐	●	●
Brakes			○	◐	◐	◐	●	●
Exhaust			◐	○	●	●	●	●
Paint/trim/rust			○	◐	●	◐	●	●
Body integrity			○	○	○	◐	●	●
Power equipment			○	◐	○	○	○	●
Body hardware			◐	○	○	◐	○	●
RELIABILITY VERDICT			✓			✓		

Prices

Year	Price
1995	–
1996	–
1997	$12,000-$14,000
1998	$14,000-$16,000
1999	$16,000-$18,000
2000	$18,000-$20,000
2001	$20,000-$22,000
2002	$24,000-$26,000

Crash-test results

Model years	Offset	Full-frontal	Side
1995	–	–	–
1996	–	–	–
1997	Accept.	◐/◐	NT
1998	Accept.	◐/◐	NT
1999	Accept.	◐/◐	○/◐
2000	Accept.	◐/◐	○/◐
2001	Accept.	◐/◐	○/◐
2002	Good	◐/●	NT

Mercury Mystique

Reliability history — Mercury Mystique V6

TROUBLE SPOTS	95	96	97	98	99	00	01	02
Engine	○	○	◐	◐	◐	●		
Cooling	●	◐	○	○	◐	●		
Fuel	●	●	●	◐	○	○		
Ignition	○	○	◐	◐	●	◐		
Transmission	○	○	◐	◐	◐	◐		
Electrical	◐	◐	○	◐	◐	◐		
Air conditioning	◐	○	◐	◐	◐	●		
Suspension	◐	◐	◐	◐	◐	◐		
Brakes	◐	◐	◐	◐	◐	◐		
Exhaust	○	◐	○	◐	◐	●		
Paint/trim/rust	◐	◐	◐	◐	◐	◐		
Body integrity	◐	◐	○	◐	●	◐		
Power equipment	○	○	◐	◐	◐	●		
Body hardware	◐	○	◐	◐	◐	◐		
RELIABILITY VERDICT					✓	✓		

Prices

Year	Price
1995	$4,000-$6,000
1996	$4,000-$6,000
1997	$6,000-$8,000
1998	$6,000-$8,000
1999	$8,000-$10,000
2000	$10,000-$12,000
2001	–
2002	–

Crash-test results

Model years	Offset	Full-frontal	Side
1995	Poor	◐/◐	NT
1996	Poor	◐/◐	NT
1997	Poor	◐/◐	○/◐
1998	Poor	◐/◐	○/◐
1999	Poor	◐/◐	○/◐
2000	Poor	◐/◐	○/◐
2001	–	–	–
2002	–	–	–

FAMILY CAR
Mercury Sable

2000 model shown

The Sable is Mercury's twin of the Ford Taurus. The early models offer good handling and comfortable seats. By 1995, the sedan and wagon still scored fairly well in our tests, but the line was getting old. A significant redesign for 1996 brought it up-to-date, with crisper handling and a firmer ride. CR also found it roomy, comfortable, and quiet. The Sable was revamped for 2000, picking up fresh styling, side air bags, adjustable pedals, and an emergency trunk release. The best choice is one that's equipped with the 200-hp V6 rather than the stodgier 155-hp V6. **Related model:** Ford Taurus.

MAJOR REDESIGN: 1996, 2000. **SAFETY EQUIPMENT:** Dual front air bags standard. Side air bags available from 2000. Safety-belt pretensioners standard from 2000. ABS available. **DRIVE WHEELS:** Front.

SMALL CAR
Mercury Tracer

1997 model shown

The Tracer shared a platform with the Mazda Protegé. It was available in sedan and wagon variations. In CR's tests, the Tracer was twitchy in emergency maneuvers, and the noisy 1.9-liter Four provided lethargic acceleration. The sophisticated Mazda-built 1.8-liter found in the LTS model is more powerful. The basic model handles sluggishly, but the LTS' taut suspension makes the car feel more nimble. A significant redesign for 1997 produced a much-improved sedan and wagon. Engine displacement climbed to 2.0 liters, and vehicle dynamics improved. The Tracer was phased out after 1999. **Related model:** Ford Escort.

MAJOR REDESIGN: 1997. **SAFETY EQUIPMENT:** Dual front air bags standard. ABS available. **DRIVE WHEELS:** Front.

Mercury Sable — Reliability history

TROUBLE SPOTS	95	96	97	98	99	00	01	02
Engine								
Cooling								
Fuel								
Ignition								
Transmission								
Electrical								
Air-conditioning								
Suspension								
Brakes								
Exhaust								
Paint/trim/rust								
Body integrity								
Power equipment								
Body hardware								
RELIABILITY VERDICT		✔	✔	✔	✔	✔	✔	✔

Mercury Sable — Prices

Year	Price
1995	$4,000-$6,000
1996	$4,000-$6,000
1997	$6,000-$8,000
1998	$8,000-$10,000
1999	$8,000-$10,000
2000	$10,000-$12,000
2001	$12,000-$14,000
2002	$14,000-$16,000

Mercury Sable — Crash-test results

Model Years	Offset	Full frontal	Side
1995	Good	○/○	NT
1996	Good	○/○	NT
1997	Good	○/○	○/○
1998	Good	○/○	○/○
1999	Good	●/○	○/○
2000	Good	●/○	○/○
2001	Good	●/○	○/○
2002	Good	●/○	○/○

Mercury Tracer — Reliability history

TROUBLE SPOTS	95	96	97	98	99	00	01	02
Engine								
Cooling								
Fuel								
Ignition								
Transmission								
Electrical								
Air-conditioning								
Suspension								
Brakes								
Exhaust								
Paint/trim/rust								
Body integrity								
Power equipment								
Body hardware								
RELIABILITY VERDICT	✔	✔	✔	✔	✔			

Mercury Tracer — Prices

Year	Price
1995	$2,000-$4,000
1996	$4,000-$6,000
1997	$4,000-$6,000
1998	$4,000-$6,000
1999	$6,000-$8,000
2000	–
2001	–
2002	–

Mercury Tracer — Crash-test results

Model Years	Offset	Full frontal	Side
1995	NT	○/○	NT
1996	NT	○/○	NT
1997	Accept.	○/○	○/○
1998	Accept.	○/○	○/○
1999	Accept.	○/○	○/○
2000	–	–	–
2001	–	–	–
2002	–	–	–

CR Good Bet

Mercury Villager

Mini Cooper

1999 model shown

2002 model shown

The Villager and its twin, the Nissan Quest, debuted in 1993 as a smaller alternative to the Chrysler mini-vans. It was initially powered by a responsive 3.0-liter V6 engine from Nissan. Ride and handling are carlike, and the interior is quiet. For 1996, conventional front safety belts and dual air bags replaced the annoying motorized shoulder belts. A 1999 redesign brought a larger V6 and added more room and a second sliding door. But overall, the improvement was modest. This version's best feature is a foldable, sliding third seat. Crash-test results are not encouraging. **Related model:** Nissan Quest.

MAJOR REDESIGN: 1993, 1999. **SAFETY EQUIPMENT:** Driver air bag standard; passenger side from 1996. ABS standard through 1998, available from 1999. **DRIVE WHEELS:** Front.

The original Mini was a low-priced urban runabout ingeniously designed to provide maximum interior space and exceptionally nimble handling. This latest incarnation, developed by BMW, manages to blend much of the old model's feisty charm with modern levels of comfort and safety. It's powered by a 1.6-liter four-cylinder engine, paired with either a five-speed manual or a continuously variable transmission (CVT). The manual-shift version CR tested offered easy shifting and extremely agile handling, but it lacked oomph. The ride is choppy and road noise is pronounced. The front seats are comfortable; the rear is cramped.

MAJOR REDESIGN: 2002. **SAFETY EQUIPMENT:** Dual front air bags standard. Side and head protection air bags standard. ABS and safety-belt pretensioners standard. **DRIVE WHEELS:** Front.

Mercury Villager

Reliability history

TROUBLE SPOTS	95	96	97	98	99	00	01	02
Engine								
Cooling								
Fuel								
Ignition								
Transmission								
Electrical								
Air conditioning								
Suspension								
Brakes								
Exhaust								
Paint/trim/rust								
Body integrity								
Power equipment								
Body hardware								
RELIABILITY VERDICT	✓	✓	✓	✓	✓		✓	*Insufficient data*

Prices

1995	$6,000-$8,000
1996	$8,000-$10,000
1997	$8,000-$10,000
1998	$10,000-$12,000
1999	$12,000-$14,000
2000	$14,000-$16,000
2001	$16,000-$18,000
2002	$18,000-$20,000

Crash-test results

Model years	Offset	Full-frontal	Side
1995	NT	◐/○	NT
1996	Marg.	◐/○	NT
1997	Marg.	◐/○	NT
1998	Marg.	◐/○	NT
1999	Poor	NT	NT
2000	Poor	◐/○	◐/◐
2001	Poor	◐/◐	◐/◐
2002	Poor	◐/◐	◐/◐

Mini Cooper

Reliability history

TROUBLE SPOTS	95	96	97	98	99	00	01	02
Engine								
Cooling								
Fuel								
Ignition								
Transmission								
Electrical								
Air conditioning								
Suspension								
Brakes								
Exhaust								
Paint/trim/rust								
Body integrity								
Power equipment								
Body hardware								
RELIABILITY VERDICT								

NOT ENOUGH DATA TO RATE

Prices

1995	–
1996	–
1997	–
1998	–
1999	–
2000	–
2001	–
2002	$20,000-$22,000

Crash-test results

Model years	Offset	Full-frontal	Side
1995	–		
1996	–		
1997	–		
1998	–		
1999	–		
2000	–		
2001	–		
2002	Good	◐/◐	◐/NA

Mitsubishi 3000GT

1995 model shown

In their sportiest forms, the Mitsubishi 3000GT and similar Dodge Stealth are loaded with gadgets. The base model with a V6 and front-wheel drive was not very exciting. The VR-4, with twin turbochargers, four-wheel steering, "active" aerodynamics, and AWD offered quick steering and strong tire grip, as well as short stops and blazing acceleration. It still wasn't that much fun to drive. The front seats are comfortable and supportive, but the rear seat is quite compact. Limited cargo space is made more useful by the split, folding rear seat backs. The 3000GT was discontinued after 1999. **Related model:** Dodge Stealth.

MAJOR REDESIGN: 1990. **SAFETY EQUIPMENT:** Dual front air bags standard. ABS available through 1998; standard in 1999. **DRIVE WHEELS:** Front or AWD.

Reliability history		
TROUBLE SPOTS		
	95 96 97 98 99 00 01 02	
Engine		
Cooling		
Fuel		
Ignition	NOT	
Transmission		
Electrical	ENOUGH	
Air-conditioning		
Suspension	DATA	
Brakes		
Exhaust	TO	
Paint/trim/rust		
Body integrity	RATE	
Power equipment		
Body hardware		
RELIABILITY VERDICT		

Prices	
1995	$12,000-$14,000
1996	$14,000-$16,000
1997	$18,000-$20,000
1998	$20,000-$22,000
1999	$24,000-$26,000
2000	–
2001	–
2002	–

Crash-test results			
Model Years	Offset	Full frontal	Side
1995	NT	NT	NT
1996	NT	NT	NT
1997	NT	NT	NT
1998	NT	NT	NT
1999	NT	NT	NT
2000	–	–	–
2001	–	–	–
2002	–	–	–

Mitsubishi Diamante

1997 model shown

Despite all its high-tech features, Mitsubishi's flagship sedan never stood out against its competitors from Acura and Lexus. The ride is controlled and quiet, but handling is not nimble. In our tests, the car provided strong acceleration only at high revs, and braking distances were long. A wagon model was introduced for 1993, but lasted only through 1995. The front-drive Diamante was redesigned for 1997, but it still didn't provide the class, room, or ability of German and other Japanese competitors. The powertrain is strong and smooth, but the Diamante's ride and handling are nothing special.

MAJOR REDESIGN: 1997. **SAFETY EQUIPMENT:** Dual front air bags standard. ABS available through 1997, standard from 1998. Safety-belt pretensioners standard from 1998. **DRIVE WHEELS:** Front.

Reliability history		
TROUBLE SPOTS		
	95 96 97 98 99 00 01 02	
Engine		
Cooling		
Fuel		
Ignition	NOT	
Transmission		
Electrical	ENOUGH	
Air-conditioning		
Suspension	DATA	
Brakes		
Exhaust	TO	
Paint/trim/rust		
Body integrity	RATE	
Power equipment		
Body hardware		
RELIABILITY VERDICT		

Prices	
1995	$8,000-$10,000
1996	$8,000-$10,000
1997	$10,000-$12,000
1998	$12,000-$14,000
1999	$14,000-$16,000
2000	$16,000-$18,000
2001	$16,000-$18,000
2002	$20,000-$22,000

Crash-test results			
Model Years	Offset	Full frontal	Side
1995	NT	NT	NT
1996	NT	NT	NT
1997	NT	NT	NT
1998	NT	NT	NT
1999	NT	NT	NT
2000	NT	NT	NT
2001	NT	NT	NT
2002	NT	NT	NT

Mitsubishi Eclipse

Mitsubishi Galant

2000 model shown

1999 model shown

The Eclipse is available in a range of performance levels, from a tame four-cylinder front-wheel-drive version to a top-of-the-line turbocharged model with AWD. The AWD GSX we tested handled well and had excellent braking, and its ride wasn't too bad for this species. For 1995, the Eclipse was redesigned with a longer wheelbase and more power. It was redesigned again for 2000, when it gained a strong, optional V6. It still isn't nimble or comfortable, the cabin is tight, and the clutch is a long reach. A convertible is also available. **Related model:** Eagle Talon.

MAJOR REDESIGN: 1990, 1995, 2000. **SAFETY EQUIPMENT:** Dual front air bags standard. Side air bags available from 2000. ABS available. **DRIVE WHEELS:** Front. AWD available until 1999.

The Galant has been a competent sedan, though always a notch below the excellent Toyota Camry and Honda Accord. Redesigned for 1994, the Galant was slightly enlarged and got new safety features. The 2.4-liter Four provides lively acceleration. The car handles securely, but its brakes are unimpressive. Redesigned again for 1999, the Galant offers an improved automatic transmission and a strong 3.0-liter V6. It has a comfortable, quiet ride and reasonably agile handling. The driver's seat provides only marginal comfort, however, and space is limited in the rear. Traction control became standard on V6 models in 2001.

MAJOR REDESIGN: 1994, 1999. **SAFETY EQUIPMENT:** Dual front air bags standard. Side air bags available from 1999. ABS available. **DRIVE WHEELS:** Front.

Reliability history — Mitsubishi Eclipse

TROUBLE SPOTS	95	96	97	98	99	00	01	02
Engine						●	●	
Cooling						●	●	
Fuel						●	●	
Ignition						●	●	
Transmission						●	●	
Electrical	Insufficient data	Insufficient data	Insufficient data	Insufficient data	Insufficient data	●	●	Insufficient data
Air conditioning						●	●	
Suspension						●	●	
Brakes						●	●	
Exhaust						●	●	
Paint/trim/rust						○	○	
Body integrity						○	●	
Power equipment						○	○	
Body hardware						○	○	
RELIABILITY VERDICT						✔		

Prices

1995	$6,000-$8,000
1996	$8,000-$10,000
1997	$10,000-$12,000
1998	$10,000-$12,000
1999	$12,000-$14,000
2000	$14,000-$16,000
2001	$14,000-$16,000
2002	$16,000-$18,000

Crash-test results

Model years	Offset	Full-frontal	Side
1995	NT	◒/◓	NT
1996	NT	◒/◓	NT
1997	NT	◒/◓	NT
1998	NT	NT	●/NA
1999	NT	NT	●/NA
2000	NT	NT	NT
2001	NT	NT	◓/NA
2002	NT	◒/◓	◓/NA

Reliability history — Mitsubishi Galant

TROUBLE SPOTS	95	96	97	98	99	00	01	02
Engine	○				●	●	●	
Cooling	○				●	●	●	
Fuel	◒				●	●	●	
Ignition	◒				●	●	●	
Transmission	○				●	◒	●	
Electrical	◒	Insufficient data	Insufficient data	Insufficient data	●	○	○	Insufficient data
Air conditioning	◒				●	●	○	
Suspension	●				◒	●	◒	
Brakes	◒				●	○	◒	
Exhaust	◒				●	●	●	
Paint/trim/rust	○				●	○	○	
Body integrity	◒				●	○	○	
Power equipment	○				●	◒	●	
Body hardware	◒				○	○	○	
RELIABILITY VERDICT	✔				✔	✔		

Prices

1995	$4,000-$6,000
1996	$6,000-$8,000
1997	$6,000-$8,000
1998	$8,000-$10,000
1999	$10,000-$12,000
2000	$10,000-$12,000
2001	$12,000-$14,000
2002	$14,000-$16,000

Crash-test results

Model years	Offset	Full-frontal	Side
1995	Poor	NA/◒	NT
1996	Poor	NA/◒	NT
1997	Poor	◒/◓	○/◒
1998	Poor	◒/◓	○/◒
1999	Accept.	◒/◓	●/◒
2000	Accept.	◒/◓	○/◒
2001	Accept.	◒/◓	○/◒
2002	Accept.	◒/◓	○/◒

SMALL CAR
Mitsubishi Mirage, Lancer

1997 model shown

The Mirage began as small car with a jumpy, uncomfortable ride. Models without ABS stopped poorly. The 1997 redesign brought vast improvements including a relatively comfortable and quiet ride. The LS model's 1.8-liter four-cylinder engine delivered better acceleration than the base model's 1.5-liter. The four-door Lancer replaced the Mirage in 2002. Among its peers it falls short in many ways. The cabin has uncomfortable seats, pronounced road noise, and unimpressive fit and finish. The ride is tolerable but unsettled. Handling is clumsy for a small car. **Related model:** Eagle Summit.

MAJOR REDESIGN: 1993, 1997, 2002. **SAFETY EQUIPMENT:** Dual front air bags standard. Side air bags available from 2002. Safety-belt pretensioners standard from 2002. ABS available from 1997. **DRIVE WHEELS:** Front.

SPORT-UTILITY VEHICLE
Mitsubishi Montero

1998 model shown

This large luxury SUV provides a well-equipped interior and commendable off-road abilities, but mediocre on-road performance. It drives competently enough but feels tippy and awkward when cornering. CR suggests leaving the selectable 4WD system engaged for better grip on wet and slippery roads. An all-new, unibody Montero debuted for 2001. CR rated the 2001 Montero Limited Not Acceptable because of a pronounced tendency to tip up on two wheels in emergency-avoidance-maneuver tests.

MAJOR REDESIGN: 2001. **SAFETY EQUIPMENT:** Driver air bag standard; passenger side from 1996. Side air bags standard from 2001. ABS standard from 1998. **DRIVE WHEELS:** Selectable 4WD. Part-time 4WD available from 2001.

Mirage, Lancer

Reliability history	95 96 97 98 99 00 01 02
TROUBLE SPOTS	
Engine	
Cooling	
Fuel	
Ignition	NOT
Transmission	
Electrical	ENOUGH
Air-conditioning	
Suspension	DATA
Brakes	
Exhaust	TO
Paint/trim/rust	
Body integrity	
Power equipment	RATE
Body hardware	
RELIABILITY VERDICT	

Prices	
1995	$2,000-$4,000
1996	$4,000-$6,000
1997	$4,000-$6,000
1998	$6,000-$8,000
1999	$6,000-$8,000
2000	$8,000-$10,000
2001	$8,000-$10,000
2002	$14,000-$16,000

Crash-test results			
Model Years	Offset	Full frontal	Side
1995	NT	NT	NT
1996	NT	○/○	NT
1997	Poor	NT	NT
1998	Poor	NT	NT
1999	Poor	NT	NT
2000	Poor	NT	NT
2001	Poor	NT	NT
2002	Good	◐/◐	◐/◐

Montero

Reliability history	95 96 97 98 99 00 01 02
TROUBLE SPOTS	
Engine	
Cooling	
Fuel	
Ignition	NOT
Transmission	
Electrical	ENOUGH
Air-conditioning	
Suspension	DATA
Brakes	
Exhaust	TO
Paint/trim/rust	
Body integrity	
Power equipment	RATE
Body hardware	
RELIABILITY VERDICT	

Prices	
1995	$12,000-$14,000
1996	$12,000-$14,000
1997	$14,000-$16,000
1998	$16,000-$18,000
1999	$18,000-$20,000
2000	$20,000-$22,000
2001	$26,000-$28,000
2002	More than $30,000

Crash-test results			
Model Years	Offset	Full frontal	Side
1995	NT	◐/◐	NT
1996	Accept.	NT	NT
1997	Accept.	○/○	NT
1998	Accept.	NT	NT
1999	Accept.	NT	NT
2000	Accept.	NT	NT
2001	Accept.	NT	NT
2002	Accept.	NT	NT

Mitsubishi Montero Sport Nissan 240SX

1998 model shown

1995 model shown

Introduced for 1997, the Montero Sport shares its underpinnings with the defunct Mitsubishi Mighty Max and is available with a choice of four- and six-cylinder engines. Pass on the Four, as even the V6 feels sluggish. Feeling more trucklike than most of its competitors, the Montero Sport delivers stiff, rubbery kicks on common road bumps. Front seats are comfortable, but access is difficult due to the high floor and low roofline. A more powerful 3.5-liter V6 became optional in 1999, and the Four was dropped by 2000. A selectable 4WD system arrived for 2002.

MAJOR REDESIGN: 1997. **SAFETY EQUIPMENT:** Dual front air bags standard. Safety-belt pretensioners standard from 2001. ABS available. **DRIVE WHEELS:** Rear or part-time 4WD. Selectable 4WD available from 2002.

The 240SX coupe and hatchback, new for 1989, performed as well as the best of the early-1990s sporty cars, except for its tricky emergency handling. The ride is fairly uncomfortable and the engine noisy. Four-wheel steering was available. While the front seats are cushy, the rear seat is practically unusable. A convertible was available from 1992 to 1994. For 1995, the coupe version was restyled and other body styles were dropped. After the redesign, the 240SX continued to provide fine handling and a reasonably comfortable ride. The 2.4-liter Four offers adequate, though noisy, acceleration. The 240SX was discontinued after 1998.

MAJOR REDESIGN: 1995. **SAFETY EQUIPMENT:** Dual front air bags standard. ABS available. **DRIVE WHEELS:** Rear.

Mitsubishi Montero Sport

Reliability history

TROUBLE SPOTS	Mitsubishi Montero Sport							
	95	96	97	98	99	00	01	02
Engine					◉			
Cooling					◉			
Fuel					◉			
Ignition					◉			
Transmission					◉			
Electrical	Insufficient data	Insufficient data	Insufficient data	Insufficient data	◉	Insufficient data	Insufficient data	Insufficient data
Air conditioning					◉			
Suspension					◉			
Brakes					◗			
Exhaust					◗			
Paint/trim/rust					◗			
Body integrity					◉			
Power equipment					◗			
Body hardware					◗			
RELIABILITY VERDICT					✔			

Prices

1995	–
1996	–
1997	$14,000-$16,000
1998	$16,000-$18,000
1999	$16,000-$18,000
2000	$18,000-$20,000
2001	$20,000-$22,000
2002	$22,000-$24,000

Crash-test results

Model years	Offset	Full-frontal	Side
1995	–	–	–
1996	–	–	–
1997	Poor	NT	NT
1998	Poor	NT	NT
1999	Poor	NT	NT
2000	Poor	NT	NT
2001	Good	◗/○	NT
2002	Good	◗/○	NT

Nissan 240SX

Reliability history

TROUBLE SPOTS								
	95	96	97	98	99	00	01	02
Engine								
Cooling								
Fuel								
Ignition			NOT					
Transmission								
Electrical			ENOUGH					
Air conditioning								
Suspension			DATA					
Brakes								
Exhaust			TO					
Paint/trim/rust								
Body integrity								
Power equipment			RATE					
Body hardware								
RELIABILITY VERDICT								

Prices

1995	$8,000-$10,000
1996	$8,000-$10,000
1997	$10,000-$12,000
1998	$12,000-$14,000
1999	–
2000	–
2001	–
2002	–

Crash-test results

Model years	Offset	Full-frontal	Side
1995	NT	○/◗	NT
1996	NT	○/◗	NT
1997	NT	○/◗	NT
1998	NT	○/◗	NT
1999	–	–	–
2000	–	–	–
2001	–	–	–
2002	–	–	–

Nissan 300ZX

1995 model shown

Introduced in 1990, the last-generation Nissan 300ZX was easy to drive, providing a fine balance of performance and comfort. Handling was very capable and secure. Even in base form, the rear-drive coupe is quick and fun. The Turbo model's four-wheel steering adds marginally to cornering capabilities. The firm ride is tolerable by sports-car standards. The interior is relatively quiet, and the seats provide good, firm support. The luggage area is also relatively roomy for a sports car. A convertible was introduced in 1993, complementing the coupe and larger 2+2 models. The 300ZX was discontinued in the U.S. after the 1996 model year.

MAJOR REDESIGN: 1990. **SAFETY EQUIPMENT:** Dual front air bags standard. ABS standard. **DRIVE WHEELS:** Rear.

Reliability history

TROUBLE SPOTS	95 96 97 98 99 00 01 02
Engine	
Cooling	
Fuel	
Ignition	NOT
Transmission	
Electrical	ENOUGH
Air-conditioning	
Suspension	DATA
Brakes	
Exhaust	TO
Paint/trim/rust	
Body integrity	
Power equipment	RATE
Body hardware	
RELIABILITY VERDICT	

Prices

Year	Price
1995	$16,000-$18,000
1996	$18,000-$20,000
1997	–
1998	–
1999	–
2000	–
2001	–
2002	–

Crash-test results

Model Years	Offset	Full frontal	Side
1995	NT	NT	NT
1996	NT	NT	NT
1997	–	–	–
1998	–	–	–
1999	–	–	–
2000	–	–	–
2001	–	–	–
2002	–	–	–

Nissan Altima

CR **Good Bet**

1998 model shown

The Altima aimed to compete with the four-cylinder Honda Accord and Toyota Camry but never stacked up to them. Handling was less than nimble and the ride was busy. The noisy engine delivered strong acceleration. The front seats were too low, rear seating was fairly cramped, and the rear seatback didn't fold down. The Altima was redesigned for 1998, evolving the same basic formula. It was slightly freshened for 2000. It remained a reliable if not very rewarding, family sedan. A 2002 redesign transformed the Altima to a roomy, quick, and competitive family sedan.

MAJOR REDESIGN: 1993, 1998, 2002. **SAFETY EQUIPMENT:** Dual front air bags standard. Side air bags available from 2000. Safety-belt pretensioners standard from 2000. ABS available. **DRIVE WHEELS:** Front.

Reliability history

TROUBLE SPOTS	Nissan Altima 95 96 97 98 99 00 01 02
Engine	
Cooling	
Fuel	
Ignition	
Transmission	
Electrical	
Air-conditioning	
Suspension	
Brakes	
Exhaust	
Paint/trim/rust	
Body integrity	
Power equipment	
Body hardware	
RELIABILITY VERDICT	✓ ✓ ✓ ✓ ✓ ✓ ✓

Prices

Year	Price
1995	$6,000-$8,000
1996	$6,000-$8,000
1997	$8,000-$10,000
1998	$8,000-$10,000
1999	$10,000-$12,000
2000	$12,000-$14,000
2001	$12,000-$14,000
2002	$18,000-$20,000

Crash-test results

Model Years	Offset	Full frontal	Side
1995	NT	NT	NT
1996	NT	◒/◒	NT
1997	NT	◒/◒	NT
1998	NT	○/◒	○/○
1999	NT	○/○	○/○
2000	Marg.	◒/●	○/○
2001	Marg.	◒/●	○/○
2002	Good	◒/●	○/◒

Nissan Maxima

2000 model shown

The 1990-to-1994 Maxima tried to be a sportier alternative to Honda and Toyota sedans. A strong and smooth 190-hp V6 was introduced on the 1992 SE model. The Maxima grew larger in a 1995 redesign. Although handling remained competent, the sedan now felt ponderous and had a stiff ride. The Maxima's best features continued to be strong performance and a roomy interior. A 2000 redesign made the Maxima considerably better. Handling was improved and the interior felt more substantial. Engine output increased to 222 hp, then to 255 in 2002. **Related models:** Infiniti I30, I35.

MAJOR REDESIGN: 1995, 2000. **SAFETY EQUIPMENT:** Dual front air bags standard. Side air bags available from 1998. Safety-belt pretensioners standard from 2000. ABS available, standard from 2000. **DRIVE WHEELS:** Front.

Reliability history

TROUBLE SPOTS	Nissan Maxima							
	95	96	97	98	99	00	01	02
Engine	◑	●	●	●	●	●	●	●
Cooling	◑	●	●	●	●	●	●	◑
Fuel	○	◑	◑	●	●	●	●	●
Ignition	○	●	●	●	●	●	●	●
Transmission	◑	●	●	●	●	●	●	●
Electrical	●	○	○	○	○	○	◑	●
Air conditioning	◑	●	◑	●	●	●	●	●
Suspension	◑	◑	◑	◑	●	●	●	●
Brakes	◑	○	○	○	○	○	◑	●
Exhaust	◑	●	●	●	●	●	●	●
Paint/trim/rust	◑	●	●	●	●	●	●	●
Body integrity	◑	◑	●	●	●	●	●	●
Power equipment	◑	◑	◑	◑	●	●	●	●
Body hardware	◑	◑	◑	●	●	●	●	●
RELIABILITY VERDICT	✓	✓	✓	✓	✓	✓	✓	✓

Prices

1995	$8,000-$10,000
1996	$8,000-$10,000
1997	$10,000-$12,000
1998	$12,000-$14,000
1999	$14,000-$16,000
2000	$16,000-$18,000
2001	$18,000-$20,000
2002	$20,000-$22,000

Crash-test results

Model years	Offset	Full-frontal	Side
1995	Poor	◑/○	NT
1996	Poor	◑/○	NT
1997	Accept.	◑/○	◑/○
1998	Accept.	◑/○	◑/○
1999	Accept.	◑/◑	◑/○
2000	Accept.	◑/◑	◑/◑
2001	Accept.	◑/◑	◑/◑
2002	Accept.	◑/◑	◑/◑

Nissan Pathfinder

2000 model shown

In our tests, the Pathfinders handling was competent in normal conditions, sloppy but controllable in emergency maneuvers. It was redesigned for 1996. Though vastly improved overall, this version suffers from so-so braking and difficult rear seat access. 2000 brought better brakes and controls as well as an efficient 3.5-liter V6 that boosted both performance and refinement. The 2001 LE model received a selectable 4WD system like that of the more expensive Infiniti QX4. **Related model:** Infiniti QX4.

MAJOR REDESIGN: 1996. **SAFETY EQUIPMENT:** Dual front air bags standard from 1996. Side air bags available from 1999. Safety-belt pretensioners standard from 1999. ABS available 1996-1997, standard from 1998. **DRIVE WHEELS:** Rear or part-time 4WD. Selectable 4WD available from 2001.

Reliability history

TROUBLE SPOTS	Nissan Pathfinder							
	95	96	97	98	99	00	01	02
Engine	◑	●	●	●	●	●	●	●
Cooling	◑	●	●	●	●	●	●	●
Fuel	○	○	○	◑	●	●	◑	●
Ignition	◑	●	●	●	●	●	●	●
Transmission	◑	●	●	●	●	●	●	●
Electrical	◑	◑	◑	◑	●	●	●	●
Air conditioning	◑	●	●	●	●	●	●	●
Suspension	○	◑	○	○	◑	●	●	●
Brakes	○	○	○	◑	◑	●	●	●
Exhaust	○	●	◑	●	●	●	●	●
Paint/trim/rust	◑	◑	◑	●	●	●	●	●
Body integrity	○	○	◑	◑	●	●	●	●
Power equipment	◑	◑	◑	●	●	●	●	●
Body hardware	○	●	○	○	◑	●	●	●
RELIABILITY VERDICT	✓	✓	✓	✓	✓	✓	✓	✓

Prices

1995	$10,000-$12,000
1996	$12,000-$14,000
1997	$12,000-$14,000
1998	$16,000-$18,000
1999	$18,000-$20,000
2000	$22,000-$24,000
2001	$24,000-$26,000
2002	$26,000-$28,000

Crash-test results

Model years	Offset	Full-frontal	Side
1995	NT	●/○	NT
1996	NT	NT	NT
1997	Marg.	○/○	NT
1998	Marg.	○/○	NT
1999	Marg.	◑/◑	◑/◑
2000	Marg.	◑/◑	◑/◑
2001	Marg.	◑/◑	◑/◑
2002	Marg.	◑/◑	◑/◑

Nissan Quest

Nissan Sentra, 200SX

1999 model shown

1995 model shown

The Quest offers a well-appointed alternative to the larger people movers. Like the Villager, it was initially powered by a responsive 3.0-liter Nissan V6. Ride and handling are carlike, and the interior is quiet. For 1996, conventional front safety belts and dual front air bags replaced the annoying motorized shoulder belts. A 1999 redesign brought a 3.3-liter V6 and added more room and a second sliding door. The Quest's best feature is its foldable, sliding third seat. Poor crash-test scores, sloppy handling, and just-adequate braking limit the Quest's appeal. **Related model:** Mercury Villager.

MAJOR REDESIGN: 1993, 1999. **SAFETY EQUIPMENT:** Driver air bag standard; passenger side from 1996. Safety-belt pretensioners standard from 2001. ABS available, standard from 1999. **DRIVE WHEELS:** Front.

Among the humdrum 1991-to-1994 Sentras, the SE-R version was a standout: a particularly good-performing, inexpensive sporty two-door. The Sentra was redesigned for 1995, and the coupe version renamed the 200SX. The Sentra series of that vintage were underpowered and the interior was cheaply made: overall a notch below the best small cars of the era. Another redesign for 2000 made substantial improvements. It has a spirited powertrain, handles fairly well, is reasonably quiet, and has a well-designed interior. A cramped rear and just-adequate brakes are its major deficiencies.

MAJOR REDESIGN: 1995, 2000. **SAFETY EQUIPMENT:** Dual front air bags standard. Side air bags available from 2000. Safety-belt pretensioners standard from 2000. ABS available. **DRIVE WHEELS:** Front.

Reliability history — Nissan Quest

TROUBLE SPOTS	95	96	97	98	99	00	01	02
Engine								
Cooling								
Fuel								
Ignition								
Transmission								
Electrical								
Air-conditioning								
Suspension								
Brakes								
Exhaust								
Paint/trim/rust								
Body integrity								
Power equipment								
Body hardware								
RELIABILITY VERDICT	✓	✓	✓	✓	✓	✓		✓

(2002 column: Insufficient data)

Prices — Nissan Quest

Year	Price
1995	$8,000–$10,000
1996	$10,000–$12,000
1997	$12,000–$14,000
1998	$12,000–$14,000
1999	$14,000–$16,000
2000	$16,000–$18,000
2001	$18,000–$20,000
2002	$20,000–$22,000

Crash-test results — Nissan Quest

Model Years	Offset	Full frontal	Side
1995	NT	⊖/○	NT
1996	Marg.	⊖/○	NT
1997	Marg.	⊖/○	NT
1998	Marg.	⊖/○	NT
1999	Poor	NT	NT
2000	Poor	⊖/○	●/○
2001	Poor	○/⊖	●/○
2002	Poor	○/⊖	●/○

Reliability history — Nissan Sentra

TROUBLE SPOTS	95	96	97	98	99	00	01	02
Engine								
Cooling								
Fuel								
Ignition								
Transmission								
Electrical								
Air-conditioning								
Suspension								
Brakes								
Exhaust								
Paint/trim/rust								
Body integrity								
Power equipment								
Body hardware								
RELIABILITY VERDICT	✓	✓	✓	✓	✓		✓	✓

Prices — Nissan Sentra

Year	Price
1995	$4,000–$6,000
1996	$4,000–$6,000
1997	$6,000–$8,000
1998	$6,000–$8,000
1999	$8,000–$10,000
2000	$10,000–$12,000
2001	$10,000–$12,000
2002	$12,000–$14,000

Crash-test results — Nissan Sentra

Model Years	Offset	Full frontal	Side
1995	NT	NT	NT
1996	NT	⊖/⊖	NT
1997	NT	⊖/⊖	NT
1998	Accept.	○/⊖	○/○
1999	Accept.	○/⊖	○/○
2000	Accept.	NT	NT
2001	Accept.	⊖/⊖	NT
2002	Accept.	⊖/⊖	NT

Nissan Truck, Frontier

Nissan Xterra

1998 model shown

2000 model shown

This basic compact pickup debuted in the mid-'80s, and had changed little by the mid-'90s. 1996 was the last year for the V6 in this model; the only engine offered for 1997 was a 2.4-liter, 134-hp Four. The new Frontier debuted for 1998, with redesigned interior and exterior styling, and improvements throughout. But the Frontier's ride is stiff, and its handling ponderous. A 3.3-liter V6 was offered beginning in 1999. A crew-cab model was added for 2000, and a supercharged version of the V6 joined the options list a year later.

MAJOR REDESIGN: 1998. **SAFETY EQUIPMENT:** Driver air bag standard from 1996; passenger side from 1998. Safety-belt pretensioners standard from 2001. ABS standard (rear only); four-wheel ABS standard with 4WD from 1998. **DRIVE WHEELS:** Rear or part-time 4WD.

The Nissan Xterra debuted as a 2000 model. Based on Nissan's Frontier pickup, it was intentionally made to be a rugged, basic, trucklike SUV, and to serve as a less expensive alternative to the Pathfinder. It boasts a large cargo area but has a fairly light load capacity. Highs include good off-road capability and towing capacity. But the ride, handling, braking, and fuel economy are subpar. The front seats aren't very supportive. The rear seating area is spacious, although the seats themselves are thinly padded. The Xterra is a useful size but not the right choice for people who value agility, comfort, or quietness.

MAJOR REDESIGN: 2000. **SAFETY EQUIPMENT:** Dual front air bags standard. ABS standard. Safety-belt pretensioners standard. **DRIVE WHEELS:** Rear or part-time 4WD.

Reliability history — Nissan Pickup, Frontier

TROUBLE SPOTS	95	96	97	98	99	00	01	02
Engine								
Cooling								
Fuel								
Ignition								
Transmission								
Electrical								
Air conditioning								
Suspension								
Brakes								
Exhaust								
Paint/trim/rust								
Body integrity								
Power equipment								
Body hardware								
RELIABILITY VERDICT	✓	✓	✓	✓	✓	✓	✓	✓

Prices

1995	$8,000-$10,000
1996	$8,000-$10,000
1997	$10,000-$12,000
1998	$12,000-$14,000
1999	$12,000-$14,000
2000	$14,000-$16,000
2001	$16,000-$18,000
2002	$20,000-$22,000

Crash-test results

Model years	Offset	Full-frontal	Side
1995	NT	○/●	NT
1996	NT	◐/●	NT
1997	NT	◐/●	NT
1998	Poor	○/●	NT
1999	Poor	○/●	●/NA
2000	Poor	○/●	●/NA
2001	Poor	●/●	●/●
2002	Poor	●/●	●/NA

Reliability history — Nissan Xterra

TROUBLE SPOTS	95	96	97	98	99	00	01	02
Engine						●	●	Insufficient data
Cooling						●	●	
Fuel						●	●	
Ignition						●	●	
Transmission						●	●	
Electrical						◐	○	
Air conditioning						◐	●	
Suspension						◐	●	
Brakes						◐	●	
Exhaust						●	●	
Paint/trim/rust						●	●	
Body integrity						○	●	
Power equipment						◐	○	
Body hardware						○	●	
RELIABILITY VERDICT						✓	✓	

Prices

1995	–
1996	–
1997	–
1998	–
1999	–
2000	$20,000-$22,000
2001	$22,000-$24,000
2002	$24,000-$26,000

Crash-test results

Model years	Offset	Full-frontal	Side
1995	–	–	–
1996	–	–	–
1997	–	–	–
1998	–	–	–
1999	–	–	–
2000	Accept.	●/●	●/●
2001	Accept.	●/●	●/●
2002	Accept.	●/●	●/●

FAMILY CAR
Oldsmobile Achieva

1995 model shown

Introduced in 1992, the Achieva was never an inspired design. It was available in two body styles, coupe and sedan. The noisy "Quad Four" four-cylinder engine performed weakly even when it was new. Look for a model equipped with the stronger V6. The steering was slow and vague, and handling was clumsy and sloppy. The front seats are low, and the interior is cramped. Consider the Achieva to be basic transportation, with all the accessories common to cars of the time but no outstanding virtues. It was dropped after the 1998 model year and replaced by the much better but still uninspiring Alero. **Related models:** Buick Skylark, Pontiac Grand Am.

MAJOR REDESIGN: 1992. **SAFETY EQUIPMENT:** Driver air bag standard; passenger side from 1996. ABS standard. **DRIVE WHEELS:** Front.

Reliability history	
TROUBLE SPOTS	95 96 97 98 99 00 01 02
Engine	
Cooling	
Fuel	
Ignition	NOT
Transmission	
Electrical	ENOUGH
Air-conditioning	
Suspension	DATA
Brakes	
Exhaust	TO
Paint/trim/rust	
Body integrity	RATE
Power equipment	
Body hardware	
RELIABILITY VERDICT	

Prices	
1995	$4,000-$6,000
1996	$4,000-$6,000
1997	$4,000-$6,000
1998	$6,000-$8,000
1999	–
2000	–
2001	–
2002	–

Crash-test results			
Model Years	Offset	Full frontal	Side
1995	NT	◐/○	NT
1996	NT	◐/○	NT
1997	NT	◐/○	●/○
1998	NT	◐/○	●/○
1999	–	–	–
2000	–	–	–
2001	–	–	–
2002	–	–	–

FAMILY CAR
Oldsmobile Alero

1999 model shown

The Alero was launched in 1999 with the intention of wooing import intenders. We found little to praise about the four-cylinder model when we tested it. Handling was unimpressive, and the ride, while taut and supple on most roads, was jittery on the highway. The standard 2.4-liter, 150-hp Four sounded noisy and rough. The available 3.4-liter, 170-hp V6 was a better choice, not only more powerful but smoother and quieter. The low front seats were reasonably comfortable, but interior appointments felt cheap. The rear seat was OK for two tall people. A poor offset-crash-test result is a noteworthy shortcoming. **Related model:** Pontiac Grand Am.

MAJOR REDESIGN: 1999. **SAFETY EQUIPMENT:** Dual front air bags standard. ABS standard. **DRIVE WHEELS:** Front.

Reliability history								
TROUBLE SPOTS	Oldsmobile Alero							
	95	96	97	98	99	00	01	02
Engine					○	○	○	
Cooling					○	○	◐	
Fuel					○	◐	○	
Ignition					○	●	○	
Transmission					○	◐	○	
Electrical					●	○	○	
Air-conditioning					○	◐	○	
Suspension					○	○	○	
Brakes					●	●	◐	
Exhaust					○	○	○	
Paint/trim/rust					○	○	○	
Body integrity					◐	○	○	
Power equipment					○	○	◐	
Body hardware					◐	◐	○	
RELIABILITY VERDICT								

Insufficient data

Prices	
1995	–
1996	–
1997	–
1998	–
1999	$10,000-$12,000
2000	$10,000-$12,000
2001	$12,000-$14,000
2002	$14,000-$16,000

Crash-test results			
Model Years	Offset	Full frontal	Side
1995	–	–	–
1996	–	–	–
1997	–	–	–
1998	–	–	–
1999	Poor	◐/●	○/○
2000	Poor	◐/●	○/○
2001	Poor	◐/●	○/○
2002	Poor	◐/●	○/○

Oldsmobile Aurora

Oldsmobile Bravada

1998 model shown

1996 model shown

The Aurora, introduced for 1995, was intended to compete with European and Japanese sports sedans. The smooth, powerful 4.0-liter V8—based on Cadillac's Northstar engine—is the car's best feature. The Aurora handles ponderously, and the steering offers little feel. The car rides harshly and rocks annoyingly on bumpy roads. The cockpit is stylish but feels tight, and the front seats are firm and lumpy. The ride was slightly improved for 1998. A 2001 redesign introduced in early 2000 improved the car considerably. The new version feels more like a luxury sports sedan, with a taut ride and sound handling. The cabin also feels more spacious.

MAJOR REDESIGN: 1995, 2001. **SAFETY EQUIPMENT:** Dual front air bags standard. Side air bags standard from 2001. Safety-belt pretensioners standard from 2001. ABS standard. **DRIVE WHEELS:** Front.

Positioned as an upscale version of the Chevrolet Blazer, the Bravada uses AWD (with no low range) instead of the Blazer's more conventional 4WD system. The Bravada always suffered from a choppy ride and cumbersome handling. As in the Blazer, the 4.3-liter V6 provided adequate acceleration. After a year's hiatus, a new Bravada was reintroduced for 1996. Like the original, this version has ponderous handling, a so-so ride, poor fit and finish, and subpar reliability. It was redesigned again for 2002, this time derived from the Chevrolet TrailBlazer. **Related models:** Chevrolet Blazer and TrailBlazer, GMC Jimmy and Envoy.

MAJOR REDESIGN: 1996, 2002. **SAFETY EQUIPMENT:** Driver air bag standard from 1996; passenger side from 1998. Side air bags standard from 2002. ABS standard. **DRIVE WHEELS:** AWD.

Reliability history — Oldsmobile Aurora

TROUBLE SPOTS	95	96	97	98	99	00	01	02
Engine	◒						●	
Cooling	●						◒	
Fuel	●						◒	
Ignition	○						◒	
Transmission	◒						●	
Electrical	●	Insufficient data	Insufficient data	Insufficient data	Insufficient data	Insufficient data	○	Insufficient data
Air conditioning	◒						○	
Suspension	◒						○	
Brakes	●						◒	
Exhaust	◒						◒	
Paint/trim/rust	○						◒	
Body integrity	○						○	
Power equipment	◒						◒	
Body hardware	●						◒	
RELIABILITY VERDICT								

Prices — Aurora

1995	$6,000-$8,000
1996	$8,000-$10,000
1997	$10,000-$12,000
1998	$12,000-$14,000
1999	$14,000-$16,000
2000	–
2001	$20,000-$22,000
2002	$24,000-$26,000

Crash-test results — Aurora

Model years	Offset	Full-frontal	Side
1995	NT	○/○	NT
1996	NT	○/○	NT
1997	NT	○/○	NT
1998	NT	○/○	NT
1999	NT	○/○	NT
2000	–	–	–
2001	Good	◒/○	○/○
2002	Good	◒/○	○/○

Reliability history — Oldsmobile Bravada

TROUBLE SPOTS	95	96	97	98	99	00	01	02
Engine				◒	○	◒		◒
Cooling				◒	○	◒		◒
Fuel				○	◒	●		◒
Ignition				◒	●	◒		◒
Transmission				○	◒	◒		○
Electrical		Insufficient data	Insufficient data	●	●	◒	Insufficient data	○
Air conditioning				○	◒	●		○
Suspension				○	◒	◒		○
Brakes				○	◒	◒		○
Exhaust				◒	●	◒		◒
Paint/trim/rust				◒	●	◒		●
Body integrity				○	◒	◒		●
Power equipment				●	○	○		
Body hardware				●	○	○		
RELIABILITY VERDICT					✓			

Prices — Bravada

1995	–
1996	$10,000-$12,000
1997	$12,000-$14,000
1998	$14,000-$16,000
1999	$16,000-$18,000
2000	$16,000-$18,000
2001	$20,000-$22,000
2002	$28,000-$30,000

Crash-test results — Bravada

Model years	Offset	Full-frontal	Side
1995	–	–	–
1996	Poor	○/●	NT
1997	Poor	○/●	NT
1998	Poor	○/○	NT
1999	Poor	○/○	○/○
2000	Poor	○/○	○/○
2001	Poor	○/○	○/○
2002	Marg.	○/○	◒/○

Oldsmobile Ciera, Cutlass

1997 model shown

Even by 1990 standards the Ciera was dated. The ride was spongy even on good roads. Replaced in 1997 by the short-lived incarnation of the Olds Cutlass moniker, it was essentially a rebadged Chevrolet Malibu. Unlike its Chevy twin, the Cutlass offered only a 3.1-liter V6. This engine provides more-than-adequate acceleration but could use an additional dose of refinement. The ride is jittery and unsettled, and handling is unexceptional. The interior is spacious, and the front seats are fairly comfortable. The rear seat is roomy enough, and the trunk is large. The Cutlass was dropped after 1999. **Related models:** Buick Century, Chevrolet Malibu.

MAJOR REDESIGN: 1997. **SAFETY EQUIPMENT:** Driver air bag standard. Passenger side not offered on Ciera, standard on Cutlass. ABS standard. **DRIVE WHEELS:** Front.

Oldsmobile Cutlass Supreme

1995 model shown

The unexceptional Cutlass Supreme was even less appealing than the related Buick Regal and Pontiac Grand Prix of the same years. A relatively large, middle-of-the-road sedan, the Cutlass Supreme had a poorly controlled ride even on smooth roads. The standard 3.1-liter V6 performed adequately. The optional 3.4-liter V6 paced more punch, but was noisier and thirstier. The Cutlass Supreme had a comfortable front seat, but the rear was much less inviting. Dual air bags became standard in 1995, and a new dash was added for 1996. This undistinguished car was replaced by the much better Oldsmobile Intrigue in mid-1997. **Related models:** Buick Regal, Pontiac Grand Prix.

MAJOR REDESIGN: 1988. **SAFETY EQUIPMENT:** Dual front air bags standard. ABS standard. **DRIVE WHEELS:** Front.

Reliability history — Oldsmobile Ciera, Cutlass

TROUBLE SPOTS	95	96	97	98	99	00	01	02
Engine	○	●	○	◑	○			
Cooling	◑	◑	◑	◑	○			
Fuel	○	◑	●	◑	◑			
Ignition	●	◑	●	◑	◑			
Transmission	○	◑	●	●	◑			
Electrical	●	●	●	●	●			
Air-conditioning	○	◑	●	◑	○			
Suspension	◑	○	◑	○	○			
Brakes	◑	●	●	●	●			
Exhaust	◑	●	◑	●	◑			
Paint/trim/rust	◑	○	◑	●	◑			
Body integrity	○	○	◑	◑	○			
Power equipment	◑	○	◑	○	○			
Body hardware	○	◑	○	◑	○			
RELIABILITY VERDICT	✔	✔						

Prices — Oldsmobile Ciera, Cutlass

1995	$4,000-$6,000
1996	$4,000-$6,000
1997	$6,000-$8,000
1998	$8,000-$10,000
1999	$10,000-$12,000
2000	–
2001	–
2002	–

Crash-test results — Oldsmobile Ciera, Cutlass

Model Years	Offset	Full frontal	Side
1995	NT	◐/◑	NT
1996	NT	◐/◑	NT
1997	Accept.	◐/◑	●/○
1998	Accept.	◐/◑	●/○
1999	Accept.	◐/◑	●/○
2000	–	–	–
2001	–	–	–
2002	–	–	–

Reliability history — Oldsmobile Cutlass Supreme

TROUBLE SPOTS	95	96	97	98	99	00	01	02
Engine	○	○	◑					
Cooling	○	○	○					
Fuel	○	◑	◑					
Ignition	○	◑	●					
Transmission	○	○	◑					
Electrical	●	●	●					
Air-conditioning	◑	○	●					
Suspension	○	◑	◑					
Brakes	●	●	●					
Exhaust	◑	●	●					
Paint/trim/rust	○	○	○					
Body integrity	◑	●	◑					
Power equipment	○	○	○					
Body hardware	◑	●	◑					
RELIABILITY VERDICT	✔	✔	✔					

Prices — Oldsmobile Cutlass Supreme

1995	$6,000-$8,000
1996	$6,000-$8,000
1997	$8,000-$10,000
1998	–
1999	–
2000	–
2001	–
2002	–

Crash-test results — Oldsmobile Cutlass Supreme

Model Years	Offset	Full frontal	Side
1995	NT	NT	NT
1996	NT	◐/○	NT
1997	NT	NT	NT
1998	–	–	–
1999	–	–	–
2000	–	–	–
2001	–	–	–
2002	–	–	–

Oldsmobile Eighty Eight

1996 model shown

Redesigned for 1992, the Olds 88 is a freeway cruiser with not much to recommend it. The standard version has a bench seat in front, allowing it to carry six passengers. A softly sprung car, the 88 suffers from sloppy handling unless fitted with the optional Touring suspension. Equipped with GM's evergreen 3.8-liter V6 engine, this front-drive Olds saw power output rise through the years, with the addition of a supercharger in 1995 and a number of engine refinements the following year. Also in 1996, the 88 was given a mild facelift. The model name celebrated its 50th birthday—and final year—with a special "Anniversary Edition" in 1999. **Related models:** Buick LeSabre, Pontiac Bonneville.

MAJOR REDESIGN: 1992. **SAFETY EQUIPMENT:** Dual front air bags standard. ABS standard. **DRIVE WHEELS:** Front.

Oldsmobile Intrigue

1998 model shown

New for 1998, the Intrigue replaced the ancient Cutlass Supreme. It was Oldsmobile's answer to cars like the Toyota Camry and Nissan Maxima. The Intrigue handles well and delivers a controlled ride, but it doesn't possess the same level of sophistication and refinement. The interior is well designed, roomy, and comfortable, and the rear seat is fairly accommodating. The trunk is also roomy. Initially, the standard engine was a responsive 3.8-liter V6. This powerplant was replaced with a smoother 3.5-liter multivalve V6 in 2000. **Related models:** Buick Century, Buick Regal, Pontiac Grand Prix.

MAJOR REDESIGN: 1998. **SAFETY EQUIPMENT:** Dual front air bags standard. ABS standard. **DRIVE WHEELS:** Front.

Oldsmobile 88

Reliability history

TROUBLE SPOTS	95	96	97	98	99	00	01	02
Engine	◐	○	○	○	○			
Cooling	○	◐	●	○	○			
Fuel	○	◐	○	○	○			
Ignition	○	○	○	○	●			
Transmission	○	○	○	○	○			
Electrical	◐	○	◐	●	○			
Air conditioning	◐	○	○	◐	◐			
Suspension	○	○	○	◐	○			
Brakes	●	○	●	○	○			
Exhaust	◐	●	◐	●	○			
Paint/trim/rust	○	○	◐	○	○			
Body integrity	○	○	◐	○	○			
Power equipment	●	○	○	○	○			
Body hardware	◐	○	○	○	○			
RELIABILITY VERDICT	✓	✓		✓	✓			

Prices

1995	$6,000-$8,000
1996	$6,000-$8,000
1997	$8,000-$10,000
1998	$10,000-$12,000
1999	$10,000-$12,000
2000	–
2001	–
2002	–

Crash-test results

Model years	Offset	Full-frontal	Side
1995	NT	●/○	NT
1996	NT	●/○	NT
1997	NT	●/○	NT
1998	NT	●/○	NT
1999	NT	●/○	NT
2000	–	–	–
2001	–	–	–
2002	–	–	–

Oldsmobile Intrigue

Reliability history

TROUBLE SPOTS	95	96	97	98	99	00	01	02
Engine				◐	●	◐	●	●
Cooling				◐	◐	○	◐	◐
Fuel				●	○	◐	◐	◐
Ignition				◐	◐	◐	●	●
Transmission				◐	◐	◐	●	●
Electrical				◐	◐	◐	◐	○
Air conditioning				◐	●	○	◐	●
Suspension				○	◐	◐	●	●
Brakes				◐	●	●	●	●
Exhaust				●	●	◐	●	●
Paint/trim/rust				○	◐	●	●	●
Body integrity				○	○	◐	◐	●
Power equipment				○	○	◐	◐	◐
Body hardware				●	○	○	◐	●
RELIABILITY VERDICT				✓	✓	✓	✓	

Prices

1995	–
1996	–
1997	–
1998	$10,000-$12,000
1999	$10,000-$12,000
2000	$12,000-$14,000
2001	$14,000-$16,000
2002	$16,000-$18,000

Crash-test results

Model years	Offset	Full-frontal	Side
1995	–	–	–
1996	–	–	–
1997	–	–	–
1998	Accept.	◐/○	○/●
1999	Accept.	◐/◐	○/●
2000	Accept.	◐/○	○/●
2001	Accept.	◐/○	○/●
2002	Accept.	◐/○	○/●

LARGE CAR

Oldsmobile Ninety Eight

1995 model shown

The front-wheel-drive 98 was for years Oldsmobile's biggest sedan. It emphasized a soft ride along with myriad power conveniences and luxury appointments. Handling, however, was always a little sloppy. The six-passenger sedan was powered by a 3.8-liter V6 engine that through the years increased from 170 horsepower to 205. A supercharged version of the V6 produced up to 225 hp. The 1994 models were updated with new styling for the front end and instrument panel. The 98 was discontinued after the 1996 model year. **Related model:** Buick Park Avenue.

MAJOR REDESIGN: 1991. **SAFETY EQUIPMENT:** Dual front air bags standard. ABS standard. **DRIVE WHEELS:** Front.

MINIVAN

Oldsmobile Silhouette

2000 model shown

Introduced as a 1990 model, the early Silhouettes were competent minivans for their time, with distinctive styling and plastic body panels. A mild 1994 redesign brought a handy optional electric sliding side door. Removable rear seats are also handy. The Silhouette was redesigned for 1997, like the Chevy Venture, and is available in standard and extended-wheelbase models. Movable seats and dual sliding doors add versatility. Poor off-set frontal crash-test results give pause for thought. **Related models:** Chevrolet Lumina Van, Chevrolet Venture, Pontiac Trans Sport/Montana.

MAJOR REDESIGN: 1994, 1997. **SAFETY EQUIPMENT:** Driver air bag standard; passenger side from 1997. Side air bags and safety-belt pretensioners standard from 1998. ABS standard. **DRIVE WHEELS:** Front. AWD available from 2002.

Reliability history

TROUBLE SPOTS	Oldsmobile 98
	95 96 97 98 99 00 01 02
Engine	○ *(Insufficient data 96–02)*
Cooling	◐
Fuel	●
Ignition	○
Transmission	○
Electrical	○
Air-conditioning	◐
Suspension	◐
Brakes	●
Exhaust	◐
Paint/trim/rust	◐
Body integrity	◐
Power equipment	●
Body hardware	◐
RELIABILITY VERDICT	✓

Prices

1995	$8,000-$10,000
1996	$10,000-$12,000
1997	–
1998	–
1999	–
2000	–
2001	–
2002	–

Crash-test results

Model Years	Offset	Full frontal	Side
1995	NT	NT	NT
1996	NT	NT	NT
1997	–	–	–
1998	–	–	–
1999	–	–	–
2000	–	–	–
2001	–	–	–
2002	–	–	–

Reliability history

TROUBLE SPOTS	Oldsmobile Silhouette (ext.)
	95 96 97 98 99 00 01 02
Engine	○ ○ ○ ◐ ○ ● ●
Cooling	○ ○ ◐ ○ ◐ ● ●
Fuel	○ ◐ ◐ ● ◐ ● ●
Ignition	◐ ◐ ◐ ◐ ◐ ● ●
Transmission	◐ ◐ ◐ ◐ ◐ ● ●
Electrical	◐ ◐ ◐ ◐ ● ● ●
Air-conditioning	○ ◐ ◐ ◐ ◐ ● ●
Suspension	○ ◐ ◐ ◐ ◐ ● ●
Brakes	◐ ◐ ◐ ○ ● ● ●
Exhaust	◐ ◐ ◐ ◐ ◐ ● ●
Paint/trim/rust	◐ ◐ ◐ ◐ ● ●
Body integrity	● ● ◐ ◐ ○ ○ ●
Power equipment	● ● ◐ ● ○ ○ ●
Body hardware	● ● ● ● ◐ ○ ●
RELIABILITY VERDICT	✓

Prices

1995	$6,000-$8,000
1996	$8,000-$10,000
1997	$10,000-$12,000
1998	$12,000-$14,000
1999	$14,000-$16,000
2000	$16,000-$18,000
2001	$18,000-$20,000
2002	$20,000-$22,000

Crash-test results

Model Years	Offset	Full frontal	Side
1995	NT	●/○	NT
1996	NT	●/○	NT
1997	Poor	●/●	NT
1998	Poor	●/●	NT
1999	Poor	●/○	●/○
2000	Poor	●/○	●/○
2001	Poor	●/○	●/○
2002	Poor	●/○	●/○

Plymouth (Chrysler) Voyager/Grand Voyager

1996 model shown

Early-1990's versions of the Voyager and extended-length Grand Voyager handled clumsily and unsteadily. A complete 1996 redesign brought substantial improvements that delivered more agile handling and a more controlled ride. A second sliding door was optional. The removable rear seats are heavy. The 3.3-liter V6 is the engine to choose. When DaimlerChrysler retired the Plymouth brand in 2000, the regular-length version became a Chrysler. **Related models:** Chrysler Town & Country, Dodge Caravan/Grand Caravan.

MAJOR REDESIGN: 1996, 2001. **SAFETY EQUIPMENT:** Dual front air bags standard. Side air bags available from 2001. Safety-belt pretensioners standard from 2001. ABS available. **DRIVE WHEELS:** Front; AWD optional to 1995.

Reliability history

TROUBLE SPOTS	Plymouth/Chrysler Voyager V6
	95 96 97 98 99 00 01 02
Engine	
Cooling	
Fuel	
Ignition	
Transmission	
Electrical	
Air conditioning	
Suspension	
Brakes	
Exhaust	
Paint/trim/rust	
Body integrity	
Power equipment	
Body hardware	
RELIABILITY VERDICT	✓ ✓

Prices

1995	$6,000-$8,000
1996	$6,000-$8,000
1997	$6,000-$8,000
1998	$10,000-$12,000
1999	$12,000-$14,000
2000	$12,000-$14,000
2001	$16,000-$18,000
2002	$18,000-$20,000

Crash-test results

Model years	Offset	Full-frontal	Side
1995	NT	○/○	NT
1996	Marg.	○/○	NT
1997	Marg.	○/○	NT
1998	Marg.	○/○	NT
1999	Marg.	○/○	○/○
2000	Marg.	○/○	○/○
2001	NT	○/○	○/○
2002	NT	○/○	○/○

Plymouth Breeze

1996 model shown

The Breeze sedan was introduced for 1996, a year after its siblings, the Chrysler Cirrus and Dodge Stratus. Initially, the Breeze was available only with a noisy, underpowered 2.0-liter four-cylinder engine, but a larger 2.4-liter Four became optional for 1998. Performance for this price leader was adequate with the top engine. Expect roomy seating and a nicely designed interior. Braking was only average, though, and the ride was jittery even on smooth roads. The Breeze handled soundly but was not very agile. It received a revised suspension for 1999 and was discontinued after 2000. **Related models:** Chrysler Cirrus, Dodge Stratus.

MAJOR REDESIGN: 1996. **SAFETY EQUIPMENT:** Dual front air bags standard. ABS available. **DRIVE WHEELS:** Front.

Reliability history

TROUBLE SPOTS	Plymouth Breeze
	95 96 97 98 99 00 01 02
Engine	
Cooling	
Fuel	
Ignition	
Transmission	
Electrical	
Air conditioning	
Suspension	
Brakes	
Exhaust	
Paint/trim/rust	
Body integrity	
Power equipment	
Body hardware	
RELIABILITY VERDICT	✓ ✓

Prices

1995	–
1996	$4,000-$6,000
1997	$4,000-$6,000
1998	$6,000-$8,000
1999	$8,000-$10,000
2000	$8,000-$10,000
2001	–
2002	–

Crash-test results

Model years	Offset	Full-frontal	Side
1995	–		
1996	Poor	○/NA	NT
1997	Poor	○/NA	○/○
1998	Poor	○/○	○/○
1999	Poor	○/○	○/○
2000	Poor	○/○	○/○
2001	–		
2002	–		

SPORTS/SPORTY CAR
Plymouth Prowler

1997 model shown

Positive response to the outrageous Prowler concept car led to its introduction in 1997. Conceived as a rolling homage to the street rods of the 1950s, it featured an open-cockpit body, outboard front wheels, and even a steering-wheel-mounted tachometer. The theme did not extend to the Prowler's powertrain, which mated a noisy, underachieving 3.5-liter V6 to a four-speed automatic. Despite a horsepower boost in 1999, the Prowler remained more of a boulevard cruiser than a serious performance car. The Prowler was rebadged as a Chrysler in 2002, and was discontinued at the end of the year.

MAJOR REDESIGN: 1997. **SAFETY EQUIPMENT:** Dual front air bags standard. ABS not offered. **DRIVE WHEELS:** Rear.

Reliability history	
TROUBLE SPOTS	95 96 97 98 99 00 01 02
Engine	
Cooling	
Fuel	
Ignition	NOT
Transmission	
Electrical	ENOUGH
Air-conditioning	
Suspension	DATA
Brakes	
Exhaust	TO
Paint/trim/rust	
Body integrity	RATE
Power equipment	
Body hardware	
RELIABILITY VERDICT	

Prices	
1995	–
1996	–
1997	$28,000-$30,000
1998	–
1999	More than $30,000
2000	More than $30,000
2001	More than $30,000
2002	More than $30,000

Crash-test results			
Model Years	Offset	Full frontal	Side
1995	–	–	–
1996	–	–	–
1997	NT	NT	NT
1998	–	–	–
1999	NT	NT	NT
2000	NT	NT	NT
2001	NT	NT	NT
2002	NT	NT	NT

SPORT-UTILITY VEHICLE
Pontiac Aztek

2001 model shown

The Aztek, introduced in the summer of 2000 as a 2001 model, is a crossover SUV based on the Montana minivan. Like the Montana, it uses GM's 3.4-liter, 185-hp V6. The Aztek is clearly aimed at the much-hyped "active lifestyle" crowd, with handy standard and optional features like removable plastic storage boxes, a removable center-console cooler, a slide-out cargo tray, and a tent that fits onto the rear of the vehicle. Negatives include so-so handling, a rear seat that's too low, no rear wiper, and a split rear gate that's awkward to operate. The GT model has a stiff ride as well.

MAJOR REDESIGN: 2001. **SAFETY EQUIPMENT:** Dual front and side air bags standard. ABS standard. Safety-belt pretensioners standard. **DRIVE WHEELS:** Front or AWD.

Reliability history	
TROUBLE SPOTS	Pontiac Aztek
	95 96 97 98 99 00 01 02
Engine	●
Cooling	●
Fuel	●
Ignition	●
Transmission	●
Electrical	○
Air-conditioning	●
Suspension	●
Brakes	●
Exhaust	●
Paint/trim/rust	●
Body integrity	◐
Power equipment	◐
Body hardware	○
RELIABILITY VERDICT	✔

Insufficient data

Prices	
1995	–
1996	–
1997	–
1998	–
1999	–
2000	–
2001	$16,000-$18,000
2002	$18,000-$20,000

Crash-test results			
Model Years	Offset	Full frontal	Side
1995	–	–	–
1996	–	–	–
1997	–	–	–
1998	–	–	–
1999	–	–	–
2000	–	–	–
2001	Marg.	○/◐	●/○
2002	Marg.	○/◐	●/○

Pontiac Bonneville

Pontiac Firebird

2000 model shown

1998 model shown

Pontiac's top sedan offers a sportier driving feel than do the similar Buick LeSabre and Oldsmobile 88. The optional sport suspension and touring tires improve the car's handling. Performance is lively with the available supercharged 3.8-liter V6, though you don't need to opt for this top-level engine to get plenty of power. It was redesigned for 2000 and was significantly improved, with taut handling, a supple ride, and optional stability control. Despite the positives, the Bonneville doesn't possess the refinement of some other cars in its class. The front seats lack support, and the rear bench is too low and soft. **Related models:** Buick LeSabre, Oldsmobile 88.

MAJOR REDESIGN: 2000. **SAFETY EQUIPMENT:** Dual front air bags standard. Side air bags standard from 2000. ABS standard. **DRIVE WHEELS:** Front.

The rear-drive Firebird is high on performance but low on refinement. Redesigned for 1993, with convertible models joining the line a year later. It was initially available with either a 160-hp V6 or a 275-hp V8. In 1995, a larger, 200-hp V6 was offered, and in 1996 the V8 gained another 10 hp. Also new for 1996 was a high-performance "WS6" package that bumped hp to 305. Expect strong acceleration (in later V6 and all V8 models) and good handling and braking, but poor driver visibility, difficult access, and an overly firm ride. Refinements in 1998 included new exterior styling and a stronger, all-aluminum V8 engine. **Related model:** Chevrolet Camaro.

MAJOR REDESIGN: 1993. **SAFETY EQUIPMENT:** Dual front air bags standard. ABS standard. **DRIVE WHEELS:** Rear.

Reliability history — Pontiac Bonneville

TROUBLE SPOTS	95	96	97	98	99	00	01	02
Engine								
Cooling								
Fuel								
Ignition								
Transmission								
Electrical								
Air conditioning								
Suspension								
Brakes								
Exhaust								
Paint/trim/rust								
Body integrity								
Power equipment								
Body hardware								
RELIABILITY VERDICT	✔		✔	✔				

Prices — Pontiac Bonneville

Year	Price
1995	$6,000-$8,000
1996	$6,000-$8,000
1997	$8,000-$10,000
1998	$10,000-$12,000
1999	$10,000-$12,000
2000	$16,000-$18,000
2001	$18,000-$20,000
2002	$20,000-$22,000

Crash-test results — Pontiac Bonneville

Model years	Offset	Full-frontal	Side
1995	NT	●/○	NT
1996	NT	●/○	NT
1997	NT	●/○	NT
1998	NT	●/○	○/○
1999	NT	●/○	◐/○
2000	Good	●/◐	◐/○
2001	Good	●/◐	◐/○
2002	Good	●/◐	◐/○

Reliability history — Pontiac Firebird

TROUBLE SPOTS	95	96	97	98	99	00	01	02
Engine						Insufficient data	Insufficient data
Cooling								
Fuel								
Ignition								
Transmission								
Electrical								
Air conditioning								
Suspension								
Brakes								
Exhaust								
Paint/trim/rust								
Body integrity								
Power equipment								
Body hardware								
RELIABILITY VERDICT	✔							

Prices — Pontiac Firebird

Year	Price
1995	$8,000-$10,000
1996	$10,000-$12,000
1997	$12,000-$14,000
1998	$14,000-$16,000
1999	$16,000-$18,000
2000	$18,000-$20,000
2001	$20,000-$22,000
2002	$22,000-$24,000

Crash-test results — Pontiac Firebird

Model years	Offset	Full-frontal	Side
1995	NT	●/○	NT
1996	NT	●/○	NT
1997	NT	●/○	○/○
1998	NT	●/○	○/○
1999	NT	●/○	○/○
2000	NT	●/○	○/○
2001	NT	●/○	○/○
2002	NT	●/○	○/○

Pontiac Grand Am

1999 model shown

The 1992 Grand Am was an uninspired design from the start. The noisy "Quad Four" four-cylinder engine performs weakly. Look for a model equipped with a V6. The handling is imprecise, the body leans a lot in turns, and the tires squeal prematurely. The front seats, at least, give fairly good support. Redesigned for 1999, the Grand Am got an improved ride and sounder handling. The cabin offers plenty of headroom, but the front seats are soft and unsupportive. The V6 continues to be the better engine choice. Overall, it still trailed most competitors, with pronounced wind noise and flimsy plastic interior trim. **Related models:** Buick Skylark, Oldsmobile Achieva, Oldsmobile Alero.

MAJOR REDESIGN: 1992, 1999. **SAFETY EQUIPMENT:** Driver air bag standard; passenger side from 1996. ABS standard. **DRIVE WHEELS:** Front.

Reliability history — Pontiac Grand Am

Trouble spots (model years 95 96 97 98 99 00 01 02): Engine, Cooling, Fuel, Ignition, Transmission, Electrical, Air-conditioning, Suspension, Brakes, Exhaust, Paint/trim/rust, Body integrity, Power equipment, Body hardware, Reliability verdict.

Prices — Pontiac Grand Am

Year	Price
1995	$4,000-$6,000
1996	$4,000-$6,000
1997	$6,000-$8,000
1998	$6,000-$8,000
1999	$8,000-$10,000
2000	$10,000-$12,000
2001	$12,000-$14,000
2002	$14,000-$16,000

Crash-test results

Model Years	Offset	Full frontal	Side
1995	NT	◐/○	NT
1996	NT	◐/○	NT
1997	NT	●/◐	●/○
1998	NT	●/◐	●/○
1999	Poor	●/◐	○/○
2000	Poor	●/◐	○/○
2001	Poor	●/◐	○/○
2002	Poor	●/◐	○/○

Pontiac Grand Prix

1998 model shown

Earlier versions of this model didn't measure up in performance or comfort. In our tests, the Grand Prix handled well in routine driving but was sluggish in emergency maneuvers. The optional 3.4-liter V6 delivers a little more punch than the 3.1-liter V6, but it's notably thirstier. Redesigned for 1997, the Grand Prix came with a 3.8-liter V6 in standard and supercharged versions. The latest Grand Prix corners crisply with little body lean, and the front seats are quite comfortable. The rear seat, however, is short on head room, and the ride is unexceptional. **Related models:** Buick Regal, Oldsmobile Cutlass Supreme, Oldsmobile Intrigue.

MAJOR REDESIGN: 1997. **SAFETY EQUIPMENT:** Dual front air bags standard. ABS available, standard from 1997. **DRIVE WHEELS:** Front.

Reliability history — Pontiac Grand Prix

Trouble spots (model years 95 96 97 98 99 00 01 02): Engine, Cooling, Fuel, Ignition, Transmission, Electrical, Air-conditioning, Suspension, Brakes, Exhaust, Paint/trim/rust, Body integrity, Power equipment, Body hardware, Reliability verdict (✔ ✔ ✔ ✔ ✔ ✔ ✔).

Prices — Pontiac Grand Prix

Year	Price
1995	$4,000-$6,000
1996	$6,000-$8,000
1997	$8,000-$10,000
1998	$10,000-$12,000
1999	$10,000-$12,000
2000	$12,000-$14,000
2001	$12,000-$14,000
2002	$16,000-$18,000

Crash-test results

Model Years	Offset	Full frontal	Side
1995	NT	◐/○	NT
1996	NT	◐/○	NT
1997	Accept.	◐/◐	NT
1998	Accept.	◐/◐	NT
1999	Accept.	◐/●	NT
2000	Accept.	◐/●	NT
2001	Accept.	◐/◐	◐/○
2002	Accept.	◐/◐	◐/○

SMALL CAR
Pontiac Sunfire

2000 model shown

The Pontiac Sunbird and early-'90s Chevrolet Cavalier handle clumsily and have a poorly controlled ride. A 3.1-liter V6, available in some models, is a better choice than the noisy base four-cylinder. In 1995, the Sunbird was replaced by the Sunfire. The steering was fairly quick, but its ride was uncomfortable. The standard 2.2-liter Four is buzzy but offers acceptable acceleration; the larger Four is stronger but even less refined. The front seats feel comfortable on short trips but are fatiguing on long journeys. The rear seat is badly shaped and uncomfortable. A minor facelift and an improved manual transmission were new for 2000. **Related model:** Chevrolet Cavalier.

MAJOR REDESIGN: 1995. **SAFETY EQUIPMENT:** Dual front air bags standard. ABS standard. **DRIVE WHEELS:** Front.

MINIVAN
Pontiac Trans Sport, Montana

1998 model shown

Early Trans Sport models were competent minivans, with distinctive styling and innovative plastic body panels. The Trans Sport was redesigned for 1997 and was available in both standard and extended-wheelbase models. Dual sliding doors and a roomy, flexible interior with movable seats provide impressive versatility. The Trans Sport was renamed the Montana after 1998. A poor showing in an insurance-industry frontal offset crash test is the Montana's greatest liability. **Related models:** Chevrolet Lumina Van, Chevrolet Venture, Oldsmobile Silhouette.

MAJOR REDESIGN: 1994, 1997. **SAFETY EQUIPMENT:** Driver air bag standard; passenger side from 1997. Side air bags and safety-belt pretensioners standard from 1998. ABS standard. **DRIVE WHEELS:** Front. AWD available from 2002.

Pontiac Sunfire — Reliability history

TROUBLE SPOTS	95	96	97	98	99	00	01	02
Engine								
Cooling								
Fuel								
Ignition								
Transmission								
Electrical								
Air conditioning								
Suspension								
Brakes								
Exhaust								
Paint/trim/rust								
Body integrity								
Power equipment								
Body hardware								
RELIABILITY VERDICT	✓			✓	✓	✓	✓	

Pontiac Sunfire — Prices

Year	Price
1995	$4,000-$6,000
1996	$4,000-$6,000
1997	$6,000-$8,000
1998	$6,000-$8,000
1999	$8,000-$10,000
2000	$8,000-$10,000
2001	$10,000-$12,000
2002	$12,000-$14,000

Pontiac Sunfire — Crash-test results

Model years	Offset	Full-frontal	Side
1995	Poor	○/○	NT
1996	Poor	○/○	NT
1997	Poor	○/○	NT
1998	Poor	○/○	●/○
1999	Poor	○/○	●/○
2000	Poor	○/○	●/○
2001	Poor	○/○	●/○
2002	Poor	○/○	●/○

Pontiac Trans Sport, Montana (ext.) — Reliability history

TROUBLE SPOTS	95	96	97	98	99	00	01	02
Engine								
Cooling								
Fuel								
Ignition								
Transmission								
Electrical								
Air conditioning								
Suspension								
Brakes								
Exhaust								
Paint/trim/rust								
Body integrity								
Power equipment								
Body hardware								
RELIABILITY VERDICT							✓	

Pontiac Trans Sport, Montana — Prices

Year	Price
1995	$6,000-$8,000
1996	$6,000-$8,000
1997	$8,000-$10,000
1998	$12,000-$14,000
1999	$12,000-$14,000
2000	$14,000-$16,000
2001	$16,000-$18,000
2002	$18,000-$20,000

Pontiac Trans Sport, Montana — Crash-test results

Model years	Offset	Full-frontal	Side
1995	NT	○/○	NT
1996	NT	○/○	NT
1997	Poor	○/○	NT
1998	Poor	○/○	NT
1999	Poor	○/○	○/○
2000	Poor	○/○	○/○
2001	Poor	○/○	○/○
2002	Poor	○/○	○/○

SPORTS/SPORTY CAR
Porsche 911

1996 model shown

The 911 has been considered among the world's most desirable sports cars. In recent years, Porsche has offered rear- and all-wheel-drive coupes, convertibles, and a Targa model with an electrically operated sliding glass roof. Exceptionally powerful AWD Turbo versions were also available. A '93 redesign improved handling considerably. A six-speed manual transmission became standard in 1995; Porsche's Tiptronic automatic was optional on rear-drive models. A 1999 redesign brought an all-new platform and a conventional water-cooled engine (earlier versions were air-cooled). The 911 offers room for tall drivers and good outward visibility.

MAJOR REDESIGN: 1993, 1999. **SAFETY EQUIPMENT:** Dual front air bags standard. Side air bags standard from 1999. ABS standard. **DRIVE WHEELS:** Rear or AWD.

Reliability history

TROUBLE SPOTS	95 96 97 98 99 00 01 02
Engine	
Cooling	
Fuel	
Ignition	NOT
Transmission	
Electrical	ENOUGH
Air-conditioning	
Suspension	DATA
Brakes	
Exhaust	TO
Paint/trim/rust	
Body integrity	
Power equipment	RATE
Body hardware	
RELIABILITY VERDICT	

Prices

1995	More than $30,000
1996	More than $30,000
1997	More than $30,000
1998	More than $30,000
1999	More than $30,000
2000	More than $30,000
2001	More than $30,000
2002	More than $30,000

Crash-test results

Model Years	Offset	Full frontal	Side
1995	NT	NT	NT
1996	NT	NT	NT
1997	NT	NT	NT
1998	NT	NT	NT
1999	NT	NT	NT
2000	NT	NT	NT
2001	NT	NT	NT
2002	NT	NT	NT

SPORTS/SPORTY CAR
Porsche Boxster

1997 model shown

New for 1997, this sporty mid-engine roadster initially used a 2.5-liter, 201-hp flat-Six engine. The transmission is either a five-speed manual or five-speed Tiptronic automatic that you can shift manually. The Boxster's handling is superb, and its ride is acceptable. The engine and manual transmission are well matched and provide quick acceleration. A powered convertible soft top is standard, and is easy to operate. A quicker, 250-hp "S" model was introduced for 2000, and featured a six-speed transmission. The base engine, meanwhile, jumped to 2.7 liters and 217 hp.

MAJOR REDESIGN: 1997. **SAFETY EQUIPMENT:** Dual front air bags standard. Side air bags standard from 1998. ABS standard. Safety-belt pretensioners standard. **DRIVE WHEELS:** Rear.

Reliability history

Porsche Boxster

TROUBLE SPOTS	95	96	97	98	99	00	01	02
Engine						◑	◑	
Cooling						◑	◑	
Fuel						◑	◑	
Ignition						◑	◑	
Transmission						◑	◑	
Electrical			Insufficient data	Insufficient data	Insufficient data	○	◑	Insufficient data
Air-conditioning						◑	◑	
Suspension						◑	◑	
Brakes						◑	◑	
Exhaust						◑	◑	
Paint/trim/rust						◑	◑	
Body integrity						◑	○	
Power equipment						◑	◑	
Body hardware						◑	◑	
RELIABILITY VERDICT						✔	✔	

Prices

1995	–
1996	–
1997	$28,000-$30,000
1998	More than $30,000
1999	More than $30,000
2000	More than $30,000
2001	More than $30,000
2002	More than $30,000

Crash-test results

Model Years	Offset	Full frontal	Side
1995	–	–	–
1996	–	–	–
1997	NT	NT	NT
1998	NT	NT	NT
1999	NT	NT	NT
2000	NT	NT	NT
2001	NT	NT	NT
2002	NT	NT	NT

Saab 900, 9-3

Saab 9000, 9-5

CR Good Bet

1999 model shown

1999 model shown

Redesigned for 1994, the 900 was available in hatchback and convertible body styles. The hatchback provided secure handling, a large and versatile cargo area, and a full complement of safety features. Engine choices included turbocharged Fours and a V6. The 900 rode stiffly and too much road noise came through to the cabin. The 900 was renamed the 9-3 for 1999. The turbo Four and automatic transmission made for a lethargic takeoff. The V6 was dropped, and a high-performance, 230-hp Viggen model was added. A stiff ride, narrow cockpit, and cramped rear seat remained.

MAJOR REDESIGN: 1994, 1999. **SAFETY EQUIPMENT:** Dual front air bags standard. Side air bags standard from 1999. ABS and safety-belt pretensioners standard. **DRIVE WHEELS:** Front.

The Saab 9000 was big and clunky but it handled pretty well, it had comfortable seats, and the hatchback had a large cargo area. The 9-5 was an improvement. Introduced for 1999, it was offered as a sedan or wagon. The 9-5 is competent and pleasant to drive, with capable and secure handling. The ride is firm and compliant, but road noise is pronounced. The turbocharged 2.3-liter, 170-hp Four provides ample acceleration. From 2000 on, this engine made 185 horsepower. The 3.0-liter, 200-hp V6 is smoother, quieter, and stronger. A higher-performance 230-hp Aero model was introduced for 2000.

MAJOR REDESIGN: 1999. **SAFETY EQUIPMENT:** Dual front air bags standard. Side air bags standard from 1999. Head protection air bags standard from 2002. ABS standard. Safety-belt pretensioners standard. **DRIVE WHEELS:** Front.

Reliability history — Saab 900, 9-3

TROUBLE SPOTS	95	96	97	98	99	00	01	02
Engine				*Insufficient data*				*Insufficient data*
Cooling								
Fuel								
Ignition								
Transmission								
Electrical								
Air conditioning								
Suspension								
Brakes								
Exhaust								
Paint/trim/rust								
Body integrity								
Power equipment								
Body hardware								
RELIABILITY VERDICT	✓		✓		✓	✓	✓	

Prices

Year	Price
1995	$6,000-$8,000
1996	$8,000-$10,000
1997	$10,000-$12,000
1998	$10,000-$12,000
1999	$18,000-$20,000
2000	$22,000-$24,000
2001	$24,000-$26,000
2002	$26,000-$28,000

Crash-test results

Model years	Offset	Full-frontal	Side
1995	Marg.	◐/◐	NT
1996	Marg.	◐/◐	NT
1997	Marg.	◐/◐	NT
1998	Marg.	◐/◐	NT
1999	Accept.	NT	NT
2000	Accept.	NT	NT
2001	Accept.	NT	NT
2002	Accept.	NT	NT

Reliability history — Saab 9-5

TROUBLE SPOTS	95	96	97	98	99	00	01	02
Engine	*Insufficient data*							
Cooling								
Fuel								
Ignition								
Transmission								
Electrical								
Air conditioning								
Suspension								
Brakes								
Exhaust								
Paint/trim/rust								
Body integrity								
Power equipment								
Body hardware								
RELIABILITY VERDICT						✓	✓	✓

Prices

Year	Price
1995	$8,000-$10,000
1996	$10,000-$12,000
1997	$12,000-$14,000
1998	$16,000-$18,000
1999	$22,000-$24,000
2000	$26,000-$28,000
2001	More than $30,000
2002	More than $30,000

Crash-test results

Model years	Offset	Full-frontal	Side
1995	NT	NT	NT
1996	NT	NT	NT
1997	NT	NT	NT
1998	NT	NT	NT
1999	Accept.	NT	NT
2000	Accept.	NT	NT
2001	Accept.	NT	NT
2002	Good	◐/◐	NT

Saturn L-Series

2000 model shown

Saturn's midsized L-Series was loosely derived from the European-market Opel Vectra. Available as either a sedan or wagon, the L-Series competes against such family-sedan mainstays as the Honda Accord and Toyota Camry. As with Saturn's smaller S-Series models, the L-Series uses dent-resistant plastic body panels. It is available with a noisy 2.2-liter four-cylinder engine or Saturn's 3.0-liter, 182-hp V6. The four-speed automatic transmission shifts well. Handling is competent but not nimble, and the ride is too stiff. The interior is roomy but the controls are not intuitive and have a low-quality feel.

MAJOR REDESIGN: 2000. **SAFETY EQUIPMENT:** Dual front air bags standard. Head protection air bags available in 2001, standard from 2002. ABS available. **DRIVE WHEELS:** Front.

Reliability history

TROUBLE SPOTS	Saturn L-Series 95 96 97 98 99 00 01 02
Engine	
Cooling	
Fuel	
Ignition	
Transmission	
Electrical	
Air-conditioning	
Suspension	
Brakes	
Exhaust	
Paint/trim/rust	
Body integrity	
Power equipment	
Body hardware	
RELIABILITY VERDICT	✔

Prices

Year	Price
1995	–
1996	–
1997	–
1998	–
1999	–
2000	$10,000-$12,000
2001	$12,000-$14,000
2002	$14,000-$16,000

Crash-test results

Model Years	Offset	Full frontal	Side
1995	–	–	–
1996	–	–	–
1997	–	–	–
1998	–	–	–
1999	–	–	–
2000	Accept.	◔/○	◔/○
2001	Accept.	◔/○	◔/○
2002	Accept.	◔/○	○/○

Saturn S-Series

1999 model shown

While Saturn's S-Series cars have been largely unremarkable, the line's appeal has been bolstered by a good reliability record and a no-haggle dealer experience. The S-Series is available in sedan (SL), coupe (SC), and wagon (SW) versions. The uplevel SL2, SC2, and SW2 are much better cars than the less expensive trim levels, with more standard features, more power, and better handling. In our tests, we've found the S-Series' four-cylinder engines noisy but fuel-efficient. The front seats are low, and the rear seat is cramped on all models. A third door was offered on the coupe in 1999, improving rear-seat access.

MAJOR REDESIGN: 1991, 1996. **SAFETY EQUIPMENT:** Dual front air bags standard. Head protection air bags available from 2001. ABS available. **DRIVE WHEELS:** Front.

Reliability history

TROUBLE SPOTS	Saturn SL/SW 95 96 97 98 99 00 01 02
Engine	
Cooling	
Fuel	
Ignition	
Transmission	
Electrical	
Air-conditioning	
Suspension	
Brakes	
Exhaust	
Paint/trim/rust	
Body integrity	
Power equipment	
Body hardware	
RELIABILITY VERDICT	✔ ✔ ✔ ✔ ✔ ✔ ✔

Prices

Year	Price
1995	$4,000-$6,000
1996	$4,000-$6,000
1997	$6,000-$8,000
1998	$6,000-$8,000
1999	$6,000-$8,000
2000	$8,000-$10,000
2001	$8,000-$10,000
2002	$10,000-$12,000

Crash-test results

Model Years	Offset	Full frontal	Side
1995	Accept.	◔/○	NT
1996	Accept.	◔/○	NT
1997	Accept.	◔/○	○/○
1998	Accept.	◕/○	○/○
1999	Accept.	◕/○	○/○
2000	Accept.	◕/○	○/◔
2001	Accept.	◕/○	○/○
2002	Accept.	◕/○	○/◔

Saturn VUE

2002 model shown

Introduced for 2002, Saturn's first SUV has potential but lacks polish. Interior fit and finish are subpar, the front seats lack support, and the rear bench is too low. The VUE handles like a car but the steering is a little numb. We also found the VUE's AWD system slow to respond on slippery surfaces, allowing the front wheels to spin noticeably before the rear wheels engaged. The available V6, also used in the L-Series sedan, provides quick but noisy acceleration. A continuously variable transmission (CVT) is offered with the base Four, while V6-powered VUEs use a five-speed automatic. Crash-test results are impressive.

MAJOR REDESIGN: 2002. **SAFETY EQUIPMENT:** Dual front air bags standard. Head protection air bags available. ABS available. **DRIVE WHEELS:** Front or AWD.

Reliability history

TROUBLE SPOTS	Saturn VUE
	95 96 97 98 99 00 01 02
Engine	02 ●
Cooling	02 ●
Fuel	02 ●
Ignition	02 ●
Transmission	02 ●
Electrical	02 ◐
Air conditioning	02 ●
Suspension	02 ◐
Brakes	02 ●
Exhaust	02 ◐
Paint/trim/rust	02 ●
Body integrity	02 ◐
Power equipment	02 ●
Body hardware	02 ●
RELIABILITY VERDICT	02 ✓

Prices

1995	–
1996	–
1997	–
1998	–
1999	–
2000	–
2001	–
2002	$16,000-$18,000

Crash-test results

Model years	Offset	Full-frontal	Side
1995	–	–	–
1996	–	–	–
1997	–	–	–
1998	–	–	–
1999	–	–	–
2000	–	–	–
2001	–	–	–
2002	Good	●/◐	●/◐

Subaru Forester

CR Good Bet

1998 model shown

The Forester, new for 1998, is one of the better small car-based SUVs. It is derived from the reliable and good-performing Subaru Impreza, but the Forester touts a taller and roomier cargo compartment and more ground clearance. The ride is compliant and handling is quite nimble. Matched to a responsive automatic transmission, the 2.5-liter four-cylinder engine provides good acceleration. Like all recent Subarus, it has an effective AWD system. The rear seat is a bit cramped, but the cabin has lots of storage compartments. It received a "good" rating in an insurance-industry frontal-offset crash test.

MAJOR REDESIGN: 1998. **SAFETY EQUIPMENT:** Dual front air bags standard. Side air bags available from 2001. ABS available, standard from 2001. **DRIVE WHEELS:** AWD.

Reliability history

TROUBLE SPOTS	Subaru Forester
	95 96 97 98 99 00 01 02
Engine	○ ● ● ● ●
Cooling	● ● ● ● ●
Fuel	● ● ○ ● ●
Ignition	● ● ● ● ●
Transmission	● ● ● ● ●
Electrical	● ◐ ● ● ●
Air conditioning	● ● ● ● ●
Suspension	● ◐ ◐ ● ●
Brakes	○ ◐ ● ● ●
Exhaust	● ● ● ● ●
Paint/trim/rust	● ◐ ◐ ● ●
Body integrity	● ● ◐ ● ●
Power equipment	● ● ● ● ●
Body hardware	● ● ● ● ●
RELIABILITY VERDICT	✓ ✓ ✓ ✓ ✓

Prices

1995	–
1996	–
1997	–
1998	$12,000-$14,000
1999	$14,000-$16,000
2000	$16,000-$18,000
2001	$18,000-$20,000
2002	$18,000-$20,000

Crash-test results

Model years	Offset	Full-frontal	Side
1995	–	–	–
1996	–	–	–
1997	–	–	–
1998	NT	NT	NT
1999	Good	●/◐	NT
2000	Good	●/◐	NT
2001	Good	●/◐	●/◐
2002	Good	●/◐	●/◐

SMALL CAR
Subaru Impreza

2002 model shown

The Impreza offered sedan and wagon models from the start. Engines have always been horizontally opposed "flat" four-cylinder types. The 2.2-liter is livelier than the base 1.8-liter. The Impreza delivers nimble handling and a relatively comfortable ride. The rear seat is cramped and cargo space is tight. In 1996, AWD became standard on all Impreza models and an "Outback Sport" SUV-inspired wagon debuted. An RS sedan followed for 2000. The sporty WRX arrived with 2002's complete redesign.

MAJOR REDESIGN: 1993, 2002. **SAFETY EQUIPMENT:** Dual front air bags standard. Side air bags available from 2002. Safety-belt pretensioners standard from 2002. ABS available, standard from 2002. **DRIVE WHEELS:** Front or AWD. From 1996, AWD.

Prices	
1995	$4,000-$6,000
1996	$6,000-$8,000
1997	$8,000-$10,000
1998	$8,000-$10,000
1999	$10,000-$12,000
2000	$12,000-$14,000
2001	$14,000-$16,000
2002	$18,000-$20,000

Reliability history — Subaru Impreza

TROUBLE SPOTS	95	96	97	98	99	00	01	02
Engine								
Cooling								
Fuel								
Ignition								
Transmission								
Electrical								
Air-conditioning								
Suspension								
Brakes								
Exhaust								
Paint/trim/rust								
Body integrity								
Power equipment								
Body hardware								
RELIABILITY VERDICT	✓	✓	✓	✓	✓	✓		✓

Insufficient data (2001 column)

Crash-test results

Model Years	Offset	Full frontal	Side
1995	NT	NT	NT
1996	NT	◐/◑	NT
1997	NT	◐/◑	NT
1998	NT	◐/◑	NT
1999	NT	◐/◑	NT
2000	NT	◐/◑	NT
2001	NT	NT	NT
2002	Good	◐/●	○/NA

FAMILY CAR
Subaru Legacy/Outback

2000 model shown

The Legacy sedan and wagon have always been well-rounded performers. The ride is supple, and routine handling is excellent, though emergency maneuvers can make the tail slide too easily. A 1995 redesign spawned the Legacy Outback, an SUV-themed wagon with added ground clearance and a slightly raised roof. Another redesign came for 2000, and the 2.5-liter Four, previously available only in the GT and Outback, became standard across the line. A 3.0-liter flat-Six engine debuted in 2001, though only in the uplevel Outback L.L. Bean and VDC models. The VDC also gets standard stability control.

MAJOR REDESIGN: 1995, 2000. **SAFETY EQUIPMENT:** Dual front air bags standard. Side air bags standard from 2000 on high-trim models. Safety-belt pretensioners standard from 2000. ABS available standard from 2000. **DRIVE WHEELS:** Front or AWD. From 1996, AWD.

Prices	
1995	$6,000-$8,000
1996	$10,000-$12,000
1997	$12,000-$14,000
1998	$14,000-$16,000
1999	$16,000-$18,000
2000	$18,000-$20,000
2001	$20,000-$22,000
2002	$22,000-$24,000

Reliability history — Subaru Legacy/Outback 4 cyl.

TROUBLE SPOTS	95	96	97	98	99	00	01	02
Engine								
Cooling								
Fuel								
Ignition								
Transmission								
Electrical								
Air-conditioning								
Suspension								
Brakes								
Exhaust								
Paint/trim/rust								
Body integrity								
Power equipment								
Body hardware								
RELIABILITY VERDICT	✓	✓	✓	✓	✓	✓	✓	✓

Crash-test results

Model Years	Offset	Full frontal	Side
1995	Accept.	◐/◑	NT
1996	Accept.	◐/◑	NT
1997	Accept.	◐/◑	NT
1998	Accept.	◐/◑	○/NA
1999	Accept.	◐/◑	○/NA
2000	Good	◐/◑	◐/◑
2001	Good	◐/●	◐/◑
2002	Good	◐/●	◐/◑

Subaru SVX

Suzuki Esteem, Aerio

1996 model shown

1998 model shown

The SVX lacks the razor-sharp performance of a true sports car, but it offers the comfort and quietness of a luxury sedan and the availability of all-wheel drive. Acceleration is ample from the horizontally opposed 3.3-liter Six, and the four-speed automatic transmission shifts smoothly. Normal handling feels very stable, but emergency handling lacks the sheer grip of dedicated sports cars. The front seats are comfortable, but two adults can tolerate the rear seat only for short periods. Aside from tiny horn buttons, the controls are well designed, and the gauges are easy to read. The tiny side windows limit access at toll booths and drive-throughs. 1997 was the SVX's final season.

MAJOR REDESIGN: 1992. **SAFETY EQUIPMENT:** Dual front air bags standard. ABS available. **DRIVE WHEELS:** Front or AWD.

The Esteem was introduced in 1995. In most respects, it provides neat packaging and thoughtful touches. Though practical and workmanlike, the car ranked below modern competitors in ride, interior noise, and powertrain smoothness. The 1.6-liter, 95-hp four-cylinder engine accelerates well enough, but sounds harsh when revved. Elbow and leg room are a little scarce front and rear. A wagon joined the lineup for 1998. The 2000 Esteem received a mild facelift, and a 1.8-liter, 122-hp four-cylinder engine became available. The Aerio replaced the Esteem and Swift in 2002, and comes as both sedan and wagon.

MAJOR REDESIGN: 1995, 2002. **SAFETY EQUIPMENT:** Dual front air bags standard. Safety-belt pretensioners standard from 2002. ABS available. **DRIVE WHEELS:** Front.

Subaru SVX

Reliability history		Prices	
TROUBLE SPOTS	95 96 97 98 99 00 01 02	1995	$6,000-$8,000
Engine		1996	$10,000-$12,000
Cooling		1997	$12,000-$14,000
Fuel		1998	–
Ignition	NOT	1999	–
Transmission		2000	–
Electrical	ENOUGH	2001	–
Air conditioning		2002	–
Suspension	DATA		
Brakes			
Exhaust	TO		
Paint/trim/rust			
Body integrity	RATE		
Power equipment			
Body hardware			
RELIABILITY VERDICT			

Crash-test results

Model years	Offset	Full-frontal	Side
1995	NT	NT	NT
1996	NT	NT	NT
1997	NT	NT	NT
1998	–	–	–
1999	–	–	–
2000	–	–	–
2001	–	–	–
2002	–	–	–

Suzuki Esteem, Aerio

Reliability history		Prices	
TROUBLE SPOTS	95 96 97 98 99 00 01 02	1995	$2,000-$4,000
Engine		1996	$4,000-$6,000
Cooling		1997	$4,000-$6,000
Fuel		1998	$4,000-$6,000
Ignition	NOT	1999	$6,000-$8,000
Transmission		2000	$6,000-$8,000
Electrical	ENOUGH	2001	$8,000-$10,000
Air conditioning		2002	$12,000-$14,000
Suspension	DATA		
Brakes			
Exhaust	TO		
Paint/trim/rust			
Body integrity	RATE		
Power equipment			
Body hardware			
RELIABILITY VERDICT			

Crash-test results

Model years	Offset	Full-frontal	Side
1995	NT	NT	NT
1996	NT	NT	NT
1997	NT	NT	NT
1998	NT	NT	NT
1999	NT	NT	NT
2000	NT	NT	NT
2001	NT	NT	NT
2002	Good	NT	NT

Suzuki Sidekick, Vitara/XL-7

1998 model shown

With its body-on-frame design, the Sidekick lacks the ride-and-handling refinement of more modern, car-based SUVs. Early models are plagued by slow steering and a weak engine. The Sidekick was discontinued in 1998 and replaced by the Vitara, which is available as a two-door soft-top and a four-door hardtop. A 2.0-liter four-cylinder engine is standard. The four-door Grand Vitara packs a stronger 2.5-liter V6 and more standard equipment. These SUVs have only part-time 4WD. Even the 2.7-liter automatic version feels sluggish. The extended-length XL-7 has a third row of seats—unique for this class. **Related model:** Geo/Chevrolet Tracker.

MAJOR REDESIGN: 1989, 1999. **SAFETY EQUIPMENT:** Dual front air bags standard from 1996. Safety-belt pretensioners standard from 2002. ABS available from 1996. **DRIVE WHEELS:** Rear or part-time 4WD.

Reliability history

TROUBLE SPOTS	Suzuki Sidekick, Vitara/XL-7							
	95	96	97	98	99	00	01	02
Engine	◑	●				◑	●	
Cooling	○	○				◑	●	
Fuel	○	○				◑	●	
Ignition	◑	●				◑	●	
Transmission	●	◑				◑	●	
Electrical	◑	○	Insufficient data	Insufficient data	Insufficient data	◑	◑	Insufficient data
Air-conditioning	◑	◑				◑	◑	
Suspension	◑	●				◑	◑	
Brakes	◑	◑				◑	◑	
Exhaust	○	◑				●	◑	
Paint/trim/rust	◑	○				◑	◑	
Body integrity	●	○				◑	◑	
Power equipment	◑	◑				○	◑	
Body hardware	○	○				◑	◑	
RELIABILITY VERDICT	✓	✓					✓	

Prices

1995	$4,000–$6,000
1996	$4,000–$6,000
1997	$6,000–$8,000
1998	$6,000–$8,000
1999	$10,000–$12,000
2000	$10,000–$12,000
2001	$12,000–$14,000
2002	$16,000–$18,000

Crash-test results

Model Years	Offset	Full frontal	Side
1995	NT	◑/○	NT
1996	NT	◑/○	NT
1997	NT	◑/○	NT
1998	NT	NT	NT
1999	Accept.	NT	NT
2000	Accept.	NT	NT
2001	Good	◑/○	NT
2002	Good	◑/○	◑/●

Suzuki Swift

1995 model shown

The Suzuki-built Swift, which was rebadged as the Geo Metro, is one of the smallest, lightest cars on the road. Available as a two-door hatchback or four-door sedan, all Swift models are powered by a four-cylinder engine (instead of the three-cylinder engine used by the Metro). In either body style, the Swift is not a car for freeway cruising, though it felt maneuverable around town. The Swift was redesigned for 1995, but was available only as a two-door hatchback. It got slightly longer, higher, and wider than its predecessor. The ride remains choppy and noisy. The Swift received a small horsepower gain for 1998. **Related model:** Geo/Chevrolet Metro.

MAJOR REDESIGN: 1995. **SAFETY EQUIPMENT:** Dual front air bags standard. ABS available. **DRIVE WHEELS:** Front.

Reliability history

TROUBLE SPOTS	Suzuki Swift							
	95	96	97	98	99	00	01	02
Engine	◑							
Cooling	◑							
Fuel	◐							
Ignition	◑							
Transmission	◑							
Electrical	◑	Insufficient data	Insufficient data	Insufficient data	Insufficient data	Insufficient data	Insufficient data	Insufficient data
Air-conditioning	●							
Suspension	◐							
Brakes	○							
Exhaust	○							
Paint/trim/rust	○							
Body integrity	○							
Power equipment	◐							
Body hardware	○							
RELIABILITY VERDICT	✓							

Prices

1995	$2,000–$4,000
1996	$2,000–$4,000
1997	$2,000–$4,000
1998	$4,000–$6,000
1999	$4,000–$6,000
2000	$6,000–$8,000
2001	$6,000–$8,000
2002	–

Crash-test results

Model Years	Offset	Full frontal	Side
1995	NT	◑/○	NT
1996	NT	◑/○	NT
1997	NT	◑/○	NT
1998	NT	◑/○	NT
1999	NT	◑/○	NT
2000	NT	◑/○	NT
2001	NT	◑/○	NT
2002	–	–	–

Toyota 4Runner

Toyota Avalon

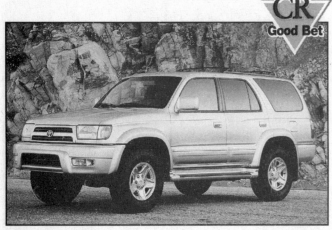

1999 model shown

1998 model shown

Based on Toyota's compact pickup, the 4Runner is a traditional truck-based SUV. In pre-'96 models, neither the four-cylinder nor the V6 engine is very strong. The rear seat and cargo area are tight. A 1996 redesign significantly improved this model's ride, powertrain, and interior packaging. A longer wheelbase and lower floor provide more cargo space and rear leg room. A low seat and high floor makes access a chore and the driving position awkward. We prefer the lively 3.4-liter V6 to the 2.7-liter Four. The V6 and stability control became standard on all models in 2001.

MAJOR REDESIGN: 1996. **SAFETY EQUIPMENT:** Dual front air bags standard from 1996. ABS available; standard from 2001. Safety-belt pretensioners standard from 2000. **DRIVE WHEELS:** Rear or part-time 4WD. Selectable 4WD available from 1999; standard in 2001.

The Avalon made its debut in 1995 as the flagship of the Toyota sedan line. Think of it as a longer, well-equipped Camry with an extra-roomy rear seat. In our tests, the Avalon cornered quite nimbly for its size. The car drives smoothly, but the light steering gives little road feel. The front bucket seats are large and comfortable. A front bench seat is optional, but it's comfortable only for two. The cabin is commendably quiet. The Avalon was redesigned for 2000. High points remain the silky-smooth V6 powertrain, Lexus-like isolation from the road, and generous accommodations.

MAJOR REDESIGN: 1995, 2000. **SAFETY EQUIPMENT:** Dual front air bags standard. Side air bags standard from 1998. ABS available; standard from 1997. Safety-belt pretensioners standard from 1998. **DRIVE WHEELS:** Front.

Toyota 4Runner — Reliability history

TROUBLE SPOTS	95	96	97	98	99	00	01	02
Engine								
Cooling								
Fuel								
Ignition								
Transmission								
Electrical								
Air conditioning								
Suspension								
Brakes								
Exhaust								
Paint/trim/rust								
Body integrity								
Power equipment								
Body hardware								
RELIABILITY VERDICT	✓	✓	✓	✓	✓	✓	✓	✓

Prices

1995	$10,000-$12,000
1996	$14,000-$16,000
1997	$16,000-$18,000
1998	$18,000-$20,000
1999	$20,000-$22,000
2000	$22,000-$24,000
2001	$24,000-$26,000
2002	$28,000-$30,000

Crash-test results

Model years	Offset	Full-frontal	Side
1995	NT	●/◐	NT
1996	Accept.	○/○	NT
1997	Accept.	○/○	NT
1998	Accept.	○/○	NT
1999	Accept.	◐/●	◐/●
2000	Accept.	◐/●	◐/●
2001	Accept.	◐/●	◐/●
2002	Accept.	◐/●	◐/●

Toyota Avalon — Reliability history

TROUBLE SPOTS	95	96	97	98	99	00	01	02
Engine								
Cooling								
Fuel								
Ignition								
Transmission								
Electrical								
Air conditioning								
Suspension								
Brakes								
Exhaust								
Paint/trim/rust								
Body integrity								
Power equipment								
Body hardware								
RELIABILITY VERDICT	✓	✓	✓	✓	✓	✓	✓	✓

Prices

1995	$8,000-$10,000
1996	$10,000-$12,000
1997	$12,000-$14,000
1998	$14,000-$16,000
1999	$16,000-$18,000
2000	$20,000-$22,000
2001	$22,000-$24,000
2002	$24,000-$26,000

Crash-test results

Model years	Offset	Full-frontal	Side
1995	Marg.	NT	NT
1996	Marg.	◐/●	NT
1997	Marg.	◐/●	NT
1998	Accept.	◐/●	◐/●
1999	Accept.	◐/●	◐/●
2000	Good	NT	◐/●
2001	Good	○/●	◐/●
2002	Good	◐/●	◐/●

Toyota Camry

CR **Good Bet**

1998 model shown

The Camry has long been one of our top choices. It has predictable handling, good brakes, a smooth, quiet ride, and excellent reliability. The wagon, available through 1996, is roomy and offers a third seat, but handling can be a bit tricky during evasive maneuvers. Redesigned for 1997, it only marginally improved. The 2.2-liter four-cylinder is somewhat sluggish, but the 3.0-liter V6 is smooth and energetic. The front seats are comfortable, and the rear is relatively roomy. Steering feels light but it's fairly quick and precise. 2002's redesign brought more room and a much better four-cylinder. **Related model:** Lexus ES300.

MAJOR REDESIGN: 1992, 1997, 2002. **SAFETY EQUIPMENT:** Dual front air bags standard. Side air bags available from 1998. ABS available. Safety-belt pretensioners standard from 1998. **DRIVE WHEELS:** Front.

Toyota Camry Solara

CR **Good Bet**

1999 model shown

Available in coupe and convertible versions, the Camry Solara is a sportier, two-door version of the Camry sedan. While the Solara's ride is comfortable and well controlled, it's noticeably tauter than that of the four-door. The Solara's handling is also more nimble, though it falls short of sports-car territory. Engine choices include a 2.2-liter four-cylinder and a smooth, strong 3.0-liter V6. The Solara's cabin is well appointed and serenely quiet, and the front seats are comfortable and supportive. The rear seat is suitable for two average-sized adults. **Related model:** Toyota Camry.

MAJOR REDESIGN: 1999. **SAFETY EQUIPMENT:** Dual front air bags standard. Side air bags and ABS available. Safety-belt pretensioners standard. **DRIVE WHEELS:** Front.

Toyota Camry

Reliability history

TROUBLE SPOTS	95	96	97	98	99	00	01	02
Engine								
Cooling								
Fuel								
Ignition								
Transmission								
Electrical								
Air-conditioning								
Suspension								
Brakes								
Exhaust								
Paint/trim/rust								
Body integrity								
Power equipment								
Body hardware								
RELIABILITY VERDICT	✓	✓	✓	✓	✓	✓	✓	✓

Prices

Year	Price
1995	$8,000-$10,000
1996	$8,000-$10,000
1997	$10,000-$12,000
1998	$12,000-$14,000
1999	$14,000-$16,000
2000	$16,000-$18,000
2001	$16,000-$18,000
2002	$20,000-$22,000

Crash-test results

Model Years	Offset	Full frontal	Side
1995	Accept.	⊖/○	NT
1996	Accept.	⊖/○	NT
1997	Good	⊖/○	○/○
1998	Good	⊖/●	○/○
1999	Good	⊖/●	○/○
2000	Good	⊖/●	○/○
2001	Good	⊖/●	○/○
2002	Good	●/⊖	⊖/●

Toyota Camry Solara

Reliability history

TROUBLE SPOTS	95	96	97	98	99	00	01	02
Engine								
Cooling								
Fuel								
Ignition								
Transmission								
Electrical								
Air-conditioning								
Suspension								
Brakes								
Exhaust								
Paint/trim/rust								
Body integrity								
Power equipment								
Body hardware								
RELIABILITY VERDICT					✓	✓	✓	✓

Prices

Year	Price
1995	–
1996	–
1997	–
1998	–
1999	$14,000-$16,000
2000	$16,000-$18,000
2001	$18,000-$20,000
2002	$20,000-$22,000

Crash-test results

Model Years	Offset	Full frontal	Side
1995	–	–	–
1996	–	–	–
1997	–	–	–
1998	–	–	–
1999	NT	NT	○/●
2000	NT	NT	○/●
2001	NT	NT	○/●
2002	NT	NT	○/●

SPORTS/SPORTY CAR

Toyota Celica

2000 model shown

Available as a coupe or a convertible, the 1994-1999 Celica was a well-rounded car that offered a combination of good handling, fuel economy, and reliability. The engine supplied zesty acceleration but overall the car wasn't especially quick. The seventh-generation Celica debuted for 2000, bringing edgier styling and more power. This iteration boasts nimble handling along with a decent ride. The top-of-the-line GT-S version features a strong-but-peaky 1.8-liter engine paired with a standard six-speed manual transmission. The base GT model offers similar real-world performance for substantially less money.

MAJOR REDESIGN: 1994, 2000. **SAFETY EQUIPMENT:** Dual front air bags standard. Side air bags available from 2000. ABS available. Safety-belt pretensioners standard from 2000. **DRIVE WHEELS:** Front.

Reliability history — Toyota Celica

TROUBLE SPOTS	95	96	97	98	99	00	01	02
Engine	○					●	●	
Cooling	◐					●	●	
Fuel	◐					●	●	
Ignition	●					●	●	
Transmission	◐					●	●	
Electrical	◐	Insufficient data	Insufficient data	Insufficient data	Insufficient data	●	◐	Insufficient data
Air conditioning	◐					●	●	
Suspension	◐					●	●	
Brakes	◐					●	●	
Exhaust	●					●	●	
Paint/trim/rust	◐					●	●	
Body integrity	○					●	●	
Power equipment	○					●	●	
Body hardware	○					●	●	
RELIABILITY VERDICT	✓				✓	✓		

Prices

1995	$8,000-$10,000
1996	$10,000-$12,000
1997	$12,000-$14,000
1998	$12,000-$14,000
1999	$14,000-$16,000
2000	$14,000-$16,000
2001	$16,000-$18,000
2002	$18,000-$20,000

Crash-test results

Model years	Offset	Full-frontal	Side
1995	NT	NT	NT
1996	NT	NT	NT
1997	NT	NT	NT
1998	NT	NT	NT
1999	NT	NT	NT
2000	NT	NT	NT
2001	NT	●/●	○/NA
2002	NT	●/●	○/NA

SMALL CAR

Toyota Corolla

1997 model shown

From 1993 through 1997 the Corolla was offered in sedan and wagon forms. Handling was safe and predictable—though not particularly nimble—in our tests. If you prefer an automatic transmission, look for a model equipped with the optional four-speed unit and 1.8-liter engine. The Corolla was redesigned for 1998, and the 1.8-liter engine became standard across the board. Some 1998 models were fitted with a front stabilizer bar that improved the car's twitchy emergency handling; this piece became standard in 1999. The Corolla's front seats are firm and supportive, but the rear is snug. **Related model:** Geo/Chevrolet Prizm.

MAJOR REDESIGN: 1993, 1998. **SAFETY EQUIPMENT:** Dual front air bags standard. Side air bags available from 1998. ABS available. Safety-belt pretensioners standard from 1998. **DRIVE WHEELS:** Front.

Reliability history — Toyota Corolla

TROUBLE SPOTS	95	96	97	98	99	00	01	02
Engine	●	●	●	●	●	●	●	●
Cooling	●	●	●	◐	●	◐	●	●
Fuel	●	●	●	●	●	●	●	●
Ignition	◐	●	●	●	●	●	●	●
Transmission	●	●	●	●	●	●	●	●
Electrical	●	○	○	●	●	●	●	●
Air conditioning	●	●	●	◐	◐	●	●	●
Suspension	◐	●	◐	●	●	◐	●	●
Brakes	○	○	◐	●	●	●	◐	●
Exhaust	●	●	●	●	●	●	●	●
Paint/trim/rust	◐	●	●	●	●	●	●	●
Body integrity	◐	●	●	●	●	●	●	●
Power equipment	●	●	●	●	●	●	●	●
Body hardware	○	◐	●	●	●	●	●	●
RELIABILITY VERDICT	✓	✓	✓	✓	✓	✓	✓	✓

Prices

1995	$6,000-$8,000
1996	$6,000-$8,000
1997	$6,000-$8,000
1998	$8,000-$10,000
1999	$8,000-$10,000
2000	$10,000-$12,000
2001	$10,000-$12,000
2002	$12,000-$14,000

Crash-test results

Model years	Offset	Full-frontal	Side
1995	NT	●/●	NT
1996	NT	●/●	NT
1997	NT	●/●	○/○
1998	Accept.	●/●	○/○
1999	Accept.	●/●	○/○
2000	Accept.	●/●	○/○
2001	Accept.	●/●	○/○
2002	Accept.	●/●	○/○

SMALL CAR
Toyota Echo

CR
Good Bet

2000 model shown

Introduced for 2000, Toyota's entry-level Echo is one of the better small cars we've tested. With its tall-roofed design, the Echo boasts a spacious, airy interior. The manual-shift Echo tested by CONSUMER REPORTS in 2000 provided good overall performance and averaged 38 mpg overall—an excellent showing. The testers found sprightly acceleration, easy access, and a roomy rear seat. Handling was sound, and the ride was reasonably quiet and comfortable. The interior is spartan, and features an instrument cluster that's curiously situated in the top center of the dash. Unfortunately, an Echo with antilock brakes can be hard to find.

MAJOR REDESIGN: 2000. **SAFETY EQUIPMENT:** Dual front air bags standard. Side air bags and ABS available. Safety-belt pretensioners standard. **DRIVE WHEELS:** Front.

Reliability history		
TROUBLE SPOTS	Toyota Echo	
	95 96 97 98 99 00 01 02	
Engine	● ● ●	
Cooling	● ● ●	
Fuel	● ● ●	
Ignition	● ● ●	
Transmission	● ● ●	
Electrical	● ● ●	
Air-conditioning	● ● ●	
Suspension	● ● ●	
Brakes	○ ● ●	
Exhaust	● ● ●	
Paint/trim/rust	◒ ● ●	
Body integrity	◒ ◒ ●	
Power equipment	● ● ●	
Body hardware	○ ● ●	
RELIABILITY VERDICT	✓ ✓ ✓	

Prices	
1995	–
1996	–
1997	–
1998	–
1999	–
2000	$8,000-$10,000
2001	$8,000-$10,000
2002	$10,000-$12,000

Crash-test results			
Model Years	Offset	Full frontal	Side
1995	–	–	–
1996	–	–	–
1997	–	–	–
1998	–	–	–
1999	–	–	–
2000	NT	NT	NT
2001	NT	◒/◒	○/◒
2002	NT	◒/◒	○/◒

SPORT-UTILITY VEHICLE
Toyota Highlander

2001 model shown

The Highlander is a car-based, five-passenger SUV that slots between Toyota's RAV4 and 4Runner. Based on Camry sedan components, it's conceptually similar to a Lexus RX300, though a tad roomier and significantly less costly. The V6 is smooth and powerful. A 2.4-liter Four is also available with front-wheel drive. As with other AWD car-based SUVs, the Highlander is intended more for rough weather and light off-pavement use. All in all, it's quiet, roomy, and pleasant, with a smooth powertrain, comfortable ride, and easy controls. Stability control is available.

MAJOR REDESIGN: 2001. **SAFETY EQUIPMENT:** Dual front air bags standard. Side air bags available. ABS standard. Safety-belt pretensioners standard. **DRIVE WHEELS:** Front or AWD.

Reliability history		
TROUBLE SPOTS	Toyota Highlander	
	95 96 97 98 99 00 01 02	
Engine	● ●	
Cooling	● ●	
Fuel	● ●	
Ignition	● ●	
Transmission	● ●	
Electrical	● ●	
Air-conditioning	● ●	
Suspension	● ●	
Brakes	◒ ●	
Exhaust	● ●	
Paint/trim/rust	● ●	
Body integrity	○ ●	
Power equipment	● ●	
Body hardware	● ●	
RELIABILITY VERDICT	✓ ✓	

Prices	
1995	–
1996	–
1997	–
1998	–
1999	–
2000	–
2001	$24,000-$26,000
2002	$26,000-$28,000

Crash-test results			
Model Years	Offset	Full frontal	Side
1995	–	–	–
1996	–	–	–
1997	–	–	–
1998	–	–	–
1999	–	–	–
2000	–	–	–
2001	Good	NT	NT
2002	Good	◒/◒	◒/◒

Toyota Land Cruiser

Toyota MR2

1997 model shown

1995 model shown

Prior to the introduction of the Sequoia, the Land Cruiser was Toyota's largest SUV. Expect a busy, rubbery ride in early versions. The Land Cruiser leans a lot in tight turns but holds the road well. The front seats are quite comfortable, the rear is roomy, and cargo space is ample. A 212-hp 4.5-liter inline six-cylinder engine was available through 1997. The Land Cruiser was extensively redesigned for 1998, when it gained a smooth V8 and an independent front suspension. Overall, it became much more refined and luxurious. Tricky emergency handling was improved with standard stability control for 2000. **Related model:** Lexus LX450/LX470.

MAJOR REDESIGN: 1991, 1998. **SAFETY EQUIPMENT:** Dual front air bags standard. ABS standard. Safety-belt pretensioners standard from 1998. **DRIVE WHEELS:** Permanent 4WD.

The mid-engined MR2 is quick, agile, and responsive. A turbo version delivers outstanding performance, with a precise five-speed manual transmission and excellent handling and braking. The ride is noisy and nervous, however, particularly at highway speeds. Passenger space is not a strong point, and cargo space is minuscule. The MR2 was discontinued after 1995. In 2000, the moniker was revived for an all-new convertible, the MR2 Spyder, which has a manually operated soft top and a 138-hp Four. The Spyder handles almost as well as a Porsche Boxster at a price closer to a Mazda Miata. Cargo space remains minuscule.

MAJOR REDESIGN: 1989, 2000. **SAFETY EQUIPMENT:** Dual front air bags standard. ABS available in 1995, standard from 2000. Safety-belt pretensioners standard from 2000. **DRIVE WHEELS:** Rear.

Toyota Land Cruiser

Reliability history

TROUBLE SPOTS	95	96	97	98	99	00	01	02
Engine						⊙		
Cooling						⊙		
Fuel						⊙		
Ignition						⊙		
Transmission						⊙		
Electrical	Insufficient data	Insufficient data	Insufficient data	Insufficient data	Insufficient data	⊙	Insufficient data	Insufficient data
Air conditioning						⊙		
Suspension						◑		
Brakes						⊙		
Exhaust						⊙		
Paint/trim/rust						⊙		
Body integrity						◑		
Power equipment						◑		
Body hardware						◑		
RELIABILITY VERDICT						✓		

Prices

1995	$20,000-$22,000
1996	$20,000-$22,000
1997	$24,000-$26,000
1998	More than $30,000
1999	More than $30,000
2000	More than $30,000
2001	More than $30,000
2002	More than $30,000

Crash-test results

Model years	Offset	Full-frontal	Side
1995	NT	NT	NT
1996	NT	NT	NT
1997	NT	NT	NT
1998	NT	NT	NT
1999	NT	NT	NT
2000	NT	NT	NT
2001	NT	NT	NT
2002	NT	NT	NT

Reliability history

TROUBLE SPOTS	95 96 97 98 99 00 01 02
Engine	
Cooling	
Fuel	
Ignition	NOT
Transmission	
Electrical	ENOUGH
Air conditioning	
Suspension	DATA
Brakes	
Exhaust	TO
Paint/trim/rust	
Body integrity	
Power equipment	RATE
Body hardware	
RELIABILITY VERDICT	

Prices

1995	$12,000-$14,000
1996	–
1997	–
1998	–
1999	–
2000	$20,000-$22,000
2001	$22,000-$24,000
2002	$24,000-$26,000

Crash-test results

Model years	Offset	Full-frontal	Side
1995	NT	NT	NT
1996	–	–	–
1997	–	–	–
1998	–	–	–
1999	–	–	–
2000	NT	NT	NT
2001	NT	NT	NT
2002	NT	NT	NT

MINIVAN

Toyota Previa

SMALL CAR

Toyota Prius

1997 model shown

2001 model shown

The Previa has proved to be a very reliable people-hauler. It has comfortable front seats, responsive steering, and a quiet ride. On early models, the mid-mounted four-cylinder engine was underpowered, particularly when hauling a full load. Starting in 1994, an optional supercharged version gave the Previa a welcome power boost. By 1996, the supercharger was standard. For hauling large cargo, seek a model with a removable second-row bench rather than captain's chairs. Available all-wheel drive provides extra traction in slippery conditions. The Previa was replaced after 1997 by the more traditionally designed Sienna.

MAJOR REDESIGN: 1991. **SAFETY EQUIPMENT:** Dual front air bags standard. ABS available. **DRIVE WHEELS:** Rear or AWD.

The Prius is a four-door hybrid-electric vehicle (HEV) that couples a 1.5-liter gasoline engine with a small electric motor. The ride is comfortable and handling is secure if not particularly agile. The brakes are touchy. The cabin feels roomy inside but a good deal of trunk space is robbed by the battery pack. The Prius automatically switches between the electric motor and gasoline engine, or runs on both as needed. Shifts are automatic via a responsive continuously variable transmission. Regenerative braking helps recharge the battery while coasting or braking. Acceleration is adequate. CR measured fuel economy at 41 mpg in mixed driving.

MAJOR REDESIGN: 2001. **SAFETY EQUIPMENT:** Dual front air bags standard. Side air bags available from 2002. ABS standard. Safety-belt pretensioners standard. **DRIVE WHEELS:** Front.

Reliability history — Toyota Previa

TROUBLE SPOTS	95	96	97	98	99	00	01	02
Engine	◒	●						
Cooling	◒	●						
Fuel	◒	●						
Ignition	◒	●						
Transmission	●	●						
Electrical	○	○						
Air-conditioning	○	○						
Suspension	◒	●						
Brakes	◒	●						
Exhaust	◒	●						
Paint/trim/rust	◒	●						
Body integrity	○	○						
Power equipment	●	●						
Body hardware	○	○						
RELIABILITY VERDICT	✓	✓						

(Columns 97 and 98 marked "Insufficient data")

Prices

1995	$10,000-$12,000
1996	$12,000-$14,000
1997	$14,000-$16,000
1998	–
1999	–
2000	–
2001	–
2002	–

Crash-test results

Model Years	Offset	Full frontal	Side
1995	Poor	◒/○	NT
1996	Poor	◒/○	NT
1997	Poor	◒/○	NT
1998	–	–	–
1999	–	–	–
2000	–	–	–
2001	–	–	–
2002	–	–	–

Reliability history — Toyota Prius

TROUBLE SPOTS	95	96	97	98	99	00	01	02
Engine							●	●
Cooling							●	●
Fuel							●	●
Ignition							●	●
Transmission							●	●
Electrical							◒	●
Air-conditioning							●	●
Suspension							◒	○
Brakes							●	●
Exhaust							●	●
Paint/trim/rust							●	●
Body integrity							●	●
Power equipment							●	●
Body hardware							◒	●
RELIABILITY VERDICT							✓	✓

Prices

1995	–
1996	–
1997	–
1998	–
1999	–
2000	–
2001	$18,000-$20,000
2002	$18,000-$20,000

Crash-test results

Model Years	Offset	Full frontal	Side
1995	–	–	–
1996	–	–	–
1997	–	–	–
1998	–	–	–
1999	–	–	–
2000	–	–	–
2001	NT	○/◒	NT
2002	NT	○/◒	○/○

Toyota RAV4

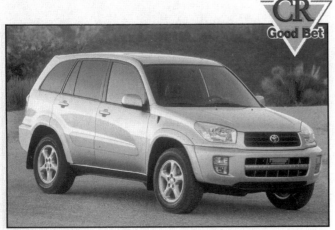

2001 model shown

Introduced for 1996, the original RAV4 ranked among the best of the small, car-based SUVs. Available in both two- and four-door versions, it delivered carlike agility and a comfortable ride, though noise from the driveline could be intrusive. Also, the engine wasn't very strong, and the rear seat was tight. A low floor made cargo loading easy. Toyota redesigned the RAV4 for 2001, dropping the two-door model from the lineup. This newer version features more interior space and improved performance. Nimble handling, excellent brakes, easy access, and good fuel economy help make this RAV4 CR's top-rated small SUV.

MAJOR REDESIGN: 1996, 2001. **SAFETY EQUIPMENT:** Dual front air bags standard. ABS available. Safety-belt pretensioners standard from 1999. **DRIVE WHEELS:** Front or AWD.

Reliability history

TROUBLE SPOTS	Toyota RAV4
	95 96 97 98 99 00 01 02
Engine	
Cooling	
Fuel	
Ignition	
Transmission	
Electrical	
Air conditioning	
Suspension	
Brakes	
Exhaust	
Paint/trim/rust	
Body integrity	
Power equipment	
Body hardware	
RELIABILITY VERDICT	✓ ✓ ✓ ✓ ✓ ✓ ✓

Prices

Year	Price
1995	–
1996	$8,000-$10,000
1997	$10,000-$12,000
1998	$12,000-$14,000
1999	$14,000-$16,000
2000	$14,000-$16,000
2001	$16,000-$18,000
2002	$18,000-$20,000

Crash-test results

Model years	Offset	Full-frontal	Side
1995	–	–	–
1996	Marg.	NT	NT
1997	Marg.	○/○	NT
1998	Marg.	●/●	NT
1999	Marg.	●/●	●/●
2000	Marg.	●/●	●/●
2001	Accept.	●/●	NT
2002	Accept.	●/●	●/●

Toyota Sequioa

2001 model shown

Introduced for 2001, the Sequoia is based on the excellent Tundra full-sized pickup. It shares the Tundra's refined 4.7-liter V8 powertrain and comes with rear- or selectable full-time four-wheel drive. The Sequoia is sized similarly to the Ford Expedition and Chevrolet Tahoe. Like those domestics, it has a third-row seat to accommodate up to eight passengers. While the Sequoia is roomier than the uplevel Land Cruiser, it doesn't ride as comfortably and has a less sophisticated four-wheel-drive system.

MAJOR REDESIGN: 2001. **SAFETY EQUIPMENT:** Dual front air bags standard. Side and head protection air bags available. ABS standard. Safety-belt pretensioners standard. **DRIVE WHEELS:** Rear or selectable 4WD.

Reliability history

TROUBLE SPOTS	Toyota Sequoia
	95 96 97 98 99 00 01 02
Engine	
Cooling	
Fuel	
Ignition	
Transmission	
Electrical	
Air conditioning	
Suspension	
Brakes	
Exhaust	
Paint/trim/rust	
Body integrity	
Power equipment	
Body hardware	
RELIABILITY VERDICT	✓ ✓

Prices

Year	Price
1995	–
1996	–
1997	–
1998	–
1999	–
2000	–
2001	More than $30,000
2002	More than $30,000

Crash-test results

Model years	Offset	Full-frontal	Side
1995	–	–	–
1996	–	–	–
1997	–	–	–
1998	–	–	–
1999	–	–	–
2000	–	–	–
2001	NT	NT	NT
2002	NT	●/●	NT

MINIVAN
Toyota Sienna

1998 model shown

A replacement for the mid-engine Previa, the more standard-design Sienna was introduced for 1998. Based on the Camry platform, the Sienna has a well-mannered suspension and refined V6 powertrain. In CR's tests, the Sienna rode quietly and handled competently. The V6 accelerated eagerly, and the transmission shifted smoothly. The front- and middle-row seats are quite comfortable; the rearmost seat is well padded but hard to access. The Sienna offers both left- and right-side sliding doors. Cargo space is less generous than in competitors such as the Honda Odyssey and Dodge Grand Caravan, but the Sienna remains a highly rated vehicle.

MAJOR REDESIGN: 1998. **SAFETY EQUIPMENT:** Dual front air bags standard. Side air bags available from 2001. ABS standard. Safety-belt pretensioners standard. **DRIVE WHEELS:** Front.

Reliability history

TROUBLE SPOTS	Toyota Sienna
	95 96 97 98 99 00 01 02
Engine	● ● ● ● ●
Cooling	● ● ● ● ●
Fuel	● ● ● ● ●
Ignition	● ● ● ● ●
Transmission	● ● ● ● ●
Electrical	◒ ◒ ● ● ●
Air-conditioning	◒ ● ● ● ●
Suspension	◒ ◒ ● ● ●
Brakes	○ ◒ ● ● ●
Exhaust	● ● ● ● ●
Paint/trim/rust	◒ ● ● ● ●
Body integrity	◒ ○ ● ◒ ●
Power equipment	● ○ ○ ◒ ●
Body hardware	● ◒ ○ ○ ◒
RELIABILITY VERDICT	✔ ✔ ✔ ✔ ✔

Prices

1995	–
1996	–
1997	–
1998	$14,000-$16,000
1999	$18,000-$20,000
2000	$20,000-$22,000
2001	$22,000-$24,000
2002	$24,000-$26,000

Crash-test results

Model Years	Offset	Full frontal	Side
1995	–	–	–
1996	–	–	–
1997	–	–	–
1998	Good	●/●	NT
1999	Good	●/●	◒/●
2000	Good	●/●	◒/●
2001	Good	●/●	◒/●
2002	Good	●/●	◒/●

SPORTS/SPORTY CAR
Toyota Supra

1995 model shown

T oyota redesigned its flagship performance coupe for 1994, transforming it into an all-out—and expensive—sports car. Compared with the model it replaced, this later Supra was a little lighter and leaner, but it still had a noisy, jarring ride. The Supra Turbo had a strong twin-turbocharged engine and a smooth-shifting six-speed manual transmission. An automatic with manual-shift capability was also offered. Steering is short on feel, but there's virtually no body lean during hard cornering. The car came well equipped and included a sophisticated traction-control system. It was discontinued in the U.S. after 1998.

MAJOR REDESIGN: 1993. **SAFETY EQUIPMENT:** Dual front air bags standard. ABS standard. **DRIVE WHEELS:** Rear.

Reliability history

TROUBLE SPOTS	
	95 96 97 98 99 00 01 02
Engine	
Cooling	
Fuel	
Ignition	NOT
Transmission	
Electrical	ENOUGH
Air-conditioning	
Suspension	DATA
Brakes	
Exhaust	
Paint/trim/rust	TO
Body integrity	
Power equipment	RATE
Body hardware	
RELIABILITY VERDICT	

Prices

1995	$22,000-$24,000
1996	$24,000-$26,000
1997	$28,000-$30,000
1998	More than $30,000
1999	–
2000	–
2001	–
2002	–

Crash-test results

Model Years	Offset	Full frontal	Side
1995	NT	NT	NT
1996	NT	NT	NT
1997	NT	NT	NT
1998	NT	NT	NT
1999	–	–	–
2000	–	–	–
2001	–	–	–
2002	–	–	–

Toyota T100, Tundra

2000 model shown

The T100, produced from 1993 through 1998, was Toyota's first large pickup but it was underpowered, underequipped, and overpriced. The Indiana-built Tundra, which debuted in 1999 as a 2000 model, has many pluses. It has a standard 190-hp V6 engine and offers an optional Lexus-derived V8 that is both smooth and powerful. Both engines attain decent fuel economy. The truck also handles fairly well, its ride is comfortable, and its cabin is very quiet. Extended-cab models have two real rear doors. The extended cab's rear bench, however, is cramped for adults.

MAJOR REDESIGN: 1993, 2000. **SAFETY EQUIPMENT:** Driver air bag only on T100. Dual front air bags standard on Tundra. ABS available. Safety-belt pretensioners standard from 2000. **DRIVE WHEELS:** Rear or part-time 4WD.

Reliability history

TROUBLE SPOTS	Toyota T100, Tundra 2WD							
	95	96	97	98	99	00	01	02
Engine				Insufficient data				
Cooling								
Fuel								
Ignition								
Transmission								
Electrical								
Air conditioning								
Suspension								
Brakes								
Exhaust								
Paint/trim/rust								
Body integrity								
Power equipment								
Body hardware								
RELIABILITY VERDICT	✓	✓	✓			✓	✓	✓

Prices

1995	$10,000–$12,000
1996	$12,000–$14,000
1997	$12,000–$14,000
1998	$14,000–$16,000
1999	–
2000	$20,000–$22,000
2001	$22,000–$24,000
2002	$24,000–$26,000

Crash-test results

Model years	Offset	Full-frontal	Side
1995	NT	◐/◕	NT
1996	NT	◐/◕	NT
1997	NT	◐/◕	NT
1998	NT	◐/◕	NT
1999	–	–	–
2000	Good	◐/○	NT
2001	Good	○/○	NT
2002	Good	◐/◐	●/NA

Toyota Tacoma

1998 model shown

Introduced for 1995, the compact Tacoma pickup is available in regular-, extended-, and, since 2001, crew-cab models, and with a choice of two- or four-wheel-drive. Two four-cylinder engines—a 2.4- and a 2.7-liter—are offered, along with the more desirable 3.4-liter, 190-hp V6. Unlike most other Toyota offerings, the Tacoma was unimpressive in our tests. It jitters uncomfortably on smooth roads, and kicks and snaps on poor ones. The steering is slow and numb. Stopping distances are long without the optional antilock brakes, which can be hard to find. The cabin is quiet, but the seats are low and lack support.

MAJOR REDESIGN: 1995. **SAFETY EQUIPMENT:** Driver air bag standard; passenger side from 1998. ABS available. Safety-belt pretensioners standard from 1999. **DRIVE WHEELS:** Rear or part-time 4WD.

Reliability history

TROUBLE SPOTS	Toyota Tacoma 2WD							
	95	96	97	98	99	00	01	02
Engine								
Cooling								
Fuel								
Ignition								
Transmission								
Electrical								
Air conditioning								
Suspension								
Brakes								
Exhaust								
Paint/trim/rust								
Body integrity								
Power equipment								
Body hardware								
RELIABILITY VERDICT	✓	✓	✓	✓	✓	✓	✓	✓

Prices

1995	$10,000–$12,000
1996	$10,000–$12,000
1997	$12,000–$14,000
1998	$12,000–$14,000
1999	$14,000–$16,000
2000	$16,000–$18,000
2001	$18,000–$20,000
2002	$18,000–$20,000

Crash-test results

Model years	Offset	Full-frontal	Side
1995	NT	◐/○	NT
1996	NT	◐/○	NT
1997	NT	●/○	NT
1998	Accept.	◐/○	NT
1999	Accept.	◐/◐	●/NA
2000	Accept.	◐/◐	●/NA
2001	Accept.	○/◐	○/NA
2002	Accept.	○/◐	○/NA

Toyota Tercel, Paseo

Volkswagen EuroVan

1995 model shown

1999 model shown

Long serving as Toyota's entry-level model, the Tercel is the quintessential economy car: relatively inexpensive to buy and sparing with fuel. It's available in sedan and coupe versions. All models come with a thrifty four-cylinder engine but a coarse ride. The seats are firm and nicely shaped, but space is in short supply. Though redesigned for 1995, the Tercel changed surprisingly little. These later models still have a rough, noisy ride, a cramped rear seat, and mediocre brakes. The engine was lively, and reliability has been very good. The Tercel was dropped after 1998. The Paseo was a short-lived coupe version.

MAJOR REDESIGN: Tercel-1991, 1995; Paseo-1992, 1996. **SAFETY EQUIPMENT:** Dual front air bags standard. ABS available. **DRIVE WHEELS:** Front.

Designed as a European commercial delivery van, the original EuroVan never quite fit into America's mainstream minivan market. It was pulled from the U.S. market after 1993, but returned for 1999 with a powerful V6 engine, a smoother automatic transmission, and updated controls. Handling is commendable for such a large box, and the ride is fairly well controlled. Available features like a kitchenette, a camper-style roof, and a two-person bed enhance the EuroVan's long-term habitability. Significant updates for 2001 included an electronic stability-control system and a 24-valve, 201-hp version of the V6.

MAJOR REDESIGN: 1993, 1999, 2001. **SAFETY EQUIPMENT:** Dual front air bags standard from 1999. ABS and safety-belt pretensioners standard from 1999. **DRIVE WHEELS:** Front.

Toyota Tercel, Paseo

Reliability history

TROUBLE SPOTS	Toyota Tercel
	95 96 97 98 99 00 01 02
Engine	○ Insufficient data Insufficient data Insufficient data
Cooling	○
Fuel	◐
Ignition	◉
Transmission	◉
Electrical	○
Air-conditioning	◐
Suspension	◉
Brakes	○
Exhaust	◉
Paint/trim/rust	◐
Body integrity	◐
Power equipment	◉
Body hardware	◐
RELIABILITY VERDICT	✓

Prices

1995	$4,000-$6,000
1996	$6,000-$8,000
1997	$6,000-$8,000
1998	$6,000-$8,000
1999	-
2000	-
2001	-
2002	-

Crash-test results

Model Years	Offset	Full frontal	Side
1995	NT	○/◐	NT
1996	NT	○/◐	NT
1997	NT	◐/◐	○/◐
1998	NT	NT	○/◐
1999	-	-	-
2000	-	-	-
2001	-	-	-
2002	-	-	-

Volkswagen EuroVan

Reliability history

TROUBLE SPOTS	95 96 97 98 99 00 01 02
Engine	
Cooling	
Fuel	
Ignition	NOT
Transmission	
Electrical	ENOUGH
Air-conditioning	
Suspension	DATA
Brakes	
Exhaust	
Paint/trim/rust	TO
Body integrity	
Power equipment	RATE
Body hardware	
RELIABILITY VERDICT	

Prices

1995	-
1996	-
1997	-
1998	-
1999	$16,000-$18,000
2000	$20,000-$22,000
2001	$22,000-$24,000
2002	$24,000-$26,000

Crash-test results

Model Years	Offset	Full frontal	Side
1995	-	-	-
1996	-	-	-
1997	-	-	-
1998	-	-	-
1999	NT	NT	NT
2000	NT	NT	NT
2001	NT	NT	NT
2002	NT	NT	NT

Volkswagen Golf

1999 model shown

The Golf can be found in two- and four-door hatch-back versions, as well as a convertible. In general, the Golf exudes a feeling of precision and solidity unusual for a small car. In 1994, a significantly updated line was introduced, increasing size and overall refinement. A responsive Four provided base power, but a stronger V6 was available in top models. The Golf was redesigned again for 1999, and became quieter and more comfortable, with a higher-quality interior. A turbocharged Four was introduced a year later. A fuel-sipping turbodiesel Four is also available.

MAJOR REDESIGN: 1994, 1999. **SAFETY EQUIPMENT:** Dual front air bags standard. Side air bags standard from 1999. Head protection air bags standard from 2001. ABS available, standard from 1999. Safety-belt pretensioners standard from 1996. **DRIVE WHEELS:** Front.

Reliability history

TROUBLE SPOTS — Volkswagen Golf 4 cyl.

Trouble Spots	95	96	97	98	99	00	01	02
Engine						○	●	
Cooling						●	●	
Fuel						●	○	
Ignition						●	●	
Transmission						●	●	
Electrical	Insufficient data	Insufficient data	Insufficient data	Insufficient data	Insufficient data	●	○	Insufficient data
Air conditioning						●	●	
Suspension						●	●	
Brakes						●	●	
Exhaust						●	●	
Paint/trim/rust						●	◐	
Body integrity						○	○	
Power equipment						◐	○	
Body hardware						◐	○	
RELIABILITY VERDICT								

Prices

Year	Price
1995	$6,000-$8,000
1996	$6,000-$8,000
1997	$8,000-$10,000
1998	$8,000-$10,000
1999	$10,000-$12,000
2000	$14,000-$16,000
2001	$14,000-$16,000
2002	$14,000-$16,000

Crash-test results

Model years	Offset	Full-frontal	Side
1995	Marg.	O/O	NT
1996	Marg.	O/O	NT
1997	Marg.	O/O	NT
1998	Marg.	NT	NT
1999	Good	NT	NT
2000	Good	●/●	NT
2001	Good	●/●	NT
2002	Good	●/●	NT

Volkswagen Jetta

1999 model shown

The Jetta is a practical car with a responsive 2.0-liter four-cylinder engine, a supple ride, and a comfortable interior. The sporty GLX packs a powerful V6, but even the plainer GL and GLS versions offer good handling and responsive steering. A 1999 redesign improved an already capable car. It picked up a host of standard safety features and well-designed interior touches, as well as a quieter and more comfortable ride. The rear seat is tight. A wagon model was added for 2001. Four, turbo-Four, turbodiesel, and V6 engines are available.

MAJOR REDESIGN: 1994, 1999. **SAFETY EQUIPMENT:** Dual front air bags standard. Side air bags available in 1998, standard from 1999. Head protection air bags standard from 2001. ABS available, standard from 1999. Safety-belt pretensioners standard from 1996. **DRIVE WHEELS:** Front.

Reliability history

TROUBLE SPOTS — Volkswagen Jetta 4 cyl.

Trouble Spots	95	96	97	98	99	00	01	02
Engine	◐	○	●	◐	●	●	◐	●
Cooling	○	◐	●	●	●	●	●	◐
Fuel	○	○	○	○	●	●	●	◐
Ignition	○	◐	◐	◐	●	◐	◐	●
Transmission	◐	○	◐	◐	●	●	◐	◐
Electrical	●	●	●	●	●	◐	◐	●
Air conditioning	○	○	◐	◐	●	●	●	◐
Suspension	◐	◐	◐	◐	●	●	◐	◐
Brakes	○	◐	○	◐	◐	◐	◐	●
Exhaust	○	◐	◐	◐	●	●	◐	●
Paint/trim/rust	●	●	◐	○	○	◐	○	●
Body integrity	○	○	○	○	○	○	○	◐
Power equipment	●	●	◐	◐	◐	◐	○	●
Body hardware	●	●	◐	◐	◐	○	○	●
RELIABILITY VERDICT								

Prices

Year	Price
1995	$6,000-$8,000
1996	$6,000-$8,000
1997	$8,000-$10,000
1998	$10,000-$12,000
1999	$10,000-$12,000
2000	$14,000-$16,000
2001	$14,000-$16,000
2002	$16,000-$18,000

Crash-test results

Model years	Offset	Full-frontal	Side
1995	Marg.	O/O	NT
1996	Marg.	O/O	NT
1997	Marg.	O/O	NT
1998	Marg.	NT	O/●
1999	Good	NT	O/●
2000	Good	●/●	●/●
2001	Good	●/●	●/●
2002	Good	●/●	●/●

SMALL CAR
Volkswagen New Beetle

1998 model shown

The New Beetle, introduced in early 1998, is a thoroughly modern car that bears a nostalgic family resemblance to the long-lived VW "Bug" discontinued in the U.S. in the 1970s. In our tests, we found the car's ride to be good, and its handling nimble. The 2.0-liter Four accelerates adequately and runs economically; a more economical diesel is also offered. The front seats are firm and supportive. The rear is cramped for passengers, though the seats fold for increased cargo space. The New Beetle has performed notably well in crash tests. A quicker turbocharged model was added for 1999.

MAJOR REDESIGN: 1998. **SAFETY EQUIPMENT:** Dual front, and side air bags standard. Head protection air bags standard from 2001. ABS available in 1998, standard from 1999. Safety-belt pretensioners standard. **DRIVE WHEELS:** Front.

Reliability history

TROUBLE SPOTS	Volkswagen New Beetle							
	95	96	97	98	99	00	01	02
Engine				◖	◖	◖	●	●
Cooling				◖	◖	◖	●	●
Fuel				◖	●	◖	○	●
Ignition				◖	◖	◖	●	●
Transmission				◖	◖	◖	●	●
Electrical				●	●	●	○	●
Air-conditioning				○	○	◖	●	●
Suspension				◖	◖	◖	●	●
Brakes				○	○	○	●	●
Exhaust				●	◖	◖	●	●
Paint/trim/rust				○	◖	◖	●	●
Body integrity				◖	○	○	◖	●
Power equipment				●	●	◖	○	●
Body hardware				●	●	●	○	●
RELIABILITY VERDICT								✓

Prices

1995	–
1996	–
1997	–
1998	$10,000-$12,000
1999	$12,000-$14,000
2000	$14,000-$16,000
2001	$14,000-$16,000
2002	$16,000-$18,000

Crash-test results

Model Years	Offset	Full frontal	Side
1995	–	–	–
1996	–	–	–
1997	–	–	–
1998	Good	NT	NT
1999	Good	◖/◗	●/○
2000	Good	◖/◗	●/○
2001	Good	◖/◗	●/○
2002	Good	◖/◗	●/○

FAMILY CAR
Volkswagen Passat

1998 model shown

The early-1990's Passat was available as both a four-door sedan and a wagon. The optional V6 was smooth and strong, but the four-speed automatic was reluctant to downshift. The Passat was completely redesigned for 1998, and a turbocharged 1.8-liter four-cylinder engine became standard. The current-generation car is related to the Audi A4 and A6, which is apparent in its attention to detail and its refinement. V6 or Four, wagon or sedan, the Passat is a top choice—comfortable, roomy, refined, and agile. 2001 brought styling revisions, more power, and additional safety features.

MAJOR REDESIGN: 1995, 1998. **SAFETY EQUIPMENT:** Dual front air bags standard. Side air bags standard from 1998. Head protection air bags standard from 2001. ABS available, standard from 1998. Safety-belt pretensioners standard. **DRIVE WHEELS:** Front or AWD.

Reliability history

TROUBLE SPOTS	Volkswagen Passat 4 cyl.							
	95	96	97	98	99	00	01	02
Engine	Insufficient data	Insufficient data	Insufficient data	○	◖	●	●	●
Cooling				◖	◖	●	●	●
Fuel				○	◖	◖	●	●
Ignition				◖	◖	●	●	●
Transmission				◖	◖	●	●	◖
Electrical				◖	◖	○	○	●
Air-conditioning				◖	●	●	●	●
Suspension				◖	●	●	●	●
Brakes				○	○	◖	●	●
Exhaust				●	●	◖	●	●
Paint/trim/rust				◖	◖	●	●	●
Body integrity				◖	◖	◖	◖	●
Power equipment				●	◖	○	◖	●
Body hardware				◖	○	○	○	◖
RELIABILITY VERDICT					✓	✓	✓	✓

Prices

1995	$8,000-$10,000
1996	$10,000-$12,000
1997	$10,000-$12,000
1998	$18,000-$20,000
1999	$20,000-$22,000
2000	$20,000-$22,000
2001	$20,000-$22,000
2002	$22,000-$24,000

Crash-test results

Model Years	Offset	Full frontal	Side
1995	Poor	◖/◗	NT
1996	Poor	◖/◗	NT
1997	Poor	◖/◗	NT
1998	Good	NT	NT
1999	Good	NT	NT
2000	Good	◖/◗	◖/◗
2001	Good	◖/◗	◖/◗
2002	Good	◖/◗	◖/◗

Volvo 850, S70/V70

Volvo 960, S90/V90

1999 model shown

1998 model shown

The 850, introduced for 1993, was offered as a four-door sedan or a wagon. The standard five-cylinder engine was available with a turbocharger, which improved acceleration dramatically. Handling was predictable. Large, comfortable front seats only partly made up for the stiff, jiggly ride. In 1998, the sedan changed its name to S70 and the wagon became the V70. From 1998, AWD versions were available, along with a sporty R model and an SUV-inspired XC (Cross Country) wagon. Overall, the midlevel GLT is our version of choice. The S60 replaced the S70 for 2001.

MAJOR REDESIGN: 1993, 1998, 2001. **SAFETY EQUIPMENT:** Dual front air bags standard. Side air bags standard from 1996. Head protection air bags standard from 2001. ABS standard. Safety-belt pretensioners standard. **DRIVE WHEELS:** Front or AWD.

The 960—and, later, the 90-Series—served as Volvo's flagship car line throughout the 1990's. The 960, available as a sedan or wagon, has a 2.9-liter inline six-cylinder engine that delivers enthusiastic performance. Handling is predictable, though not nimble, and the ride is smooth. The 960 sedan provides exceptional comfort for five and a huge trunk. The 1995 model received new styling and suspension changes to improve both handling and ride. In 1997, the cars were renamed the S90 (sedan) and V90 (wagon). They were replaced by the S80 sedan for 1999, when the wagon version was discontinued.

MAJOR REDESIGN: 1996. **SAFETY EQUIPMENT:** Dual front air bags standard. Side air bags standard from 1996. ABS standard. Safety-belt pretensioners standard. **DRIVE WHEELS:** Rear.

Reliability history — Volvo 850, V70 Cross Country

TROUBLE SPOTS	95	96	97	98	99	00	01	02
Engine								
Cooling								
Fuel								
Ignition								
Transmission								
Electrical								
Air conditioning								
Suspension								
Brakes								
Exhaust								
Paint/trim/rust								
Body integrity								
Power equipment								
Body hardware								
RELIABILITY VERDICT	✓	✓	✓				✓	✓

Insufficient data

Prices — Volvo 850, S70/V70

1995	$12,000–$14,000
1996	$14,000–$16,000
1997	$16,000–$18,000
1998	$16,000–$18,000
1999	$18,000–$20,000
2000	$22,000–$24,000
2001	$26,000–$28,000
2002	More than $30,000

Crash-test results

Model years	Offset	Full-frontal	Side
1995	Good	⊘/○	NT
1996	Good	⊘/○	NT
1997	Good	⊘/○	⊖/NA
1998	Good	⊘/○	⊖/NA
1999	Good	⊘/○	⊖/NA
2000	Good	⊘/○	⊖/NA
2001	NT	NT	NT
2002	NT	NT	NT

Reliability history — Volvo 960, S90/V90

TROUBLE SPOTS	95	96	97	98	99	00	01	02
Engine								
Cooling								
Fuel								
Ignition								
Transmission								
Electrical								
Air conditioning								
Suspension								
Brakes								
Exhaust								
Paint/trim/rust								
Body integrity								
Power equipment								
Body hardware								
RELIABILITY VERDICT	✓							

Prices — Volvo 960, S90/V90

Year	Price
1995	$10,000–$12,000
1996	$12,000–$14,000
1997	$14,000–$16,000
1998	$16,000–$18,000
1999	—
2000	—
2001	—
2002	—

Crash-test results

Model years	Offset	Full-frontal	Side
1995	NT	NT	NT
1996	NT	NT	NT
1997	NT	⊘/○	NT
1998	NT	⊘/○	NT
1999	—	—	—
2000	—	—	—
2001	—	—	—
2002	—	—	—

Volvo C70

Volvo S40/V40

1998 model shown

2000 model shown

New in 1998, the C70 coupe was based on Volvo's front-drive 70-Series. It performed well, with nicely weighted steering and good brakes. Initially the engine was a fairly unresponsive 2.3-liter turbocharged five-cylinder that produced 236 horsepower. In 1999, a 2.4-liter, 190-hp turbo Five was introduced. Despite its lower total output, that engine felt more responsive in everyday driving. Both automatic and manual transmissions were offered. Handling was capable and braking was good but the ride was stiff. A premium sound system was a noteworthy option. A convertible was introduced in the latter part of the 1998 model year.

MAJOR REDESIGN: 1998. **SAFETY EQUIPMENT:** Dual front air bags standard. Side air bags standard. ABS standard. Safety-belt pretensioners standard. **DRIVE WHEELS:** Front.

The S40 sedan and V40 wagon debuted in the U.S. for 2000, although the car had been available in Europe since 1996. It's Volvo's smallest and least expensive model. These vehicles are the result of a joint venture between Volvo and Mitsubishi and are manufactured in the Netherlands. The 40 Series comes well equipped, with antilock brakes and other safety features. It handled well in CR tests but didn't feel sporty, and the ride was stiff. Engine noise from the turbocharged Four intruded into the cabin during acceleration. The front seats were firm and comfortable; the rear was cramped.

MAJOR REDESIGN: 2000. **SAFETY EQUIPMENT:** Dual front and side air bags standard. Head protection air bags standard from 2001. ABS and safety-belt pretensioners standard. **DRIVE WHEELS:** Front.

Volvo C70

Reliability history		Prices	
TROUBLE SPOTS	95 96 97 98 99 00 01 02	1995	–
		1996	–
		1997	–
Engine		1998	$20,000-$22,000
Cooling		1999	$24,000-$26,000
Fuel		2000	$28,000-$30,000
Ignition	NOT	2001	More than $30,000
Transmission		2002	More than $30,000
Electrical	ENOUGH		
Air-conditioning			
Suspension	DATA		
Brakes			
Exhaust	TO		
Paint/trim/rust			
Body integrity	RATE		
Power equipment			
Body hardware			
RELIABILITY VERDICT			

Crash-test results			
Model Years	Offset	Full frontal	Side
1995	–	–	–
1996	–	–	–
1997	–	–	–
1998	NT	NT	NT
1999	NT	NT	NT
2000	NT	NT	NT
2001	NT	NT	NT
2002	NT	NT	NT

Volvo S40/V40

Reliability history		Prices	
TROUBLE SPOTS	Volvo S40/V40 95 96 97 98 99 00 01 02	1995	–
		1996	–
		1997	–
Engine	◐ ◐	1998	–
Cooling	◐ ◐	1999	–
Fuel	○ ◐	2000	$16,000-$18,000
Ignition	◐ ◐	2001	$20,000-$22,000
Transmission	◐ ◐	2002	$22,000-$24,000
Electrical	◐ ○		
Air-conditioning	◐ ◐		
Suspension	○ ◐		
Brakes	● ○		
Exhaust	◐ ◐		
Paint/trim/rust	◐ ◐		
Body integrity	○ ◐		
Power equipment	◐ ◐		
Body hardware	○ ◐		
RELIABILITY VERDICT	✔		

Insufficient data

Crash-test results			
Model Years	Offset	Full frontal	Side
1995	–	–	–
1996	–	–	–
1997	–	–	–
1998	–	–	–
1999	–	–	–
2000	NT	NT	NT
2001	NT	NT	NT
2002	Good	NT	NT

Volvo S60

2001 model shown

Introduced for 2001, the midlevel S60 is smaller and more boldly styled than the boxy S70 sedan it replaced. The ride, though improved, is still a bit jiggly, and handling is not really agile or sporty. With its 197-hp turbocharged five-cylinder engine, the 2.4T version provides fairly brisk acceleration. CR also drove the higher-performance T5, which didn't feel as quick as its 247-hp rating would suggest. Braking is strong, though the pedal feels touchy. The cabin is quiet, the climate-control system excellent, and the seats very comfortable, though the rear is cramped. The unintuitive audio controls are a nuisance. An AWD option arrived for 2002.

MAJOR REDESIGN: 2001. **SAFETY EQUIPMENT:** Dual front, side, and head protection air bags standard. ABS standard. Safety-belt pretensioners standard. **DRIVE WHEELS:** Front. AWD available from 2002.

Reliability history

TROUBLE SPOTS	Volvo S60							
	95	96	97	98	99	00	01	02
Engine							●	●
Cooling							●	●
Fuel							●	●
Ignition							●	●
Transmission							●	●
Electrical							○	◐
Air conditioning							●	●
Suspension							●	●
Brakes							●	●
Exhaust							●	●
Paint/trim/rust							◐	●
Body integrity							◐	●
Power equipment							◐	●
Body hardware							○	●
RELIABILITY VERDICT							✓	✓

Prices

1995	–
1996	–
1997	–
1998	–
1999	–
2000	–
2001	$24,000-$26,000
2002	$26,000-$28,000

Crash-test results

Model years	Offset	Full-frontal	Side
1995	–	–	–
1996	–	–	–
1997	–	–	–
1998	–	–	–
1999	–	–	–
2000	–	–	–
2001	Good	◐/◐	●/◐
2002	Good	◐/◐	●/◐

Volvo S80

1999 model shown

Volvo's current flagship debuted for 1999. The front-wheel-drive S80 has lots of interior room and many neat little details. You can expect a comfortable ride and fairly nimble handling. The numerous modern safety systems include side-curtain air bags and integrated whiplash protection in the front seats. The optional premium audio system offers exceptional sound, but its controls are awkward. The standard engine is a lively 2.9-liter inline six-cylinder mounted transversely. With 268 hp, the turbocharged T6 version offers even more abundant and effortless acceleration. Reliability has been disappointing.

MAJOR REDESIGN: 1999. **SAFETY EQUIPMENT:** Dual front, side, and head protection air bags standard. ABS standard. Safety-belt pretensioners standard. **DRIVE WHEELS:** Front.

Reliability history

TROUBLE SPOTS	Volvo S80							
	95	96	97	98	99	00	01	02
Engine					●	●	●	
Cooling					○	●	●	
Fuel					◐	○	●	
Ignition					●	●	●	
Transmission					●	●	◐	
Electrical					●	◐	◐	
Air conditioning					●	●	●	
Suspension					○	◐	◐	
Brakes					○	◐	●	
Exhaust					●	●	●	
Paint/trim/rust					●	●	◐	
Body integrity					○	○	◐	
Power equipment					◐	●	○	
Body hardware					◐	○	○	
RELIABILITY VERDICT								

Insufficient data

Prices

1995	–
1996	–
1997	–
1998	–
1999	$22,000-$24,000
2000	$24,000-$26,000
2001	$28,000-$30,000
2002	More than $30,000

Crash-test results

Model years	Offset	Full-frontal	Side
1995	–	–	–
1996	–	–	–
1997	–	–	–
1998	–	–	–
1999	NT	NT	◐/◐
2000	Good	NT	◐/◐
2001	Good	◐/◐	◐/◐
2002	Good	◐/◐	◐/◐

Recalls & Technical Service Bulletins

ABOUT SAFETY RECALLS

For more than 20 years the federal government has operated a vehicle recall system in co-operation with the auto industry, principally for safety-related defects. The National Highway Traffic Safety Administration (NHTSA) oversees the program. Sometimes cars are recalled for emissions problems, under a separate program administered by the U.S. Environmental Protection Administration.

When a defect is identified, auto companies have to alert all the vehicle's current owners and "recall" the defective vehicle for a free repair. In some rare cases, the manufacturer has had to buy back the entire vehicle. Vehicle owners have eight years from the time the defect is determined to have the repair made free of charge.

Since the program started, more than 140 million cars and trucks have been recalled for safety reasons. The majority of recalls are initiated by the manufacturers themselves, who may note a defect from an upsurge of warranty work performed by their dealers. Others are initiated by NHTSA, in response to consumer complaints. Most of the recalls that involved large numbers of vehicles have been prompted by the government.

Still, nearly all recalls are called "voluntary," even the ones initiated by the government. Once in a while a carmaker balks when the government suggests to them that they recall a group of their cars. Those cases normally wind up in court.

Other ways carmakers can remedy a problem are with a "service action" or an "information campaign." The manufacturer might persuade the government that a formal recall is unnecessary. Basically, the manufacturer contacts the affected vehicle's owners and tells them they can come in and have a part fixed if it's causing trouble, or just to be on the safe side.

Service actions initiated by automakers are common enough, but such programs negotiated by the government in lieu of a safety recall are very rare. When they do hap-

TO REPORT A SAFETY DEFECT

Call NHTSA's Toll-free hotline: 888-327-4236. For the latest recall information you can call NHTSA's Traffic Safety Hotline, at 888-327-4236. Have as much identifying information about the car as you can, including make, model, year, and VIN number. It's printed on a strip of metal on the driver's side of the dashboard, where the dashboard meets the windshield. The vehicle's date of manufacturer can help, too. It's usually located on a label on the door jamb of the driver's door.

Recall information is also available at NHTSA's web site, *www.NHTSA.DOT.gov*. You can use NHTSA's web page to find recall information, to report safety problems you've had with your own car, and to find crash-test scores and other information. NHTSA's web site also has a handy database of "Consumer Complaints" that you can search by make, model, and year. That listing summarizes individual problems people have reported.

Complaints from consumers are one of the government's primary means of spotting a defect trend that might lead to a recall.

If you discover that a recall did apply to the car you're considering buying, find out if the repair was ever made. Many people ignore recall notices if they think the problem is unimportant. Some people are never notified. Manufacturers keep track of the current owners of their cars by using information supplied by state motor-vehicle departments. It's not uncommon for a car to slip through the cracks.

The vehicle's owner may have a record of recall repairs. If not, check with a car dealer that services that brand. You may even be able to do this over the phone. The service department normally has access to computerized records of which cars have had recall work done. You'll need the car's VIN to see if the repair was made.

---

pen, they tend to be notorious. One case involved Chrysler's 1984-1994 minivans. Some of those vans had a rear-liftgate latch that could give way too easily in a rear-end collision, allowing occupants to be thrown from the vehicle. After months of wrangling, the government agreed to let Chrysler perform a "service action" which amounted to a recall in all but name. Chrysler embarked on a program to alert owners and offer a stronger replacement for the van latch, at no charge.

If you're buying a used car, check to see if it was ever recalled. Then ask the seller if the repair was made and for a written receipt for verification.

On the following pages we list important safety-related recalls applying to passenger vehicles, by make, for 1995-2002 models.

HIDDEN WARRANTIES AND FREE REPAIRS

Besides safety recalls, there is a far longer list of known problems that manufacturers have decided to fix free of charge. For non-safety-related defects, a manufacturer will frequently adjust or lengthen the warranty on a part that's proved troublesome. Federal law doesn't require that owners be notified of such policies. Instead, manufacturers alert their dealers by means of so-called Technical Service Bulletins. TSBs are also issued to alert service departments to updated repair techniques and other technical advice.

The TSBs spell out any special remedies the manufacturer is prepared to offer, such as free or discounted parts and labor.

The trouble with these "secret warranties" is that you often have to ask for them to get them. However, they are public documents, by law.

How to find Technical Service Bulletins

You can find all TSBs relating to any car on NHTSA's web site (*www.nhtsa.dot.gov/cars/problems*). Scanning any TSBs on your car could point the way to a free fix. NHTSA gives only summaries of the TSBs on its web site, though. The full text is available by mail for a nominal copying charge.

Another option is to print out the summary, which has identifying numbers on it, and take it to a franchised dealer. The service department will usually look it up for you on request.

You might also check with the nonprofit Center for Auto Safety (*www.autosafety.org*), which keeps TSB information and can advise on other actions you can take. Finally you can check with an organization called Lemon-Aid (*www.lemonaidcars.com*). The site lists a variety of hidden warranties and defects on selected models.

VEHICLE RECALLS

On the following pages, you'll find a list of recent recalls on 1995 to 2002 models, as published monthly in CONSUMER REPORTS through December 2002.

Acura

'96-99 Acura (various models)
Bolt in transmission case could fall out, resulting in sudden loss of power to wheels. Also, vehicle could roll even though shifter is placed in "park." Either condition could cause accident.
Models: 96,616 cars made 12/95-4/98 including '96-99 3.5RL and '96-98 3.2TL.
What to do: Have dealer install redesigned bolt.

'98 Acura CL and Honda Accord
Vehicle could roll away even when shifter is in park.
Models: 33,966 cars made 9/97-1/98.
What to do: Have dealer install collar on transmission parking pawl.

Audi

'93-95 Audi 90, 100, and Cabriolet
Fuel injectors could leak and cause engine fire.
Models: 37,200 cars with V6 engine made 1/92-7/95.
What to do: Have dealer replace fuel injectors.

'94-96 Audis (various models)
Electrical accessories, including lights, wipers, turn-signal indicators, power windows, and air-conditioner could malfunction when engine is started.
Models: 24,000 cars made 1/94-12/95 including the following models: 90, 100, A6, Cabriolet, S4, and S6.
What to do: Have dealer replace ignition switch.

'95-97 Audi (various models)
Driver's-side air bag could deploy suddenly, possibly causing injury.
Models: 39,300 cars made 7/94-9/96, including Audi 90, Cabriolet, A4, A6, and A8. In low humidity, static electricity could trigger air bag when driver touches steering wheel.
What to do: Have dealer install ground wire on driver's-side air bag.

'98 Audi A4 and A6 and Volkswagen Passat
Engine backfire during cold start could dislodge and break air screen in airflow meter and prevent engine from slowing fully when accelerator is released.
Models: 19,800 cars made 2/97-2/98.
What to do: Have dealer install ring to secure air screen.

'98-00 Audi A6
Fuel gauge could read full even though tank is running dry.
Models: 48,500 cars made 8/98-11/99. Hazard exists because sulfur in fuel may interact with certain gasoline additives. If that happens, sulfur deposits could confound the fuel- sending units, causing the incorrect reading.
What to do: Have dealer replace all three sending units in fuel tank.

BMW

'88-95 BMWs (various models)
If engine overheats, cooling system could spew hot coolant into passenger compartment.
Models: 340,000 cars made 1/88-11/94 including: '88-95 M5, 735i, 735iA, 735iLA, 740iA, 740iLA, 750iLA, 840CiA,850Ci, 850CiA, 850CSi, 850iA; '89-95 525i, 525iA, 525iTA, 530i, 530iA, 530iTA, 540i, 540iA; '92-95 M3, 318C, 318iCA, 318i, 318iA, 318is, 318iSA, 325i, 325iA, 325ic, 325iCA, 325is, and 325isA.
What to do: Have dealer install redesigned radiator cap.

'90-95 BMWs (various models)
Brake lights may be lit continuously or not at all.
Models: 180,000 cars made 1/90-3/94, including '90-92 535i, 735i, 735iL, and 750i; '90-94 525i; '92-94 325i, 325iS, and 525iT; '93-94 740i and 740iL; '94 325iC, 530i, 530iT, and 540i; and '95 M3.
What to do: Have dealer replace brake-light switch.

'94-95 BMW 525i, 525iA, and 525iTA
Double-locking feature could prevent occupants from opening windows and

doors and exiting car, and would prevent engine from starting.
Models: 2,180 cars made 1-8/94.
What to do: Have dealer replace general control module.

'95 BMW 318iC and 318iCA
Label in door jamb overstates car's vehicle load and seating capacity. Overloading could damage tires or mechanical components and cause accident.
Models: 5,200 sedans and convertibles made 1/94-3/95.
What to do: If you don't get revised label by mail, contact dealer.

'95 BMW 740i and 740iL, and '95-96 750iL
Fuel leak could cause fire hazard.
Models: 18,000 cars made 9/94-10/95.
What to do: Have dealer replace two fuel hoses, four metal fuel lines, and clamps.

'95-97 BMW 740i, 740iL, and 750iL
Front springs could break and cause loss of control.
Models: 29,000 cars made 9/94-8/96.
What to do: Have dealer replace front springs and lower spring mounts.

'97-99 BMW M3
Side air bags and other safety systems could deploy if car strikes curb or pothole, causing possible loss of vehicle control. Also, electrical system could malfunction, resulting in inability to restart engine after stopping.
Models: 17,000 cars made 3/97-8/99.
What to do: Have dealer reprogram central computer-control module that regulates performance of all occupant-protection systems.

'99 BMW 323i and 328i
Air bags could deploy inadvertently, causing driver to lose control and crash.
Models: 32,500 cars made 6/98-3/99.
What to do: Have dealer reprogram central computer control module regulating occupant-protection systems.

'01 BMW cars (various models)
Engine auxiliary/cooling fan could fail, resulting in overheating and, possibly, fire.

Models: 22,345 cars made 11/00 to 4/01, including 7 Series, 3 Series, X5, and Z8.
What to do: Have dealer replace engine auxiliary/cooling fan

'01 BMW cars (various models)

Cooling fan could fail, resulting in engine overheating and, possibly, fire.
Models: 22,345 cars made 11/00 to 4/01, including 7 Series; 3 Series; X5; and Z8.
What to do: Have dealer replace engine auxiliary/cooling fan.

Buick

'89-96 Buicks, Chevrolets, Oldsmobiles, and Pontiacs

Rear outboard safety belts may not hold in crash.
Models: 2.2 million cars made 4/88-8/95, including '89-96 Buick Century, '89-90 Chevrolet Celebrity, '89-96 Oldsmobile Ciera, and '89-91 Pontiac 6000.
What to do: Have dealer install new bolt and thread-locking adhesive for each belt. Dealer will also apply washer-like patch to each anchor point to reduce noise as belt pivots.

'93-95 Buick Regal

Clear bulbs instead of amber ones may have been installed in side-marker lights. That could confuse other drivers.
Models: 39,849 cars made 6/91-2/95.
What to do: Have dealer replace bulbs.

'94-95 Buick Regal and '94 Oldsmobile Cutlass

Brake hoses could wear through and leak, causing loss of stopping ability.
Models: 199,572 cars made 6/93-10/94.
What to do: Have dealer inspect and, if necessary, replace rear brake hoses.

'94-95 Buick Roadmaster, Cadillac Fleetwood, and Chevrolet Caprice

At low temperatures, engine might not return to idle speed when accelerator is released.
Models: 87,039 cars made 4/94-12/94.
What to do: Have dealer replace accelerator-pedal assembly.

'95 Buick Regal

Front turn-signal lights aren't bright enough to be seen by other motorists.
Models: 1,022 cars made 9/94.
What to do: Have dealer replace bulbs.

'95 Buick Regal and Chevrolet Lumina minivan

Steering could fail.
Models: 420 vehicles made 10/94.
What to do: Have dealer tighten bolts on steering-column support bracket.

'95 Buick Regal, Chevrolet Lumina, Oldsmobile Cutlass, Pontiac Grand Prix

Center-rear safety belt might not provide adequate protection in crash.

Models: 111,470 cars made 11/94-1/95
What to do: Have dealer replace safety-belt assembly.

'95 Buick Roadmaster, Cadillac Fleetwood, and Chevrolet Caprice

Shifter could be moved out of Park with ignition key removed. That could allow parked vehicle to roll away.
Models: 83,400 cars made 11/94-8/95.
What to do: Have dealer adjust transmission linkage.

'95 Buick, Chevrolet, Oldsmobile, and Pontiac models

Center-rear safety belt could fail in crash.
Models: 50,709 cars made 2/95, including Buick Regal, Chevrolet Lumina and Monte Carlo, Oldsmobile Cutlass, and Pontiac Grand Prix.
What to do: Have dealer replace center-rear safety belt.

'95-96 Buick Roadmaster, Cadillac Fleetwood, and Chevrolet Caprice

Wheels could come off.
Models: 21,582 cars made 8/95.
What to do: Have dealer tighten lug nuts to specifications.

'96 Buick Park Avenue and '97 Le Sabre

Safety belts may not latch properly and may not provide protection in crash.
Models: 15,122 cars made 1/96-2/96.
What to do: Have dealer inspect all safety belts and replace any incorrect parts.

'96 Buick Skylark and Oldsmobile Achieva

During deployment, air bag could snag inside dash and provide inadequate protection in crash.
Models: 48,689 cars made 8/95-2/96.
What to do: Have dealer inspect dash and, if necessary, install plastic edge protector on dash reinforcement. On some models, dealer will replace entire dash-panel pad.

'96 Buicks, Chevrolets, Oldsmobiles, and Pontiacs

Interior lamps could come on unexpectedly, startling driver and increasing risk of crash.
Models: 249,420 cars made 4/95-1/96, including Buick Skylark, Chevrolet Beretta and Cavalier, Oldsmobile Achieva, and Pontiac Grand Am and Sunfire.
What to do: Have dealer check and, if necessary, replace light-control module.

'96-97 Buicks, Oldsmobiles, and Pontiacs

Engine backfire could break upper intake manifold and cause fire or prevent engine from running.
Models: 275,811 cars with 3.8-liter V6, including '96 Buick Park Avenue, Regal,

and Riviera, Oldsmobile 88 and 98, and Pontiac Bonneville; also, ''96-97 Buick LeSabre.
What to do: Have dealer reprogram engine control module. Until repair is made, don't start engine when hood is open.

'97 Buick Skylark, Oldsmobile Achieva, and Pontiac Grand Am

Cover of underhood fuse center may have been omitted, leaving terminal bolt exposed. Battery cable could contact terminal bolt, abrade insulation, and short out, causing fire hazard.
Models: 3,464 cars made 12/96-1/97.
What to do: Have dealer install cover if it's missing.

'97 Buicks and Cadillacs

Antilock-brake system could engage during routine braking and increase stopping distance.
Models: 77,449 cars made 4/96-12/96, including Buick Park Avenue and Cadillac Seville, Deville, and El Dorado.
What to do: Have dealer replace electronic brake-control module or electronic brake- and traction-control module.

'99 Buick Century and Regal

Electrical short in antilock-brakes motor could cause brake hose to overheat and melt plastic fuel line, resulting in gasoline leak and fire.
Models: 168,035 cars made 3/98-4/99
What to do: Have dealer install ground cable from electronic brake-control module to engine-compartment body rail.

'99 Buick LeSabre, Oldsmobile 88, Pontiac Bonneville

Transmission indicator may not show proper gear position. For example, indicator could show drive position when transmission is actually in reverse.
Models: 99,269 cars made 8/98-1/99.
What to do: Have dealer install manual valve-link assembly kit with spring-type retainer.

'00 Buick Century, Regal, and Chevrolet Lumina

Rear wheels could shift out of position, causing loss of control.
Models: 18,754 cars with rear drum brakes made 11/99-2/00.
What to do: Have dealer replace bolts on rear spindle rod.

'00 Buick, Chevrolet, GMC, Oldsmobile, Pontiac, and Saturn vehicles

Rear safety belts may not provide adequate protection in a crash.
Models: 156,305 vehicles with TRW safety-belt buckle, made 4/00-5/00, including Buick Century and Regal; Chevrolet Blazer, Impala, Lumina, Monte Carlo, Venture, and S10/T10; GMC

Jimmy; Oldsmobile Intrigue and Silhouette; Pontiac Grand Prix and Montana; and Saturn L-Series.
What to do: Have dealer inspect and, if necessary, replace rear safety-belt buckles.

Cadillac

'94-95 Cadillac Fleetwood, Buick Roadmaster, and Chevrolet Caprice
At low temperatures, engine might not return to idle speed when accelerator is released.
Models: 87,039 cars made 4/94-12/94.
What to do: Have dealer replace accelerator-pedal assembly.

'95 Cadillac (various models)
Air bag could deploy when it shouldn't and cause loss of control.
Models: 102,627 Concours, Deville, Eldorado, and Seville models made 4/94-2/95.
What to do: Have dealer seal electronic module under driver's seat to keep out moisture.

'95 Cadillac Fleetwood, Buick Roadmaster, and Chevrolet Caprice
Shifter could be moved out of Park with ignition key removed. That could allow parked vehicle to roll away.
Models: 83,400 cars made 11/94-8/95.
What to do: Have dealer adjust transmission linkage.

'95-96 Cadillac Fleetwood, Buick Roadmaster, and Chevrolet Caprice
Wheels could come off.
Models: 21,582 cars made 8/95.
What to do: Have dealer tighten lug nuts to specifications.

'96 Cadillac Concours and DeVille
Hood could pop open unexpectedly, block driver's view, and hit windshield.
Models: 12,783 cars made 7/95-9/95.
What to do: Have dealer adjust secondary hood latch.

'96 Cadillac Eldorado and Seville
Short circuit in dashboard could disable gauges and most warning indicators and could prevent engine from starting.
Models: 1,408 cars made 10/95-11/95.
What to do: Have dealer inspect and, if necessary, replace instrument-panel cluster.

'97 Cadillacs and Buicks
Antilock-brake system could engage during routine braking and increase stopping distance.
Models: 77,449 cars made 4/96-12/96, including Buick Park Avenue and Cadillac Seville, Deville, and El Dorado.
What to do: Have dealer replace electronic brake-control module or electronic brake- and traction-control module.

'98 Cadillac DeVille
Instead of buckling in crash, hood could penetrate windshield, increasing risk of injury to occupants.
Models: 14,423 cars made 9/97-11/97.
What to do: Have dealer replace hood hinge-pivot bolts.

'98 Cadillac Seville
Windshield wipers could fail.
Models: 1,059 cars made 6/98.
What to do: Have dealer replace wiper-motor cover, which contains microprocessor that controls wiper speed.

'98-99 Cadillac DeVille
Side-impact air bags could deploy suddenly and unexpectedly.
Models: 224,000 cars made 3/4/97 to 8/2/99.
What to do: Have dealer will replace side-impact sensing modules.

Chevrolet

'89-96 Chevrolets, Buicks, Oldsmobiles, and Pontiacs
Rear outboard safety belts may not hold in crash.
Models: 2.2 million cars made 4/88-8/95, including '89-96 Buick Century, '89-90 Chevrolet Celebrity, '89-96 Oldsmobile Ciera, and '89-91 Pontiac 6000.
What to do: Have dealer install new bolt and thread-locking adhesive for each belt. Dealer will also apply washer-like patch to each anchor point to reduce noise as belt pivots.

'91-96 Chevrolet Blazer and S10, and GMC Jimmy and Sonoma, with four-wheel drive
In two-wheel-drive mode, antilock brake system may not perform as expected, resulting in increased stopping distances.
Models: 1.1 million pickup trucks and sport-utility vehicles, with EBC4 antilock brake system, made 9/89-8/96.
What to do: Have dealer make necessary repairs (at press time, General Motors hadn't announced the specific remedy).

'91-96 Chevrolet and GMC light trucks, sport-utility vehicles, and vans
Antilock brake system could malfunction, resulting in increased stopping distances.
Models: Approx. 1.1 million '91-96 4-wheel-drive vehicles, including Chevrolet Blazer and S-10, and GMC Jimmy and Sonoma. Also subject to corrective action are about 2.4 million 2-wheel-drive vehicles, including '93-96 Chevrolet Blazer and GMC Jimmy, '94-96 Chevrolet S-10 and GMC Sonoma, and '92-95 Chevrolet Astro and GMC Safari. According to General Motors, braking problems are much less likely to occur in the 2-wheel-drive vehicles because of a combination of unusual circumstances necessary to precipitate them.
What to do: Have dealer replace sensor switch in ABS system of 4-wheel-drive vehicles. With 2-wheel-drive models, dealer will modify computer-control unit in ABS system.

'94-95 Chevrolet Beretta
Right-side panel may not be reinforced properly. That subjects occupants to increased injury in side crash.
Models: 1,604 cars made 8/94.
What to do: Contact dealer. Chevrolet will replace car.

'94-95 Chevrolet Caprice and Buick Roadmaster, Cadillac Fleetwood
At low temperatures, engine might not return to idle speed when accelerator is released.
Models: 87,039 cars made 4/94-12/94.
What to do: Have dealer replace accelerator-pedal assembly.

'95 Chevrolet Astro and GMC Safari
Hoses from fuel tank could leak, creating fire hazard.
Models: 3,037 minivans made 9/94.
What to do: Have dealer tighten hoses to fuel tank.

'95 Chevrolet Blazer and GMC Jimmy
Brakes could fail.
Models: 262 vehicles made 11/94.
What to do: Have dealer inspect break pedal pivot bolt in weld nut and tighten adequately.

'95 Chevrolet Blazer and S10 and GMC Jimmy and S15 pickup trucks and sport-utility vehicles
Radiator fan could break apart. If hood is open, blades could strike anyone nearby.
Models: 73,163 light-duty trucks and sport-utility vehicles with 4.3-liter V6 and air-conditioning, made 9/94-11/94.
What to do: Have dealer inspect and, if necessary, replace fan.

'95 Chevrolet Caprice and Buick Roadmaster, Cadillac Fleetwood
Shifter could be moved out of Park with ignition key removed. That could allow parked vehicle to roll away.
Models: 83,400 cars made 11/94-8/95.
What to do: Have dealer adjust transmission linkage.

'95 Chevrolet Cavalier and Pontiac Sunfire
Front suspension components could separate, resulting in loss of vehicle control.
Models: 21,340 cars made 2/94-1/95.
What to do: Have dealer inspect lower-control-arm assemblies and, if necessary, replace.

'95 Chevrolet Lumina APV, Oldsmobile Silhouette, and Pontiac Trans Sport

Brake-pedal arm could fracture in use, resulting in diminished stopping ability.
Models: 6,523 minivans made 11/94-2/95.
What to do: Have dealer replace all suspect brake-pedal assemblies.

'95 Chevrolet Lumina and Monte Carlo

Steering could fail.
Models: 221 cars made 8/94.
What to do: Have dealer replace right lower control arm and ball-joint stud.

'95 Chevrolet Lumina and Pontiac Trans Sport minivans

Engine may not slow down sufficiently when accelerator is released.
Models: 6,772 minivans, with 3.1-liter V6, made 5/95-9/95.
What to do: Have dealer replace throttle-cable support bracket.

'95 Chevrolet Lumina minivan and Buick Regal

Steering could fail.
Models: 420 vehicles made 10/94.
What to do: Have dealer tighten bolts on steering-column support bracket.

'95 Chevrolet Lumina, Buick Regal, Oldsmobile Cutlass, Pontiac Grand Prix

Center-rear safety belt might not provide adequate protection in crash.
Models: 111,470 cars made 11/94-1/95
What to do: Have dealer replace safety-belt assembly.

'95 Chevrolet Tahoe and GMC Yukon

Center-rear safety belt might not provide adequate protection in crash.
Models: 8,323 sport-utility vehicles with 2 doors and 4-wheel drive made 4/94-12/94.
What to do: Owners will receive instructions on rerouting belt—or have dealer reroute it.

'95 Chevrolet and GMC light trucks

When shifter is placed in Park, indicator light may not go on.
Models: 36,641 sport-utility vehicles and pickup trucks with M30/MT1 automatic transmission made 3/94-10/94, including Chevrolet and GMC C3500HD and Suburban; Chevrolet Tahoe; and GMC Sierra and Yukon.
What to do: Have dealer adjust transmission shift cable and install lock clip.

'95 Chevrolet and GMC pickup trucks and vans

Transmission fluid could leak onto hot exhaust manifold and cause possible fire.
Models: 13,853 vehicles, with 4L80-E automatic transmission, made 12/94-1/95 including Chevrolet C20, C30, G30, K20, K30, P, Sportvan, Suburban, and GMC C25, C35, G35, K25, K35, P, Rally, Sierra, and Suburban.
What to do: Have dealer inspect transmission-case assembly to determine if casting is too thin and, if necessary, replace transmission.

'95 Chevrolet, Buick, Oldsmobile, and Pontiac models

Center-rear safety belt could fail in crash.
Models: 50,709 cars made 2/95, including Buick Regal, Chevrolet Lumina and Monte Carlo, Oldsmobile Cutlass, and Pontiac Grand Prix.
What to do: Have dealer replace center-rear safety belt.

'95-96 Chevrolet Caprice and Buick Roadmaster, Cadillac Fleetwood

Wheels could come off.
Models: 21,582 cars made 8/95.
What to do: Have dealer tighten lug nuts to specifications.

'95-96 Chevrolet, Pontiac, and Oldsmobile (various models)

Four-way hazard-warning flashers may not work.
Models: 270,014 cars made 7/95-8/95 including '95-96 Chevrolet Cavalier and Pontiac Sunfire, and '96 Pontiac Gran Am and Oldsmobile Achieva.
What to do: Check whether flashers are working properly. If not, have dealer replace hazard switch.

'95-98 Chevrolet C10 and C15 crew-cab pickups

Fuel tank could leak, causing fire hazard.
Models: 55,272 trucks made 9/94-9/97.
What to do: Have dealer install spacer between tank and front crossmember. Also, dealer will replace tank if necessary.

'96 Chevrolet S10 and GMC S15 and Sonoma pickup trucks

Transmission could seize, lock up rear wheels, and cause loss of control.
Models: 24,906 two-wheel-drive pickups, with four-cylinder engine and 5-speed manual transmission, made 8/95-1/96.
What to do: Have dealer inspect and, if necessary, replace transmission.

'96 Chevrolets, Buicks, Oldsmobiles, and Pontiacs

Interior lamps could come on unexpectedly, startling driver and increasing risk of crash.
Models: 249,420 cars made 4/95-1/96, including Buick Skylark, Chevrolet Beretta and Cavalier, Oldsmobile Achieva, and Pontiac Grand Am and Sunfire.
What to do: Have dealer check and, if necessary, replace light-control module.

'96-97 Chevrolet Astro and GMC Safari

Right-rear safety belt could fail in crash.
Models: 18,972 minivans made 7/95-6/96.

What to do: Have dealer install "protector" on frame of seat cushion to keep safety-belt webbing from coming apart.

'96-97 Chevrolet Cavalier and Pontiac Sunfire

Air bag could deploy when it shouldn't—in low-speed crash or if road debris kicks up against floor.
Models: 675,302 cars made 4/95-5/97.
What to do: Have dealer recalibrate air-bag module.

'96-97 Chevrolet S10 and GMC Sonoma pickup trucks

Front brake hose could chafe against left side of engine oil pan, leak, and reduce stopping ability.
Models: 146,851 light pickups, with V6 engine, made 3/95-8/96.
What to do: Have dealer check brake-hose clearance and, if necessary, install extra brake-hose clip and replace hose.

'97 Chevrolet Corvette

Safety belts might not protect adequately in crash.
Models: 4369 cars made 9/96-5/97.
What to do: Have dealer replace both safety-belt retractors.

'97 Chevrolet Corvette

Fuel leak could cause fire hazard.
Models: 3,792 cars made 9/96-4/97.
What to do: Have dealer replace left and right fuel-tank assemblies, including sending unit and pump.

'97-01 Chevrolet, Pontiac, and Oldsmobile minivans

Even though power-sliding door is closed, it may not latch properly. If so, door could open unexpectedly while vehicle is moving, causing occupant to fall out.
Models: 477,011 minivans with passenger side sliding door made 5/95 to 12/00, including the following: '97-01 Chevrolet Venture and Oldsmobile Silhouette; '98-01 Pontiac Montana; and '97-98 Pontiac Trans Sport.
What to do: Have dealer replace actuator assembly to power sliding door.

'97-98 Chevrolet Malibu and Oldsmobile Cutlass

Snow or ice buildup could damage passenger-side windshield wiper, causing wiper to fail.
Models: 129,427 cars made 1/96 to 1/98 and registered or located in Ala., Colo., Conn., Del., Idaho, Ill., Ind., Iowa, Maine, Md., Mass., Mich., Minn., Mont., Neb., N.H., N.J., N.Y., N.D., Ohio, Pa., R.I., S.D., Utah, Vt., W. Va., Wis., and Wyo.
What to do: Have dealer replace wiper's pivot housing.

'97-98 Chevrolet Venture and Oldsmobile Silhouette

Passenger's fingers could be severed by latch mechanism that moves seat fore and aft.

Models: 125,990 minivans, made 4/96-3/98, with bucket seats or split bench seat in second or third row.

What to do: Have dealer install protective covers on seat-latch mechanisms.

'98 Chevrolet Venture, Oldsmobile Silhouette, and Pontiac Trans Sport

Vehicle could roll when shifter is in "park."

Models: 38,540 minivans made 12/97-4/98.

What to do: Have dealer inspect and, if necessary, replace transaxle range-selector cable.

'99 Chevrolet Silverado and GMC Sierra

Steering could fail.

Models: 8,367 extended cab pick-up trucks with four-wheel drive made 4/98-8/98.

What to do: Have dealer tighten bolts attaching steering gear to frame.

'99 Chevrolet Tracker

Steering could fail.

Models: 1,158 sport-utility vehicles made 11/98-12/98.

What to do: Have dealer replace steering-shaft coupling.

'99-00 Chevrolet and GMC pickup trucks and sport-utility vehicles

Brake pipe could leak fluid.

Models: 1,383,922 vehicles, including '99-00 Chevrolet Silverado and GMC Sierra, '00 Chevrolet Tahoe and Suburban, and '00 GMC Yukon and Yukon XL.

What to do: Have dealer inspect right front brake pipe for wear from contact with body and install redesigned section of pipe if necessary. In the absence of wear, spacer clip should be installed to maintain adequate clearance between brake pipe and body cross sill.

'00 Chevrolet Lumina and Buick Century, Regal,

Rear wheels could shift out of position, causing loss of control.

Models: 18,754 cars with rear drum brakes made 11/99-2/00.

What to do: Have dealer replace bolts on rear spindle rod.

'00 Chevrolet Suburban, Tahoe, and Silverado; GMC Yukon, Yukon XL, and Sierra

Air bags may not deploy in a frontal crash.

Models: 525,254 vehicles made 2/99 to 2/00.

What to do: Have dealer recalibrate air bag sensing-diagnostic module (SDM).

'00 Chevrolet, Buick, GMC, Oldsmobile, Pontiac, and Saturn vehicles

Rear safety belts may not provide adequate protection in a crash.

Models: 156,305 vehicles with TRW safety-belt buckle, made 4/00-5/00, including Buick Century and Regal; Chevrolet Blazer, Impala, Lumina, Monte Carlo, Venture, and S10/T10; GMC Jimmy; Oldsmobile Intrigue and Silhouette; Pontiac Grand Prix and Montana; and Saturn L-Series.

What to do: Have dealer inspect and, if necessary, replace rear safety-belt buckles.

'00-02 General Motors sport-utility vehicles (various makes)

Rear stop and hazard lamps could become inoperative, increasing risk of crash with another vehicle, whose driver doesn't realize SUV is slowing.

Models: Models: 506,377 sport-utility vehicles made 9/99 to 8/01, including '00-01 GMC Jimmy and Oldsmobile Bravada, and '00-02 Chevrolet Blazer.

What to do: What to do: At press time, General Motors had not provided a remedy or owner-notification schedule. If you have not been contacted, call 800-462-8782 (for a GMC vehicle), 800-442-6537 (Oldsmobile), or 800-222-1020 (Chevrolet).

'01 General Motors minivans and sport-utility vehicles

May not accommodate child safety seats.

Models: 75,816 vehicles with second-row 50/50-split bench seats or captain's chairs, made 4/00 to 10/00, including Chevrolet Venture, Pontiac Aztec and Montana, and Oldsmobile Silhouette.

What to do: Have dealer inspect and, if necessary, repair seat-latch anchor wires.

'02 Chevrolet TrailBlazer, GMC Envoy, and Oldsmobile Bravada

Fuel-filter fitting could become disconnected. If that occurs during start-up, engine might not turn over and fuel would be pumped onto ground, creating a fire hazard. If fitting comes off while vehicle is moving, engine would stop, possibly resulting in crash.

Models: 60,044 sport-utility vehicles made 9/01 to 11/01.

What to do: Have dealer replace fuel-filter quick-connect retainers.

'02 Chevrolet Trailblazer and GMC Envoy

Vehicle could roll even though shifter is in Park.

Models: 78,004 sport-utility vehicles, with four-wheel drive, made 1/01 to 8/01.

What to do: Have dealer recalibrate transfer-case control module.

Chrysler

'95 Chrysler Cirrus and Dodge Stratus

Rear safety belts could fail in crash.

Models: 91,544 cars made 7/94-5/95.

What to do: Have dealer inspect and, if necessary, reposition outboard floor attachment for rear belts.

'95-96 Chrysler Cirrus and Dodge Stratus

Oil could leak from engine and create fire hazard.

Models: 40,000 cars, with 2.4-liter Four, made 12/94-9/95.

What to do: Have dealer install expansion plug and retaining bracket on cylinder head.

'95-96 Chrysler Cirrus, Dodge Stratus, and '96 Plymouth Breeze

Valves in antilock brake system could stick and cause car to veer to one side when stopping.

Models: 90,000 cars made 8/94-8/95.

What to do: Have dealer install a plate and inject silicone grease into solenoid cavity of ABS hydraulic control unit.

'95-96 Chrysler Sebring, Dodge Avenger, and Eagle Talon

Ball joint could separate and cause suspension to collapse, resulting in sudden loss of power and reduced steering control.

Models: 170,000 cars made 6/94-6/96.

What to do: Have dealer inspect and, if necessary, replace rubber ball-joint boots on lower lateral arm.

'95-96 Chrysler, Dodge, and Plymouth cars with "ACR" competition package

Brake master cylinder could leak fluid, resulting in decreased stopping ability.

Models: 151,800 cars made 8/94-10/95 including '95-96 Chrysler Cirrus, Dodge Neon and Stratus, and Plymouth Neon, and '96 Plymouth Breeze.

What to do: Have dealer replace rear brake master-cylinder piston assembly.

'95-97 Chrysler, Dodge, and Plymouth models

Ball joints in front suspension could corrode and fail, causing loss of steering control.

Models: 599,000 cars, including '95-97 Chrysler Cirrus, Dodge Stratus, and Plymouth Breeze, and '96-97 Chrysler Sebring convertibles.

What to do: Have dealer inspect and, if necessary, replace ball-joints.

'95-98 Chrysler Cirrus and Sebring, Dodge Stratus, and Plymouth Breeze

Car could roll even if shifter is in park position.

Models: 685,000 cars with automatic transmission made 7/94-1/98.

What to do: Have dealer inspect interlock system and, if necessary, install self-adjusting shift mechanism and cable.

'96 Chrysler Sebring JX convertible

Brakes could lose power assist, making car harder to stop.
Models: 22,500 cars with V6, made 8/95-5/96.
What to do: Have dealer make sure vacuum hose is firmly secured to engine manifold.

'96 Chrysler Sebring convertible

Water and road salt could short-circuit power mirror and pose fire hazard.
Models: 39,000 cars made 8/96.
What to do: Have dealer replace power-mirror switch.

'96 Chrysler, Dodge, and Plymouth minivans

Fire or explosion could occur during refueling because of static buildup on fuel-filler tube.
Models: 265,000 minivans, including Chrysler Town & Country, Dodge Caravan and Grand Caravan, and Plymouth Voyager and Grand Voyager, made 1/95-12/95.
What to do: Have dealer install ground strap for filler tube.

'96 Chrysler, Dodge, and Plymouth minivans

Fuel could leak from tank and cause fire.
Models: 622,000 minivans including Chrysler Town and Country, Dodge Caravan and Grand Caravan, and Plymouth Voyager and Grand Voyager.
What to do: Have dealer replace nut holding fuel-pump module in place.

'96 Chrysler, Dodge, and Plymouth minivans

Fuel tank could leak, creating fire hazard.
Models: 80,000 minivans made 1/95-8/95, including Chrysler Town & Country, Dodge Caravan and Grand Caravan, and Plymouth Voyager and Grand Voyager.
What to do: Have dealer install redesigned fuel-tank filler tube and reroute rollover-valve vapor hoses.

'96-97 Chrysler, Dodge, and Plymouth minivans with built-in child safety seat

Shoulder-harness latch could stick, making it difficult to remove child in emergency.
Models: 157,000 minivans made 1/95-7/97 including Chrysler Town & Country, Dodge Caravan and Grand Caravan, and Plymouth Voyager and Grand Voyager.
What to do: Have dealer clean latch mechanism and add extender to emergency release on safety-belt anchor.

'96-00 Chrysler, Dodge, and Plymouth minivans

Fuel-injector system could leak, possibly causing fire.
Models: 1,163,000 minivans, with 3.3- and 3.8-liter engines, made 2/95-9/99, including Dodge Caravan and Grand Caravan, Plymouth Voyager and Grand Voyager, and Chrysler Town and Country. Hazard exists because fuel could seep through O-ring seals in fuel-injection rail.
What to do: Have dealer install seal on fuel rails to prevent leakage from fuel-rail crossover tube. If fuel is already leaking from O-rings or cracked fuel line, have dealer make necessary repairs as soon as possible.

'98 Chrysler, Dodge, and Plymouth minivans with built-in child safety seat

Seat may not restrain child adequately in crash.
Models: 25,900 minivans made 11/97, including Chrysler Town & Country, Dodge Caravan and Grand Caravan, and Plymouth Voyager and Grand Voyager.
What to do: Have dealer inspect and, if necessary, reroute seat's harness webbing.

'98-99 Chrysler Cirrus, Dodge Stratus, Plymouth Breeze

Rear brake hose could abrade and leak from contact with exhaust system clamp, causing increased stopping distances.
Models: 367,000 cars made 6/97-5/99.
What to do: Have dealer replace any brake hose that shows wear from contact with clamp. If no evidence of contact exists, dealer will attach clip to hose to prevent future occurrence.

'99-00 Chrysler, Dodge, and Jeep

Safety belts might not provide adequate protection in crash.
Models: 204,000 vehicles made 9/99, including Chrysler Concorde, 300M, and LHS; Dodge Intrepid; and Jeep Grand Cherokee. There is a manufacturing defect in the belt's shoulder-height adjustable turning loop (ATL).
What to do: Have dealer replace upper ATL bolt.

'01 Chrysler Town & Country, Dodge Caravan and Grand Caravan, and Plymouth Voyager

Suspension components could come apart.
Models: 41,587 minivans made 3/01 to 4/01.
What to do: Have dealer replace nuts and bolts on lower control arm.

'02 Chrysler PT Cruiser and Jeep Grand Cherokee

Gauges, warning lamps, and illumination lamps could become inoperative and become a distraction that could lead to crash.

Models: 43,000 vehicles made 7/01 to 8/01.
What to do: Have dealer correct software error in instrument-cluster microprocessor.

Daewoo

'98-01 Daewoo Leganza

Occupants could suffer head injury in crash because front roof pillar lacks adequate padding.
Models: 58,691 cars. Date of manufacture was not available.
What to do: Have dealer install padding to pillar at edge of windshield.

Dodge

'94 Dodge Dakota and '94-95 Dodge Ram

Extra keys on ring could jam in screw-access holes in back cover of steering wheel and impair steering or turn off ignition.
Models: Models: 293,043 light and club-cab trucks made 7/93-7/94.
What to do: Have dealer replace back cover of steering wheel.

'94-95 Dodge Ram pickup truck

Secondary hood latch might not engage properly. That could cause hood to fly up suddenly and unexpectedly.
Models: 175,000 pickups made 1-12/94.
What to do: Have dealer replace secondary hood-latch bracket.

'94-96 Dodge Ram

When climate-control blower motor is on high setting for extended period, ignition switch and wiring could overheat and cause fire.
Models: 690,000 pickup trucks made 6/93-4/96.
What to do: Have dealer install a relay and overlay harness.

'94-96 Dodge Ram pickup trucks

Fuel could leak from tank and create fire hazard.
Models: 497,000 pickup trucks. Hazard exists when fuel tank is full and when truck is parked on slope or weather is hot.
What to do: Have dealer replace fuel-tank valve.

'94-97 Dodge Ram pickup trucks

Under certain hard-driving conditions, overheated transmission fluid could melt hose connections and spray onto exhaust manifold, possibly causing a fire.
Models: 96,000 light-duty trucks made 1/94-2/97.
What to do: Have dealer replace high-temperature side of transmission-fluid cooler-hose connector fittings with

connectors that incorporate stainless-steel retainer.

'94-99 Dodge Ram pickup

Hood could open unexpectedly.
Models: 701,000 pickup trucks made 7/93 to 3/99 and registered or located in Conn., Del., Ill., Ind., Iowa, Maine, Mass., Md., Mich., Minn., Mo., N.H., N.J., N.Y., Ohio, Pa., R.I., Vt., Washington, D.C., W. Va., and Wis. Hazard exists if the primary hood latch is not engaged and secondary latch is corroded.
What to do: Have dealer replace secondary hood latch.

'95 Dodge Stratus and Chrysler Cirrus

Rear safety belts could fail in crash.
Models: 91,544 cars made 7/94-5/95.
What to do: Have dealer inspect and, if necessary, reposition outboard floor attachment for rear belts.

'95 Dodge and Plymouth Neon

Driver could lose steering control if car runs over object that strikes underbody.
Models: 375,000 cars made 1/94-8/95.
What to do: Have dealer install new steering-column coupler.

'95-96 Dodge Avenger, Chrysler Sebring, and Eagle Talon

Ball joint could separate and cause suspension to collapse, resulting in sudden loss of power and reduced steering control.
Models: 170,000 cars made 6/94-6/96.
What to do: Have dealer inspect and, if necessary, replace rubber ball-joint boots on lower lateral arm.

'95-96 Dodge Ram diesel pickup trucks

Engine oil seeping into vacuum hose could make it collapse partially, making vehicle harder to stop.
Models: 58,000 light pickup trucks with diesel engines made 6/95-6/96.
What to do: Have dealer install check valve to keep oil out of hose. Also, have dealer replace vacuum hose with one that's oil-resistant.

'95-96 Dodge Stratus and Chrysler Cirrus

Oil could leak from engine and create fire hazard.
Models: 40,000 cars, with 2.4-liter Four, made 12/94-9/95.
What to do: Have dealer install expansion plug and retaining bracket on cylinder head.

'95-96 Dodge Stratus, Chrysler Cirrus, and '96 Plymouth Breeze

Valves in antilock brake system could stick and cause car to veer to one side when stopping.
Models: 90,000 cars made 8/94-8/95.
What to do: Have dealer install a plate

and inject silicone grease into solenoid cavity of ABS hydraulic control unit.

'95-96 Dodge, Chrysler, and Plymouth cars with "ACR" competition package

Brake master cylinder could leak fluid, resulting in decreased stopping ability.
Models: 151,800 cars made 8/94-10/95 including '95-96 Chrysler Cirrus, Dodge Neon and Stratus, and Plymouth Neon, and '96 Plymouth Breeze.
What to do: Have dealer replace rear brake master-cylinder piston assembly.

'95-97 Dodge, Chrysler, and Plymouth models

Ball joints in front suspension could corrode and fail, causing loss of steering control.
Models: 599,000 cars, including '95-97 Chrysler Cirrus, Dodge Stratus, and Plymouth Breeze, and '96-97 Chrysler Sebring convertibles.
What to do: Have dealer inspect and, if necessary, replace ball-joints.

'95-98 Dodge Stratus, Chrysler Cirrus and Sebring, and Plymouth Breeze

Car could roll even if shifter is in park position.
Models: 685,000 cars with automatic transmission made 7/94-1/98.
What to do: Have dealer inspect interlock system and, if necessary, install self-adjusting shift mechanism and cable.

'96 Dodge Caravan and Grand Caravan and Plymouth Voyager and Grand Voyager

Rear bench seat could could break loose in accident, increasing risk of injury.
Models: 20,000 minivans, made 10/95-11/95, with bench seat rather than captain's chairs in rear.
What to do: Check vehicle identification number atop dashboard or on registration certificate. If 11th character is letter "R," have dealer replace bolts connecting rear bench seat to riser.

'96 Dodge and Plymouth Neon

Engine-wiring harness could short and cause various electrical malfunctions, including engine stalling.
Models: 15,000 cars made 7/95-11/95 at Toluca, Mexico, assembly plant.
What to do: Have dealer replace damaged wire and reroute wiring harness away from exhaust-gas-recirculation tube.

'96 Dodge, Chrysler, and Plymouth minivans

Fuel tank could leak, creating fire hazard.
Models: 80,000 minivans made 1/95-8/95, including Chrysler Town & Country, Dodge Caravan and Grand Caravan, and Plymouth Voyager and Grand Voyager.
What to do: Have dealer install

redesigned fuel-tank filler tube and reroute rollover-valve vapor hoses.

'96 Dodge, Chrysler, and Plymouth minivans

Fuel could leak from tank and cause fire.
Models: 622,000 minivans including Chrysler Town and Country, Dodge Caravan and Grand Caravan, and Plymouth Voyager and Grand Voyager.
What to do: Have dealer replace nut holding fuel-pump module in place.

'96 Dodge, Chrysler, and Plymouth minivans

Fire or explosion could occur during refueling because of static buildup on fuel-filler tube.
Models: 265,000 minivans, including Chrysler Town & Country, Dodge Caravan and Grand Caravan, and Plymouth Voyager and Grand Voyager, made 1/95-12/95.
What to do: Have dealer install ground strap for filler tube.

'96-97 Dodge, Chrysler, and Plymouth minivans with built-in child safety seat

Shoulder-harness latch could stick, making it difficult to remove child in emergency.
Models: 157,000 minivans made 1/95-7/97 including Chrysler Town & Country, Dodge Caravan and Grand Caravan, and Plymouth Voyager and Grand Voyager.
What to do: Have dealer clean latch mechanism and add extender to emergency release on safety-belt anchor.

'96-00 Dodge, Chrysler, and Plymouth minivans

Fuel-injector system could leak, possibly causing fire.
Models: 1,163,000 minivans, with 3.3- and 3.8-liter engines, made 2/95-9/99, including Dodge Caravan and Grand Caravan, Plymouth Voyager and Grand Voyager, and Chrysler Town and Country. Hazard exists because fuel could seep through O-ring seals in fuel-injection rail.
What to do: Have dealer install seal on fuel rails to prevent leakage from fuel-rail crossover tube. If fuel is already leaking from O-rings or cracked fuel line, have dealer make necessary repairs as soon as possible.

'97 Dodge Ram diesel pickup trucks

Hot exhaust pipe could start fire.
Models: 6,400 light-duty trucks made 3/97-5/97.
What to do: Have dealer remove dash silencer pad and install heat shield on exhaust pipe.

'97-01 Dodge pickup trucks (various models)

Driver's air bag could fail.
Models: 216,100 pickups made 8/96 to

4/01 including the '97-00 Dakota and Durango and '97-01 Ram. Sound-deadening material inside steering wheel could become detached from cover and housing. It could then interfere with clockspring ribbon that controls air bag, causing it to become inoperative and triggering air-bag warning lamp.
What to do: Have dealer replace clockspring assembly.

'98 Dodge Durango
Wiring in engine compartment could overheat and cause fire.
Models: 25,000 sport-utility vehicles made 9/97-1/98.
What to do: Have dealer inspect and, if necessary, tighten wiring connection.

'98 Dodge Ram pickup trucks
Safety belts might not protect adequately in crash.
Models: 4,200 pickup trucks made 4/98.
What to do: Have dealer replace front outer safety-belt buckles.

'98 Dodge, Chrysler, and Plymouth minivans with built-in child safety seat
Seat may not restrain child adequately in crash.
Models: 25,900 minivans made 11/97, including Chrysler Town & Country, Dodge Caravan and Grand Caravan, and Plymouth Voyager and Grand Voyager.
What to do: Have dealer inspect and, if necessary, reroute seat's harness webbing.

'98-99 Dodge Durango
Fuel-tank strap could separate from tank, increasing risk of fuel leak and fire.
Models: 150,000 trucks made 8/97-9/98.
What to do: Have dealer install strap with single (instead of double) toggle-lock design.

'98-99 Dodge Stratus, Chrysler Cirrus, Plymouth Breeze
Rear brake hose could abrade and leak from contact with exhaust system clamp, causing increased stopping distances.
Models: 367,000 cars made 6/97-5/99.
What to do: Have dealer replace any brake hose that shows wear from contact with clamp. If no evidence of contact exists, dealer will attach clip to hose to prevent future occurrence.

'99 Dodge Ram pickup trucks
Hydraulic fluid could leak onto hot exhaust and cause underbody fire.
Models: 9,000 pickup trucks made 2/99-6/99.
What to do: Have dealer install longer heat shield for hydraulic clutch line.

'99-00 Dodge, Chrysler, and Jeep
Safety belts might not provide adequate protection in crash.

Models: 204,000 vehicles made 9/99, including Chrysler Concorde, 300M, and LHS; Dodge Intrepid; and Jeep Grand Cherokee. There is a manufacturing defect in the belt's shoulder-height adjustable turning loop (ATL).
What to do: Have dealer replace upper ATL bolt.

'00 Dodge and Plymouth Neon
Passenger-side air bag may not inflate adequately.
Models: 380 cars made 11/98-1/99.
What to do: Have dealer replace passenger-side air-bag module.

'00-01 Dodge Ram van
Road salt, water, or other debris could cause electrical short in power-seat connector beneath driver's seat, posing fire hazard.
Models: 98,000 vans and wagons made 8/99 to 3/01 and not equipped with power front seats. Extraneous material could cause short circuit that prompts circuit breaker to cycle for extended period, which could lead to overheating and fire.
What to do: Have dealer remove the circuit breaker from the fuse panel.

'00-01 Dodge and Plymouth Neon
Loss of power-brake assist could cause increased stopping distances and increased engine idle speed.
Models: 353,000 cars made 7/99 to 3/01.
What to do: Have dealer replace brake-booster vacuum hose.

'01 Dodge Caravan and Grand Caravan, Chrysler Town & Country, and Plymouth Voyager
Suspension components could come apart.
Models: 41,587 minivans made 3/01 to 4/01.
What to do: Have dealer replace nuts and bolts on lower control arm.

Eagle

'92-96 Eagle Summit and Plymouth Colt with all-wheel drive
Wheels could lockup and cause loss of control.
Models: 6,198 vehicles made 7/91-6/96, including '92-96 Summit and '92-94 Colt.
What to do: Have dealer inspect transfer case and, if necessary, add oil or replace case.

'95-96 Eagle Talon
Fuel-tank could leak, creating fire hazard.
Models: 9,616 cars made 3/94-7/96.
What to do: Have dealer inspect and, if necessary, replace fuel tank, cap, and gaskets.

'95-96 Eagle Talon and Chrysler Sebring, Dodge Avenger
Ball joint could separate and cause suspension to collapse, resulting in sudden loss of power and reduced steering control.
Models: 170,000 cars made 6/94-6/96.
What to do: Have dealer inspect and, if necessary, replace rubber ball-joint boots on lower lateral arm.

Ford

'86-95 Ford Taurus, Mercury Sable, and Lincoln Continental
Corrosion from road salt could make subframes drop, suddenly making the car very hard to steer.
Models: 2.7 million cars made 10/85-6/95 including '86-95 Ford Taurus and Mercury Sable and '88-94 Lincoln Continental. Recall affects vehicles sold or currently registered in Conn., Dela., D.C., Ill., Ind., Iowa, Kan., Ky., Maine, Md., Mass., Mich., Minn., Mo., Neb., N.H., N.J., N.Y., Ohio, Pa., R.I., Vt., Va., W.Va., and Wis.
What to do: Have dealer reinforce subframe with nuts, bolts, and plates.

'91-95 Ford, Lincoln, and Mercury
Water could freeze in cruise-control cable and prevent driver from disengaging cruise control.
Models: 212,700 cars with 3.8-liter V6, including '91-94 Lincoln Continental and '91-95 Ford Taurus and Mercury Sable. Recall applies only to cars registered in Alaska, Colo., Idaho, Ill., Ind., Iowa, Kan., Maine, Mass., Mich., Minn., Mo., Mont., Neb., N.H., N.Y., N.D., Ohio, Pa., S.D., Vt., Wisc., and Wyo. Affected vehicles were made 7/90-11/94.
What to do: Have dealer install cable boot to keep out water.

'92-95 Ford, Lincoln, and Mercury
Snow could clog engine-cooling fan and make it overheat, posing fire hazard.
Models: 75,200 cars, with 2.3-liter Four, 3.0-liter V6, or 3.8-liter V6, including '92-94 Ford Tempo, Mercury Topaz, and Lincoln Continental and '92-95 Ford Taurus and Mercury Sable. Recall applies only to cars registered in Alaska, Iowa, Minn., Neb., N.D., and S.D. are being recalled. Dates of manufacture are: Tempo, 8/5/91-5/20/94; Topaz, 8/5/91-5/16/94; Continental, 8/12/91-11/17/94; Taurus, 5/3/91-6/26/95; Sable, 6/19/91-6/16/95.
What to do: Have dealer install wiring with circuit breaker to prevent fan motor from overheating.

'92-97 Ford Aerostar
Electrical short in accessory power circuit could cause fire. Also, electrical connection at fuel pump in some '94-95

Aerostar minivans could short out, resulting in power loss and fire.
Models: 887,000 '92-97 models made 5/8/91-8/22/97 and 29,000 '94-95 models made 6/27/94-8/31/94.
What to do: Dealer will install relaying wiring harness on '92-97 models, and fuse jumper harness on '94-95 models.

'93-95 Ford Explorer
In open position, liftgate could fall unexpectedly, possibly injuring anyone beneath it.
Models: 506,600 sport-utility vehicles made 4/1/93-2/17/95 at Louisville, Ky., plant and 12/21/94-2/14/95 at St. Louis plant.
What to do: Have dealer install liftgate reinforcement bracket.

'94-95 Ford Escort and Mercury Tracer
Driver's-side air bag might not deploy properly in crash, and hot gasses could cause burns.
Models: 240 cars made 9-10/94.
What to do: Have dealer replace air-bag module.

'95 Ford Aerostar
Spare tire could rub against rear-axle brake hoses, damaging hose and resulting in reduced stopping ability.
Models: 9,400 light-duty vans, with spare mounted in underbody tire carrier, made 10-11/94.
What to do: Have dealer install "low profile" mini-spare tire on existing mini-spare wheel.

'95 Ford Contour and Mercury Mystique
If rear passenger-side door windows break, glass could shatter into large fragments, a violation of Federal safety standard.
Models: 2,512 cars made 11/94.
What to do: Have dealer replace windows.

'95 Ford Contour and Mercury Mystique
Fuel could seep through weld at filler pipe opening, creating fire hazard.
Models: 28,500 cars made 7-10/94.
What to do: Have dealer inspect and, if necessary, replace fuel tank.

'95 Ford Contour and Mercury Mystique
Fuel could leak from filler pipe and create fire hazard.
Models: 167,784 cars made 7/94-4/95.
What to do: Have dealer install redesigned fuel-tank assembly.

'95 Ford Contour and Mercury Mystique
Outside front safety belts might fail in crash.
Models: 229,500 cars made 7/94-5/95. A

few cars made 9/4/95-9/8/95 in Ford's Mexican plant are also included.
What to do: Have dealer reinforce belts' anchor tabs—or, if tab is cracked, have dealer replace entire safety-belt assembly.

'95 Ford Crown Victoria and Mercury Grand Marquis
Improper circuit breaker could make headlights go out unexpectedly.
Models: 45,000 cars made 8/94-11/94.
What to do: Have dealer switch circuit breakers.

'95 Ford Crown Victoria and Mercury Grand Marquis
Rear left and right safety belts may not provide adequate protection in crash.
Models: 49,000 cars made 8/94-10/94.
What to do: Have dealer add reinforcement plate to rear safety-belt anchors.

'95 Ford Crown Victoria, Lincoln Town Car, and Mercury Grand Marquis
Fuel could leak from tank and pose fire hazard.
Models: 100,000 cars made 6/94-12/94.
What to do: Have dealer replace seal at fuel-filler pipe.

'95 Ford Escort
Bolts securing passenger-side air-bag module may be missing. If so, air bag might not provide adequate protection in crash.
Models: 29,000 cars made 8-9/94.
What to do: Have dealer install bolts, if necessary.

'95 Ford Escort and Mercury Tracer
Plastic fuel tank could crack and cause fire hazard.
Models: 69,100 cars built 4/95-10/95 and originally sold or currently registered in Ala., Ariz., Ark., Calif., Fla., Ga., Hawaii, La., Miss., Nev., Okla., S.C., and Tex.
What to do: Have dealer remove spacer block between fuel tank and its heat shield.

'95 Ford Explorer
Steering components could break and cause vehicle to shake or shimmy at low speeds. That increases likelihood of accident.
Models: 49,300 sport-utility vehicles made 11/94-2/95.
What to do: Have dealer inspect and, if necessary, replace inner tie rods.

'95 Ford Mustang
Suspension components could fracture, causing vehicle to shake and wheels to tuck inward or outward. That could result in crash.
Models: 1,300 cars made 2/95.
What to do: Have dealer inspect outer tie-rod ends and, if necessary, replace incorrectly tapered ball studs.

'95 Ford Mustang and Taurus, and Mercury Sable
Engine cooling fan could overheat, melt, and cause fire under hood.
Models: 695,260 Taurus and Sable cars with 3.0- and 3.8-liter engine and Mustangs with 3.8- and 5.0-liter engine made 4/94 to 8/95.
What to do: Have dealer inspect engine cooling-fan assembly and install circuit breaker. If fan is inoperative, dealer will replace fan and motor assembly.

'95 Ford Taurus and Mercury Sable
Brakes could fail.
Models: 1,500 cars made 9/94.
What to do: Have dealer check brake lin kage and, if necessary, install retainer clip that links master cyclinder to brake pedal.

'95 Ford Windstar
Fuel tank could crack and leak, causing fire.
Models: 93,654 minivans originally sold or currently registered in the following hot-weather states: Ala., Ariz., Ark. Calif. (10 southern counties), Fla., Ga., Hawaii., La., Miss., Nev. (Clark County only), Okla., S.C., and Texas. Cracks could develop in forward strap area of standard 20-gallon fuel tank due to a combination of factors that exist in very hot regions.
What to do: Have dealer install a brace at strap-bolt hole and a longer strap.

'95 Ford Windstar
Wiring harness could short out, creating fire hazard.
Models: 72,000 light-duty minivans made 1-6/94.
What to do: Have dealer insulate wiring harnesses to prevent abrasion.

'95 Ford Windstar
Alternator-output wire in power-distribution box could overheat and cause fire.
Models: 112,000 minivans made 1/94-9/94.
What to do: Have dealer inspect and tighten connection, and, if necessary, replace power distribution box and underhood harness.

'95 Ford, Lincoln, and Mercury cars, vans, and sport-utility vehicles
Passenger-side air bag might not deploy properly in crash. Also, air-bag ignitor could spew hot gases, possibly resulting in fire and burn injuries to anyone nearby.
Models: 8,600 vehicles made 1-2/95 including Ford Contour, Crown Victoria, Explorer, Mustang, Probe, and Windstar; Lincoln Town Car; and Mercury Grand Marquis and Mystique.
What to do: Have dealer replace air-bag module.

'95-96 Ford Contour and Mercury Mystique

In cars with traction control, engine may not slow to idle when driver removes foot from accelerator.
Models: 38,000 cars made 4/94-8/96.
What to do: Have dealer replace throttle cable.

'95-96 Ford Crown Victoria, Mercury Grand Marquis, and Lincoln Town Car

Front-suspension welds could break, causing creaking and clanking noises and pulling to one side during braking. Eventually, steering could deteriorate.
Models: 231,000 cars made 6/15/95-3/29/96.
What to do: Have dealer inspect and, if necessary, repair welds. (After 3/1/97, cars may not be eligible for recall program after basic warranty has expired.)

'95-96 Ford Windstar

Vehicles built at Oakville, Ontario, assembly plant and registered in certain states could lose some stopping ability because of brake-fluid leakage.
Models: 250,283 minivans made 1/94 to 5/96 and sold or currently registered in the state of Conn., Del., Ill., Ind., Iowa, Maine, Mass., Md., Mich., Minn., Mo., N.H., N.J., N.Y, Ohio, Pa., R.I., Vt., Wis., or W.Va, or in Washington, D.C. Hazard exists because brake lines may have been installed in twisted position, causing contact with dash-panel insulator above catalytic converter. If contact occurs, insulation on brake lines could become worn, allowing road salt or water to seep in and cause leak.
What to do: Have dealer inspect brake lines for corrosion and clearance conditions. Corroded or leaking lines will be replaced with nylon-coated ones and secured with retaining clips to ensure proper clearance from insulator. Brake lines that show no sign of damage will be repositioned.

'96 Ford Explorer and '97 Mercury Mountaineer

Raised liftgate could drop and injure anyone underneath.
Models: 2200 sport-utility vehicles made 6/96.
What to do: Have dealer reinforce liftgate's gas-cylinder bracket with two pop rivets.

'96 Ford Taurus

Gasoline could be expelled from engine air cleaner or exhaust system, creating fire hazard.
Models: 4,700 cars made 10/95-7/96.
What to do: Have dealer inspect and, if necessary, replace fuel-pressure regulator.

'96 Ford Taurus and Mercury Sable

Warning indicator for low brake fluid could remain lit continuously or fail to light.
Models: 76,500 cars made 6/85-9/95.
What to do: Have dealer replace indicator light switch.

'96 Ford Taurus and Mercury Sable sedans and Ford Windstar minivan

Vehicle could roll even when shifter is in Park position.
Models: 99,700 vehicles, which can be identified by contacting Ford's customer service-line at 800 392-3673 or any Ford dealer. Note vehicle identification number before you call.
What to do: Have dealer inspect and, if necessary, replace parking-pawl mechanism.

'96 Ford Taurus, Lincoln Continental, and Mercury Sable

Vehicle could roll away even though transmission shifter is in Park.
Models: 340,000 cars made 4/95-8/96.
What to do: Have dealer inspect and, if necessary, replace park-pawl shaft.

'96 Ford Thunderbird and Mercury Cougar with semiautomatic climate-control system

Climate-control blower could fail to defrost or defog windshield, reducing driver's vision.
Models: 10,600 cars made 8/95-12/95.
What to do: Have dealer replace temperature-control modules.

'96-97 Ford Explorer and Mercury Mountaineer

In extreme cold, ice could form in throttle housing and prevent engine from slowing when driver lifts foot off accelerator.
Models: 23,000 sport-utility vehicles made 2/96-2/97 and registered in the following states: Alaska, Idaho, Iowa, Maine, Mich. (Upper Peninsula only), Minn., Mont., Neb., N.H., N.Y., N.D., S.D., Vt., Wisc., and Wyo.
What to do: Have dealer install redesigned positive-crankcase-ventilation (PCV) system with heated vacuum source. (Note that even if engine races, driver can control vehicle by shifting into neutral and braking.)

'96-97 Ford pickup trucks, minivans, and sport-utility vehicles

Rear tires could wear prematurely if inflated according to incorrect labeling.
Models: 134,770 vehicles made 12/95-3/96, including '96 Aerostar, F350, Explorer, and Ranger, and '96-97 F250.
What to do: Have dealer install correct label.

'96-97 Ford, Lincoln, and Mercury (various models)

Vehicle could roll even though transmission shifter is in Park.
Models: 380,000 vehicles, including '96 Ford Windstar made 8/96; 96 Lincoln Continental made 4/95-8/96; and '96-97 Ford Taurus and Mercury Sable made 4/95-8/96.
What to do: Have dealer inspect and, if necessary, repair park pawl assembly.

'96-98 Ford Contour, Mercury Mystique

Pressure-conscious reducing valve (PCRV)that controls rear brakes could corrode from exposure to road salt.
Models: 250,000 cars with standard brakes, made 4/96-8/98. Recall does not apply to vehicles with antilock brakes.
What to do: Have dealer install redesigned PCRV in rear brake system.

'97 Ford Expedition

Rear axle components could come loose from frame and cause accident.
Models: 25,000 sport-utility vehicles made 7/96-10/96.
What to do: Have dealer install track-bar bracket reinforcement kit. Dealer will also inspect axle tubes and replace those without stamped date code.

'97 Ford F-150 pickup trucks

Safety belts could fail in a crash.
Models: 133,000 light-duty pickup trucks made 8/95-4/96.
What to do: Have dealer inspect and, if necessary, repair safety-belt anchorage attachments.

'97 Ford F150 light pickup trucks

Fuel lines could leak, possibly causing fire.
Models: 670,509 pickups made 11/95-8/97. Front fuel-line assembly could develop hole because mounting brackets were incorrectly installed. In trucks equipped with manual 4x4 transfer-case shifter, shifter linkage could rub against steel fuel lines while changing gears.
What to do: Have dealer inspect front fuel-line assembly and replace it if necessary.

'97 Ford Taurus and Windstar and Mercury Sable

Transmission fluid could leak onto hot catalytic coverter, causing fire hazard.
Models: 100,000 vehicles made 11/96-3/97.
What to do: Have dealer inspect transmission and, if necessary, replace servo cover.

'97-98 Ford Explorer and Mercury Mountaineer

Fuel hose could pose fire hazard during jump-starting.
Models: 320,000 V6-powered sport-utility vehicles made 8/96-2/98. If ground cable is attached to fuel-line bracket near bat-

tery during jump-starting, fuel hose could act as a ground, overheat, and leak.
What to do: Have dealer install warning label on fuel-line bracket advising against its use as jump-start ground. Dealer will also replace bolt in alternator bracket to provide convenient ground for jump-starting.

'97-98 Ford F-150 and F-250 pickup trucks and '97-98 Ford Expedition and Lincoln Navigator sport-utility vehicles

Transmission shifter could jam or indicate wrong gear position. Either condition could result in unintended vehicle movement.
Models: 973,000 vehicles made 11/95 to 8/97.
What to do: Have dealer inspect and, if necessary, replace shift cable. Also, have dealer install retention strap.

'97-98 Ford F-150 and F-250 pickup trucks and '97-98 Ford Expedition and '98 Lincoln Navigator sport-utility vehicles

Insulation on battery cable could chafe against body panel in trunk and eventually wear away. Short circuit could cause loss of electrical power and create fire hazard.
Models: 866,000 vehicles made 11/95-9/97.
What to do: Have dealer reposition and, if necessary, replace main battery cable.

'97-98 Ford F-150 and F-250 pickups, and Ford Expedition and Lincoln Navigator sport-utility vehicles

Wheels could come off.
Models: 1,520,000 pickups made 12/95-4/98 and sport-utility vehicles made 5/96-4/98.
What to do: Have dealer inspect wheel studs and replace lug nuts.

'97-98 Ford F150 pickup trucks

If truck is overloaded, rear springs could break and damage fuel tank, causing fire hazard.
Models: 202,000 four-wheel-drive trucks made 11/95-2/98.
What to do: Have dealer install clip on forward end of rear springs to prevent contact with fuel tank if spring breaks. Also, dealer will replace any broken springs.

'97-99 Ford and Mercury vehicles with automatic speed control

Vehicle might not decelerate when speed control is disengaged.
Models: 945,000 cars and trucks with speed control, including: '97-99 right-hand-drive Ford Explorer with single-overhead-cam V6, made 5/29/96-3/4/99; '98-99 Ford Ranger (all engines) made 1/5/98-3/4/99; '98-99 Ford Explorer and Mercury Mountaineer with single-overhead-cam V6 or V8, made 1/5/98-3/4/99; '98-99 Ford Mustang (all engines) made

3/2/98-3/4/99; '99 Ford F250, F350, F450, and F550 (over 8,500 lbs.) with 5.4-liter or 6.8-liter V8, made 3/2/98-3/4/99; F-53 stripped chassis with 5.4-liter or 6.8-liter V8, made 3/2/98-3/4/99.
What to do: Have dealer replace speed-control cable.

'97-00 Ford Expedition, Lincoln Navigator

Trailer hitch could detach, causing vehicle in tow to break free.
Models: 565,800 sport-utility vehicles made 7/96-12/99.
What to do: Have dealer replace trailer hitch mounting bolts and nut plates.

'98 Ford Contour and Mercury Mystique

Over time, front coil springs could break from road-salt corrosion and flatten tires, increasing risk of crash.
Models: 108,000 cars made at the Kansas City assembly plant 9/96 to 4/98 and registered in Conn., Del., Iowa, Ill., Ind., Mass., Md., Maine., Mich., Minn., Mo., N.H., NJ., N.Y., Ohio, Pa., R.I., Vt., W.Va., Wis., and Washington, D.C.
What to do: Have dealer install spring catcher brackets.

'98 Ford Contour and Mercury Mystique

Accelerator may not return to idle when foot is removed from pedal, which could lead to crash.
Models: 153,000 cars made 7/97-4/98.
What to do: Have dealer install redesigned accelerator cable.

'98 Ford Mustang GT

Fuel system could leak, creating fire hazard.
Models: 8,300 V8 models made 8/4/97-10/31/97.
What to do: Have dealer replace fuel rail.

'98 Ford Ranger pickup

Fuel hose could leak, creating fire hazard.
Models: 2,600 V6 pickup trucks made 8/5/97-9/19/97.
What to do: Have dealer install extra clip to keep hose away from hot exhaust manifold.

'98-99 Ford Explorer and Mercury Mountaineer

Hood could fly open suddenly if primary latch isn't engaged or hood release is inadvertently triggered.
Models: 845,000 sport-utility vehicles made 4/97-5/99.
What to do: Have dealer install secondary hood latch that's been coated for improved corrosion resistance.

'99 Ford Expedition and Lincoln Navigator

Brake system may be missing hardware, resulting in increased stopping distances.

Models: 4,000 sport-utility vehicles made 10/98-11/98.
What to do: Have dealer check retainer clip that holds master-cylinder pushrod to brake-pedal arm.

'99 Ford Expedition and Lincoln Navigator

Wheels could fall off.
Models: 57,200 4x4 sport-utility vehicles, with optional 17-inch chromed-steel wheels, made through 4/11/98.
What to do: Have dealer tighten lugs and install warning label on each wheel under hubcap.

'99-00 Ford Contour, Mercury Mystique, and Cougar

Rear wheels could lock up during braking, hampering steering ability and increasing risk of crash.
Models: 186,200 cars with standard (not antilock) brakes, made 8/98 to 3/00. Pressure-conscious reducing valve (PCRV) in rear brakes could corrode and malfunction when operated in areas where road salt is used.
What to do: Have dealer install redesigned PCRVs in rear brake system.

'00 Ford Focus

Left rear wheel and brake drum could come off. Automatic speed control could become stuck and prevent car from decelerating.
Models: 232,500 cars made 3/99 to 2/00.
What to do: For rear-wheel problem, dealer will inspect rear wheel bearings and install retention cap to prevent wheel separation. Dealer will inspect and, if necessary, replace speed-control cable on other vehicles.

'00 Ford Focus

Water could enter speed-control assembly and prevent throttle from returning to idle. If so, car could unexpectedly accelerate, increasing risk of crash.
Models: 33,292 cars with automatic speed control, made 3/8/99-10/29/99 at Wayne, Mich. plant. Only about half the suspect vehicles are in customers' hands; the rest remain in dealer inventory, according to Ford.
What to do: Have dealer inspect assembly for water corrosion and install redesigned speed-control cable. Owners are advised not to use speed control until repairs are made.

'00-01 Ford, Lincoln, and Mercury cars and sport-utility vehicles

Windshield wipers could fail.
Models: 1.1 million vehicles made 2/00 to 9/00, including the following: Ford Focus, Taurus, Expedition, Excursion, and F150 through F650 trucks; Lincoln Continental, Town Car, and Navigator; and Mercury Sable. Suspect vehicles were made at the

following assembly plants: Atlanta (dates of manufacture 2/11-7/31); Chicago (2/14-8/4); Kansas City (2/26-9/4); Kentucky truck plant (2/18-8/31); Michigan truck plant (2/23-8/3); Norfolk (2/21-7/27); Wayne stamping and assembly plant (2/25-8/15); and Wixom (2/15-8/8). Hazard exists because switch in plastic cover of wiper-motor gear case could malfunction and overheat. Overheating could cause smoking, or plastic cover material could catch fire. Malfunction is most likely to occur when wipers are set for intermittent operation or when snow or ice prevents blades from returning to "parked" position at bottom of windshield.

What to do: Have dealer check date code on wiper motor and replace motor gear-case cover if necessary.

'01 Ford Focus
Front seatbacks could unexpectedly recline, causing driver to lose control of vehicle.
Models: 8,500 cars made 3/01.
What to do: Have dealer replace driver and passenger seatback recliner-handle springs.

'01 Ford, Mercury, and Lincoln vehicles
Front safety belts may not provide adequate protection in crash.
Models: 1.4 million vehicles made 9/99 to 6/01, including the following: Ford Crown Victoria and Mercury Grand Marquis made at St. Thomas, Ontario, assembly plant 4/17/00 to 5/29/01; Lincoln Town Car built at Wixom, Mich., assembly plant 3/27/00 to 5/30/01; Lincoln Navigator built at Wayne, Mich., truck plant 4/11/00 to 5/31/01; Ford Windstar built at Oakville, Ontario, plant 3/23/00 to 5/30/01; Ford Ranger built at Twin Cities (St. Paul, Minn.) plant 3/28/00 to 5/30/01 and at Edison, N.J., plant 3/13/00 to 5/25/01. Also Ford F-150 trucks built at Norfolk, Va., plant 4/18/00 to 5/25/00, at Oakville plant 5/10/00 to 5/28/01, at Kansas City, Mo., plant 9/11/99 to 5/25/01 and at Cuautitlan, Mexico, plant 5/16/00 to 6/9/01; Ford Super Duty F-250, F-350, F-450, and F-550 built at Louisville, Ky., plant 4/17/00 to 5/27/01 and at Cuautitlan plant 5/16/00 to 6/19/01; Ford Excursion built at Louisville plant 4/17/00 to 10/2/00; Ford Expedition built at Wayne truck plant 4/11/00 to 5/31/01.
What to do: Have dealer inspect and, if necessary, replace front outboard safety-belt buckles.

'02 Ford SVT Focus
On cars with a manual transmission, the throttle can stick in the wide-open position.
Models: 534 cars made 11/01 to 4/02. (The Focus tested for the report in this issue did not exhibit this problem.)

What to do: Have dealer replace the throttle body and check for proper operation.

Geo

'93-95 Geo Prizm and Toyota Corolla
If liquid should spill around center console box, air bag could deploy, creating accident hazard.
Models: 627,858 cars made 6/92-1/95.
What to do: Have dealer install protective cover over air-bag sensor and replace any sensor damaged by previous spill.

'95 Geo Prizm and Toyota Corolla cars and Toyota Tacoma pickup trucks
Defective terminal could cause dead battery and could make battery explode, spraying acid.
Models: 14,363 cars and trucks made 6/95-7/95.
What to do: Have dealer replace battery.

'96 Geo Tracker and Suzuki Sidekick
In rear-end crash, fuel tank could puncture, creating fire hazard.
Models: 18,121 Trackers and 4325 Sidekicks, four-door models only, made 8/95-6/96.
What to do: Have dealer install two shield gussets between fuel tank and attachment brackets.

GMC

'91-96 GMC Jimmy and Sonoma Chevrolet Blazer and S10, with four-wheel drive
In two-wheel-drive mode, antilock brake system may not perform as expected, resulting in increased stopping distances.
Models: 1.1 million pickup trucks and sport-utility vehicles, with EBC4 antilock brake system, made 9/89-8/96.
What to do: Have dealer make necessary repairs (at press time, General Motors hadn't announced the specific remedy).

'91-96 GMC and Chevrolet light trucks, sport-utility vehicles, and vans
Antilock brake system could malfunction, resulting in increased stopping distances.
Models: Approx. 1.1 million '91-96 4-wheel-drive vehicles, including Chevrolet Blazer and S-10, and GMC Jimmy and Sonoma. Also subject to corrective action are about 2.4 million 2-wheel-drive vehicles, including '93-96 Chevrolet Blazer and GMC Jimmy, '94-96 Chevrolet S-10 and GMC Sonoma, and '92-95 Chevrolet Astro and GMC Safari. According to General Motors, braking problems are much less likely to occur in the 2-wheel-

drive vehicles because of a combination of unusual circumstances necessary to precipitate them.
What to do: Have dealer replace sensor switch in ABS system of 4-wheel-drive vehicles. With 2-wheel-drive models, dealer will modify computer-control unit in ABS system.

'95 GMC Jimmy and Chevrolet Blazer
Brakes could fail.
Models: 262 vehicles made 11/94.
What to do: Have dealer inspect break pedal pivot bolt in weld nut and tighten adequately.

'95 GMC Jimmy and S15 pickup trucks and sport-utility vehicles and Chevrolet Blazer and S10
Radiator fan could break apart. If hood is open, blades could strike anyone nearby.
Models: 73,163 light-duty trucks and sport-utility vehicles with 4.3-liter V6 and air-conditioning, made 9/94-11/94.
What to do: Have dealer inspect and, if necessary, replace fan.

'95 GMC Safari and Chevrolet Asto
Hoses from fuel tank could leak, creating fire hazard.
Models: 3,037 minivans made 9/94.
What to do: Have dealer tighten hoses to fuel tank.

'95 GMC Yukon and Chevrolet Tahoe
Center-rear safety belt might not provide adequate protection in crash.
Models: 8,323 sport-utility vehicles with 2 doors and 4-wheel drive made 4/94-12/94.
What to do: Owners will receive instructions on rerouting belt—or have dealer reroute it.

'95 GMC and Chevrolet light trucks
When shifter is placed in Park, indicator light may not go on.
Models: 36,641 sport-utility vehicles and pickup trucks with M30/MT1 automatic transmission made 3/94-10/94, including Chevrolet and GMC C3500HD and Suburban; Chevrolet Tahoe; and GMC Sierra and Yukon.
What to do: Have dealer adjust transmission shift cable and install lock clip.

'95 GMC and Chevrolet pickup trucks and vans
Transmission fluid could leak onto hot exhaust manifold and cause possible fire.
Models: 13,853 vehicles, with 4L80-E automatic transmission, made 12/94-1/95 including Chevrolet C20, C30, G30, K20, K30, P, Sportvan, Suburban, and GMC C25, C35, G35, K25, K35, P, Rally, Sierra, and Suburban.
What to do: Have dealer inspect transmission-case assembly to determine if casting is too thin and, if necessary, replace transmission.

'96 GMC S15 and Sonoma pickup trucks and Chevrolet S10

Transmission could seize, lock up rear wheels, and cause loss of control.
Models: 24,906 two-wheel-drive pickups, with four-cylinder engine and 5-speed manual transmission, made 8/95-1/96.
What to do: Have dealer inspect and, if necessary, replace transmission.

'96-97 GMC Safari and Chevrolet Astro

Right-rear safety belt could fail in crash.
Models: 18,972 minivans made 7/95-6/96.
What to do: Have dealer install "protector" on frame of seat cushion to keep safety-belt webbing from coming apart.

'96-97 GMC Sonoma pickup trucks and Chevrolet S10

Front brake hose could chafe against left side of engine oil pan, leak, and reduce stopping ability.
Models: 146,851 light pickups, with V6 engine, made 3/95-8/96.
What to do: Have dealer check brake-hose clearance and, if necessary, install extra brake-hose clip and replace hose.

'99 GMC Sierra and Chevrolet Silverado

Steering could fail.
Models: 8,367 extended cab pick-up trucks with four-wheel drive made 4/98-8/98.
What to do: Have dealer tighten bolts attaching steering gear to frame.

'99-00 GMC and Chevrolet pickup trucks and sport-utility vehicles

Brake pipe could leak fluid.
Models: 1,383,922 vehicles, including '99-00 Chevrolet Silverado and GMC Sierra, '00 Chevrolet Tahoe and Suburban, and '00 GMC Yukon and Yukon XL.
What to do: Have dealer inspect right front brake pipe for wear from contact with body and install redesigned section of pipe if necessary. In the absence of wear, spacer clip should be installed to maintain adequate clearance between brake pipe and body cross sill.

'00 GMC Yukon, Yukon XL, and Sierra; Chevrolet Suburban, Tahoe, and Silverado

Air bags may not deploy in a frontal crash.
Models: 525,254 vehicles made 2/99 to 2/00.
What to do: Have dealer recalibrate air bag sensing-diagnostic module (SDM).

'00 GMC, Buick, Chevrolet, Oldsmobile, Pontiac, and Saturn vehicles

Rear safety belts may not provide adequate protection in a crash.
Models: 156,305 vehicles with TRW safety-belt buckle, made 4/00-5/00, including Buick Century and Regal; Chevrolet Blazer, Impala, Lumina, Monte Carlo, Venture, and S10/T10; GMC Jimmy; Oldsmobile Intrigue and Silhouette; Pontiac Grand Prix and Montana; and Saturn L-Series.
What to do: Have dealer inspect and, if necessary, replace rear safety-belt buckles.

'00-02 General Motors sport-utility vehicles (various makes)

Rear stop and hazard lamps could become inoperative, increasing risk of crash with another vehicle, whose driver doesn't realize SUV is slowing.
Models: Models: 506,377 sport-utility vehicles made 9/99 to 8/01, including '00-01 GMC Jimmy and Oldsmobile Bravada, and '00-02 Chevrolet Blazer.
What to do: What to do: At press time, General Motors had not provided a remedy or owner-notification schedule. If you have not been contacted, call 800-462-8782 (for a GMC vehicle), 800-442-6537 (Oldsmobile), or 800-222-1020 (Chevrolet).

'02 GMC Envoy and Chevrolet Tralblazer

Vehicle could roll even though shifter is in Park.
Models: 78,004 sport-utility vehicles, with four-wheel drive, made 1/01 to 8/01.
What to do: Have dealer recalibrate transfer-case control module.

'02 GMC Envoy, Chevrolet TrailBlazer, and Oldsmobile Bravada

Fuel-filter fitting could become disconnected. If that occurs during start-up, engine might not turn over and fuel would be pumped onto ground, creating a fire hazard. If fitting comes off while vehicle is moving, engine would stop, possibly resulting in crash.
Models: 60,044 sport-utility vehicles made 9/01 to 11/01.
What to do: Have dealer replace fuel-filter quick-connect retainers.

Honda

'95 Honda Accord

Air bag could deploy unexpectedly and cause injury or loss of control.
Models: 164,139 cars made 4/94-2/95.
What to do: Have dealer replace air bag electronic control unit.

'96 Honda Civic

Brakes could lose power assist, making car harder to stop.
Models: 160,689 hatchbacks, sedans, and coupes made 8/95-5/96.
What to do: Have dealer clean soapy lubricant from inside of brake-booster vacuum hose with hot water.

'96-98 Honda Civic

Floor mat could prevent accelerator pedal from returning to idle when foot is removed, possibly causing crash.
Models: 931,000 cars made 8/95-8/98. Recall involves only those vehicles with genuine Honda floor mats.
What to do: Have dealer install positive floor-mat retention system consisting of grommet in mat and pin bracket attached to car.

'98 Honda Accord and Acura CL

Vehicle could roll away even when shifter is in park.
Models: 33,966 cars made 9/97-1/98.
What to do: Have dealer install collar on transmission parking pawl.

'98-99 Honda CR-V

Wire harness under dash could abrade from contact with brake switch, resulting in failure of interior and exterior lamps, windshield wipers, antilock functioning of brakes, and battery-charging system.
Models: 101,159 cars made 11/97-11/98.
What to do: Have dealer repair damaged wires and install protective corrugated plastic tube over wire harness near brake-stop switch.

'99 Honda Odyssey

In freezing weather, vehicle might not decelerate when driver removes foot from accelerator, possibly causing crash. Also, sliding doors could open unexpectedly, allowing unrestrained rear passenger to fall out of vehicle.
Models: 46,162 EX and LX model minivans made 8/98-4/99.
What to do: For vehicles with deceleration problem, dealer will drill two additional holes in bottom of air-intake resonator to prevent ice from forming in throttle body. Dealer will replace door-latch assembly in minivans whose doors don't close properly.

'00-01 Honda Accord and Civic

Rear safety belts may not unfasten after crash.
Models: 16,459 sedans and coupes made 7/00 to 9/00. Only buckles marked with assembly numbers beginning with 00185, 00186, or 00187 are subject to recall. Number appears on back of buckle.
What to do: Have dealer inspect and, if necessary, replace safety-belt assemblies.

'02 Honda CR-V

Front safety belts could unlatch in crash.
Models: 6,744 sport-utility vehicles made 9/01 to 10/01.
What to do: Have dealer repair front safety-belt pretensioners.

'02 Honda TL

"Auto-up" power window feature on driver's door could fail.
Models: 10,575 sedans made 2/01 to

4/01. Problem may keep window from opening or cause it to move spontaneously.
What to do: Have dealer replace power-window control unit.

Hyundai

'94-95 Hyundai Elantra
Air bag could fail.
Models: 14,651 cars made 6/94-10/94.
What to do: Have dealer inspect air-bag assembly wiring-harness connector; if terminal holder is missing, dealer will install one.

'95 Hyundai Accent
Depressing clutch could abrade insulation on engine control module wiring harness. That could result in sudden engine stall.
Models: 5,306 cars, with manual transmission, made 8/94-2/95.
What to do: Have dealer inspect wiring harness for damage and reposition harness to avoid contact with clutch-pedal lever.

'95 Hyundai Sonata
Label on left rear door overstates car's weight capacity. Label should read 860 pounds, not 1100 pounds. Overloading could damage tires or mechanical components and cause accident.
Models: 4,842 cars made 11/93-3/94.
What to do: If you don't get correct label by mail, contact dealer.

'95 Hyundai Sonata GLS
Defective rear gas-filled shock absorbers could cause loss of control.
Models: 356 cars made 3/95-7/95.
What to do: Have dealer check and, if necessary, replace rear shock-absorber and spring-seat assemblies.

'95-97 Hyundai Accent
Road salt could make front springs to rust, break, and puncture tire.
Models: 64,967 cars made 5/94-11/96 and registered in the following states: Conn., Del., Ill., Ind., Iowa, Maine., Md., Mass., Mich., Minn., Mo., N.H., N.J., N.Y., Ohio, Pa., R.I., Vt., W.Va., and Wisc.
What to do: Have dealer install spring guide to keep broken coil spring from damaging tire.

'96-97 Hyundai Elantra and '97 Tiburon
Fuel tank could crack and leak, resulting in possible fire.
Models: 84,020 cars made 9/95-8/97.
What to do: Have dealer pressure-check fuel tank for cracks and replace it if necessary. Also confirm that new fuel filler cap has been installed.

'96-97 Hyundai models
Windshield wipers could fail.
Models: 74,965 cars made 4/95-10/96, including '96-97 Accent, Elantra, and Sonata and '97 Tiburon.
What to do: Have dealer clean contacts on wiper circuit breaker.

'97-01 Hyundai Tiburon
Front safety belts may not extend and retract smoothly, discouraging occupants from wearing belts and subjecting them to increased risk of injury in crash.
Models: 42,782 cars made 3/96 to 8/00.
What to do: Have dealer install stopper over front safety belts' D-ring guides to facilitate smooth operation.

'99 Hyundai Accent, Elantra, Tiburon
Transmission fluid could leak and prevent vehicle from accelerating as expected when accelerator pedal is depressed.
Models: 11,530 cars with automatic transmission made 3/99-4/99.
What to do: Have dealer replace automatic transmission pressure-control solenoid valve.

'99-00 Hyundai Elantra and Sonata
Engine could stall suddenly at low speeds.
Models: 165,977 Sonatas with 2.5-liter V6 engine and all Elantras made 7/98-7/00.
What to do: Have dealer reroute MAF (mass air flow) sensor-connector wiring harness.

'99-01 Hyundai Sonata
Air-bag warning lamp could illuminate unexpectedly.
Models: 86,513 cars made 3/98 to 11/00.
What to do: Have dealer make necessary alterations to front-seat, side-impact air-bag wiring harness.

'01 Hyundai Santa Fe
Engine could stall suddenly and unexpectedly.
Models: 15,241 sport-utility vehicles made 3/00 to 2/01.
What to do: Have dealer replace crankshaft position sensors.

Infiniti

'91-96 Infiniti G20
Fuel-filler- tube assembly could rust and leak, posing fire hazard. Problem is most likely in areas where road salt is used.
Models: 85,000 cars made 7/90-5/96.
What to do: Have dealer replace filler tube and other assembly components as needed.

'97-98 Infiniti Q45
Key can be removed from ignition switch when shifter isn't in park. If driver does so, parked car could roll and crash.
Models: 22,000 cars made 7/96-6/98.
What to do: Have dealer replace shift-lock control unit. (In any car, you should apply parking brake when parking.)

'97-98 Infiniti Q45 and '98 Infiniti I30
Electrical short could occur in alternator and cause engine-compartment fire.
Models: 17,000 cars made 4/97-7/97.
What to do: Have dealer replace alternator.

Isuzu

'96 Isuzu Trooper
Center rear safety belt may not latch properly.
Models: 2,345 vehicles made 2/96.
What to do: Have dealer inspect center rear safety belt and, if necessary, replace buckle.

'96-97 Isuzu Trooper
Brake fluid could leak from hose, lengthening stopping distances.
Models: 6,667 sport-utility vehicles made 2/96-6/96.
What to do: Have dealer inspect clearance between brake hose and upper control arm and, if necessary, replace hose.

'98 Isuzu Amigo
Rear safety belts might not provide adequate protection in crash.
Models: 3,044 sport-utility vehicles made 12/97-3/98.
What to do: Have dealer install rear safety-belt anchor bolts.

'98 Isuzu Amigo
Sunroof sunshade could fall and stike occupant.
Models: 5,361 sport-utility vehicles made 12/97-6/98.
What to do: Have dealer remove sunshade holder, reapply adhesive, and rebond to sunroof.

'98 Isuzu Amigo and Rodeo
Engine could stall or fail to start.
Models: 38,637 vehicles made 7/97-2/98.
What to do: Have dealer replace wiring harness.

Jeep

'92-95 Jeep Cherokee and '94-95 Grand Cherokee
Extensive exposure to road salt could corrode brake components and hamper stopping ability.
Models: 490,000 sport-utility vehicles originally sold or currently registered in the following "salt belt" states: Conn., Ill., Ind., Me., Md., Mass., Mich., N.H., N.J., N.Y., Ohio, Pa., R.I., Vt., and Wisc. as

well as Washington, D.C.

What to do: Have dealer install corrosion-coated front disc-brake rotors with stainless-steel center section.

'95 Jeep Cherokee

Driver-side air bag might not deploy in crash.

Models: 70,000 sport-utility vehicles made 6/94-2/95.

What to do: Have dealer inspect air-bag module for presence of arming lever and replace module if lever is missing.

'95 Jeep Cherokee and Grand Cherokee

Release button could come off parking-brake handle, rendering brake inoperative.

Models: 135,000 sport-utility vehicles made 10/94-2/95.

What to do: Have dealer replace parking-brake handle assembly.

'96 Jeep Cherokee and Grand Cherokee

Sparking at alternator-circuit fuse could cause under-hood fire.

Models: 32,000 sport-utility vehicles made 7/95-8/95.

What to do: Have dealer replace fuse with fuse link and repair any damage to power-distribution center.

'96-99 Jeep Cherokee and '96-98 Grand Cherokee

Road salt could corrode front disc-brake rotors, resulting in reduced stopping ability.

Models: 637,973 sport-utility vehicles made 7/95-10/98 and sold or registered in the following states: Conn., Ill., Ind., Maine., Md., Mass., Mich., N.H., N.J., N.Y., Ohio, Pa., R.I., Vt., Wis., and D.C.

What to do: Have dealer install rotors with a stainless-steel hub.

'97-99 Jeep Cherokee

Air bag could deploy unexpectedly and injure driver. Alternatively, air bag warning light could come on for no apparent reason.

Models: 391,623 sport-utility vehicles made 7/96-6/99.

What to do: Have dealer replace air-bag control module, positioning it on top of transmission tunnel.

'99 Jeep Grand Cherokee

Rear left and right safety belts might not provide adequate protection in crash.

Models: 13,000 sport-utility vehicles made 7/98-9/98.

What to do: Have dealer replace safety-belt retractors.

'99-00 Jeep, Chrysler and Dodge

Safety belts might not provide adequate protection in crash.

Models: 204,000 vehicles made 9/99, including Chrysler Concorde, 300M, and LHS; Dodge Intrepid; and Jeep Grand Cherokee. There is a manufacturing defect in the belt's shoulder-height adjustable turning loop (ATL).

What to do: Have dealer replace upper ATL bolt.

'99-02 Jeep Wrangler, Cherokee, and Grand Cherokee

Debris could accumulate near one of engine cylinders and cause fire under hood.

Models: 1,115,322 sport-utility vehicles, with 4.0-liter engine, made 6/98 to 3/02, including the following: '00-01 Cherokee, '99-02 Grand Cherokee, and '00-02 Wrangler.

What to do: Have dealer install manifold shield to modify the intake and exhaust airflow and to prevent debris from building up near No. 3 cylinder.

'02 Jeep Grand Cherokee

Gasoline could spill from filler tube during refueling and pose fire hazard.

Models: 38,700 sport-utility vehicles made 7/01 to 9/01.

What to do: Have dealer inspect and, if necessary, reroute vapor-recovery-system vent hose. Dealer will also replace canister assembly if vent hose is bent and vehicle has been driven more than 20 miles.

'02 Jeep Grand Cherokee and Chrysler PT Cruiser

Gauges, warning lamps, and illumination lamps could become inoperative and become a distraction that could lead to crash.

Models: 43,000 vehicles made 7/01 to 8/01.

What to do: Have dealer correct software error in instrument-cluster microprocessor.

'02 Jeep Liberty

Air bags may not deploy quickly enough in a crash.

Models: 102,000 sport-utility vehicles made 1/01 to 11/01. Hazard exists because sharp edge of power-steering pressure hose could cut front air bag's impact-sensor wiring insulation in crash. That could cause an electrical short, which could then delay deployment.

What to do: Have dealer wrap harness of front-impact-sensor wire with protective insulation.

Kia

'95 Kia Sportage

Rear brakes could fail or rear wheel and axle shaft could come off.

Models: 1,319 sport/utility vehicles made 10/94-1/95.

What to do: Have dealer inspect and tighten rear-axle bearing oil-seal retainers and brake backing plates.

'97-99 Kia Sportage

Engine could stall.

Models: 76,986 cars made 8/96-2/99. Wires attached to connectors can loosen as a result of engine movement.

What to do: Have dealer install spring clips, to lock connectors together, and solder a splice in wiring harness.

'98-99 Kia Sephia

Engine could stall.

Models: 102,944 cars made 9/97-5/99.

What to do: Have dealer replace connectors that channel electrical current to fuel pump and reposition those connectors so they won't come in contact with moisture.

'01 Kia Optima

Driver's side air bag may not deploy in crash.

Models: 16,231 cars made 10/00 to 3/01. Air-bag wire harness may have been misrouted, causing it to be pinched or cut by seat-cushion tilt mechanism.

What to do: Have dealer check for proper routing of side-air-bag wire harness and secure it with plastic tie-wrap. If harness is damaged, dealer will replace it.

Land Rover

'94-98 Land Rover Discovery and '95 Range Rover

Cruise-control wiring could abrade from contact with steering components and trigger air bag.

Models: 54,488 sport-utility vehicles made 12/93-12/97.

What to do: Have dealer install fusible link to protect steering-wheel rotary coupler from overheating.

'95 Range Rover

Flexible brake hose connecting hydraulic pump to antilock brake system could leak, severely hampering stopping ability and creating fire hazard.

Models: 2,114 vehicles made 6/94-4/95.

What to do: Have dealer inspect and, if necessary, replace flexible hose.

'95 Range Rover 4.0SE

Power steering could fail and suddenly make steering much heavier.

Models: 2,946 sport-utility vehicles made 6/94-7/95.

What to do: Have dealer replace idler pulley in engine serpentine-belt system.

'95-96 Land Rover Discovery

Right front door could open unexpectedly.

Models: 20,889 vehicles made 4/95-6/96.

What to do: Have dealer install hardware to make door latch properly. (Dealer will check other door latches as well.).

'95-98 Range Rover
Hoses could leak engine coolant, automatic-transmission fluid, or windshield-wiper fluid and cause underhood fire.
Models: 22,870 sport-utility vehicles made 10/94-5/98.
What to do: Have dealer inspect and, if necessary, replace hose and tubing components.

'95-99 Range Rover
If moisture freezes in transmission breather tube and blocks it, transmission fluid could leak out from dipstick tube and create fire hazard.
Models: 26,250 sport-utility vehicles made 10/94-8/98.
What to do: Have dealer cut breather tube at angle to keep it away from pooled water.

Lexus

'97 Lexus ES300, Toyota Avalon, and Toyota Camry
In extreme cold, icing could disable brakes' power assist. Brakes would then require more distance and much greater pedal pressure to stop car.
Models: 18,746 cars made 7/96-2/97 and originally sold or currently registered in Alaska, Colo., Idaho, Ill., Iowa, Kan., Me., Mich., Minn., Mont., Neb., Nev., N.H., N.Y., N.D., S.D., Vt., Wisc., and Wyo.
What to do: Have dealer install redesigned brake vacuum hose. Owners of cars in other states who drive in extremely cold weather should also ask dealer for redesigned hose.

'99 Lexus RX300
When switch is set to "auto," headlights and taillights may not turn themselves on in low-light conditions. Also, in cars with optional traction-control system, brake hose could fail and make braking action feel unsteady, increasing risk of crash.
Models: 23,441 cars made 1/98-7/99.
What to do: Have dealer install modified body electronic control unit. On cars with traction-control system, have dealer install modified brake hoses.

'02 Lexus ES300 and Toyota Camry
On vehicles equipped with certain steering wheels, horn cover could detach and injure driver during air-bag deployment.
Models: 19,587 cars, with three-spoke-style steering wheel, made 7/01 to 11/01.
What to do: Have dealer replace driver's side air-bag module.

Lincoln

'86-95 Lincoln Continental, Ford Taurus, and Mercury Sable
Corrosion from road salt could make subframes drop , suddenly making the car very hard to steer.
Models: 2.7 million cars made 10/85-6/95 including '86-95 Ford Taurus and Mercury Sable and '88-94 Lincoln Continental. Recall affects vehicles sold or currently registered in Conn., Dela., D.C., Ill., Ind., Iowa, Kan., Ky., Maine., Md., Mass., Mich., Minn., Mo., Neb., N.H., N.J., N.Y., Ohio, Pa., R.I., Vt., Va., W.Va., and Wis.
What to do: Have dealer reinforce subframe with nuts, bolts, and plates.

'91-95 Lincoln, Ford, and Mercury
Water could freeze in cruise-control cable and prevent driver from disengaging cruise control.
Models: 212,700 cars with 3.8-liter V6, including '91-94 Lincoln Continental and '91-95 Ford Taurus and Mercury Sable. Recall applies only to cars registered in Alaska, Colo., Idaho, Ill., Ind., Iowa, Kan., Maine, Mass., Mich., Minn., Mo., Mont., Neb., N.H., N.Y., N.D., Ohio., Pa., S.D., Vt., Wisc., and Wyo. Affected vehicles were made 7/90-11/94.
What to do: Have dealer install cable boot to keep out water.

'92-95 Lincoln, Ford, and Mercury
Snow could clog engine-cooling fan and make it overheat, posing fire hazard.
Models: 75,200 cars, with 2.3-liter Four, 3.0-liter V6, or 3.8-liter V6, including '92-94 Ford Tempo, Mercury Topaz, and Lincoln Continental and '92-95 Ford Taurus and Mercury Sable. Recall applies only to cars registered in Alaska, Iowa, Minn., Neb., N.D., and S.D. are being recalled. Dates of manufacture are: Tempo, 8/5/91-5/20/94; Topaz, 8/5/91-5/16/94; Continental, 8/12/91-11/17/94; Taurus, 5/3/91-6/26/95; Sable, 6/19/91-6/16/95.
What to do: Have dealer install wiring with circuit breaker to prevent fan motor from overheating.

'95 Lincoln Town Car, Ford Crown Victoria, and Mercury Grand Marquis
Fuel could leak from tank and pose fire hazard.
Models: 100,000 cars made 6/94-12/94.
What to do: Have dealer replace seal at fuel-filler pipe.

'95 Lincoln, Ford, and Mercury cars, vans, and sport-utility vehicles
Passenger-side air bag might not deploy properly in crash. Also, air-bag ignitor could spew hot gases, possibly resulting in fire and burn injuries to anyone nearby.
Models: 8,600 vehicles made 1-2/95 including Ford Contour, Crown Victoria,

Explorer, Mustang, Probe, and Windstar; Lincoln Town Car; and Mercury Grand Marquis and Mystique.
What to do: Have dealer replace air-bag module.

'95-96 Lincoln Continental
Headlights and other exterior lights could go out suddenly when "autolamp" system is being used.
Models: 40,000 cars made 11/94-11/95.
What to do: Have dealer replace "autolamp" control module. Until repair is made, use manual switch to turn on headlights.

'95-96 Lincoln Town Car, Ford Crown Victoria, and Mercury Grand Marquis
Front-suspension welds could break, causing creaking and clanking noises and pulling to one side during braking. Eventually, steering could deteriorate.
Models: 231,000 cars made 6/15/95-3/29/96.
What to do: Have dealer inspect and, if necessary, repair welds. (After 3/1/97, cars may not be eligible for recall program after basic warranty has expired.)

'96 Lincoln Continental, Ford Taurus, and Mercury Sable
Vehicle could roll away even though transmission shifter is in Park.
Models: 340,000 cars made 4/95-8/96.
What to do: Have dealer inspect and, if necessary, replace park-pawl shaft.

'96-97 Lincoln, Ford, and Mercury (various models)
Vehicle could roll even though transmission shifter is in Park.
Models: 380,000 vehicles, including '96 Ford Windstar made 8/96; 96 Lincoln Continental made 4/95-8/96; and '96-97 Ford Taurus and Mercury Sable made 4/95-8/96.
What to do: Have dealer inspect and, if necessary, repair park pawl assembly.

'97-98 Lincoln Navigator sport-utility vehicles, Ford F-150 and F-250 pickup trucks and '97-98 Ford Expedition
Transmission shifter could jam or indicate wrong gear position. Either condition could result in unintended vehicle movement.
Models: 973,000 vehicles made 11/95 to 8/97.
What to do: Have dealer inspect and, if necessary, replace shift cable. Also, have dealer install retention strap.

'97-98 Lincoln Navigator sport-utility vehicles, Ford F-150 and F-250 pickups, and Ford Expedition
Wheels could come off.
Models: 1,520,000 pickups made 12/95-4/98 and sport-utility vehicles made 5/96-4/98.
What to do: Have dealer inspect wheel studs and replace lug nuts.

'97-98 '98 Lincoln Navigator sport-utility vehicles, Ford F-150 and F-250 pickup trucks and '97-98 Ford Expedition

Insulation on battery cable could chafe against body panel in trunk and eventually wear away. Short circuit could cause loss of electrical power and create fire hazard.

Models: 866,000 vehicles made 11/95-9/97.

What to do: Have dealer reposition and, if necessary, replace main battery cable.

'97-00 Lincoln Navigator, Ford Expedition

Trailer hitch could detach, causing vehicle in tow to break free.

Models: 565,800 sport-utility vehicles made 7/96-12/99.

What to do: Have dealer replace trailer hitch mounting bolts and nut plates.

'99 Lincoln Continental

Fuel hose could leak and cause engine fire.

Models: 2,500 cars made 9/98-10/98.

What to do: Have dealer install revised fuel-rail assembly.

'99 Lincoln Navigator and Ford Expedition

Wheels could fall off.

Models: 57,200 4x4 sport-utility vehicles, with optional 17-inch chromed-steel wheels, made through 4/11/98.

What to do: Have dealer tighten lugs and install warning label on each wheel under hubcap.

'99 Lincoln Navigator and Ford Expedition

Brake system may be missing hardware, resulting in increased stopping distances.

Models: 4,000 sport-utility vehicles made 10/98-11/98.

What to do: Have dealer check retainer clip that holds master-cylinder pushrod to brake-pedal arm.

'00-01 Lincoln, Ford, and Mercury cars and sport-utility vehicles

Windshield wipers could fail.

Models: 1.1 million vehicles made 2/00 to 9/00, including the following: Ford Focus, Taurus, Expedition, Excursion, and F150 through F650 trucks; Lincoln Continental, Town Car, and Navigator; and Mercury Sable. Suspect vehicles were made at the following assembly plants: Atlanta (dates of manufacture 2/11-7/31); Chicago (2/14-8/4); Kansas City (2/26-9/4); Kentucky truck plant (2/18-8/31); Michigan truck plant (2/23-8/3); Norfolk (2/21-7/27); Wayne stamping and assembly plant (2/25-8/15); and Wixom (2/15-8/8). Hazard exists because switch in plastic cover of wiper-motor gear case could malfunction and overheat. Overheating could cause smoking, or plastic cover

material could catch fire. Malfunction is most likely to occur when wipers are set for intermittent operation or when snow or ice prevents blades from returning to "parked" position at bottom of windshield.

What to do: Have dealer check date code on wiper motor and replace motor gear-case cover if necessary.

'01 Lincoln, Ford, and Mercury vehicles

Front safety belts may not provide adequate protection in crash.

Models: 1.4 million vehicles made 9/99 to 6/01, including the following: Ford Crown Victoria and Mercury Grand Marquis made at St. Thomas, Ontario, assembly plant 4/17/00 to 5/29/01; Lincoln Town Car built at Wixom, Mich., assembly plant 3/27/00 to 5/30/01; Lincoln Navigator built at Wayne, Mich., truck plant 4/11/00 to 5/31/01; Ford Windstar built at Oakville, Ontario, plant 3/23/00 to 5/30/01; Ford Ranger built at Twin Cities (St. Paul, Minn.) plant 3/28/00 to 5/30/01 and at Edison, N.J., plant 3/13/00 to 5/25/01. Also Ford F-150 trucks built at Norfolk, Va., plant 4/18/00 to 5/25/00, at Oakville plant 5/10/00 to 5/28/01, at Kansas City, Mo., plant 9/11/99 to 5/25/01 and at Cuautitlan, Mexico, plant 5/16/00 to 6/9/01; Ford Super Duty F-250, F-350, F-450, and F-550 built at Louisville, Ky., plant 4/17/00 to 5/27/01 and at Cuautitlan plant 5/16/00 to 6/19/01; Ford Excursion built at Louisville plant 4/17/00 to 10/2/00; Ford Expedition built at Wayne truck plant 4/11/00 to 5/31/01.

What to do: Have dealer inspect and, if necessary, replace front outboard safety-belt buckles.

Mazda

'86-95 Mercury Sable, Ford Taurus, and Lincoln Continental

Corrosion from road salt could make subframes drop , suddenly making the car very hard to steer.

Models: 2.7 million cars made 10/85-6/95 including "86-95 Ford Taurus and Mercury Sable and '88-94 Lincoln Continental. Recall affects vehicles sold or currently registered in Conn., Dela., D.C., Ill., Ind., Iowa, Kan., Ky., Maine., Md., Mass., Mich., Minn., Mo., Neb., N.H., N.J., N.Y., Ohio, Pa., R.I., Vt., Va., W.Va., and Wis.

What to do: Have dealer reinforce subframe with nuts, bolts, and plates.

'92-95 Mazda MX3

Road salt could corrode front suspension spring. If spring breaks, it could puncture tire.

Models: 25,000 cars made 8/91-8/94 and registered in Conn., Del., Ill., Ind., Iowa, Me., Md., Mass., Mich., Minn., N.H.,

N.J., N.Y., Ohio, Pa., R.I., Vt., Washington D.C., W. Va., and Wisc.

What to do: Have dealer install guard assembly to keep broken suspension spring from contacting and puncturing tire.

'93-95 Mazda RX-7

Oil mist could collect in brake vacuum check valve and reduce brakes' power assist, so that stopping would require more pedal effort.

Models: 13,900 cars made 12/91-12/95.

What to do: Have dealer replace two vacuum hoses and check valve.

'95 Mazda Protege

Engine valve springs could break, damaging pistons and causing engine to stall.

Models: 5,760 cars, with 1.5-liter engine, made 10-11/94.

What to do: Have dealer replace all 16 valve springs in engine.

'95-97 Mazda 626 and MX6

Air bag could deploy unexpectedly and cause injury or loss of control.

Models: 213,000 cars made 6/94-9/96, including '95-97 626 and '95-96 MX6.

What to do: Have dealer reprogram air-bag sensor to reduce likelihood of deployment if road debris hits undercarriage.

'98 Mazda 626

Condensation could short-circuit audio system and cause fire.

Models: 73,000 cars made 8/97-8/98. Hazard exists when car is driven in hot, humid weather, with windows open and air conditioner running.

What to do: Have dealer apply aluminum tape to audio system to keep out moisture.

'98 Mazda 626

Spring in timing-belt tensioner could break and become jammed in belt, causing engine to stall.

Models: 31,000 cars with 2.0-liter engine made 8/97-8/98.

What to do: Have dealer inspect and, if necessary, replace timing-belt tensioner.

'99 Mazda Miata

Fuel-injector harness could contact engine manifold and blow fuse, stalling the engine.

Models: 8,000 cars made 11/97-3/98.

What to do: Have dealer reroute and, if necessary, replace injector harness.

'99-00 Mazda 626

Brakes could partially fail.

Models: 71,000 cars made 2/99-1/00.

What to do: Have dealer inspect reservoir-tank cap on brake master cylinder and replace it if necessary.

'00 Mazda MPV minivan

Door could be opened even though

childproof locking system is in use.
Models: 12,000 minivans made 3/99-7/99.
What to do: Have dealer repair latching assembly in door-lock mechanism.

'00 Mazda MPV minivan
Fuel could leak and cause fire under hood.
Models: 5,600 minivans made 3/99-6/99.
What to do: Have dealer replace lower intake manifold assembly.

Mercedes-Benz

'92-95 Mercedes-Benz 124
Front passenger metal footrest could abrade wiring harness underneath and cause electrical short. That could result in engine stall or inadvertent air-bag deployment.
Models: 50,000 cars made 2/92-10/94.
What to do: Have dealer install additional wiring harness cable-fastener ties and protective covering for sharp edges of metal footrest.

'92-95 Mercedes-Benz 300- and E-Class
Front passenger's footrest could abrade wiring harness underneath. Short circuit could stall engine or deploy air bag.
Models: Models: 50,000 cars made 2/92-10/94.
What to do: What to do: Have dealer cover sharp edges of footrest and install additional cable ties to secure harness.

'97 Mercedes S
Driver's air bag could deploy suddenly and unexpectedly, causing possible loss of vehicle control.
Models: 4,402 cars made 6/96-7/97. Hazard exists when car is operated in areas of high humidity which could cause ignition filament of gas generator to corrode and airbag to deploy spontaneously.
What to do: Have dealer replace air-bag module.

'98-99 Mercedes M-Class
Front safety-belt buckles could unlatch unexpectedly and increase risk of injury in crash.
Models: 85,970 cars made 1/97-11/99.
What to do: Have dealer inspect and, if necessary, replace, safety-belt buckles.

'98-99 Mercedes Benz C-Class
Battery could explode.
Models: 65,731 cars with Hoppecke battery made 4/97 to 6/99. Hazard exists because battery maintenance schedule might let too much time pass between servicing to maintain proper electrolyte levels. Low electrolyte levels could cause battery to spark or cells to rupture, possibly resulting in explosion.
What to do: Have dealer inspect and, if necessary, replace battery. Dealer will

also provide labeling for owner's manual and engine compartment that reminds owner and service technician of the need to perform periodic maintenance.

'00 Mazda MPV minivan
Door could be opened even though childproof locking system is in use.
Models: 12,000 minivans made 3/99-7/99.
What to do: Have dealer repair latching assembly in door-lock mechanism.

Mercury

'86-95 Ford Taurus, Mercury Sable, and Lincoln Continental
Corrosion from road salt could make subframes drop, suddenly making the car very hard to steer.
Models: 2.7 million cars made 10/85-6/95 including '86-95 Ford Taurus and Mercury Sable and '88-94 Lincoln Continental. Recall affects vehicles sold or currently registered in Conn., Dela., D.C., Ill., Ind., Iowa, Kan., Ky., Maine., Md., Mass., Mich., Minn., Mo., Neb., N.H., N.J., N.Y., Ohio, Pa., R.I., Vt., Va., W.Va., and Wis.
What to do: Have dealer reinforce subframe with nuts, bolts, and plates.

'91-95 Mercury, Ford, and Lincoln
Water could freeze in cruise-control cable and prevent driver from disengaging cruise control.
Models: 212,700 cars with 3.8-liter V6, including '91-94 Lincoln Continental and '91-95 Ford Taurus and Mercury Sable. Recall applies only to cars registered in Alaska, Colo., Idaho, Ill., Ind., Iowa, Kan., Maine, Mass., Mich., Minn., Mo., Mont., Neb., N.H., N.Y., N.D., Ohio, Pa., S.D., Vt., Wisc., and Wyo. Affected vehicles were made 7/90-11/94.
What to do: Have dealer install cable boot to keep out water.

'92-95 Mercury, Ford, and Lincoln
Snow could clog engine-cooling fan and make it overheat, posing fire hazard.
Models: 75,200 cars, with 2.3-liter Four, 3.0-liter V6, or 3.8-liter V6, including '92-94 Ford Tempo, Mercury Topaz, and Lincoln Continental and '92-95 Ford Taurus and Mercury Sable. Recall applies only to cars registered in Alaska, Iowa, Minn., Neb., N.D., and S.D. are being recalled. Dates of manufacture are: Tempo, 8/5/91-5/20/94; Topaz, 8/5/91-5/16/94; Continental, 8/12/91-11/17/94; Taurus, 5/3/91-6/26/95; Sable, 6/19/91-6/16/95.
What to do: Have dealer install wiring with circuit breaker to prevent fan motor from overheating.

'94-95 Mercury Tracer and Ford Escort
Driver's-side air bag might not deploy

properly in crash, and hot gasses could cause burns.
Models: 240 cars made 9-10/94.
What to do: Have dealer replace air-bag module.

'95 Mercury cars, vans, and sport-utility vehicles, Ford, and Lincoln
Passenger-side air bag might not deploy properly in crash. Also, air-bag ignitor could spew hot gases, possibly resulting in fire and burn injuries to anyone nearby.
Models: 8,600 vehicles made 1-2/95 including Ford Contour, Crown Victoria, Explorer, Mustang, Probe, and Windstar; Lincoln Town Car; and Mercury Grand Marquis and Mystique.
What to do: Have dealer replace air-bag module.

'95 Mercury Grand Marquis and Ford Crown Victoria
Improper circuit breaker could make headlights go out unexpectedly.
Models: 45,000 cars made 8/94-11/94.
What to do: Have dealer switch circuit breakers.

'95 Mercury Grand Marquis and Ford Crown Victoria
Rear left and right safety belts may not provide adequate protection in crash.
Models: 49,000 cars made 8/94-10/94.
What to do: Have dealer add reinforcement plate to rear safety-belt anchors.

'95 Mercury Grand Marquis, Ford Crown Victoria, and Lincoln Town Car
Fuel could leak from tank and pose fire hazard.
Models: 100,000 cars made 6/94-12/94.
What to do: Have dealer replace seal at fuel-filler pipe.

'95 Mercury Mystique and Ford Contour
Fuel could leak from filler pipe and create fire hazard.
Models: 167,784 cars made 7/94-4/95.
What to do: Have dealer install redesigned fuel-tank assembly.

'95 Mercury Mystique and Ford Contour
Outside front safety belts might fail in crash.
Models: 229,500 cars made 7/94-5/95. A few cars made 9/4/95-9/8/95 in Ford's Mexican plant are also included.
What to do: Have dealer reinforce belts' anchor tabs—or, if tab is cracked, have dealer replace entire safety-belt assembly.

'95 Mercury Mystique and Ford Contour
If rear passenger-side door windows break, glass could shatter into large fragments, a violation of Federal safety standard.

Models: 2,512 cars made 11/94.
What to do: Have dealer replace windows.

'95 Mercury Mystique and Ford Contour

Fuel could seep through weld at filler pipe opening, creating fire hazard.
Models: 28,500 cars made 7-10/94.
What to do: Have dealer inspect and, if necessary, replace fuel tank.

'95 Mercury Sable and Ford Taurus

Brakes could fail.
Models: 1,500 cars made 9/94.
What to do: Have dealer check brake linkage and, if necessary, install retainer clip that links master cyclinder to brake pedal.

'95 Mercury Sable and Ford Mustang and Taurus

Engine cooling fan could overheat, melt, and cause fire under hood.
Models: 695,260 Taurus and Sable cars with 3.0- and 3.8-liter engine and Mustangs with 3.8- and 5.0-liter engine made 4/94 to 8/95.
What to do: Have dealer inspect engine cooling-fan assembly and install circuit breaker. If fan is inoperative, dealer will replace fan and motor assembly.

'95 Mercury Tracer and Ford Escort

Plastic fuel tank could crack and cause fire hazard.
Models: 69,100 cars built 4/95-10/95 and originally sold or currently registered in Ala., Ariz., Ark., Calif., Fla., Ga., Hawaii, La., Miss., Nev., Okla., S.C., and Tex.
What to do: Have dealer remove spacer block between fuel tank and its heat shield.

'95 Mercury Villager

Tail lights and brake lights could fail. (High center-mounted brake light isn't affected.)
Models: 36,000 minivans made 4/95-9/96.
What to do: Have dealer install redesigned rear light sockets and wiring assemblies.

'95-96 Mercury Grand Marquis, Ford Crown Victoria, and Lincoln Town Car

Front-suspension welds could break, causing creaking and clanking noises and pulling to one side during braking. Eventually, steering could deteriorate.
Models: 231,000 cars made 6/15/95-3/29/96.
What to do: Have dealer inspect and, if necessary, repair welds. (After 3/1/97, cars may not be eligible for recall program after basic warranty has expired.)

'95-96 Mercury Mystique and Ford Contour

In cars with traction control, engine may not slow to idle when driver removes

foot from accelerator.
Models: 38,000 cars made 4/94-8/96.
What to do: Have dealer replace throttle cable.

'96 Mercury Cougar with semiautomatic climate-control system and Ford Thunderbird

Climate-control blower could fail to defrost or defog windshield, reducing driver's vision.
Models: 10,600 cars made 8/95-12/95.
What to do: Have dealer replace temperature-control modules.

'96 Mercury Sable and Ford Taurus

Warning indicator for low brake fluid could remain lit continuously or fail to light.
Models: 76,500 cars made 6/85-9/95.
What to do: Have dealer replace indicator light switch.

'96 Mercury Sable, Ford Taurus, and Lincoln Continental

Vehicle could roll away even though transmission shifter is in Park.
Models: 340,000 cars made 4/95-8/96.
What to do: Have dealer inspect and, if necessary, replace park-pawl shaft.

'96 Mercury Sable sedans and Ford Taurus and Ford Windstar minivan

Vehicle could roll even when shifter is in Park position.
Models: 99,700 vehicles, which can be identified by contacting Ford's customer service-line at 800 392-3673 or any Ford dealer. Note vehicle identification number before you call.
What to do: Have dealer inspect and, if necessary, replace parking-pawl mechanism.

'96-97 Mercury (various models), Ford, and Lincoln

Vehicle could roll even though transmission shifter is in Park.
Models: 380,000 vehicles, including '96 Ford Windstar made 8/96; '96 Lincoln Continental made 4/95-8/96; and '96-97 Ford Taurus and Mercury Sable made 4/95-8/96.
What to do: Have dealer inspect and, if necessary, repair park pawl assembly.

'96-97 Mercury Mountaineer and Ford Explorer

In extreme cold, ice could form in throttle housing and prevent engine from slowing when driver lifts foot off accelerator.
Models: 23,000 sport-utility vehicles made 2/96-2/97 and registered in the following states: Alaska, Idaho, Iowa, Maine, Mich. (Upper Peninsula only), Minn., Mont., Neb., N.H., N.Y., N.D., S.D., Vt., Wisc., and Wyo.
What to do: Have dealer install redesigned positive-crankcase-ventilation (PCV) system with heated vacuum

source. (Note that even if engine races, driver can control vehicle by shifting into neutral and braking.)

'96-98 Mercury Mystique, Ford Contour

Pressure-conscious reducing valve (PCRV)that controls rear brakes could corrode from exposure to road salt.
Models: 250,000 cars with standard brakes, made 4/96-8/98. Recall does not apply to vehicles with antilock brakes.
What to do: Have dealer install redesigned PCRV in rear brake system.

'97 Mercury Mountaineerand '96 Ford Explorer

Raised liftgate could drop and injure anyone underneath.
Models: 2200 sport-utility vehicles made 6/96.
What to do: Have dealer reinforce liftgate's gas-cylinder bracket with two pop rivets.

'97 Mercury Sable and Ford Taurus and Windstar

Transmission fluid could leak onto hot catalytic coverter, causing fire hazard.
Models: 100,000 vehicles made 11/96-3/97.
What to do: Have dealer inspect transmission and, if necessary, replace servo cover.

'97-98 Mercury Mountaineer and Ford Explorer

Fuel hose could pose fire hazard during jump-starting.
Models: 320,000 V6-powered sport-utility vehicles made 8/96-2/98. If ground cable is attached to fuel-line bracket near battery during jump-starting, fuel hose could act as a ground, overheat, and leak.
What to do: Have dealer install warning label on fuel-line bracket advising against its use as jump-start ground. Dealer will also replace bolt in alternator bracket to provide convenient ground for jump-starting.

'97-98 Mercury Villager

Battery could rupture and cause fire or prevent engine from starting.
Models: 4,945 minivans made 8/28/97-9/24/97.
What to do: Have dealer inspect and, if needed, replace battery.

'97-99 Mercury vehicles with automatic speed control and Ford

Vehicle might not decelerate when speed control is disengaged.
Models: 945,000 cars and trucks with speed control, including: '97-99 right-hand-drive Ford Explorer with single-overhead-cam V6, made 5/29/96-3/4/99; '98-99 Ford Ranger (all engines) made 1/5/98-3/4/99; '98-99 Ford Explorer and Mercury Mountaineer with single-over-head-cam V6 or V8, made 1/5/98-3/4/99;

'98-99 Ford Mustang (all engines) made 3/2/98-3/4/99; '99 Ford F250, F350, F450, and F550 (over 8,500 lbs.) with 5.4-liter or 6.8-liter V8, made 3/2/98-3/4/99; F-53 stripped chassis with 5.4-liter or 6.8-liter V8, made 3/2/98-3/4/99.
What to do: Have dealer replace speed-control cable.

'98 Mercury Mystique and Ford Contour

Accelerator may not return to idle when foot is removed from pedal, which could lead to crash.
Models: 153,000 cars made 7/97-4/98.
What to do: Have dealer install redesigned accelerator cable.

'98 Mercury Mystique and Ford Contour

Over time, front coil springs could break from road-salt corrosion and flatten tires, increasing risk of crash.
Models: 108,000 cars made at the Kansas City assembly plant 9/96 to 4/98 and registered in Conn., Del., Iowa, Ill., Ind., Mass., Md., Maine., Mich., Minn., Mo., N.H., NJ., N.Y., Ohio, Pa., R.I., Vt., W.Va., Wis., and Washington, D.C.
What to do: Have dealer install spring catcher brackets.

'98-99 Mercury Mountaineer and Ford Explorer

Hood could fly open suddenly if primary latch isn't engaged or hood release is inadvertently triggered.
Models: 845,000 sport-utility vehicles made 4/97-5/99.
What to do: Have dealer install secondary hood latch that's been coated for improved corrosion resistance.

'99-00 Mercury Cougar

Misrouted battery cable could lead to short circuit, resulting in fire, stall, or inability to start car.
Models: 120,000 cars, with 2.5-liter V-6, made 12/97 to 9/00.
What to do: Have dealer inspect and, if necessary, replace battery cable to alternator, reposition cable, install routing clip, and tighten cable attachment to alternator.

'99-00 Mercury Mystique, Ford Contour, and Cougar

Rear wheels could lock up during braking, hampering steering ability and increasing risk of crash.
Models: 186,200 cars with standard (not antilock) brakes, made 8/98 to 3/00. Pressure-conscious reducing valve (PCRV) in rear brakes could corrode and malfunction when operated in areas where road salt is used.
What to do: Have dealer install redesigned PCRVs in rear brake system.

'00-01 Mercury cars and sport-utility vehicles and Ford, Lincoln

Windshield wipers could fail.
Models: 1.1 million vehicles made 2/00 to 9/00, including the following: Ford Focus, Taurus, Expedition, Excursion, and F150 through F650 trucks; Lincoln Continental, Town Car, and Navigator; and Mercury Sable. Suspect vehicles were made at the following assembly plants: Atlanta (dates of manufacture 2/11-7/31); Chicago (2/14-8/4); Kansas City (2/26-9/4); Kentucky truck plant (2/18-8/31); Michigan truck plant (2/23-8/3); Norfolk (2/21-7/27); Wayne stamping and assembly plant (2/25-8/15); and Wixom (2/15-8/8). Hazard exists because switch in plastic cover of wiper-motor gear case could malfunction and overheat. Overheating could cause smoking, or plastic cover material could catch fire. Malfunction is most likely to occur when wipers are set for intermittent operation or when snow or ice prevents blades from returning to "parked" position at bottom of windshield.
What to do: Have dealer check date code on wiper motor and replace motor gear-case cover if necessary.

'01 Mercury, Ford, and Lincoln vehicles

Front safety belts may not provide adequate protection in crash.
Models: 1.4 million vehicles made 9/99 to 6/01, including the following: Ford Crown Victoria and Mercury Grand Marquis made at St. Thomas, Ontario, assembly plant 4/17/00 to 5/29/01; Lincoln Town Car built at Wixom, Mich., assembly plant 3/27/00 to 5/30/01; Lincoln Navigator built at Wayne, Mich., truck plant 4/11/00 to 5/31/01; Ford Windstar built at Oakville, Ontario, plant 3/23/00 to 5/30/01; Ford Ranger built at Twin Cities (St. Paul, Minn.) plant 3/28/00 to 5/30/01 and at Edison, N.J., plant 3/13/00 to 5/25/01. Also Ford F-150 trucks built at Norfolk, Va., plant 4/18/00 to 5/25/00, at Oakville plant 5/10/00 to 5/28/01, at Kansas City, Mo., plant 9/11/99 to 5/25/01 and at Cuautitlan, Mexico, plant 5/16/00 to 6/9/01; Ford Super Duty F-250, F-350, F-450, and F-550 built at Louisville, Ky., plant 4/17/00 to 5/27/01 and at Cuautitlan plant 5/16/00 to 6/19/01; Ford Excursion built at Louisville plant 4/17/00 to 10/2/00; Ford Expedition built at Wayne truck plant 4/11/00 to 5/31/01.
What to do: Have dealer inspect and, if necessary, replace front outboard safety-belt buckles.

Mini

'02 Mini Cooper with manual transmission

On certain vehicles with a manual transmission, the shift cable can detach from the linkage while the driver is changing gears. If the transmission moves into neutral, the driver will lose the ability to accelerate or maintain speed, increasing the risk of a crash.
Models: 3,531 cars made 9/01 to 5/02.
What to do: Have dealer inspect shift cable and, if necessary, install retaining clip over end of cable to prevent detachment.

Mitsubishi

'91-95 Mitsubishis (various models)

Brake hose could crack, leak fluid, and reduce effectiveness of brakes.
Models: 93,000 coupes, sedans, and station wagons with antilock brakes, and sport-utility vehicles with or without ABS, made 7/90-5/95, including '91-94 3000GT; '92-95 Diamante; and '92-93 Montero.
What to do: Have dealer replace left and right front brake hoses.

'95-96 Mitsubishi Eclipse

Fuel-tank gaskets could leak, posing fire hazard.
Models: 5,731 cars made 3/94-7/96.
What to do: Have dealer inspect fuel tank and, if necessary, replace faulty parts.

'98 Mitsubishi Spyder and Eclipse

Engine speed may not drop to idle when driver releases accelerator pedal.
Models: 20,974 cars made 7/97-1/98.
What to do: Have dealer trim dashboard-panel pad to clear throttle cable.

'99-00 Mitsubishi Galant and '00 Eclipse

Heat from exhaust manifold may damage battery-cable wire harness, causing inability to start car or use air conditioner, turn-signals, or hazard lamps; oil-pressure warning light may stay on constantly.
Models: 19,789 cars made 5/98-11/99.
What to do: Have dealer remove and discard metal manifold bracket (from Galant only) and install heat insulator and heat-resistant wire harness clips or new harness with integral heat protection as appropriate.

'99-00 Mitsubishi Gallant and '00 Eclipse

Headlights, directional signals, and windshield wipers could malfunction, causing them to operate all the time or not at all.

Models: 101,360 cars made 5/98-10/99.

What to do: Have dealer install new multifunction switch on steering column.

'01-02 Mitsubishi Montero

Driver may have to apply extra brake pressure to stop if vehicle has been parked for a while.

Models: 39,020 sport-utility vehicles made 12/99 to 6/01. Problem exists because accumulator installed on hydraulic brake booster may be faulty. If so, gas pressure inside accumulator could decrease, resulting in abnormal noise from left side of dashboard when brakes are applied and possible delay in brake-boost assist the first time the brakes are applied after the vehicle has been sitting unused for a period of time.

What to do: Have dealer replace accumulator.

Nissan

'95 Nissan Altima

Transmission can suddenly shift from Park to Drive or Neutral, making car move unexpectedly.

Models: 1,000 cars, with automatic transmission, made 7-8/94.

What to do: Have dealer install bracket to prevent breakage of shift-lever lock plate.

'95 Nissan Quest

Taillights and brake lights could fail.

Models: 25,000 minivans made 4/95-9/95. (Center high-mounted brake light is unaffected.)

What to do: Have dealer install redesigned sockets and wiring.

'95-98 Nissan Sentra and 200SX

Windshield wipers could fail.

Models: 512,387 cars made 11/94-12/97.

What to do: Have dealer modify wiper-linkage assembly to keep out moisture.

'96 Nissan Pathfinder

Steering wheel could become difficult to turn in very cold weather. Also, carpeting on transmission tunnel could snag driver's foot and hamper braking.

Models: 1,775 sport-utility vehicles made 8/95-1/96.

What to do: Have dealer install new steering-gear assembly with appropriate lubricant. Also, have dealer remove carpet padding on transmission tunnel near accelerator to prevent driver's foot from getting caught.

'97 Nissan Altima

Rear safety belts could fail in crash.

Models: 36,000 cars made 6/96-9/96.

What to do: Have dealer inspect buckle

assemblies and replace buckles with lot no. 023 or 029.

'98 Nissan Frontier

Shifter could inadvertently be moved out of park, allowing vehicle to roll away.

Models: 3,000 pickup trucks with automatic transmission, made 10/97-12/97.

What to do: Have dealer inspect and, if necessary, replace transmission-control assembly.

'98 Nissan Frontier

Safety belts could be severed in frontal crash.

Models: 20,000 pickup trucks, with bucket seats, made 9/97-1/98. Sharp metal edge of seatback-recliner lever could sever safety belt.

What to do: Have dealer replace plastic handle on reclining lever to keep belt from slipping between seat and lever.

'00-01 Nissan Sentra

Engine could stall out suddenly and unexpectedly, possibly resulting in crash. Also, "Service Engine Soon" warning light could come on or engine could suffer loss of power, which could increase risk of accident as well.

Models: 103,000 cars, with 1.8-liter engine, made 1/00 to 5/01.

What to do: Have dealer replace crankshaft position sensors.

'01 Nissan Sentra

Front suspension could fail.

Models: 80,000 cars made 7/00 to 4/01. Improperly manufactured bolts used to attach each front-suspension lower control arm to body could crack.

What to do: Have dealer replace lower control-arm attachment bolts.

Oldsmobile

'89-96 Oldsmobiles, Buicks, Chevrolets, and Pontiacs

Rear outboard safety belts may not hold in crash.

Models: 2.2 million cars made 4/88-8/95, including '89-96 Buick Century, '89-90 Chevrolet Celebrity, '89-96 Oldsmobile Ciera, and '89-91 Pontiac 6000.

What to do: Have dealer install new bolt and thread-locking adhesive for each belt. Dealer will also apply washer-like patch to each anchor point to reduce noise as belt pivots.

'94-95 '94 Oldsmobile Cutlass and Buick Regal

Brake hoses could wear through and leak, causing loss of stopping ability.

Models: 199,572 cars made 6/93-10/94.

What to do: Have dealer inspect and, if necessary, replace rear brake hoses.

'95 Oldsmobile, Buick, Chevrolet, and Pontiac models

Center-rear safety belt could fail in crash.

Models: 50,709 cars made 2/95, including Buick Regal, Chevrolet Lumina and Monte Carlo, Oldsmobile Cutlass, and Pontiac Grand Prix.

What to do: Have dealer replace center-rear safety belt.

'95 Oldsmobile 98 and Pontiac Bonneville

Headlights and parking lights could go out suddenly. Also, headlights could go on by themselves after being switched off, draining battery.

Models: 1,997 cars, with Twilight Sentinel lights, made 6-7/94.

What to do: Have dealer replace headlight module.

'95 Oldsmobile Cutlass, Buick Regal, Chevrolet Lumina, Pontiac Grand Prix

Center-rear safety belt might not provide adequate protection in crash.

Models: 111,470 cars made 11/94-1/95

What to do: Have dealer replace safety-belt assembly.

'95 Oldsmobile Silhouette, Chevrolet Lumina APV, and Pontiac Transport

Brake-pedal arm could fracture in use, resulting in diminished stopping ability.

Models: 6,523 minivans made 11/94-2/95.

What to do: Have dealer replace all suspect brake-pedal assemblies.

'95-96 Oldsmobile (various models), and Chevrolet, Pontiac

Four-way hazard-warning flashers may not work.

Models: 270,014 cars made 7/95-8/95 including '95-96 Chevrolet Cavalier and Pontiac Sunfire, and '96 Pontiac Gran Am and Oldsmobile Achieva.

What to do: Check whether flashers are working properly. If not, have dealer replace hazard switch.

'96 Oldsmobile Achieva and Buick Skylark

During deployment, air bag could snag inside dash and provide inadequate protection in crash.

Models: 48,689 cars made 8/95-2/96.

What to do: Have dealer inspect dash and, if necessary, install plastic edge protector on dash reinforcement. On some models, dealer will replace entire dash-panel pad.

'96 Oldsmobiles, Buicks, Chevrolets, and Pontiacs

Interior lamps could come on unexpectedly, startling driver and increasing risk of crash.

Models: 249,420 cars made 4/95-1/96, including Buick Skylark, Chevrolet Beretta and Cavalier, Oldsmobile Achieva, and

Pontiac Grand Am and Sunfire.
What to do: Have dealer check and, if necessary, replace light-control module.

'96-97 Oldsmobiles, Buicks, and Pontiacs

Engine backfire could break upper intake manifold and cause fire or prevent engine from running.
Models: 275,811 cars with 3.8-liter V6, including '96 Buick Park Avenue, Regal, and Riviera, Oldsmobile 88 and 98, and Pontiac Bonneville; also, '96-97 Buick LeSabre.
What to do: Have dealer reprogram engine control module. Until repair is made, don't start engine when hood is open.

'97 Oldsmobile Achieva, Buick Skylark, and Pontiac Grand Am

Cover of underhood fuse center may have been omitted, leaving terminal bolt exposed. Battery cable could contact terminal bolt, abrade insulation, and short out, causing fire hazard.
Models: 3,464 cars made 12/96-1/97.
What to do: Have dealer install cover if it's missing.

'97-98 Oldsmobile Cutlass and Chevrolet Malibu

Snow or ice buildup could damage passenger-side windshield wiper, causing wiper to fail.
Models: 129,427 cars made 1/96 to 1/98 and registered or located in Ala., Colo., Conn., Del., Idaho, Ill., Ind., Iowa, Maine, Md., Mass., Mich., Minn., Mont., Neb., N.H., N.J., N.Y., N.D., Ohio, Pa., R.I., S.D., Utah, Vt., W. Va., Wis., and Wyo.
What to do: Have dealer replace wiper's pivot housing.

'97-98 Oldsmobile Silhouette and Chevrolet Venture

Passenger's fingers could be severed by latch mechanism that moves seat fore and aft.
Models: 125,990 minivans, made 4/96-3/98, with bucket seats or split bench seat in second or third row.
What to do: Have dealer install protective covers on seat-latch mechanisms.

'97-01 Oldsmobile minivans and Chevrolet, Pontiac

Even though power-sliding door is closed, it may not latch properly. If so, door could open unexpectedly while vehicle is moving, causing occupant to fall out.
Models: 477,011 minivans with passenger side sliding door made 5/95 to 12/00, including the following: '97-01 Chevrolet Venture and Oldsmobile Silhouette; '98-01 Pontiac Montana; and '97-98 Pontiac Trans Sport.
What to do: Have dealer replace actuator assembly to power sliding door.

'98 Oldsmobile Silhouette, Chevrolet Venture, and Pontiac Trans Sport

Vehicle could roll when shifter is in "park."
Models: 38,540 minivans made 12/97-4/98.
What to do: Have dealer inspect and, if necessary, replace transaxle range-selector cable.

'99 Oldsmobile 88, Buick LeSabre, Pontiac Bonneville

Transmission indicator may not show proper gear position. For example, indicator could show drive position when transmission is actually in reverse.
Models: 99,269 cars made 8/98-1/99.
What to do: Have dealer install manual valve-link assembly kit with spring-type retainer.

'99 Oldsmobile Intrigue

Coolant could leak onto hot exhaust manifold and cause fire.
Models: 2,732 cars, with 3.8-liter engine, made 4/98-8/98.
What to do: Have dealer install heater-hose clip.

'99-00 Oldsmobile Alero and Pontiac Grand Am

In violation of Federal safety standard, cover of console between front seats may open in crash, allowing contents of console or cover itself to injure occupants.
Models: 487,400 cars made 10/97-9/99.
What to do: Have dealer replace console latch mechanism.

'00 Oldsmobile, Buick, Chevrolet, GMC, Pontiac, and Saturn vehicles

Rear safety belts may not provide adequate protection in a crash.
Models: 156,305 vehicles with TRW safety-belt buckle, made 4/00-5/00, including Buick Century and Regal; Chevrolet Blazer, Impala, Lumina, Monte Carlo, Venture, and S10/T10; GMC Jimmy; Oldsmobile Intrigue and Silhouette; Pontiac Grand Prix and Montana; and Saturn L-Series.
What to do: Have dealer inspect and, if necessary, replace rear safety-belt buckles.

'00-02 General Motors sport-utility vehicles (various makes)

Rear stop and hazard lamps could become inoperative, increasing risk of crash with another vehicle, whose driver doesn't realize SUV is slowing.
Models: Models: 506,377 sport-utility vehicles made 9/99 to 8/01, including '00-01 GMC Jimmy and Oldsmobile Bravada, and '00-02 Chevrolet Blazer.
What to do: What to do: At press time, General Motors had not provided a remedy or owner-notification schedule. If you have not been contacted, call 800-

462-8782 (for a GMC vehicle), 800-442-6537 (Oldsmobile), or 800-222-1020 (Chevrolet).

'01 General Motors minivans and sport-utility vehicles

May not accommodate child safety seats.
Models: 75,816 vehicles with second-row 50/50-split bench seats or captain's chairs, made 4/00 to 10/00, including Chevrolet Venture, Pontiac Aztec and Montana, and Oldsmobile Silhouette.
What to do: Have dealer inspect and, if necessary, repair seat-latch anchor wires.

'02 Oldsmobile Bravada, Chevrolet TrailBlazer, and GMC Envoy

Fuel-filter fitting could become disconnected. If that occurs during start-up, engine might not turn over and fuel would be pumped onto ground, creating a fire hazard. If fitting comes off while vehicle is moving, engine would stop, possibly resulting in crash.
Models: 60,044 sport-utility vehicles made 9/01 to 11/01.
What to do: Have dealer replace fuel-filter quick-connect retainers.

Plymouth

'92-96 Plymouth Colt and Eagle Summit with all-wheel drive

Wheels could lockup and cause loss of control.
Models: 6,198 vehicles made 7/91-6/96, including '92-96 Summit and '92-94 Colt.
What to do: Have dealer inspect transfer case and, if necessary, add oil or replace case.

'95 Plymouth and Dodge Neon

Driver could lose steering control if car runs over object that strikes underbody.
Models: 375,000 cars made 1/94-8/95.
What to do: Have dealer install new steering-column coupler.

'95-96 Plymouth cars with "ACR" competition package, Chrysler, and Dodge

Brake master cylinder could leak fluid, resulting in decreased stopping ability.
Models: 151,800 cars made 8/94-10/95 including '95-96 Chrysler Cirrus, Dodge Neon and Stratus, and Plymouth Neon, and '96 Plymouth Breeze.
What to do: Have dealer replace rear brake master-cylinder piston assembly.

'95-97 Plymouth, Chrysler, and Dodge models

Ball joints in front suspension could corrode and fail, causing loss of steering control.
Models: 599,000 cars, including '95-97 Chrysler Cirrus, Dodge Stratus, and Plymouth Breeze, and '96-97 Chrysler Sebring convertibles.

What to do: Have dealer inspect and, if necessary, replace ball-joints.

'95-98 Plymouth Breeze, Chrysler Cirrus and Sebring, and Dodge Stratus

Car could roll even if shifter is in park position.
Models: 685,000 cars with automatic transmission made 7/94-1/98.
What to do: Have dealer inspect interlock system and, if necessary, install self-adjusting shift mechanism and cable.

'96 Plymouth Breeze, and '95-96 Chrysler Cirrus and Dodge Stratus

Valves in antilock brake system could stick and cause car to veer to one side when stopping.
Models: 90,000 cars made 8/94-8/95.
What to do: Have dealer install a plate and inject silicone grease into solenoid cavity of ABS hydraulic control unit.

'96 Plymouth, Chrysler, and Dodge minivans

Fire or explosion could occur during refueling because of static buildup on fuel-filler tube.
Models: 265,000 minivans, including Chrysler Town & Country, Dodge Caravan and Grand Caravan, and Plymouth Voyager and Grand Voyager, made 1/95-12/95.
What to do: Have dealer install ground strap for filler tube.

'96 Plymouth, Chrysler, and Dodge minivans

Fuel tank could leak, creating fire hazard.
Models: 80,000 minivans made 1/95-8/95, including Chrysler Town & Country, Dodge Caravan and Grand Caravan, and Plymouth Voyager and Grand Voyager.
What to do: Have dealer install redesigned fuel-tank filler tube and reroute rollover-valve vapor hoses.

'96 Plymouth, Chrysler, and Dodge minivans

Fuel could leak from tank and cause fire.
Models: 622,000 minivans including Chrysler Town and Country, Dodge Caravan and Grand Caravan, and Plymouth Voyager and Grand Voyager.
What to do: Have dealer replace nut holding fuel-pump module in place.

'96 Plymouth and Dodge Neon

Engine-wiring harness could short and cause various electrical malfunctions, including engine stalling.
Models: 15,000 cars made 7/95-11/95 at Toluca, Mexico, assembly plant.
What to do: Have dealer replace damaged wire and reroute wiring harness away from exhaust-gas-recirculation tube.

'96 Plymouth Voyager and Grand Voyager and Dodge Caravan and Grand Caravan

Rear bench seat could could break loose in accident, increasing risk of injury.
Models: 20,000 minivans, made 10/95-11/95, with bench seat rather than captain's chairs in rear.
What to do: Check vehicle identification number atop dashboard or on registration certificate. If 11th character is letter "R," have dealer replace bolts connecting rear bench seat to riser.

'96-97 Plymouth, Chrysler, and Dodge, minivans with built-in child safety seat

Shoulder-harness latch could stick, making it difficult to remove child in emergency.
Models: 157,000 minivans made 1/95-7/97 including Chrysler Town & Country, Dodge Caravan and Grand Caravan, and Plymouth Voyager and Grand Voyager.
What to do: Have dealer clean latch mechanism and add extender to emergency release on safety-belt anchor.

'96-00 Plymouth, Chrysler and Dodge minivans

Fuel-injector system could leak, possibly causing fire.
Models: 1,163,000 minivans, with 3.3- and 3.8-liter engines, made 2/95-9/99, including Dodge Caravan and Grand Caravan, Plymouth Voyager and Grand Voyager, and Chrysler Town and Country. Hazard exists because fuel could seep through O-ring seals in fuel-injection rail.
What to do: Have dealer install seal on fuel rails to prevent leakage from fuel-rail crossover tube. If fuel is already leaking from O-rings or cracked fuel line, have dealer make necessary repairs as soon as possible.

'98 Plymouth, Chrysler and Dodge minivans with built-in child safety seat

Seat may not restrain child adequately in crash.
Models: 25,900 minivans made 11/97, including Chrysler Town & Country, Dodge Caravan and Grand Caravan, and Plymouth Voyager and Grand Voyager.
What to do: Have dealer inspect and, if necessary, reroute seat's harness webbing.

'98-99 Plymouth Breeze, Chrysler Cirrus, and Dodge Stratus,

Rear brake hose could abrade and leak from contact with exhaust system clamp, causing increased stopping distances.
Models: 367,000 cars made 6/97-5/99.
What to do: Have dealer replace any brake hose that shows wear from contact with clamp. If no evidence of contact exists, dealer will attach clip to hose to prevent future occurrence.

'00 Plymouth and Dodge Neon

Passenger-side air bag may not inflate adequately.
Models: 380 cars made 11/98-1/99.
What to do: Have dealer replace passenger-side air-bag module.

'00-01 Plymouth and Dodge Neon

Loss of power-brake assist could cause increased stopping distances and increased engine idle speed.
Models: 353,000 cars made 7/99 to 3/01.
What to do: Have dealer replace brake-booster vacuum hose.

'01 Plymouth Voyager, Dodge Caravan and Grand Caravan, and Chrysler Town & Country

Suspension components could come apart.
Models: 41,587 minivans made 3/01 to 4/01.
What to do: Have dealer replace nuts and bolts on lower control arm.

Pontiac

'89-96 Pontiacs, Buicks, Chevrolets, and Oldsmobiles

Rear outboard safety belts may not hold in crash.
Models: 2.2 million cars made 4/88-8/95, including '89-96 Buick Century, '89-90 Chevrolet Celebrity, '89-96 Oldsmobile Ciera, and '89-91 Pontiac 6000.
What to do: Have dealer install new bolt and thread-locking adhesive for each belt. Dealer will also apply washer-like patch to each anchor point to reduce noise as belt pivots.

'95 Pontiac Bonneville and Oldsmobile 98

Headlights and parking lights could go out suddenly. Also, headlights could go on by themselves after being switched off, draining battery.
Models: 1,997 cars, with Twilight Sentinel lights, made 6-7/94.
What to do: Have dealer replace headlight module.

'95 Pontiac, Buick, Chevrolet, and Oldsmobile and models

Center-rear safety belt could fail in crash.
Models: 50,709 cars made 2/95, including Buick Regal, Chevrolet Lumina and Monte Carlo, Oldsmobile Cutlass, and Pontiac Grand Prix.
What to do: Have dealer replace center-rear safety belt.

'95 Pontiac Grand Prix, Buick Regal, Chevrolet Lumina, and Oldsmobile Cutlass

Center-rear safety belt might not provide adequate protection in crash.
Models: 111,470 cars made 11/94-1/95.

What to do: Have dealer replace safety-belt assembly.

'95 Pontiac Sunfire and Chevrolet Cavalier

Front suspension components could separate, resulting in loss of vehicle control.
Models: 21,340 cars made 2/94-1/95.
What to do: Have dealer inspect lower-control-arm assemblies and, if necessary, replace.

'95 Pontiac Sunfire with automatic transmission

Sagging trim plate could obscure lighted pointer indicating shifter position, and driver might inadvertently shift into wrong gear.
Models: 28,068 cars made 7/94-6/95.
What to do: Have dealer replace trim plate on instrument panel.

'95 Pontiac Trans and Chevrolet Lumina Sport minivans

Engine may not slow down sufficiently when accelerator is released.
Models: 6,772 minivans, with 3.1-liter V6, made 5/95-9/95.
What to do: Have dealer replace throttle-cable support bracket.

'95 Pontiac Transport, Chevrolet Lumina APV, and Oldsmobile Silhouette

Brake-pedal arm could fracture in use, resulting in diminished stopping ability.
Models: 6,523 minivans made 11/94-2/95.
What to do: Have dealer replace all suspect brake-pedal assemblies.

'95-96 Pontiac, Chevrolet, and Oldsmobile (various models)

Four-way hazard-warning flashers may not work.
Models: 270,014 cars made 7/95-8/95 including '95-96 Chevrolet Cavalier and Pontiac Sunfire, and '96 Pontiac Gran Am and Oldsmobile Achieva.
What to do: Check whether flashers are working properly. If not, have dealer replace hazard switch.

'96 Pontiacs, Buicks, Chevrolets, and Oldsmobiles

Interior lamps could come on unexpectedly, startling driver and increasing risk of crash.
Models: 249,420 cars made 4/95-1/96, including Buick Skylark, Chevrolet Beretta and Cavalier, Oldsmobile Achieva, and Pontiac Grand Am and Sunfire.
What to do: Have dealer check and, if necessary, replace light-control module.

'96-97 Pontiacs, Buicks, and Oldsmobiles

Engine backfire could break upper intake manifold and cause fire or prevent engine from running.
Models: 275,811 cars with 3.8-liter V6, including '96 Buick Park Avenue, Regal,

and Riviera, Oldsmobile 88 and 98, and Pontiac Bonneville; also, '96-97 Buick LeSabre.
What to do: Have dealer reprogram engine control module. Until repair is made, don't start engine when hood is open.

'96-97 Pontiac Sunfire and Chevrolet Cavalier

Air bag could deploy when it shouldn't—in low-speed crash or if road debris kicks up against floor.
Models: 675,302 cars made 4/95-5/97.
What to do: Have dealer recalibrate air-bag module.

'97 Pontiac Grand Am and Buick Skylark, Oldsmobile Achieva

Cover of underhood fuse center may have been omitted, leaving terminal bolt exposed. Battery cable could contact terminal bolt, abrade insulation, and short out, causing fire hazard.
Models: 3,464 cars made 12/96-1/97.
What to do: Have dealer install cover if it's missing.

'97-01 Pontiac, Chevrolet, and Oldsmobile minivans

Even though power-sliding door is closed, it may not latch properly. If so, door could open unexpectedly while vehicle is moving, causing occupant to fall out.
Models: 477,011 minivans with passenger side sliding door made 5/95 to 12/00, including the following: '97-01 Chevrolet Venture and Oldsmobile Silhouette; '98-01 Pontiac Montana; and '97-98 Pontiac Trans Port.
What to do: Have dealer replace actuator assembly to power sliding door.

'98 Pontiac Trans Sport, Chevrolet Venture, and Oldsmobile Silhouette

Vehicle could roll when shifter is in "park."
Models: 38,540 minivans made 12/97-4/98.
What to do: Have dealer inspect and, if necessary, replace transaxle range-selector cable.

'99 Pontiac Bonneville, Buick LeSabre, and Oldsmobile 88

Transmission indicator may not show proper gear position. For example, indicator could show drive position when transmission is actually in reverse.
Models: 99,269 cars made 8/98-1/99.
What to do: Have dealer install manual valve-link assembly kit with spring-type retainer.

'99-00 Pontiac Grand Am and Oldsmobile Alero

In violation of Federal safety standard, cover of console between front seats may open in crash, allowing contents of console or cover itself to injure occupants.

Models: 487,400 cars made 10/97-9/99.
What to do: Have dealer replace console latch mechanism.

'00 Pontiac, Buick, Chevrolet, GMC, Oldsmobile, and Saturn vehicles

Rear safety belts may not provide adequate protection in a crash.
Models: 156,305 vehicles with TRW safety-belt buckle, made 4/00-5/00, including Buick Century and Regal; Chevrolet Blazer, Impala, Lumina, Monte Carlo, Venture, and S10/T10; GMC Jimmy; Oldsmobile Intrigue and Silhouette; Pontiac Grand Prix and Montana; and Saturn L-Series.
What to do: Have dealer inspect and, if necessary, replace rear safety-belt buckles.

'01 General Motors minivans and sport-utility vehicles

May not accommodate child safety seats.
Models: 75,816 vehicles with second-row 50/50-split bench seats or captain's chairs, made 4/00 to 10/00, including Chevrolet Venture, Pontiac Aztec and Montana, and Oldsmobile Silhouette.
What to do: Have dealer inspect and, if necessary, repair seat-latch anchor wires.

Saab

'94-95 Saab 900

Missing welds on front-seat recliners could allow seatback to fall backwards suddenly.
Models: 10,584 cars made 3/94-10/94.
What to do: Have dealer inspect seats and, if necessary, replace frames and recliners.

'94-95 Saab 900

Transmission may be in Neutral when shifter is in Reverse. Car could roll away if it's parked with parking brake disengaged.
Models: 8,993 cars with manual transmission made 8/93-9/94.
What to do: Have dealer reair transmission linkage.

'95 Saab 900

Engine speed could fluctuate dramatically for up to half a minute after engine is started, possibly causing unexpected movement if transmission is in gear.
Models: 5,383 nonturbocharged cars made 7/94-12/94.
What to do: Have dealer replace engine-control module.

Saturn

'94-95 Saturn
Front seatback could slip backward and cause loss of control.
Models: 136,300 cars (all versions) made 1/94-8/94.
What to do: Have dealer replace recliner mechanisms.

'95 Saturn SL
Driver could completely lose steering control.
Models: 931 cars, with nonpower steering, made 8/94.
What to do: Have dealer replace steering assembly.

'95 Saturn models with automatic transmission
Shifter could be moved out of Park with ignition key removed, or key could be removed with shifter in position other than Park, allowing vehicle to move unexpectedly.
Models: 20,518 cars made 7-8/94.
What to do: If either condition exists in your car, have dealer adjust Park-lock cable.

'96-97 Saturn
Horn assembly could overheat and cause fire under hood. Also, horn could fail or go on unexpectedly.
Models: 64,199 cars made 7/95-2/97.
What to do: Have dealer replace horn assembly.

'96-97 Saturn SL
Steering could fail.
Models: 14,580 cars with manual steering made 12/95-6/96.
What to do: Have dealer replace steering-gear assembly.

'97 Saturn SC1 and SC2
If front safety belts are repeatedly pulled out very quickly, belt could fail.
Models: 26,135 cars made 5/96-11/96.
What to do: Have dealer replace driver' and front passenger' safety belts.

'97 Saturn SC1 and SC2
Right front seat could slide forward in frontal crash, increasing risk of injury.
Models: 3,472 cars made 5/96-7/96.
What to do: Have dealer replace seat's inboard fore-aft seat adjuster.

'99-00 Saturn SC, SL, and SW
Safety belts may not work.
Models: 265,522 vehicles made 4/98-8/99.
What to do: Have dealer inspect safety belts and properly tighten shoulder-guide anchor bolts.

'00 Saturn, Buick, Chevrolet, GMC, Oldsmobile, and Pontiac vehicles
Rear safety belts may not provide adequate protection in a crash.
Models: 156,305 vehicles with TRW safety-belt buckle, made 4/00-5/00, including Buick Century and Regal; Chevrolet Blazer, Impala, Lumina, Monte Carlo, Venture, and S10/T10; GMC Jimmy; Oldsmobile Intrigue and Silhouette; Pontiac Grand Prix and Montana; and Saturn L-Series.
What to do: Have dealer inspect and, if necessary, replace rear safety-belt buckles.

Subaru

'94-95 Subaru Impreza and '95-96 Legacy
Over pothole or bump, front tow hooks could hit pavement deploy air bag, and cause injury or crash.
Models: 95,693 cars made 2/94-7/95.
What to do: Have dealer remove front tow hooks.

'94-97 Subaru Impreza and Legacy
Air bag could deploy unexpectedly if front tow hooks come in contact with pavement.
Models: 95,000 '94-95 Imprezas and '95-96 Legacys (excluding Outback models).
What to do: Have dealer remove tow hooks.

'95-99 Subaru Legacy sedan, wagon, and Outback and '97-98 Ford Windstar
Road salt could cause front coil springs to corrode, break, and flatten tires, resulting in loss of vehicle control or crash.
Models: 180,000 Subaru vehicles made 1/94 to 1/98 and 198,583 Ford minivans made 8/96 to 7/98. Vehicles were sold or are currently registered in the following states: Conn., Del., Ill., Ind., Iowa, Ky., Maine, Mass., Md., Mich., Minn., Mo., N.H., N.J., N.Y., Ohio, Pa., R.I., Va., Vt., W.Va., Wis., and the District of Columbia
What to do: Have Subaru dealer install protective spring guards on front struts and replace any broken springs. Have Ford dealer install protective shields around springs.

'96-97 Subaru Legacy and Outback
Suspension could fail, causing loss of control.
Models: 29,442 vehicles made 6/96-9/96.
What to do: Have dealer inspect and, if necessary, replace front-suspension support brackets.

'98-99 Subaru Forester and Legacy with antilock brakes
In extreme cold, seals on brake master cylinder could fail and increase stopping distances.
Models: 221,987 vehicles made 4/97-3/99.
What to do: Have dealer replace master cylinder.

'98-99 Subaru Legacy
Oil filter could crack, spray oil, and cause fire.
Models: 20,603 cars made 1/98-4/98.
What to do: Have dealer replace oil filter.

Suzuki

'97 Suzuki Swift
Automatic shifter can be moved out of park position easily with key removed from ignition lock. That could allow parked car to roll and crash.
Models: 1,198 cars made 7/96-3/97.
What to do: Have dealer replace shifter assembly.

Toyota

'93-95 Toyota Corolla and Geo Prizm
If liquid should spill around center console box, air bag could deploy, creating accident hazard.
Models: 627,858 cars made 6/92-1/95.
What to do: Have dealer install protective cover over air-bag sensor and replace any sensor damaged by previous spill.

'95 Toyota Corolla cars and Toyota Tacoma pickup trucks and Geo Prizm
Defective terminal could cause dead battery and could make battery explode, spraying acid.
Models: 14,363 cars and trucks made 6/95-7/95.
What to do: Have dealer replace battery.

'95-98 Toyota Camry and '94-98 Lexus ES300
Steering wheel could loosen or come off.
Models: 540,037 cars made 7/94-7/98.
What to do: Have dealer tighten steering-wheel set nut.

'96-98 Toyota 4Runner
The combination of a heavy load and severe steering maneuvers could cause vehicle to lose directional stability, possibly resulting in loss of control and crash.
Models: 273,743 sport-utility vehicles, with two- and four-wheel drive, made 11/95 to 2/98.
What to do: Have dealer replace rear-suspension parts.

'97 Toyota Avalon, Toyota Camry and Lexus ES300
In extreme cold, icing could disable brakes' power assist. Brakes would then require more distance and much greater pedal pressure to stop car.
Models: 18,746 cars made 7/96-2/97 and originally sold or currently registered in Alaska, Colo., Idaho, Ill., Iowa, Kan., Me., Mich., Minn., Mont., Neb., Nev., N.H., N.Y., N.D., S.D., Vt., Wisc., and Wyo.

What to do: Have dealer install redesigned brake vacuum hose. Owners of cars in other states who drive in extremely cold weather should also ask dealer for redesigned hose.

'97 Toyota Camry
In extremely cold climates, icing could disable brake vacuum assist, increasing pedal effort and lengthening stopping distances.
Models: 18,746 cars registered in the following states: Alaska, Colo., Idaho, Ill., Iowa, Kan., Me., Mich., Minn., Mont., Neb., Nev., N.H., N.Y., N.D., S.D., Vt., Wisc., and Wyo.
What to do: Have dealer install redesigned brake vacuum hose.

'02 Toyota Camry and Lexus ES300
On vehicles equipped with certain steering wheels, horn cover could detach and injure driver during air-bag deployment.
Models: 19,587 cars, with three-spoke-style steering wheel, made 7/01 to 11/01.
What to do: Have dealer replace driver's side air-bag module.

Volkswagen

'93-95 Volkswagen Corrado, Golf, Jetta, and Passat
Radiator-fan motor could fail, making engine overheat and stall.
Models: 34,000 cars, with V6 engine, made 4/93-2/95.
What to do: Have dealer inspect and, if necessary, replace fan blade and lock nut or complete cooling-fan assembly.

'93-95 Volkswagen Golf and Jetta
Jack could collapse in use.
Models: 104,000 cars made 4/93-10/94.
What to do: Have dealer replace jack.

'93-95 Volkswagen Golf, GTI, and Jetta
Brake hose could leak, reducing stopping ability.
Models: 153,000 cars made 2/92-6/95.
What to do: Have dealer inspect right rear brake hose and, if necessary, reroute and replace it.

'97-00 Volkswagen Jetta and Passat
If car is driven on a flat until tire disinte-grates, fuel-tank filler neck may become damaged and leak fuel, causing fire.
Models: 311,047 cars made 8/96 to 11/99, including '97-99 Jetta and '98-00 Passat.
What to do: Have dealer fit Passat with new wheelhouse liner that will better protect filler neck. The Jetta will be fitted with a metal shield designed to enhance abrasion protection in the event of tire disintegration.

'98 Volkswagen Beetle
Electrical wiring could abrade from contact with battery tray, disable fuel injection, stall engine, and start engine-compartment fire.
Models: 8,500 cars made 1/98-5/98.
What to do: Have dealer install modified battery tray, and inspect, properly route, and secure wiring.

'98 Volkswagen Passat and Audi A4 and A6
Engine backfire during cold start could dislodge and break air screen in airflow meter and prevent engine from slowing fully when accelerator is released.
Models: 19,800 cars made 2/97-2/98.
What to do: Have dealer install ring to secure air screen.

'01-02 Volkswagen Beetle, Golf, and Jetta
Electronic control unit of antilock brake system (ABS) could short circuit and cause fire.
Models: 55,000 cars made 10/00 to 9/01.
What to do: Have dealer replace ABS control unit.

Volvo

'93-96 Volvo 850 with engine-block heater
Heater could separate from engine and rub through fuel hose, creating fire hazard.
Models: 400 cars made through 8/96.
What to do: Have dealer inspect and secure or, if necessary, replace block heater.

'95 Volvo 850, 854, and 855
Jack may lack sufficient load capacity. If so, device could collapse in use.
Models: 31,315 cars made 6/94-1/95.

What to do: Have dealer make sure jack is sufficient to support vehicle load and, if not, replace.

'95 Volvo 854 and 855
Front safety belts might not provide adequte protection in severe crash.
Models: 475 sedans and stations wagons, with one or two power seats, made 2/95.
What to do: Have dealer replace threaded insert that connects safety-belt catch to front seat.

'95 Volvo 964 and 965
Spare tire could fail if inflated according to incorrect labeling. Also, label lists wrong tire size.
Models: 5,199 sedans and station wagons made 6/94-11/94.
What to do: Have dealer supply label noting correct size (T125/90R15) and pressure (60 psi).

'96-97 Volvo 850 and 960 series cars
Engine may not slow to idle when accelerator is released.
Models: 13,221 late '96 and early '97 sedans and station wagons made 4/96-7/96. Affected cars can be identified by last six digits of vehicle identification number. 850 models bear numbers 256997 to 311340; 338213 to 380371; 332305 to 376485; and 339561 to 372831 (numbers run sequentially). 960 models bear numbers 036243 to 039442 and 098612 to 107701.
What to do: Have dealer replace throttle body in fuel system.

'98-99 Volvo V70 station wagon
Tailpipe may extend too far beyond rear bumper, posing hazard to anyone exiting from third-row seat.
Models: 50,835 station wagons made 1/97-10/98.
What to do: Check tailpipe, and if necessary, have dealer modify it.

'01 Volvo S80 and V70
Rear safety belts may not provide adequate protection in crash.
Models: 3,276 cars and station wagons made 11/00 to 1/01.
What to do: Have dealer inspect and, if necessary, tighten rear outboard anchorage bolts.

Index

PROFILES AND ROAD-TEST REPORTS This index tells you which page a model's profile is on. It also notes CONSUMER REPORTS issues between 1995 and 2002 that carry the full road-test reports on that model. Some reports covered an essentially similar twin or triplet of the model listed. Subscribers to ConsumerReports.org *(www.consumerreports.org)* can access recent road tests, including other tested versions not listed on the profile page.

Consumer Reports

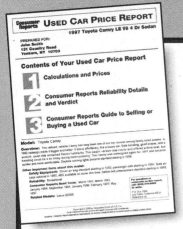

How to BUY, SELL or TRADE IN a USED CAR without getting taken for a ride.

Cars, Minivans, Vans, Sport-Utility Vehicles, and Pickup Trucks

Consumer Reports gives you access to our extensive used-car database so you can:

get the inside scoop on dealers' selling and trade-in prices • make the best deal in a private sale • figure out how a vehicle's mileage and options affect its value • see how your vehicle compares in our annual reliability tests • learn tips and techniques to help you negotiate the best deal.

Arm yourself with our customized **Consumer Reports Used Car Price Report** to help you negotiate the best deal.

Here's a sample of what you'll find.

BUYERS Beware.

→ Don't pay for the vehicle twice: now, and again in repair bills. Our 14-Point Reliability Summary evaluates your entire vehicle from transmission to suspension, brakes to exhaust systems (available for most models). As a bonus, if we reviewed your vehicle in our magazine, we'll give you our Model Overview, which alerts you to potential trouble spots.

→ Why pay the price for negotiating without a safety net? Check our up-to-date dealer selling prices and negotiate from a position of strength to get the best deal possible.

Setting the SELLING Price.

In three simple steps, learn how to determine the base price for vehicles from 1991–2002, how to compensate for important features and options, and ultimately how to get the best possible price.

Timing Your TRADE-IN.

Although selling your vehicle privately is often the way to get top dollar, many sellers prefer the ease and convenience of trading in. If you're trading in your vehicle, you stand to get a better deal if you settle on a price for the new vehicle first — before you reveal your plans to trade in.

Consumer Reports
1-USED CAR PRICE SERVICE
1-800-422-1079

Up-to-date information you can trust — all in one report.

Each report costs just $10, and the call is free.

Call today to order a customized report on the vehicle you want to buy, sell or trade in:

1-800-422-1079

We'll rush your report to you by fax or mail.

Here's all you do:

- Tell us the year, make, model, and trim line of the vehicle you want to buy, sell or trade in (e.g., **1995 Nissan Pathfinder XE 4-door 4WD**).

- Have your credit card handy. (We accept Visa, MasterCard, Discover, or American Express.)

No service in Canada.

4/03